Memory and Justice in Post-Genocide Rwanda

Following times of great conflict and tragedy, many countries implement programs and policies of transitional justice, none more extensive than in post-genocide Rwanda. Placing Rwanda's transitional justice initiatives in their historical and political context, this book examines the project undertaken by the post-genocide government to shape the collective memory of the Rwandan population, both through political and judicial reforms but also in public commemorations and memorials. Drawing on over two decades of field research in Rwanda, Longman uses surveys and comparative local case studies to explore Rwanda's response, both at governmental and local level. He argues that despite good intentions and important innovations, Rwanda's authoritarian political context has hindered the ability of transitional justice to bring the radical social and political transformations that its advocates hoped. Moreover, it continues to heighten the political and economic inequalities that underline ethnic divisions and are an important ongoing barrier to reconciliation.

Timothy Longman is Director of the African Studies Center and Associate Professor of Political Science and International Relations at Boston University. He has previously held teaching and research positions at Vassar College, the University of California, Berkeley, the University of the Witwatersrand, and the National University of Rwanda. He has conducted over twenty years of research in Rwanda, and is the author of *Christianity and Genocide in Rwanda* (Cambridge, 2010).

Memory and Justice in Post-Genocide Rwanda

Timothy Longman

Boston University

CAMBRIDGE
UNIVERSITY PRESS

University Printing House, Cambridge CB2 8BS, United Kingdom

One Liberty Plaza, 20th Floor, New York, NY 10006, USA

477 Williamstown Road, Port Melbourne, VIC 3207, Australia

314–321, 3rd Floor, Plot 3, Splendor Forum, Jasola District Centre,
New Delhi – 110025, India

79 Anson Road, #06-04/06, Singapore 079906

Cambridge University Press is part of the University of Cambridge.

It furthers the University's mission by disseminating knowledge in the pursuit of
education, learning, and research at the highest international levels of excellence.

www.cambridge.org
Information on this title: www.cambridge.org/9781107017993
DOI: 10.1017/9781139086257

© Timothy Longman 2017

This publication is in copyright. Subject to statutory exception
and to the provisions of relevant collective licensing agreements,
no reproduction of any part may take place without the written
permission of Cambridge University Press.

First published 2017
Reprinted 2019

Printed in the United Kingdom by TJ International Ltd. Padstow, Cornwall

A catalogue record for this publication is available from the British Library.

Library of Congress Cataloging-in-Publication Data
Names: Longman, Timothy Paul, author.
Title: Memory and justice in post-genocide Rwanda /
Timothy Longman (Boston University).
Description: Cambridge, United Kingdom; New York, NY: Cambridge
University Press, 2017. | Includes bibliographical references and index.
Identifiers: LCCN 2017003644| ISBN 9781107017993 (hardback) |
ISBN 9781107678095 (paperback)
Subjects: LCSH: Rwanda – Politics and government – 1994– | Genocide –
Political aspects – Rwanda. | Collective memory – Political aspects –
Rwanda. | Transitional justice – Rwanda. | Social change – Rwanda. |
Political culture – Rwanda. | Authoritarianism – Rwanda. |
Ethnic conflict – Rwanda. | Rwanda – Ethnic relations – Political aspects. |
BISAC: POLITICAL SCIENCE / Government / General.
Classification: LCC DT450.44.L66 2017 | DDC 967.57104/3–dc23
LC record available at https://lccn.loc.gov/2017003644

ISBN 978-1-107-01799-3 Hardback
ISBN 978-1-107-67809-5 Paperback

Cambridge University Press has no responsibility for the persistence or
accuracy of URLs for external or third-party internet websites referred to in
this publication and does not guarantee that any content on such websites is,
or will remain, accurate or appropriate.

To my husband, Tracy Keene, who has put up with far too many trips during the process of research and writing this book. It was always a joy to come home to you.

"Much has been made of the doom of not remembering. But remembering has its limitations. Believe me, it is good to forget."

"Yes," I said. Though everything that I ever forgot I always remembered again later, so perhaps it didn't count.

Lorrie Moore
A Gate at the Stairs

Administrative map of Rwanda 1996–2006 with case studies highlighted.

Contents

List of Figures   *page* x
Acknowledgments   xi
List of Abbreviations   xiii

1   Introduction: The Meaning of Murambi   1

**Part I   Creating What You Are Afraid of: The Rwandan
Patriotic Front's Transitional Justice Program**   27

2   Rewriting History in Post-Genocide Rwanda   33

3   Symbolic Struggles   65

4   Justice as Memory   91

5   From Violent Repression to Political
Domination: Transitional Justice, Political Reform, and
Development   135

Part II   Popular Narratives   187

6   Political Reform in Three Rwandan Communities   189

7   Popular Narratives of Memory and History   231

8   Politics by Other Means: Popular Opinion about
"Transitional Justice"   271

Part III   Conclusion   311

9   "We Pretend to Live Together": Assessing the Impact of
Transitional Justice Mechanisms in Rwanda   313

Bibliography   341
Index   365

Figures

1 Coffins exposed at the Kigali Memorial Centre
  (Photo by author)   *page* 66
2 Skulls on display at Ntarama memorial site
  (Photo by author)   69
3 The debris-strewn floor of Ntarama memorial site
  (Photo by author)   69
4 The room of victim photos at the Kigali Memorial
  Centre (Photo by author)   81
5 Kibeho genocide memorial and church (Photo by author)   86
6 Rwanda's new national flag (Photo by author)   160

Acknowledgments

In the long process of researching and writing this book, I have accumulated numerous debts of gratitude. Between my first research trip to Rwanda for this book in March 2001 until its ultimate publication sixteen years later, I traveled to Rwanda at least fifteen times, oversaw nine distinct research projects that involved more than three dozen researchers, interviewed hundreds of individuals, and presented elements of the data and analysis at numerous conferences, workshops, and lectures. In this long process, I have benefitted from the insight, skill, and generosity of countless individuals. My colleagues from the Human Rights Center at the University of California, Berkeley – particularly Harvey Weinstein, Eric Stover, and Sarah Freedman – provided the opportunity for this research and offered important support and inspiration. From 2001 to 2003, Théoneste Rutagengwa ably led a team of Rwandan researchers in conducting individual and focus group interviews. Alice Karekezi, from the National University of Rwanda, and Phuong Pham, now at Harvard University, oversaw the 2002 survey. Several Rwandans, I hesitate to name over concern for their safety, directed important aspects of the research. I wish in particular to thank BN, DF, and JM for their dedicated work and helpful insight.

Several students have provided important support as research assistants. Vassar College undergraduates, Evan White and Zachary Moon, conducted helpful secondary research. Whitney Flanagan conducted careful systematic analysis of the interviews and media reports. Erica Beidelman and Courtney Kramer, Masters students at Boston University's Pardee School of Global Affairs, worked on the bibliography.

The research for this book was funded by the John D. and Catherine T. MacArthur Foundation, the Sandler Foundation, the Hewlett Foundation, and the United States Institute for Peace. Additional support came from research funds from Vassar College and Boston University.

I received helpful feedback on earlier drafts of this book from Susan Thomson, Noel Twagiramungu, Théoneste Ganza, Benjamin Twagira, and Anuradha Chakravarty. An early version of Chapter 3 was helpfully workshopped with my colleagues at Vassar College. Over the years, I have greatly benefited from the exceptionally congenial community of scholars working on Rwanda. An earlier generation of Rwanda experts, including Catharine and David Newbury, the late Alison Des Forges, Filip Reyntjens, René Lemarchand, Villia Jefremovas, Johan Pottier, and Danielle DeLame have offered consistent wisdom and guidance, while a younger generation of scholars, including Jennie Burnet, Susan Thomson, Lars Waldorf, Bert Ingelaere, Scott Straus, Noel Twagiramungu, An Ansoms, Aimable Twagilimana, Anu Chakravarty, Jens Meierenrich, Jude Murison, Aloys Habimana, Phil Clark, and Christopher Huggins, have provided continuing intellectual stimulation, information, and inspiration. My colleagues at Vassar College and Boston University have also provided important support over the years. I am particularly grateful to Patrick Vinck for creating the map at the beginning of this text.

Finally, I must thank my family for all of their support and understanding over the years. My research has taken me away from home far too many times, and the writing has taken far too much of my attention. I thank them for their patience.

Abbreviations

ANC	African National Congress
CDR	Coalition for the Defense of the Republic
FIDH	International Federation of Human Rights
HRW	Human Rights Watch
ICC	International Criminal Court
ICTR	International Criminal Tribunal for Rwanda
IDP	internally displaced people
LIPRODHOR	*Ligue Rwandaise pour la Promotion et la Défense des Droits de l'Homme*
MRND	National Revolutionary Movement for Development (*Mouvement Révolutionaire National pour le Développement*)
NUR	National University of Rwanda
PTSD	post-traumatic stress disorder
RPA	Rwandan Patriotic Army
RPF	Rwandan Patriotic Front
RTLM	Radio-Television of the Thousand Hills (*Radio-Télévision Libre des Milles Collines*)
TRC	Truth and Reconciliation Commission

1   Introduction: The Meaning of Murambi

The stench of death reached us long before we arrived at the summit of Murambi hill. The odor was surprisingly sweet but cloying and syrupy, and it hung in the air like a thick fog. The day was April 7, 1996, two years exactly since the beginning of a genocide that killed an estimated 80 percent of Rwanda's minority Tutsi population. In April 1994, several thousand Tutsi who had sought refuge from the violence in an unfinished school complex here were instead slaughtered. Now, two years later, a crowd was once again gathering at Murambi, but this time there were no militia groups or death squads. Instead, the president was there, along with the prime minister, most of the cabinet, and much of Rwanda's expatriate community. The elite of Rwanda had come to Murambi this day two years after the genocide to commemorate the hundreds of thousands of innocent civilians who were killed in Rwanda from April to July 1994.

Murambi is a tall hill just northwest of the capital of Gikongoro, long Rwanda's poorest province. In this mountainous area now part of Southern Province, the steep slopes of the Congo-Nile continental divide make the soil infertile and the land difficult to farm.[1] Rwanda has experienced ethnic tensions and violence since the late colonial period, and in two earlier waves of anti-Tutsi violence, in 1963 and again in 1973, Gikongoro suffered some of the country's most brutal attacks.[2] When ethnic tensions re-emerged in Rwanda in the early 1990s, Gikongoro's poverty, large Tutsi population, and strong ties with the former Tutsi monarchy made ethnic relations in the province particularly precarious.

---

[1] On social and economic conditions in Gikongoro just prior to the genocide, see Jennifer M. Olson, *Land Degradation in Gikongoro Rwanda: Problems and Possibilities in the Integration of Household Survey Data and Environmental Data*, Rwanda society environment project, working paper 5, East Lansing: Michigan State University, 1994. Olson conducted extensive research with farmers in the region in the early 1990s.

[2] René Lemarchand, *Rwanda and Burundi*, New York: Praeger Publishers, 1970, 223–224. Lemarchand reports that the December 1963 massacres instigated by the Gikongoro prefect killed about 5,000 Tutsi, including men, women, and children. Several people I interviewed in Gikongoro in 1996 and again in 2004 recounted this earlier violence.

After Rwandan President Juvénal Habyarmimana was killed in a plane crash on April 6, 1994, Gikongoro was among the first places outside the national capital, Kigali, where violence broke out. Taking cues from the new extremist Hutu ethno-nationalist regime in Kigali, government officials, military officers, and others in Gikongoro with ties to the regime organized "civil self-defense" programs to protect against a supposed internal Tutsi threat. They armed and mobilized local civilian militia to attack Tutsi and burn their homes, driving thousands to flee in search of refuge. Throughout the prefecture, officials, a few apparently seeking sincerely to protect the Tutsi, but most cynically intending to facilitate their elimination by gathering them together with false promises of sanctuary, directed displaced Tutsi to central locations such as the churches at Kibeho, Kaduha, and Cyanika. In central Gikongoro, Tutsi initially sought refuge at the Anglican cathedral at Kigeme and the Gikongoro Catholic cathedral, but around April 11, the day militias began to attack Tutsi gathered at nearby Kibeho parish, officials brought Tutsi under police escort from the cathedrals and other locations to Murambi, where a technical high school was under construction. With a remote location on a high hill and available buildings – several small classroom structures and a large administrative building were completed but not yet in use – Murambi offered an ideal location for housing and protecting the Tutsi or, as it eventually turned out, for isolating and eliminating them. Over the next week, the number of refugees increased as Tutsi who fled Kibeho and others who sought to escape along the main highway toward still peaceful Butare prefecture were stopped and redirected to Murambi.[3]

On April 17, 1994, civilian militia launched a first assault against those gathered at the Murambi Technical School, but the refugees repulsed them by throwing stones. The refugees successfully defended themselves from attacks for several days, even as more Tutsi continued to arrive at Murambi, fleeing massacres in other communities. By April 20, however, with some 40,000 people gathered at the school and water and food supplies depleted, conditions had become squalid, and the refugees were increasingly weak and sick. Early in the morning of April 21, several hundred militia members returned, this time backed by soldiers and gendarmes. They surrounded Murambi hill, tossed grenades and shot into the crowd, and followed up with clubs and machetes. They killed several thousand, while thousands more fled, many to nearby Cyanika

---

[3] Details on the genocide in Gikongoro are drawn from Alison Des Forges, *Leave None to Tell the Story: Genocide in Rwanda*, New York: Human Rights Watch, 1999, 303–352, as well as interviews that I conducted (some for the Des Forges text) in 1996.

parish, where they were massacred a few days later. After all the Tutsi at Murambi were either killed or dispersed, government officials came to inspect the results and reward the most brutal militia groups with cattle looted from the slaughtered Tutsi. In the next few days, Gikongoro prison inmates dug mass graves where the bodies of the victims were unceremoniously dumped, and the site was abandoned as the violence moved on to Cyanika, Kaduha, and elsewhere.[4]

Two years exactly after the beginning of the 1994 genocide, a huge crowd gathered at Murambi to commemorate the terrible slaughter that Rwanda experienced. Despite the rainy weather, several hundred people had turned out, and cars lined the mud roads leading to the abandoned school-turned-memorial site. A new government was now in place in Rwanda, a government installed by the largely Tutsi former rebel movement, the Rwandan Patriotic Front (RPF), that drove out the genocidal government and put a stop to the genocide in July 1994.[5] The government had declared an annual week of remembrance of the genocide, with a national day of commemoration, which this year was being held at Murambi. Government ministers, UN employees, international diplomats, prominent Rwandan citizens, foreign visitors, journalists, and others had come to Murambi to show their respects at the official annual ceremony commemorating the 1994 genocide. As the director of the office of Human Rights Watch (HRW) and the International Federation of Human Rights (FIDH) in Rwanda, I attended the ceremony with a few American and Rwandan colleagues. We parked our pick-up far down the hill and hiked some distance up the muddy road. The day was fittingly dark and gray, and we could smell the strange odor of decomposing bodies even before we reached the crowd gathered at the site.

A large field stood at the top of the hill, with the two-story main building at one end where the official ceremony would take place. To the side of this building was a small memorial garden, where victims' bodies were to be given a proper burial after the commemoration. As part of the national program of recovery, the bodies of Tutsi killed in the genocide were being disinterred around the country and reburied with appropriate ceremonies in marked graves. One mass grave for victims of the genocide had already been completed at Murambi,

---

[4] Specifics on Murambi come from interviews in Gikongoro, Kaduha, and Butare in 1995, 1996, 2001, and 2004, and from the International Criminal Tribunal for Rwanda, *The Prosecutor vs. Aloys Simba*, Case No. ICTR-01-76-T, Judgement and Sentence, Arusha, December 13, 2005.

[5] In this text, I do not make a distinction between the Rwandan Patriotic Front and the Rwandan Patriotic Army. Technically, the former is a political movement while the latter is its armed wing, but in practice the two have always been closely interconnected and their personnel overlap.

covered with cement and surrounded by blooming flowers; another large hole had been dug beside it, where more bodies would be interred following the day's commemoration. At Murambi, the bodies of victims had been unearthed for reburial, and for this day of commemoration, the bodies had been laid out in the classroom buildings, a short distance down the hill from the main building. As the crowds waited for the commemoration ceremonies to begin, people walked down the hill to view the bodies of the victims and bear witness to the crimes committed in this place.[6]

My colleagues and I joined the line filing past the narrow cement classroom buildings. Inside each of the rooms, bodies were laid out, covered with powdered lime to preserve them. Even so, the stench of decaying flesh was still so strong that most people covered their noses and mouths as they passed. The display of bodies was meant to resemble one of the other memorial sites in the country, like the Catholic parish of Nyamata, where bodies had been left as they had fallen when the swift RPF advance drove out the local population before they could dispose of the evidence of their crimes. But here at Murambi the bodies were laid out carefully on display, each room with a theme serving a didactic purpose. The ghostly lime-covered bodies, skeletons with mummified skin and bits of cloth clinging to them, were laid side by side in tightly packed rows. In one room were bodies with visible machete scars, in another bodies missing feet or hands, apparently amputated, and in yet another, piles of flesh-less bones. One room held the small corpses of children and another held bodies with remnants of dresses that showed the victims were women. One woman was laid out with her legs spread wide and a stick inserted between them to demonstrate how Tutsi women were brutally raped during the genocide.

The sight of the bodies and bones was shocking and horrific. Yet as someone with a deep connection to Rwanda, someone who had lost friends in the genocide, I was also deeply troubled by the very fact that the bodies were being placed on display, that they were being laid out in a fashion calculated to shock observers. In Rwandan tradition, the proper treatment of the body of the deceased is important, as it represents the connection between the living and the dead. Rwandans have traditionally been buried on their own land or, for chiefs, on the land of clients, representing their physical link to the land. Although some cemeteries did exist in Rwanda prior to the genocide, few families buried their dead in these communal graves, preferring a more intimate and immediate connection

[6] Fieldnotes on visit to Murambi, April 7, 1996.

to the dead.[7] In the aftermath of the genocide, when so many people had been lost and their bodies disposed of carelessly in rivers and lakes, pit latrines, and hastily dug mass graves, the fact that identifying each body and returning it to its family might not be possible was understandable. Yet the public exhibition of the bodies at Murambi seemed particularly offensive, insensitive to the families of those killed. The use of bodies to manufacture a scene of horror and provoke a reaction seemed to contradict the intent of remembering the genocide and honoring the dead.

As the commemoration ceremony began, the crowds of Rwandan and international visitors gathered in the main building, overflowing into the surrounding yard. With a backdrop of bodies and bones, the politicians who spoke in the commemoration event invoked the genocide, the need to never forget, the shame this genocide brings not only to the Rwandan perpetrators but also to the international community that actively supported the genocidal government as the RPF was fighting to bring the genocide to an end. This massacre site and this commemoration, I realized, allowed the government installed by the RPF to promote a crucial political message: the genocide was so horrible that it justified any actions that the new government had to take to maintain security. The bodies of genocide victims were being used to make a political point.

Whatever reservations I had, the macabre display at Murambi seems to have served a valuable purpose. While most of the churches and schools where Rwanda's Tutsi were slaughtered in 1994 have been scrubbed clean and returned to their original purposes, Murambi is one of only a few massacre sites that the post-genocide government decided to preserve as an official national memorial to the genocide. Along with the Catholic churches at Nyarubuye, Nyamata, and Ntarama in southeastern Rwanda, where the bodies of slaughtered Tutsi were initially left as they were found by troops of the advancing RPF; Bisesero, the hill above the shores of Lake Kivu where Tutsi maintained a long and valiant resistance against the genocidal militias; the museum built with funding from the UK-based Aegis Trust, the Kigali Genocide Memorial Centre, where victims of the genocide in Kigali have been buried, Murambi has come to represent the Rwandan genocide. The bones on display at Murambi are presented as evidence of the horrible tragedy that Rwanda experienced, and they have become iconic symbols of the genocide. In fact, a novel set at Murambi by Senegalese writer Boubacar Boris Diop, part of an African

---

[7] Gerard van't Spijker, *Les usages funéraires et la mission de l'Église: une etude anthropologique et théologique des rites funéraires au Rwanda*, Kampen: Uitgeversmaatschappij J.H. Kok, 1990, 51–128; Jennie Burnet, *Genocide Lives in Us: Women, Memory, and Silence in Rwanda*, Madison: University of Wisconsin Press, 2012.

artists project to commemorate the genocide, is called *Murambi: the Book of Bones*.[8] The Aegis Trust, which has taken responsibility for preserving the site and developing programming, writes on their website, "Survivors returning to the site preserved some of the bodies in lime; these remain visible today, a stark memorial and warning to the world."[9] Murambi has become an obligatory stop for visitors to Rwanda, whether international aid workers or tourists who drop by Murambi on their way to see the monkeys of Nyungwe Forest.[10]

I returned to Murambi in November 2001, over five years after my initial visit, as part of my research for this book. Since my research program worked in cooperation with the National University of Rwanda, a guide from the public relations office at the university was sent to host me and another colleague on our visit to Murambi. Like most of those in official positions in post-genocide Rwanda, Susan had not been in Rwanda at the time of the genocide, but she lectured us on the genocide nevertheless. She told us that, "The genocide happened because there are so many ignorant, illiterate people who could easily be misled."[11] She went on to claim that children had learned bigotry, because in schools Hutu and Tutsi students had been segregated into separate classrooms – something that was factually untrue.[12] Arriving at the site, we were met by a man who reported that he was one of only four survivors of the massacre. He had a bullet scar in his skull, across his forehead. He told us that five to six thousand people were killed at Murambi. As he led us down to the classroom buildings, I asked about the bodies that had been on display in 1996. Our guide told us that they had indeed been placed in the mass grave as promised, but that other mass graves had been unearthed around Gikongoro and the bodies had been brought here to replace those previously interred, so cadavers were still on exhibit.[13] In fact, there were now several additional classrooms with bodies on display. Perhaps

---

8   Boubacar Boris Diop, *Murambi: The Book of Bones*, Bloomington: Indiana University Press, 2006. On the project, '"Rwanda": ecrire par devoir de mémoire', see Odile Cazenave and Patricia Célérier, *Contemporary Francophone African Writers and the Burden of Commitment*, Charlottesville: University of Virginia Press, 2011, especially Chapter 2.

9   www.aegis.tv/index.php?option=content&task=view&id=218&Itemid=222,   accessed on June 26, 2006.

10   An internet search for Murambi turns up mentions of the site on the itinerary of numerous tourist junkets to Rwanda.

11   Fieldnotes, November 13, 2001, Murambi, Gikongoro.

12   The number of Tutsi allowed into each school was limited by quota, and Tutsi faced discrimination and harassment, but schools were not segregated. Elisabeth King, *From Classrooms to Conflict in Rwanda*, New York: Cambridge University Press, 2014.

13   This account differs slightly from Claudine Vidal, "Les commémorations du génocide au Rwanda," *Les Temps Modernes* 613, 1–46, who reports that the bodies now on display were some that had never been buried.

as a nod to the sensibilities of survivors, the new corpses were not placed on the cold cement floor, but on wooden pallets built for the purpose of exhibiting them. Yet the site remained gruesome and shocking, with bodies still organized and displayed in a calculated fashion, like a demented museum diorama.[14]

I found myself wondering about the purpose of this memorial site, with its contrived, grisly exhibition of bodies. The Aegis Trust description suggests that genocide survivors themselves were behind the exhibit, but my research indicated that in reality the government organized both the initial display of bodies and the subsequent location of more bodies. That survivors would ever choose to have the bodies of their families put on display is hard to believe, particularly given Rwanda's cultural attitudes toward treatment of the dead. In fact, every conversation I have had with survivors about memorial sites suggests that they find the display of bodies offensive. I had an opportunity a few months after my visit to Murambi to speak with a woman whose family was killed at Murambi, when I interviewed two Rwandan nuns in Butare, both Tutsi, one of whom had come back to Rwanda from Congo after the genocide, the other, a native of Gikongoro, who had survived the genocide in hiding in Butare. When I asked what they thought about the memorials, the nun from Gikongoro spoke with considerable pain.

"It is not good to leave the bodies like that," she said, grief visible in her eyes. "They need to find the means to bury them. We can't leave them like that."

Her colleague quickly jumped in to defend the Murambi site. "But it has another role. It helps to show those who said that there was no genocide what happened. It acts as a proof to the international community." The other nun looked on with a sorrowful expression but said nothing more.[15]

If Murambi is not for the survivors, who, then, is the audience for this gruesome exhibit? When we were at Murambi in 2001, I asked our guide who visited the site.

"Foreigners," he said, "and sometimes people from Kigali or Byumba," by which I understood him to mean urban people, mostly Rwanda's new elite, the returned refugees.

"Do local people come here?" I asked.

"Never local people," he said. In fact, most of the names in the guest book that he asked us to sign were foreigners – Americans, Germans, Japanese – and a few others were from Kigali.

---

[14] Field notes on visit to Murambi, November 13, 2001.

[15] Interview in Butare, June 10, 2002, in French. All translations from French to English by the author.

Murambi stands, then, as a symbol of the genocide for the international community. As the nun from Congo told me, "It stands as a proof *to the international community.*" The bones are meant to demonstrate to the world that the genocide actually occurred and to remind the international community of its extraordinary moral and political failure in the face of the genocide. Murambi tells the international community that whatever faults there may be in the current regime, they are understandable, given the genocide, and they cannot compare to the horrible atrocities that the country experienced in 1994.

Yet the bones of Murambi have another audience as well: members and supporters of the current regime, the former Tutsi refugees who have returned to Rwanda and now dominate Rwandan social, political, and economic life. To the returnees, the horrific display of bodies is a reminder of the terrible atrocities committed against their people. It reassures them of their moral right to rule, and it also warns them of the consequences of allowing themselves once again to become victims. As a symbol of the genocide, Murambi is much less about remembering the past than about paving the way for a particular political agenda in the present.

But what does it mean when the proof has been falsified? There is no denying that Murambi was the site of a terrible massacre in 1994. But the Murambi memorial site shows a level of disrespect and deception that is indicative of a wider problem with efforts by the post-genocide government to confront Rwanda's past. Rather than honestly presenting the horrors of what happened at Murambi, bodies are used for their shock effect. The fact that the bodies currently on display at Murambi did not even come from this site is not made evident. As one person familiar with the site told me, "we do not even know what these bodies are, how they died. Some of them may even be Hutu killed by the RPF."[16] The truth of the tragedy at Murambi is secondary to the need for a political symbol.

The discussion of numbers killed at Murambi is a prime example of the careless (or calculated) deception used to prove a point. Our guide at Murambi in 2001, himself a survivor of the massacre, told us that between 5,000 and 6,000 people died at Murambi. The bodies exhumed at the site for the 1996 commemoration confirmed this figure.[17] Yet published estimates have been rising since a Rwandan government commission in 1995 estimated that 20,000 were killed at Murambi.[18] The Aegis website for Murambi says that, "An estimated 40,000 victims perished

---

[16] Interview in Butare, November 15, 2001.
[17] Des Forges, *Leave None to Tell the Story*, p. 16.
[18] Ibid.

on this site in 48 hours."[19] A photo-journalist who visited the site in
late 2005 reports that 60,000 Tutsi sought refuge at Murambi and that
45,000 were killed.[20] Another website claims that "more than 50,000
people were killed" at Murambi.[21] Never Again International, an organization that seeks to promote awareness of the Rwandan genocide, uses
the corpses on display and inflated numbers to illustrate the horrors at
Murambi on their website:

The stench Of corpses Covered with a crispy white preservative In positions of
self defense: Hands to heads. Heads in hands. Babies. Squashed skulls. Flattened
rib cages. Battering – holes, dents, damage. Teeth missing. And teeth. Lives taken.
Brutally. And a Survivor. There were 4 out of 50–60 thousand. He wore a blue
shirt and has a hole is his head where the bullet entered and failed to kill him. He
fell to the ground and lay under the bodies of his dead family and neighbors. He
moved himself to the surrounding forests where he hid for four months. He lives
on. With no one he loves left. Now he lives far from Murambi but returns to the
site when he needs to feel close to his family.[22]

As I have found in my research and advocacy, to question these numbers or to challenge the appropriateness of placing bodies on display is
quickly dismissed as an attempt to negate the seriousness of the genocide.
When I said to the Director of Memorials in the Ministry of Youth and
Culture, the chief government official charged with overseeing memorials, that Rwanda does not have a tradition of leaving bodies exposed, he
responded vehemently, "Rwanda does not have a tradition of genocide
either!"[23] There is little room for the quiet voice of a survivor that says,
"It is not good to leave the bodies like that."

The Politics of Memory and the Rwandan Genocide

The massacre at Murambi was unfortunately only one small chapter in the terrible cataclysm of violence that shook Rwanda in 1994.
Beginning in 1990, the combined pressures of an economic downturn,
a pro-democracy movement, and an invasion by Rwandan refugees,
mostly Tutsi who had fled earlier waves of violence and were now seeking the right to return to their country of origin, disrupted Rwandan
society. These pressures forced the government of long-time president

[19] www.aegis.tv/index.php?option=content&task=view&id=218&Itemid=222, accessed on
June 26, 2006.
[20] www.geoffbugbee.com, accessed on June 27, 2006.
[21] www.findarticles.com/p/articles/mi_m0438/is_3_38/ai_n16118531/pg_22, accessed on
June 27, 2006.
[22] www.neveragaininternational.org/news/murambi.html, accessed on June 27, 2006.
[23] Interview in Kigali, June 2003.

Habyarimana to offer concessions allowing an expansion of press freedom, a blossoming of civil society, and the emergence of new political parties and their inclusion in government. Over time, however, the fact that the army attacking the country was comprised mostly of members of the Tutsi ethnic group provided an opportunity for supporters of the regime to exploit popular resentment of the war. Building on a history of ethnic violence dating back to 1959, regime supporters fostered suspicion of Tutsi still living in Rwanda and portrayed themselves as defenders of majority Hutu interests. From late 1990 through 1993, extremist Hutu ethno-nationalists, acting with government support, carried out a series of massacres of Tutsi (and in a few cases moderate Hutu) in several parts of the country that helped to heighten ethnic tensions. They painted Hutu who challenged the regime as traitors to their people.[24]

When President Habyarimana was assassinated in a plane crash on April 6, 1994, Hutu extremists used his death as justification for launching a long-planned attack on regime opponents – opposition politicians, civil society activists, journalists, intellectuals – under the guise of ethnic violence. Initially focused in the capital, the international community's failure to condemn their actions inspired the extremists to expand their plan into the rest of the country.[25] While continuing to target Hutu who resisted the genocide, the organizers focused the violence more specifically on Tutsi, creating an incentive for Hutu to support, or at least acquiesce to, the violence – making ethnic solidarity the easiest route to survival. Officials and others supporting the genocide lured Tutsi to central locations, such as churches or schools, like Murambi, then trained local militia groups with backing from police or soldiers attacked the ostensible places of sanctuary, systematically slaughtering those inside, often over a period of several days. In the weeks that followed the major massacres, leaders organized the general population to work barricades and carry out "security" patrols in communities throughout the country to find Tutsi survivors and prevent their fleeing. In three months, more than 500,000 Tutsi and several thousand moderate Hutu were murdered,

---

[24] The best general sources on the genocide and its causes are Des Forges, *Leave None to Tell the Story* and Gerard Prunier, *The Rwanda Crisis: History of a Genocide*, New York: Columbia, 1995. Nigel Eltringham, *Accounting for Horror: Post-Genocide Debates in Rwanda*, London: Pluto Press, 2005, challenges the use of the terms "extremist Hutu" and "moderate Hutu," arguing that they obscure the complexities within the Hutu population. In the absence of better terms, however, I refer to Hutu who embraced an anti-Tutsi ideology as "extremists" and those who supported ethnic unity and opposed Tutsi scapegoating as "moderates."

[25] The transformation of the violence into genocide is a central theme in André Guichaoua, *From War to Genocide: Criminal Politics in Rwanda 1990–1994*, Madison: University of Wisconsin Press, 2015.

thousands of Tutsi women were raped, countless houses and other Tutsi-owned buildings were destroyed, and communities were devastated.

When the genocide began, the Rwandan Patriotic Front, the predominantly Tutsi rebel group that had been attacking the country from October 1990 until an August 1993 peace accord, responded almost immediately by renewing their assault on Rwanda. Where they occupied territory, first in the capital and the north and east of the country, then pushing south and west, the RPF stopped the genocide, saving thousands of Tutsi. Yet the RPF invasion also lent credence to the ideological claims of the leaders of the genocide in areas still under their control, particularly as refugees fleeing the RPF advances reported massacres carried out by the RPF. The Rwandan Armed Forces (*Forces Armées Rwandaise*, FAR), meanwhile, were so focused on eliminating imaginary internal enemies that they were incapable of fending off the RPF advance. The RPF quickly drove the Rwandan forces back, sending over one million mostly Hutu refugees fleeing into neighboring Tanzania and another million into the Democratic Republic of Congo (then known as Zaire). By July, RPF troops had occupied all of the country except a section in the southwest (including Gikongoro) occupied by French troops.

After taking power, the RPF named a new multi-ethnic, multi-party government and over the next several months used considerable force to subdue the population remaining in Rwanda. While RPF violence was much less systematic than the genocide, as they advanced across the country, the RPF opened fire on civilians in communities they occupied, carried out hundreds of summary executions, looted property, and engaged in other human rights abuses. Such abuses continued fairly intensely for a few months following the RPF rise to power, while thousands of people were imprisoned under accusations of participation in the genocide. After the French forces left Rwanda in late 1994, RPF troops used force to close camps housing thousands of displaced people.[26] Within a year after the genocide, however, levels of state-sponsored violence within Rwanda diminished.

In many ways, Rwandan society has made significant advances in the two decades since 1994. To casual observers, Rwanda may seem to have recovered from the genocide with extraordinary speed. The infrastructure of the country has been rebuilt, so that most of the physical scars of the war and genocide have been erased. Within the capital, at least, the country seems quite prosperous, with extensive new construction, both private and public, newly paved roads and sidewalks, new parks and

---

[26] On RPF human rights abuses, see Des Forges, *Leave None to Tell the Story*, 692–735; Prunier, *The Rwanda Crisis*, 304–334.

monuments, and many new homes, stores, and restaurants. Investment in the agricultural sector has increased yields of grains and potatoes and helped to drive an annual gross domestic product growth rate averaging around six percent for the past decade.[27] More significantly, the country appears to have made much political and social progress. Refugees from the anti-Tutsi violence that began in 1959 and those Rwandans, mostly Hutu, who fled to Tanzania and Congo in 1994 have returned home and been reintegrated into their communities. Hutu and Tutsi live together as neighbors. Public discussion of ethnicity is now illegal, and most people today will claim they are neither Hutu nor Tutsi but Rwandan. A new constitution has been adopted, elections held, and a multi-ethnic government is now in power, one that includes a higher percentage of women in parliament than any other country on earth. The government espouses a strong rhetoric of national unity and reconciliation. On the surface, Rwanda appears to have made a remarkable recovery from the bitter ethnic violence that rent the country a decade earlier.

Yet the actual state of social relations in Rwanda today is much less tranquil than it appears. As I describe in this book, the post-genocide government of Rwanda has undertaken an extraordinarily far-reaching program of social engineering, surely one of the most extensive by any modern state. Using commemorations and memorials, judicial processes, historical revision, re-education camps, curricular reform, popular mobilization, political restructuring, electoral activity, land reform, and many other programs, the government has sought not simply to reshape relations between the population and the state, or even between groups within the society, but to transform the ways in which individual Rwandans understand their own social identities. Using memorial sites such as Murambi, the government of Rwanda, with support from the international community, has attempted what the Aegis Trust calls "shaping the memory of the Rwandan genocide."[28] In reinterpreting the past – both recent traumatic events and the more distant past – the regime and its supporters have sought to reshape the very ways in which Rwandans understand their own historical experience. The genocide is placed at the center of Rwandan history, the ultimate outcome of the historical process of colonization. Any other tragic experiences – like RPF attacks on Hutu refugees in Congo – are, while perhaps regrettable, peripheral to Rwandan history. The RPF's rule is legitimized by the fact that they brought the genocide to an end and subsequently

---

[27] World Bank, "Rwanda," April 22, 2016, available at www.worldbank.org/en/country/rwanda.

[28] Aegis Trust – Rwanda, "10 Years After: Shaping the Memory of the Rwandan Genocide," Press Release, Kigali, April 7, 2004.

established a multi-ethnic government rather than seeking revenge or dominance. In promoting these various ideas, the regime sought to create a cohesive collective memory to unify the country by minimizing the historic importance of ethnicity, while simultaneously protecting the Tutsi minority from further persecution and violence and maintaining the control of the current power elite, who are overwhelmingly drawn from a limited demographic – former Tutsi refugees, primarily from Uganda and Congo.

How one views the Rwandan government's project of aggressively shaping collective memory depends in large part on whether one regards the regime's primary goal as avoiding future ethnic violence or, in contrast, merely preventing opposition in order to preserve personal power. Much of the international community seems to take at face value the regime's claims of eschewing ethnic discrimination and supporting unity. When I worked for Human Rights Watch and FIDH in Rwanda in 1995–1996, although my primary task was researching the 1994 genocide, I also collected extensive testimony from individuals who had lost family members to RPF attacks or who had been unjustly imprisoned, and I investigated a number of cases of ongoing abuse – disappearances, politically motivated arrests, torture, and murder. The regime in Kigali, however, rejected human rights criticisms, easily brushing aside concerns that did not fit their self-promoted public image as a non-prejudicial, unifying regime that backed rule of law. The international diplomatic corps overwhelmingly backed the government position, often responding harshly to those of us who raised questions about RPF abuses. Johann Pottier has convincingly exposed the degree to which the Rwandan Patriotic Front's project of "knowledge construction" has persuaded the international community.[29] According to Pottier, "[J]ournalists unfamiliar with the region, ... newcomer academics, diplomats, and aid workers ... have helped, although to varying degrees, to popularise and spread an RPF-friendly but empirically questionable narrative."[30] The RPF interpretation of Rwandan society and history has become the standard means for the international community to approach Rwanda.

The primary audience for the government's policies, however, is not the international community but the Rwandan population itself. Both the government and international community have expended considerable energy and money to rebuild Rwandan society, fight impunity, promote rule of law, maintain peace, and encourage reconciliation, and

---

[29] Johan Pottier, *Re-Imagining Rwanda: Conflict, Survival and Disinformation in the Late Twentieth Century*, Cambridge: Cambridge University Press, 2002, p. 109.
[30] Ibid., p. 53.

a specific interpretation of the past lies at the heart of this effort. If the government is successful in creating a coherent collective memory that erases ethnic identity from public consciousness, then ethnic conflict will indeed become impossible. Yet the contradictions between the government's perspective and the lived experience of much of the population challenge the possibilities of developing a common understanding of the past. How can a coherent collective memory be developed when individual experiences – or, in fact, the experiences of various social groups – diverge so widely? The choice is much more complex than, as both the government and much of the international community seem to suggest, a choice between accepting the government's perspective, which is tantamount to supporting unity and peace, or rejecting the government line and embracing bigotry and violence. The ways in which Rwandans have responded to efforts to create a collective memory and unified national identity is the main focus of this book.

Collective Memory, Transitional Justice, and the Limits of State Power

While the 1994 genocide in Rwandan was remarkable for its intensity and rapidity, mass violence is an unfortunately widespread phenomenon in the modern world. From the relatively limited violence of authoritarian regimes in places like Chile, Argentina, and Brazil to the more widespread brutality of El Salvador, Bosnia-Herzegovina, East Timor, and the Democratic Republic of Congo, violence has disrupted numerous societies, rupturing social networks, undermining the rule of law, and alienating populations from the state. In the past two decades, finding means to help societies recover from the legacies of authoritarianism and violence has become a major focus of both diplomatic action and academic attention. The term "transitional justice" has come to encompass a wide range of policies and approaches applied in post-authoritarian and post-conflict societies.

While transitional justice has emerged quickly as a major political and academic focus, the concept remains loosely defined, and diverse disciplines approach the topic in divergent ways.[31] Legal scholars have focused on the contributions that accountability can make to social reconstruction. Considerable debate exists over the comparative advantages of trials and truth commissions. The emphasis in trials on retributive justice is

---

[31] Ruti Teitel, *Transitional Justice*, Oxford: Oxford University Press, 2002, is the most widely read introduction to the field, though it approaches transitional justice primarily from a legal/philosophical perspective.

said to build rule of law, while the focus in truth commissions on truth telling is said to promote reconciliation. An increasing number of post-conflict countries have sought to combine the two types of institution to promote both accountability and reconciliation.[32] Many political scientists interested in post-conflict societies have explored identity politics, focusing in particular on how to construct unifying national identities in contexts of deep social division.[33] Others have studied the reform of political institutions – democratization, federalism, the adoption of consociational governmental models – as means of easing social tensions and avoiding future conflicts.[34] Scholars in cultural studies (and, increasingly, other fields) have looked at the construction of collective memory in the aftermath of violence. The role that memorials and commemorations can play in shaping collective understandings of past atrocities has been a particular focus.[35] Specialists in education have looked at the role that schools can play in promoting dialogue and reshaping social attitudes.[36] Researchers in psychology and public health have studied means of addressing trauma and post-traumatic stress disorder (PTSD) and have taken an increasing interest in the role that the legacies of trauma

[32] Martha Minow, *Between Vengeance and Forgiveness: Facing History after Genocide and Mass Violence*, Boston: Beacon Press, 1998; Naomi Roht Arriaza and Javier Mariencurrena, eds., *Transitional Justice in the Twenty-First Century: Beyond Truth versus Justice*, Cambridge: Cambridge University Press, 2006.

[33] Charles T. Call, ed., *Building States to Build Peace*, Boulder: Lynne Rienner, 2008; Aidan Hehir and Neil Robinson, eds., *State Building: Theory and Practice*, New York: Routledge, 2007; Kate Jenkins and William Plowden, *Governance and Nationbuilding: The Failure of International Intervention*, Northampton, MA: Edward Elgar, 2006; Wayne Norman, *Negotiating Nationalism: Nation-building, Federalism, and Secession in the Multinational State*, Oxford: Oxford University Press, 2006.

[34] Donald L. Horowitz, *Ethnic Groups in Conflict*, Berkeley: University of California Press, 2000; Crawford Young, ed., *Ethnic Diversity and Public Policy: A Comparative Inquiry*, New York: Palgrave, 1998; Crawford Young, H. Edwin Young, and Ruppert Emmerson, eds., *The Accommodation of Cultural Diversity: Case Studies*, New York: St. Martin's Press, 1999; Arend Lijphart, *Thinking About Democracy: Power Sharing and Majority Rule in Theory and Practice*, New York: Routledge, 2008.

[35] James Edward Young, *The Texture of Memory: Holocaust Memorials and Meaning*, New Haven: Yale University Press, 1993; Mieke Bal, Jonathan Crewe, and Leo Spitzer, eds., *Acts of Memory: Cultural Recall in the Present*, Hanover, NH: Dartmouth University Press, 1999; Béatrice Pouligny, Simon Chesterman and Albrecht Schnabel, eds., *After Mass Crime: Rebuilding States and Communities*, New York: United Nations University Press, 2007.

[36] Elizabeth Cole, "Transitional Justice and the Reform of History Education," *The International Journal of Transitional Justice*, no. 1, 2007, 115–137; Elizabeth Cole and Judy Barsalou, *Unite or Divide? The Challenges of Teaching History in Societies Emerging from Violent Conflict*, Washington, DC: United States Institute of Peace, Special Report, 2006; Wolfgang Hoepken, "War, Memory, and Education in a Fragmented Society: The Case of Yugoslavia," *East European Politics and Societies*, 13, no. 1, 1999, 190–227; Sobhi Tawil and Alexandra Harley, eds., *Education, Conflict and Social Cohesion: Studies in Comparative Education*, International Bureau of Education/UNESCO, 2004.

may have on societies recovering from mass violence.[37] Economists have looked at the impact of economic deprivation and development on social relations.[38]

Little of the academic work on transitional justice provides an overall analysis of how societies recover from mass violence – or why they fail to recover. Each aspect of recovery is treated (at least to a degree) in isolation, when in reality violence has widespread social consequences that leave legacies throughout society. Recovery from violence, thus, requires broad interconnected social transformations. Policies addressing one element of the legacies of violence – the attempt to build rule of law, for example – will be affected by other social factors – for example, the widespread presence of PTSD in the population. Without studying the broad spectrum of legacies of violence and diverse processes of recovery, researchers might not understand the actual reasons for the success or failure of a given program. Even more problematic, much of the work on transitional justice is normative and theoretical, advocating policies that should contribute to peace and reconciliation without providing empirical evidence that the policies actually achieve their desired results. Yet the belief that transitional justice helps societies rebuild has become a cornerstone of post-conflict politics.

Because of the wide range of programs undertaken by the government and international community to promote social reconstruction in Rwanda, much of the post-conflict and transitional justice literature is relevant, and Rwanda represents an important empirical case for understanding the possibilities and interconnections of post-conflict rebuilding initiatives. Both the international community and the government of Rwanda have organized trials of genocide perpetrators, while the local-level gacaca courts instituted by the government drew on ideas from restorative justice and truth commissions. The Rwandan government has actively sought to create a national identity that will eclipse ethnic particularities. A decade-long period of transition culminated in 2003 in a new constitution, a reformed system of government, and national elections.

---

[37] B. Lopes Cardozo, et al, "Mental Health, Social Functioning, and Attitudes of Kosovar Albanians following the War in Kosovo," *Journal of the American Medical Association*, 286, 2001, 555–562; A Dyregrov, LRG Gupta, et al., "Trauma Exposure and Psychological Reactions to Genocide among Rwandan Children," *Journal of Traumatic Stress*, 13, 2000, 3–21.

[38] Brian Shoup, *Conflict and Cooperation in Multi-ethnic States: Institutional Incentives, Myths, and Counter-Balancing*, New York: Routledge, 2008; N. Shanmugaratnam, ed., *Between War and Peace in Sudan and Sri Lanka: Deprivation and Livelihood Revival*, Oxford: James Currey, 2008; Alexander Costy, "The Peace Dividend in Mozambique, 1987–1997," in Taisier M. Ali and Robert O. Matthews, eds., *Durable Peace: Challenges for Peacebuilding in Africa*, Toronto: University of Toronto Press, 2004, 142–182.

The government created a number of genocide memorials and each year organizes a period of genocide commemoration. Education reform was a major focus of the regime. While no comprehensive policies to deal with the trauma of genocide survivors were instituted, the therapeutic value of trials, memorials, and other activities is often lauded.[39] The government has also greatly emphasized economic development and policies to fight poverty, in part under the understanding that prosperity can help to prevent future violence.

Each of these policies is interesting in itself and worthy of study, and each discipline offers a useful lens through which to analyze post-genocide Rwanda. Yet to take each approach by itself and analyze each policy and institution in isolation from the others produces at best a partial understanding of the process of social reconstruction and at worst an inaccurate and distorted picture. This text thus takes an interdisciplinary approach to explore the range of government initiatives to clarify how reconciliation and social reconstruction programs interact and interrelate. Looking at how the population reacts to these programs provides a better understanding of which policies are most effective and why reconstruction policies succeed or fail to help societies overcome violence.

Methodology

In this book, I draw on an extremely rich body of empirical evidence gathered over the course of more than a decade of research to analyze both how the Rwandan government has sought to confront the legacies of violence and also how the Rwandan population has reacted to government programs for social reconstruction. To explore these questions, I draw on a number of research projects, some designed specifically to inform the writing of this book, others focused on related issues that nonetheless help to broaden and deepen the analysis. From 2001–2005, I oversaw five related research projects on social reconstruction in Rwanda.[40] The most substantial project for this book was a study of memory, justice, and identity that combined national-level monitoring of the press and interviews of government officials and other national leaders with case studies of three communes (equivalent to counties in

---

[39] Susanne Buckley-Zistel, "Between Past and Future: An Assessment of the Transition from Conflict to Peace in Post-genocide Rwanda," *Deutsche Stiftung Friedensforschung,* 2008, explores the government's claim truth heals

[40] These studies were part of the project Communities in Crisis: Social Reconstruction after Genocide and Ethnic Cleansing in Rwanda and the Former Yugoslavia, based at the Human Rights Center of the University of California, Berkeley, and funded by the John D. and Catherine T. MacArthur Foundation and the Sandler Foundation.

the United States) chosen to reflect several key variables – region, ethnic composition, genocide onset, genocide intensity, and involvement in post-genocide justice. Ngoma, the commune for the City of Butare, in what is today Southern Province, had a higher than average Tutsi population. It resisted the genocide longer than many areas, but the genocide ultimately had devastating results. Butare also experienced substantial RPF violence. The commune of Mabanza was in Kibuye Prefecture, now part of Western Province, and had a larger Tutsi population than the country as a whole. It experienced the genocide intensely and early on, but because it was in the French protection Zone Turquoise, Mabanza was spared extensive RPF violence. Buyoga was in the prefecture of Byumba, now in Northern Province, and had a small Tutsi population. The genocide started early, but most of the commune was in the demilitarized zone, so the genocide took place in only three of the commune's sectors, yet Buyoga experienced considerable RPF violence. Mabanza had cases completed at the International Criminal Tribunal for Rwanda (ICTR) at the time of the research, while ICTR cases for Butare were underway. Buyoga had no ICTR cases. In each of these communities, a team of researchers conducted ethnographic observation, individual interviews, and focus group interviews over a two and a half year period. A survey of 2,071 individuals was also conducted in these three communities plus one additional commune in northern Rwanda. In 2015, one of my long-time research assistants returned to two case study communities to conduct several dozen follow-up interviews a decade after the main research.

This study was complemented by several other studies of specific issues in post-genocide Rwanda that were directed by other researchers with my assistance and guidance. A team of researchers conducted extended observation of the function of gacaca courts in one locality, while another researcher studied the role of identity politics in Rwandan civil society groups. A study of the role of education in schools combined interviews and focus groups in six schools located in or near the case study communes.[41]

In addition to the studies formally conducted for this book, my analysis draws from a number of other projects in which I have been involved. From 1995–1996, I served as a human rights researcher, based in Rwanda, gathering information on both the genocide and ongoing human rights abuses. In 2002, I served on a team that conducted a democracy and

---

[41] The project Education and Social Reconstruction was directed by Sarah Warshauer Freedman of the University of California, Berkeley, and funded by the Hewlett Foundation.

governance assessment for USAID and the State Department. In 2004–2006, I was a principal investigator in a project to work on developing a new history curriculum for Rwandan secondary schools.[42] In 2004–2005, I conducted an assessment of a documentary news film project focused on promoting justice and good journalism in Rwanda.[43] In these projects, I benefited from collaboration with a wide range of researchers whose diverse disciplinary backgrounds in law, psychiatry, education, epidemiology, journalism, and history helped to augment my own formal training in political science and allowed me to bring a unique level of interdisciplinary analysis to this project.

Although I have conducted extensive research for this book and attempted to respect principles of social scientific rigor, employing a wide range of methodologies, I do not pretend to approach the subject of social reconstruction in Rwanda as a dispassionate observer, if such an attitude is even possible in the face of such a horrible tragedy. My connection to the country predates the genocide, and thus violence affected me personally. I first came to Rwanda in 1992 as a graduate student to spend a year conducting dissertation research on church-state relations.[44] I lived for several months in Kirinda, a small village in Kibuye prefecture and spent several more months teaching at the Protestant seminary in Butare and researching in Butare and the neighboring community of Save. I traveled through much of the rest of the country, observing public life and conducting hundreds of interviews. I developed close friendships with students, workers, and activists in the communities where I worked. The many principled people I met in Rwanda impressed me with their vision and their bravery – agronomists working to combat rural poverty, women's organizers standing up for women's rights, intellectuals fighting for democracy and human rights, students speaking out against ethnic discrimination, many people willing to risk their lives to make Rwanda a better place.

When I left Rwanda in mid-1993, however, I was pessimistic and deeply worried about the country's future. During my year in Rwanda, I saw a gradual unraveling of the social fabric and a descent into violence.[45]

---

[42] The project was funded by the United States Institute for Peace, with additional funding by the John D. and Catherine T. MacArthur Foundation. I was a principal researcher along with Sarah Freedman and Harvey Weinstein.

[43] I conducted an assessment of the Internews Newsreel project for the International Center for Transitional Justice.

[44] The 1992–1993 research project provides the core data for Longman, *Christianity and Genocide in Rwanda*.

[45] Danielle de Lame, *A Hill Among a Thousand: Transformations and Ruptures in Rural Rwanda*, Madison: University of Wisconsin Press, 2005, made a similar observation based on her research in the same period.

Even as some people were struggling to effect positive change, the leaders of the country were working to preserve their wealth and positions by undermining every reform they had been forced to accept. The ongoing civil war between the government and the RPF became an excuse for ethnic scapegoating of Rwanda's Tutsi and for calling into question the patriotism of Hutu who criticized the regime. Even at the local level, the divisions were stark: between the moderates who envisioned a democratic country where ethnicity did not matter, and Hutu ethno-nationalists who sought to make Rwanda a homeland for Hutu alone. I heard stories of discrimination and threats, and several Tutsi students asked advice on whether they should flee the country. I learned that some people I knew were embracing the extremist line. I traveled through communities ravaged by the civil war, including some where massacres of the local Tutsi had taken place. Witnessing the lynching of a rapist and robber by a vigilante mob that included people I knew made a deep impression on me. When I left the country, it seemed clear to me that extremism was on the rise, violence was becoming normalized, and the prospects of democracy were fading. I worried that, if the international community provided no support, Rwanda could descend into violence.

In the end, of course, the international community offered no support, and Rwanda fell into mass violence. In the aftermath of the 1994 genocide, I struggled from my position in the United States to discover what had happened to my friends – the news trickled out in letters and phone calls. Many friends were dead, some had fled the country, while others had survived but were scarred, physically and emotionally. In some cases I personally knew not only those murdered but also those who had killed them. So the Rwandan genocide touched me deeply and personally, and cannot avoid shaping how I approach and analyze post-genocide Rwanda.

In 1995, a little over a year after the genocide, I returned to Rwanda to work in the office of HRW and FIDH in Butare. My main task was to conduct research for a major report on the genocide.[46] I spoke with survivors, visited genocide sites, scoured government archives, and interviewed prisoners accused of complicity in the genocide, collecting convincing evidence of the careful organization of the killing and proof that it was in fact genocide. I returned to Kirinda and Butare and other communities where I had previously researched, found friends from before the genocide, and learned of their experiences. In the process, I also heard many stories of massacres carried out by the RPF, either

---

[46] I also wrote drafts of the two chapters on Nyakizu Commune in Des Forges, *Leave None to Tell the Story*.

as they advanced across the country or after they took power in July 1994. Several people told me of massacres in the provinces of Byumba and Kibungo, which the RPF occupied in April 1994. Others testified about the killings by RPF troops after they took control of Butare, or some months later at the camp for displaced people at Kibeho in March 1995. While the level of active violence had diminished considerably by the time I returned to Rwanda, complaints of summary executions, disappearances, arrests without charge, and other human rights problems persisted. Friends and associates who had experienced persecution under the Habyarimana regime told of harassment and intimidation by the current regime. As I became known in the community as a human rights researcher, an increasing number of people came to me seeking help with family members who had disappeared, friends arrested under false accusations, or threats by government officials or soldiers. Some expatriates working in Rwanda for Oxfam or Concern or Care spoke of the threats against their Hutu employees and the pressure they faced to hire Tutsi, particularly former refugees who were returning to Rwanda by the thousands from Uganda, Congo, and Burundi.

Yet most expatriates, particularly those who came to the country on short visits, were only interested in the genocide. Journalists came to Rwanda looking for parallels to the Holocaust, and their interest in Rwanda was entirely shaped by the events of 1994.[47] Most diplomats were little better. The United States government, whose leaders felt guilt over their failure in the 1994 genocide, strongly backed the new RPF-installed regime, and attempts to raise concerns over the current human rights situation with the US embassy or most other diplomatic missions were met not with indifference but with open hostility. To accuse the RPF of human rights abuses, many people suggested, was to equate the actions of the current government with the genocide and thereby deny the genocide.[48]

Living and working in Rwanda after the genocide, it became clear to me that even the voices and experiences of genocide survivors had been quashed by the post-genocide regime. Tutsi friends I knew from before 1994 complained about their sense of disempowerment and alienation.

---

[47] Philip Gourevitch, *We Wish to Inform You That Tomorrow We Will be Killed Along with our Families: Stories from Rwanda*, Picador, 1999. During his research in Rwanda I suggested to Gourevitch that if he wanted to understand the genocide, he needed to speak not simply with the government nor even with survivors, but also with the Hutu population, some of whom had supported the genocide, others of whom had opposed it, and many of whom were frustrated by the current state of events. Yet he, like many others, had little interest in the Hutu perspective.

[48] For more on the international perspective on Rwanda as influenced by the RPF, see Pottier's excellent, *Re-Imagining Rwanda*.

The new government, survivor friends complained, had little room for them, except as symbols used to justify the new regime. Survivors who were struggling to find housing and employment, who had descended into dire poverty because of the destruction of their homes and possessions and the loss of their families and support system, looked on as newly returned refugees took control of the economy and prospered, taking over businesses and building lavish new homes. Other survivors complained that the returned refugees had little understanding of Rwandan culture, bringing with them styles and tastes developed in Kampala and Kinshasa. Worse, many survivors felt that they were forced to justify their survival under the suspicious eye of those who assumed that they must have betrayed their people to stay alive.

My approach to the subject of social reconstruction in Rwanda is, thus, colored by my own long association with the country and its people. My goal is to apply the tools of social science to the process of social reform and reconciliation in the hope of contributing to the search for a durable peace, the struggle for understanding, and the development of a just and equitable society in Rwanda. I have employed social scientific methodologies with the purpose of understanding life in post-genocide Rwanda, thereby to inform future policymaking in the country and beyond. While much that I say may be controversial and may challenge accepted orthodoxies both within and outside Rwanda, my conclusions are based on careful and extensive research rather than ideology. My arguments are based on empirical evidence and rooted in careful historical method,[49] and I have attempted to speak honestly, even when my conclusions will likely draw the wrath of those currently in power and their supporters. The current climate in which a hegemonic discourse is imposed on all discussions of Rwanda while people must censor themselves for fear of the political consequences does not contribute to an honest assessment of post-genocide policy and its impact. A similar orthodoxy by some opponents of the regime, one that denies or justifies the genocide and recognizes no positive developments in Rwanda since 1994, is equally unhelpful. While keeping in mind the interests of the Rwandan population, I have attempted to set aside political considerations and allow the empirical evidence to dictate the conclusions, believing that an honest assessment of the process of reconstruction will be most useful for helping Rwanda chart its future and for contributing to the scholarly understanding of societies struggling to recover from mass violence.

---

[49] Following the advice from David Newbury, "Canonical Conventions in Rwanda: Four Myths of Recent Historiography of Central Africa," *History in Africa*, 39, 2012, 41–76, my work draws on a deep reading of the existing literature on Rwanda, including the rich historiography of the country.

The Argument and Plan of the Book

The first section of this book reviews the transitional justice initiatives undertaken by the post-genocide government and its supporters to shape the collective memory of the Rwandan population. In Chapter 2, I review the uses of history in Rwanda's past and outline the key elements of the historical narrative developed by Rwanda's new elite. Through the popular media, academic publications, political speeches, public meetings, re-education camps, and public education, the new political, social, and intellectual elite, both inside and outside the government, have articulated a modified historical narrative that emphasizes the historic unity of the Rwandan people, the divisive effects of colonialism, the neo-colonial corruption of the post-independence governments, the centrality of the genocide to Rwandan history, and the heroic position of the RPF. This narrative lies at the heart of the country's post-genocide transitional justice efforts that have sought to reshape Rwandan understandings of the past – remote and recent – to eliminate the ideas that rationalized the exclusion of the country's Tutsi minority while at the same time justifying the RPF's right to rule Rwanda today.

In the following chapters, I look at the ways that the government's transitional justice programs seek to promote this new historical narrative and thereby forge national unity. In Chapter 3, I contend that genocide commemorations and memorials, as well as "sites of forgetting," events and sites that are intentionally *not* memorialized, seek to promote the idea that the genocide is central to Rwandan history and that RPF abuses are insignificant and should be forgotten. In Chapter 4, I look at judicial responses to the genocide, including the grassroots gacaca courts. I argue that the RPF attempted to use the justice system to construct memory, both within Rwanda and abroad, that places the genocide in the center of Rwandan history while erasing any memory of RPF atrocities. By trying virtually every case of wrongdoing by Hutu during the genocide and trying almost no cases of wrongdoing by Tutsi against Hutu, they seek to establish the collective guilt of the Hutu population, effectively justifying their exclusion from power and opportunity and solidifying RPF political, social, and economic domination.

In Chapter 5, I analyze the political, social, and economic context within which transitional justice has been implemented and explore the ways in which political reforms have been framed as an aspect of transitional justice. The RPF used extensive coercive force in the first years after taking power, and even though the RPF shifted to less violent means after taking directly control of government, the history of coercion created a context of fear and submission that shaped responses to the widespread reforms implemented since 2000, including transitional justice programs. Despite the RPF's ambitious reform and development agenda, many Rwandans distrust the regime. The political reforms that the regime characterized as a "democratic transition," actually represented an assertion of state power that helped solidify RPF control. The extensive government programs for political, social, and economic reform have been implemented in a top-down and authoritarian fashion, involving ever greater extension of the state into the lives of individuals. The heavy hand of the state has further deepened the culture of fear and obedience that prevents real democracy from taking place and hinders reconciliation. At the same time, the growing concentration of economic and social power in the hands of the country's elite and the gap between the wealthy and powerful – primarily Tutsi former refugees – and the masses serves to emphasize ethnic and other forms of differentiation.

In the second section of the book, I assess the impact of the government's transitional justice initiatives on popular perceptions by looking in depth at three case study communities. Chapter 6 introduces these communities, providing an overview of their demographics and experience during the genocide and since 1994. I describe the manipulation of the supposedly decentralized political system in each community to maneuver strong regime supporters into positions and suppress real democratic choice. I also look at popular reactions to the political reforms undertaken by the regime and argue that the population supports some of the reforms at least in principle but that people feel increasingly oppressed by the heavy hand of the state.

Based on interviews, focus groups, and survey research in these three communities, Chapter 7 considers how the population has reacted to the government's effort to shape the historical narrative. The population was well informed about the official narrative, but they adopted it only to the extent that it resonated with their lived experience. Most people acknowledged and condemned the genocide as a horrific and unjustified event that brought shame and tragedy to Rwandans regardless of their ethnicity. Yet people regarded RPF efforts to shape memory cynically. They continued to sustain the memory of killings carried out by the RPF and did not see the genocide as justification for their own suffering.

Chapter 8 looks specifically at issues of judicial action. I find that the public widely embraced the idea of accountability – even retributive punishment – for those guilty of committing atrocities, but they believed that accountability should be for all people, not merely those guilty of genocide crimes. People felt little connection to the formal judicial system, which was removed from their daily lives and had little relevance for the processes of reconciliation. In contrast, the public was initially widely enthusiastic about the gacaca courts – despite some concerns – largely because they regarded them as something more relevant to their community. While gacaca provided important opportunities for communities to confront some of the violence they experienced and provided information about what happened during the genocide, the trials actually heightened ethnic tensions in many communities rather than promoting reconciliation. The exclusion of RPF violence and interference by government officials undermined the ultimate effect of the gacaca courts, leaving many Rwandans with the impression that trials were corrupt and biased. Perceptions of growing economic inequality undermined popular support for trials, as many Rwandans believe that they were used to benefit the wealthy and powerful.

In the concluding chapter, I reflect on the impact of Rwanda's transitional justice programs on social transformation. An important argument in this book is that the success of post-conflict social reconstruction programs is determined not simply by the policies directed at the past but by ongoing political, social, and economic developments. While the literatures on political transition and transitional justice tend to be teleological, assuming a straightforward development from authoritarian rule to democracy and from violence to peace, the Rwandan case indicates that in an authoritarian context, transitional justice mechanisms may actually undermine democratic transition. Both the national and local-level research presented in this book indicates that transitional justice in Rwanda helped the RPF consolidate its control rather than promoting democracy.

The contributions of transitional justice to peace, reconciliation, and justice have also been limited. While recognizing that transitional justice programs made some positive contributions to social reconstruction – for example, by providing important information about what happened in 1994 and promoting rapprochement between some survivors and perpetrators – my research demonstrates that overall the regime's programs of historical revision, memorialization, commemoration, judicial accountability, and political reform heightened rather than diminished ethnic identity. Over the course of my research for this book from 2001 to 2015, ethnic tensions increased, in part due to the divisive nature of the transitional justice programs. Economic stratification since the genocide further reinforced ethnic differences and undermined the ability of transitional justice mechanisms to promote reconciliation. For all the official rhetoric about a unified Rwandan identity, access to political and economic opportunity is still dictated by identity, including ethnic identity, and by personal connections, which reinforces the importance of family, region, origin, and ethnicity.

In short, transitional justice in Rwanda has provided little justice and no transition. The Rwandan public lumps transitional justice initiatives together with numerous other government programs that are implemented with a heavy hand and create onerous burdens of time and money. Gacaca trials, genocide commemoration ceremonies, and other initiatives are understood not as attempts to promote social reconstruction but as tools to increase compliance of the population, allowing those in power to further increase their political, social, and economic control. In an authoritarian context in which people are unable safely to express dissent or organize opposition, the long-term effect of Rwanda's growing inequality is to lay the seeds for future violence. Sadly, rather than helping to prevent this eventuality, transitional justice has increased the possibility that Rwanda may once again face a violent future.

Creating What You Are Afraid of: The Rwandan Patriotic Front's Transitional Justice Program

There is a group of leaders who have their own project for society, and they want you to join into this project. If you fall outside, they are afraid that you will go in a different direction. There is also a visceral reaction that if you leave these lines that they have set, it could lead us into what happened before. … But you create what you are afraid of.

– Rwandan Civil Society Leader, 2002

Introduction to Part I: The RPF as a Janus-Faced Movement

Two widely divergent images have emerged of post-genocide Rwanda and the party that has dominated Rwandan politics since 1994. Development experts praise the Rwandan Patriotic Front's efficiency, resistance to corruption, and commitment to economic growth.[1] Many diplomats praise the RPF for promoting national unity, advocating reconciliation rather than revenge, and seeking to eliminate the ethnic differences that have divided the country. The seriousness of purpose of leaders impresses outside observers. For much of the world, the RPF represents a model of good governance in the aftermath of a terrible disaster, not only bringing order and economic development but also altruistically promoting forgiveness and reconciliation in the face of horrific violence.[2] Journalist

---

[1] Praise from the head of the United Nations Development Program in Rwanda is typical of the views of many development experts. "Rwanda has made tremendous socio-economic progress and institutional transformation since the 1994 Genocide. Today Rwanda is a peaceful state enjoying a steady progress toward the achievement of national development goals under a visionary and dedicated leadership." Aurélien A. Agbénonci, "Introductory Remarks," *Delivering as One: Annual Report 2009*, Kigali: United Nations Rwanda, 2010, p. v.

[2] C.f., Margee Ensign, "Rwanda at 50: Reflections, Reconstruction, and Recovery," *Huffington Post*, July 3, 2012; Michael Fairbanks, "Nothing Good Comes Out of Africa,"

Stephen Kinzer, for example, contrasts Rwanda with Somalia and contends that against expectations, Rwanda has become peaceful and unified:

Rwanda … rebelled against its destiny. It has recovered from civil war and genocide more fully than anyone imagined possible and is united, stable, and at peace. Its leaders are boundlessly ambitious. Rwandans are bubbling over with a sense of unlimited possibility. Outsiders, drawn by the chance to help transform a resurgent nation, are streaming in … Rwanda is not being torn apart by civil war, like Somalia, or by criminal violence, like Kenya. Instead, it is stable, its people groping their way toward modernity and liberation.[3]

Paul Farmer, whose organization Partners in Health has worked closely with the government to implement health sector reforms, is a particularly strong defender of the regime:

Today Rwanda has been transformed. Mass violence has not recurred within the country's borders, and its gross domestic product has more than tripled over the past decade. Growth has been less uneven than in other countries in the region, partly because both local and national governments have made equity and human development guiding principles of recovery. Recent studies suggest that more than one million Rwandans were lifted out of poverty between 2005 and 2010, as the proportion of the population living below the poverty line dropped from 77.8% in 1994 to 58.9% in 2000 and 44.9% in 2010. Life expectancy climbed from 28 years in 1994 to 56 years in 2012. It is the only country in sub-Saharan Africa on track to meet most of the millennium development goals by 2015. Although metrics for equity are disputed, it is an increasingly well known fact that Rwanda today has the highest proportion of female civil servants in the world.[4]

For Kinzer, Farmer, and many others, the RPF's success at building peace and stability is due largely to the influence of the RPF leader, President Paul Kagame. Kinzer writes that, "President Kagame … has accomplished something truly remarkable. The contrast between where Rwanda is today and where most people would have guessed it would be today in the wake of the 1994 genocide is astonishing."[5] Phillip Gourevitch, the most widely-read author on Rwanda, similarly portrays

Huffington Post, May 3, 2010; Emily Holland, "Dispatches from a Humanitarian Journalist: Dispatch I: Kibuye, Rwanda," *McSweeney's*, September 4, 2007; "Rwanda: Trying to Move on," Public Radio International's *The World*, Jeb Sharp, producer, 2007.

[3] Stephen Kinzer, *A Thousand Hills: Rwanda's Rebirth and the Man Who Dreamed It*, Hoboken, NJ: John Wiley and Sons, 2008, pp. 1–2.

[4] Paul Farmer, et al., "Reduced Premature Mortality in Rwanda: Lessons from Success," *BMJ*, January 2013, pp.

[5] Ibid, p. 337.

Kagame as a moderate leader who has embraced former adversaries and promoted forgiveness and reconciliation. He cites a genocide survivor referring to her *génocidaire* neighbors, "It's because of the President that they don't kill. Forgiveness came from a Presidential order. If he were not there, we would all be killed."[6] Both Kinzer and Gourevitch praise Kagame's deft management of the economy, having attracted considerable foreign investment, aggressively fought corruption, and brought about impressive economic growth. Kinzer writes that, "Kagame has set out to do something that has never been done before: pull an African country from misery to prosperity in the space of a generation."[7]

In contrast, among human rights activists and many scholars of Rwanda, a much less sanguine perspective on post-genocide Rwanda prevails.[8] Human Rights Watch and Amnesty International, who raised the alarm early about the 1994 genocide, also denounced human rights abuses perpetrated by the RPF as it fought its way to power and sought to establish authority, and both organizations have remained consistent critics of the post-genocide regime.[9] A growing body of academic publications based on recent fieldwork conducted in Rwanda portrays a heavy-handed state that uses fines, arrests, and other forms of intimidation to force the population into mobilizing for government programs and implementing far-reaching plans to restructure social relations, economic activity, political engagement, and even personal hygiene.[10] Longtime Rwanda observer Filip Reyntjens argues that, "The [RPF] regime

---

[6] Philip Gourevitch, "The Life After: 15 Years after the Genocide in Rwanda, the Reconciliation Defies Expectations," *The New Yorker*, May 4, 2009.

[7] Kinzer, *A Thousand Hills*, p. 336.

[8] A recent collection of essays in honor of the late Alison Des Forges by a group of twenty-eight Rwanda scholars was uniformly bleak in its portrayal of post-genocide state and society. Scott Straus and Lars Waldorf, eds., *Remaking Rwanda: State Building and Human Rights after Mass Violence*, Madison: University of Wisconsin Press, 2011.

[9] Amnesty International, "Rwanda: Reports of Killings and Abductions by Rwandese Patriotic Army, April-August 1994," AFR 47/16/94, London: Amnesty International, October 19, 1994; Amnesty International, "Rwanda: Human Rights May be the Main Casualty of Tensions in the Rwandese Government," AFR 47/18/95, London: Amnesty International, August 30, 1995; Des Forges, *Leave None to Tell the Story*.

[10] An Ansoms, "Striving for growth, bypassing the poor: a critical review of Rwanda's rural sector policies," *Journal of Modern African Studies*, 46, no. 1, 2008, 1–32; An Ansoms, "Re-engineering rural society: the visions and ambitions of the Rwandan elite," *African Affairs*, 108, no. 431, 2009, 289–309; An Ansoms and Stefaan Marysse, eds., *Natural Resources and Local Livelihoods in the Great Lakes Region in Africa: A Political Economy Perspective*, New York: Palgrave Macmillan, 2011; Larissa Begley, "'Resolved to Fight the Ideology of Genocide and all of its Manifestations': The Rwandan Patriotic Front, Violence and Ethnic Marginalisation in Post-Genocide Rwanda and Eastern Congo," PhD Dissertation, University of Sussex, March 2011; Burnet, *Genocide Lives in Us*; Anuradha Chakravarty, *Investing in Authoritarian Rule: Punishment and Patronage in Rwanda's Gacaca Courts for Genocide Crimes*, New York: Cambridge University Press, 2016; Christopher Huggins, "Seeing Like a Neoliberal State? Authoritarian High

seeks full control over people and space: Rwanda is an army with a state, rather than a state with an army."[11]

The contrast between these two perspectives of post-genocide Rwanda could hardly be more stark, yet ample evidence exists to support each. Any reasonable observer of Rwanda cannot ignore the numerous accomplishments of the post-genocide regime. The RPF-led government has consistently employed a discourse of national unity, justice, and reconciliation. Since the suppression of the uprising in northwestern Rwanda in 1998, the country has been free from large-scale violence. Strong promotion of women's rights has given Rwanda the distinction of having the highest percentage of women in parliament of any country in the world, the first where women are a majority of members of parliament.[12] The regime has placed considerable emphasis on education, leading to a proliferation of schools at all levels, raising the elementary school completion rate from 51.1 percent in 1991 to 79.0 percent in 2011 and the adult literacy rate from 58 percent in 1991 to 70 percent in 2008. Investments in healthcare have helped to lower child malnutrition from 24.3 percent in 1991 to 18.0 percent in 2008.[13]

Shortly after Kagame became president in 2000, the government released *Rwanda Vision 2020*, an ambitious economic program "to raise the people of Rwanda out of poverty and transform the country into a middle-income economy" in twenty years.[14] The government has since aggressively promoted policies to attract international

Modernism, Commercialization and Governmentality in Rwanda's Agricultural Reform," PhD Dissertation, Carleton University, 2013; Bert Ingelaere, "Do We Understand Life After Genocide: Center and Periphery in the Construction of Knowledge on Rwanda," *African Studies Review*, 53, no. 1, April 2010, 41–59; Bert Ingelaere, "Peasants, Power and Ethnicity: A Bottom-Up Perspective on Rwanda's Political Transition," *African Affairs*, 109, no. 435, 2010, 273–292; Andrea Purdeková, *Making* Ubumwe: *Power, State, and Camps in Rwanda's Unity-Building Project*, New York: Berghan Books, 2015; Marc Sommers, *Stuck: Rwandan Youth and the Struggle for Adulthood*, Athens, GA: The University of Georgia Press, 2012; Susan Thomson, *Whispering Truth to Power: Everyday Resistance to Reconciliation in Post-Genocide Rwanda*, Madison: University of Wisconsin Press, 2013.

[11] Filip Reyntjens, "Constructing the Truth, Dealing with Dissent, Domesticating the World: Governance in Post-Genocide Rwanda," *African Affairs*, 2010, 1–34, citation p. 2. See also Filip Reyntjens, "Rwanda Ten Years On: From Genocide to Dictatorship," *African Affairs*, 103, 2004, 177–210; and René Lemarchand, "Bearing Witness to Mass Murder," *African Studies Review*, 48, no. 3, December 2005, 93–101.

[12] Timothy Longman, "Rwanda: Achieving Equality or Serving an Authoritarian State?" in Gretchen Bauer and Hannah Britton, eds., *Women in African Parliaments*, Boulder: Lynne Rienner, 2005.

[13] "Rwanda," World Bank, http://data.worldbank.org/country/rwanda.

[14] Ministry of Finance and Economic Planning, "Rwanda Vision 2020," Kigali: Government of Rwanda, July 2000.

investment, and the economy has enjoyed annual gross domestic product growth rates as high as 11.2 percent. The government has thoroughly embraced neo-liberal economic reforms, privatizing numerous public assets and adopting extensive regulatory reforms to ease international investment. In 2010, the World Economic Forum's Global Competitiveness Report ranked Rwanda as having the third lowest burden of government regulation and the twelfth most efficient government overall.[15] Rwanda's ranking in Transparency International's annual Corruption Perceptions Index was 44th in 2015, among the best in Africa and far ahead of any other East African state.[16] Rwanda was welcomed into the East African Community in 2007 and the British Commonwealth in 2009.[17]

Yet strong evidence also indicates that extensive human rights abuses have simultaneously occurred. The RPF used widespread violence to establish its initial authority, perpetrating massacres, summary executions, and numerous arbitrary arrests in its first years in power, and carrying out a bloody counter-insurgency operation in the northwest in 1997–1998.[18] Since 2000, even as the RPF has gained an international reputation for competence and moderation, the leadership has used more subtle means to maintain its power, tightly constraining public space and tolerating little dissent, while coercing the general population to implement sweeping social changes.[19] Security forces regularly harassed, arrested, and even killed civil society activists, journalists, and politicians who dared to criticize the government, while average Rwandans who objected to the apparently arbitrary imposition of onerous new regulations or resisted the regime's constant mobilization programs (such as those for villagization, constitutional reform, elections, gacaca, public works, and land reform) also faced punishment. Beginning with the First Congo War in 1996, while the level of active violence declined inside Rwanda, the RPF carried out massive attacks on civilians in the

---

[15] World Economic Forum, "The Global Competitiveness Report 2010–2011," http://gcr.weforum.org/gcr2010/, 2010.

[16] Transparency International, "Corruption Perceptions Index," www.transparency.org.

[17] "Keep Looking Ahead Rwanda," *The Economist*, January 13, 2007; Josh Kron, "Rwanda Joins British Commonwealth," *New York Times*, November 29, 2009.

[18] Des Forges, *Leave None to Tell the Story*, pp. 692–735; Amnesty International, "Rwanda: The Hidden Violence: 'Disappearances' and Killings Continue, London: Amnesty International, June 22, 1998.

[19] Chakravarty, *Investing in Authoritarian Rule*, contends that "Although its tight grip in the early transition years depended on the use of blatant force through killings and arbitrary arrests, the RPF has entrenched itself over the years, becoming thoroughly able to project power at the grassroots without over-reliance on these tools of repression" (p. 2).

Democratic Republic of Congo (DRC), where violence and instability continue to reverberate.[20]

In this first part of the book, I explore an aspect of public policy that reveals the Janus-faced nature of RPF rule – transitional justice. I review the government's diverse programs to shape popular understandings of Rwanda's past and thus promote a unified national identity. The regime has developed a narrative that emphasizes the historic unity of the Rwandan people, highlights the centrality of the 1994 genocide, and portrays the RPF in a favorable light. It has promoted these ideas through education and propaganda, trials, political reform, and memorialization and commemoration. While the RPF has created these programs in part to promote justice, accountability, and reconciliation, their implementation has also been influenced by the leadership's suspicion of the Rwandan population and the belief in the absolute necessity that they stay in power. As I explore in the second section of the book, the contradictions in these motivations ultimately undermine their ability to transform Rwandan society.

---

[20] Jason K. Stearns, *Dancing in the Glory of Monsters: The Collapse of the Congo and the Great War of Africa*, New York: Public Affairs, 2011; René Lemarchand, *The Dynamics of Violence in Central Africa*, Philadelphia: University of Pennsylvania Press, 2009; Filip Reyntjens, *The Great African War: Congo and Regional Geopolitics, 1996–2006*, Cambridge: Cambridge University Press, 2009.

    Rewriting History in Post-Genocide Rwanda

> To contest the past is also, of course, to pose questions about the present,
> and what the past means in the present. Our understanding of the past has
> strategic, political, and ethical consequences. Contests over the meaning
> of the past are also contests over the meaning of the present and over ways
> of taking the past forward.
>
> – Katharine Hodgkin and Susannah Rodstone, "Contested Pasts"

In the aftermath of the 1994 genocide, the government put into
office in Rwanda by the victorious Rwandan Patriotic Front undertook a wide-reaching program of social reform aimed, in part, at
preventing future ethnic violence. Among their social programs, the
post-genocide government placed a major emphasis on promoting
education, believing that low levels of education and high illiteracy
had fostered ignorance in the population that increased its vulnerability to manipulation by those who wished to foment ethnic violence.
A better-educated population, government officials reasoned, would
be more capable of seeing through the false consciousness that, from
the perspective of Rwanda's new rulers, ethnicity represented. The
government thus sought not only to increase enrollments in schools
from primary through university levels but also to increase the quality of education by revamping the curriculum and raising standards
for teachers.[1] The results are impressive, with rates of enrollment by
primary-age children rising from 66 percent in 1991 to 96.5 percent

---

[1] From 2001 to 2003, I worked with a team of researchers headed by Sarah Freedman
of the University of California, Berkeley School of Education on a project called
"Education for Reconciliation," part of the Communities in Crisis program that
I directed in Rwanda. The information about the schools in this chapter is drawn from
that research project. An analysis of this research can be found in Sarah Warshauer
Freedman, Déo Kambanda, Beth Lewis Samuelson, et al., "Confronting the Past
in Rwandan Schools," in Eric Stover and Harvey Weinstein, eds., *My Neighbor, My
Enemy: Justice and Community in the Aftermath of Mass Atrocity*, Cambridge: Cambridge
University Press, 2004, pp. 248–264.

in 2012, and enrollment in secondary schools rising from 8 to 28 percent of eligible youth during the same period.[2]

At the same time, however, the Ministry of Education struggled over the appropriate content of education, particularly in the area of history. Shortly after taking power, the government placed a moratorium on the teaching of history in schools. Believing that distorted historical narratives promulgated by schools since the colonial era had promoted the anti-Tutsi ideology that drove the genocide, the Ministry of Education determined that history courses would be removed from the secondary school schedule until a new curriculum could be developed that corrected the distortions of the previous history curriculum.[3]

Writing a new history for Rwandan schools proved to be a challenging task. History in post-genocide Rwanda is a highly sensitive topic in which the government has expressed a clear vested interest. Those who endeavored to write history entered a political minefield in which their analysis was constrained by the government's expectations of a "correct" version of history. Yet even those historians who shared the government's vision of the past were confronted by the sheer magnitude of the task of developing a new narrative entirely at odds with ideas previously accepted as fact by the majority of Rwanda's people. Although a group of both professional and amateur historians had dedicated considerable attention since 1994 to publishing new interpretations of Rwanda's past, when conferences were held at the National University of Rwanda (NUR) in 1998 and 1999 to begin the process of developing a definitive history of the country, participants felt that insufficient scholarly groundwork had been laid.

The research project that I participated in from 2001 to 2003 to study Rwandan secondary schools found that participants in both individual and focus group interviews – whether teachers, administrators, parents, or students – uniformly expressed a strong interest in bringing history back into the schools. But when we received funding to work with the Rwandan government to develop a new history curriculum and launched a curriculum development project in 2004, we confronted a contradiction inherent to official attitudes toward history in Rwanda today. The desire to foster critical thinking skills that would allow students to reason for themselves and thereby be capable of resisting manipulation ran into direct conflict with the idea that there was a "correct" version of Rwandan history that anyone who supported the ideals of reconciliation and peace must adopt. In two years of working with a diverse group of

[2] UNESCO Institute for Statistics, "UIS Statistics in Brief: Education in Rwanda," www.stats.uis.unesco.org/unesco/TableViewer/document.aspx?ReportId=121&IF_Language=eng&BR_Country=6460; and UNICEF, "Rwanda: Education," www.unicef.org/rwanda/education.html.
[3] Freedman, et al, "Confronting the Past in Rwandan Schools."

high school teachers and students, education and history professors, government officials, and civil society activists, we found repeatedly that the articulated support for the idea of history as a series of problems and opportunities for debate collided with the reality of a highly authoritarian society. Participants appreciated the idea of free discussion of history, but most did not feel sufficiently free in Rwanda's contemporary political climate to challenge the newly developed orthodox version of Rwandan history. Debate could be tolerated, but only if it led to predetermined answers.[4]

Memory, History, and Identity

That national histories are not sets of established facts but rather socially constructed narratives of the past is widely accepted in academic circles today. Popular historical narratives are not unbiased descriptions of events but subjective accounts shaped by the present needs and interests of societies. While history may be "a fable agreed upon,"[5] the manner in which historical narratives are constructed has social and political significance. The process by which societies collectively develop and accept myths about the past that become their national history is not benign. The statement attributed to Winston Churchill that, "History is written by the victors," emphasizes the ways in which the powerful shape history for their own political purposes. Not only do the victors in great wars interpret history in a way that ennobles their cause and vilifies their defeated enemies, but social victors – the rich and powerful who dominate societies – write history to justify their domination and undercut the pretensions to power of society's losers.[6] The construction of historical narrative thus has a coercive nature.

Scholars have employed the concept of collective memory to enlighten discussions of historical narratives and their social impact. Maurice Halbwachs first developed the idea of collective memory in the 1920s, arguing that an individual's memories are developed in a social context that shapes the content of memory.[7] Applying the lens of social

---

[4] Sarah Warshauer Freedman, Henry M. Weinstein, Karen Murphy and Timothy Longman, "Teaching History after Identity-Based Conflicts: The Rwanda Experience," *Comparative Education Review*, 52, no. 4, 2008, 663–669.

[5] This quote is attributed to Napoleon Bonaparte by Ralph Waldo Emerson in "History," *The Essays of Emerson*, vol. 1, London: Arthur L. Humphries, 1899, p. 8.

[6] George Orwell, "As I Please," February 4, 1944, for example, asserted in reference to the Spanish Civil War, that, "if Franco or anyone at all resembling him remains in power, the history of the war will consist quite largely of 'facts' which millions of people now living know to be lies."

[7] Maurice Halbwachs, *On Collective Memory*, edited and translated by Lewis A. Coser, Chicago and London: University of Chicago Press, 1992, p. 40.

psychology, Halbwachs contended that, "the mind reconstructs its memories under pressure of society. ... Society from time to time obligates people not just to reproduce in thought previous events of their lives, but also to touch them up, to shorten them, or to complete them so that, however convinced we are that our memories are exact, we give them a prestige that reality did not possess."[8] Even events that we have personally experienced are shaped by the society within which we live.

The concept of collective memory gained new currency in the 1980s when Pierre Nora applied it to the study of nationalism, looking at the "sites of memory" – the memorials, holidays, anthems, and other symbols – that helped shape French Republican identity.[9] Nora's analysis contributed to a growing literature that regards nationalities as "imagined communities," in which people are tied together not by any real fundamental social, cultural, or historical unity but rather by the *idea* that they share a common connection.[10] Eric Hobsbawm argued that nations cannot ultimately be defined by racial differences or such cultural differences as language or religion but rather by a sense of shared history, "the consciousness of having belonged to a lasting political entity ... a 'historical nation.'"[11]

Developing a collective historical memory is key to developing national identities, but the process carries coercive tendencies. To build a shared national identity, a population must be re-educated and may ultimately need to be forced into accepting a particular vision of the past. Karl Deutsch's classic study of nationalism in the aftermath of the Second World War noted that nationalism involves, "processes of social learning and control which are particularly subject to risks of pathological developments and trends to self-destruction."[12] Those engaged in a nationalist project seek to promote a particular collective memory about the past that serves to support their definition of national identity. Such nationalist projects are notoriously intolerant of open debate and discussion. As Katharine Hodgkin and Susannah Rodstone argue in the epigraph, arguments about the past reflect conflicts over the present.[13] Nationalists

---

[8] Ibid., p. 51.
[9] Pierre Nora, ed., *Les Lieux de Mémoire*, Vols. 1–3, Paris: Gallimard, 1984–1992.
[10] Benedict Anderson, *Imagined Communities: Reflections on the Origin and Spread of Nationalism*, New York: Verso, 1983.
[11] Eric J. Hobsbawm, *Nations and Nationalism since 1780: Programme, Myth, Reality*, Cambridge: Cambridge University Press, 1990, p. 73.
[12] Karl W. Deutsch, *Nationalism and Social Communication: An Inquiry into the Foundations of Nationality*, New York: John Wiley and Sons, 1953, p. 163.
[13] Katharine Hodgkin and Susannah Rodstone, "Introduction: Contested Pasts," in Katharine Hodgkin and Susannah Radstone, eds., *Contested Pasts: The Politics of Memory*, London and New York: Routledge, pp. 1–21, citation p. 1.

who seek to marshal the past to promote a unified national identity do so ultimately to achieve a particular political goal, and as such they generally cannot tolerate individuals and ideas that seek to complicate the past or challenge aspects of the proposed collective memory.

In Rwanda, the post-genocide government has actively sought to shape collective memory, using a focus on the 1994 genocide as a focal point for constructing a new national identity. In subsequent chapters, I explore the various mechanisms being used to build collective memory, such as genocide memorials and genocide trials. In this chapter, I focus on the more obvious aspects of shaping collective memory, the development and promulgation of a new historical narrative. I first review the ways in which historical narratives served to justify the Rwandan genocide. While the historical myths central to the genocidal ideology did not push most people to participate in the violence, historical narratives did serve to delineate the distinctions between Hutu, Tutsi, and Twa without which the genocide could not have occurred, and for a small core group, the ideas that Tutsi did not belong in Rwanda and that Hutu needed to redeem their besmirched honor motivated participation. As I then analyze, since taking power in 1994, the RPF regime and its supporters have undertaken a major project to re-write Rwandan history. They have completely rejected previous historical narratives and sought to develop new ones; but these are no more based on historical fact than those that preceded them. Just as previous history overemphasized the centrality of ethnicity, the more recent history overemphasizes the historical unity of Rwanda's population, inaccurately denying any historic social significance at all to ethnicity. More problematic is the attempt to re-imagine the RPF in heroic terms, seeking to expunge from popular memory abuses carried out by the RPF and portray RPF violence as motivated exclusively by the attempt to end genocide and bring peace and democracy to Rwanda. As I will develop in later chapters, this portrayal of the RPF – which is directly at odds with the lived experience of many Rwandans – ultimately undermines the public's willingness to embrace the new official historical narrative.

History, Ideology, and the Rwandan Genocide

History played a key role in the 1994 genocide in Rwanda. The ideology used to justify the genocide drew on a historical narrative developed during the colonial period that saw Hutu, Tutsi, and Twa as clear and distinct racial groups and characterized Tutsi as recent arrivals in the region which had conquered and dominated the other groups. Based on this narrative, the instigators of the genocide asserted that Tutsi were foreigners who had no right to be in Rwanda and needed to be feared and opposed because of their history of dominating the majority Hutu.[14]

While the exact meaning of the categories "Hutu," "Tutsi," and "Twa" in pre-colonial Rwanda remains contentious, most scholars today agree that they were not ethnic groups in the modern sense. Current scholarship indicates that the terms reflected a status difference even in pre-colonial times,[15] but the groups shared a common culture, spoke the same language, Kinyarwanda, and lived in integrated communities or in close proximity. Furthermore, Hutu and Tutsi were somewhat flexible categories, since intermarriage was possible and a family's status could change as their fortunes rose or fell.[16] The identities emerged as centralizing monarchies sought to extend their control by implanting a Tutsi aristocracy throughout the territory as representatives of the crown.[17] Patterns of migration within the region were complex, and each group included both recent migrants and those long in Rwanda.[18] Hutu or Tutsi were only one of a number of significant identities for Rwandans along with lineage, region, clan, and sub-clan.

When European missionaries and colonial administrators arrived in Rwanda around the turn of the twentieth century, their perspective on Rwandan society was shaped by then-contemporary European ideas about race and identity. Ignoring the actual complexity of identity within Rwanda, they believed that the Hutu, Tutsi, and Twa identities were paramount, regarding them as three distinct ethnic, or even

[14] Eltringham, *Accounting for Horror*, pp. 147–179, provides a helpful review of the meta-narratives represented in the ways in which Rwandans inside and outside the country have discussed Rwandan history since 1994.

[15] The majority of scholars today argue that Hutu and Tutsi were status differences that were gaining in significance even before the advent of colonialism. C.f., Catharine Newbury, *The Cohesion of Oppression: Clientship and Ethnicity in Rwanda, 1860–1960*, New York: Columbia University Press, 1988; Catharine Newbury, "Ethnicity and the Politics of History in Rwanda," *Africa Today*, 45, no. 1, January–March 1998, 7–24; Jan Vansina, *Le Rwanda ancien: Le Royaume Nyinginya*, Paris: Karthala, 2001.

[16] Alison Des Forges, "The Ideology of Genocide," *Issue: A Journal of Opinion*, 23, no. 2, 1995, 44–47.

[17] Newbury, *The Cohesion of Oppression*, provides an excellent study of how ethnic differentiation was used to extend central court control into an outlying region of the Rwandan kingdom. "[T]he categories of Hutu and Tuutsi assumed new hierarchical overtones associated with proximity to the central court – proximity to power ... More than simply conveying the connotation of cultural difference from Tuutsi, Hutu identity came to be associated with and eventually defined by inferior status" (p. 51).

[18] Des Forges, "The Ideology of Genocide," writes, "the elite that we now call Tutsi encompassed a number of competing lineages who had arrived in Rwanda at different times over a period of centuries and who had different interests as well as varied backgrounds. In the same way, the masses that are now known as Hutu included both peoples long resident within Rwanda and those who had just arrived from Zaire or Uganda" (p. 44).

racial, categories. Influenced by ideas of social Darwinism, that considered identity not merely social but biological, with each ethnic and racial group naturally possessing specific talents and characteristics, they saw in the Tutsi a superior Hamitic group, distant relatives of Caucasians who were more intelligent than their fellow countrymen and therefore natural rulers. They regarded the Hutu as a Bantu group, sturdy and simple, best suited for physical work such as farming, while they considered the Twa a Pygmy group, inferior, lazy, and untrustworthy, never having evolved beyond hunting and gathering.[19]

The Tutsi elite played on European prejudices to their own advantage, helping develop a historical narrative of Rwanda's past adapted to European racist assumptions. As Des Forges wrote:

Not only did they use European backing to extend and intensify their control over the Hutu – whose faults they exaggerated to the gullible Europeans – they also joined with the Europeans to create the ideological justification for this exploitation. ... In a great and unsung collaborative enterprise over a period of decades, European and Rwandan intellectuals created a history that fit European assumptions and accorded with Tutsi interests.[20]

According to this history, the Twa, the region's original inhabitants, were subdued by Hutu who migrated from the west at the beginning of the first millennium. The Tutsi supposedly arrived from the northeast over a millennium later bringing with them cattle and a complex, centralized political system and, because of their natural intelligence and military superiority, subdued the other groups.[21]

Far from being merely of academic interest, this ideologically shaped historical narrative became a basis for public policy. The German and Belgian administrations established a system of indirect rule that left the Rwandan monarchy in place to facilitate their administration of the

---

[19] For the definitive explanation of the development of the ideas of a Hamitic race, see Edith R. Sanders, "The Hamitic Hypothesis: Its Origin and Functions in Time Perspective," *Journal of African History*, 10, no. 4, 1969. For more general discussions of the application of European racial ideas to Rwanda, see Mahmood Mamdani, *When Victims Become Killers: Colonialism, Nativism, and the Genocide in Rwanda*, Princeton: Princeton University Press, 2001, especially chapter three, and Eltringham, *Accounting for Horror*, pp. 1–33.

[20] Des Forges, "The Ideology of Genocide," pp. 44–45.

[21] Examples of this historical narrative can be found in Louis de Lacger, *Le Ruanda: Aperçu historique*, Kabgayi, 1959; Alexis Kagame, *La Poésie Dynastique au Rwanda*, Brussels: Institute Royal du Congo Belge (IRCB), 1951; Alexis Kagame, *Le code des institutions politiques du Rwanda précolonial* Brussels: IRCB, 1952; Alexis Kagame, *L'histoire des armées Bovines dans l'Ancien Rwanda* Brussels: ARSOM, 1963; Jacques J. Maquet, *The Premise of Inequality in Ruanda: A Study of Political Relations in a Central African Kingdom*, London: Oxford University Press, 1961; Albert Pagès, *Un Royaume Hamite au Centre de l'Afrique: Au Rwanda sur les Bos du Lac Kivu*, Brussels: Van Campenhout, 1933.

territory. At the same time, they reshaped the existing system, consolidating Tutsi social position and centralizing the power of the monarchy, eliminating existing vestiges of Hutu power. Much of Rwanda, and particularly the Hutu, experienced what Catharine Newbury has called "dual colonialism" of both the colonial administration and the central court.[22] Both the government and Christian churches reserved most educational and salaried employment opportunities for Tutsi. In the 1930s, the colonial administration required all residents to carry identity cards that listed their ethnicity, hence administratively fixing group identities and eliminating their flexibility.[23] These policies effectively increased the salience of Hutu, Tutsi, and Twa identities over other social identities, since they helped determine life chances, while the ideology provided different historical imaginaries for the groups that ultimately helped to convert them into ethnic identities.

For much of the colonial period, the myth of Tutsi conquest and superiority served successfully to justify the group's privileged position. But following the Second World War, colonial administrators and missionaries influenced by social democratic political ideas began to change their sympathies to the Hutu, whom they now characterized as an oppressed working class who had suffered under the yoke of Tutsi domination for centuries. The same erroneous historical narrative that had been used to support Tutsi dominance was now used to support the emergence of a Hutu counter-elite and justify a shift in political control to Hutu hands following anti-Tutsi violence in 1959. The democratic principle of "majority rule" got distorted in Rwanda to mean rule by the Hutu ethnic majority, and after independence, the government of Kayibanda continued to draw on the historical narrative of Tutsi conquest and exploitation of the Hutu to justify his own consolidation of power as the defender of Hutu interests.[24] The false histories of migration as the source of ethnic differentiation in Rwanda and of Tutsi as the long-time oppressors of Hutu continued to be taught in schools after independence.

After Juvénal Habyarimana became president in a 1973 coup, he sought to quell ethnic violence by implementing an ethnic quota system that limited Tutsi access to education and employment, but the

---

[22] Newbury, *The Cohesion of Oppression*.

[23] Timothy Longman, "Nation, Race, or Class? Defining the Hutu and Tutsi of East Africa," in Joseph Feagin and Pinar Batur-Vanderlippe, eds., *The Global Color Line: Racial and Ethnic Inequality and Struggle from a Global Perspective*, JAI Press: Bingley, UK, 1999, pp. 103–130.

[24] The best source on the 1959 "revolution" and the early independence era is René Lemarchand, *Rwanda and Burundi*, New York: Palgrave, 1970. See also Jean-Paul Kimonyo, *Rwanda's Popular Genocide: A Perfect Storm*, Boulder: Lynne Reinner, 2016 on the conflation of majority rule with Hutu rule.

basic ideology of Hutu majority rule remained unchanged. When both an internal movement for democratization and the invasion by the Rwandan Patriotic Front challenged the Habyarimana regime in the early 1990s, his supporters returned to the ideology of the Kayibanda years and sought to regain popular support by recasting themselves as the defenders of the Hutu majority against an attempt to re-establish a minority Tutsi dictatorship. They used targeted violence against the Tutsi to heighten ethnic polarization[25] and undermined their critics by portraying them as traitors to Hutu interests. This strategy of using ethnic violence to mobilize Hutu support ultimately culminated in the 1994 genocide.[26]

The ideology used to justify the 1994 genocide and inspire popular participation drew heavily on the historical narrative developed during colonial rule. The message was promulgated as propaganda through meetings of Habyarimana's political party, the National Revolutionary Movement for Development (*Mouvement Révolutionaire National pour le Développement*, MRND), and even more extreme Coalition for the Defense of the Republic (CDR), extremist publications, and both the official radio station, Radio Rwanda, and the ostensibly independent Radio-Television of the Thousand Hills (*Radio-Télévision Libre des Milles Collines*, RTLM), founded by MRND and CDR supporters. The ideology claimed that Tutsi were aliens who did not belong in Rwanda. In a notorious November 1992 speech to an MRND meeting in Gisenyi Prefecture recorded on a cassette and much replayed, Léon Mugesera, the prefecture's party vice-president, said of members of the largely Tutsi Liberal Party, "I am telling you that your home is Ethiopia, that we are going to send you back there quickly, by the Nyabarongo" [a tributary of the Nile].[27] Another major theme was the history of Tutsi conquest and the need for Hutu to revenge their humiliation and emasculation at Tutsi hands. Mugesera asserted that, "At whatever cost, you will leave here with these words ... do not let yourselves be invaded. ... I know

---

[25] Research by both a team of international human rights investigators and a leading Rwandan human rights group revealed that ethnic massacres that occurred between October 1990 and February 1993 were not, as they were portrayed, spontaneous expressions of popular anger but rather actions undertaken by government officials with the approval of higher authorities. Africa Watch, Fédération Internationale des Droits de l'Homme (FIDH), Union Inter-Africaine des Droits de l'Homme et des Peuples (UIDH), et al., "Rapport de la Commission Internationale d'Enquête sur les Violations des Droits de l'Homme au Rwanda depuis le 1er Octobre 1990 (7–21 Janvier 1993)," Paris: FIDH, March 1993; Association Rwandaise Pour la Defense des Droits de la Personne et des Libertés Publiques (ADL), "Rapport sur les Droits de l'Homme au Rwanda," Kigali: ADL, December 1992.

[26] On the early 1990s, see Prunier, *The Rwanda Crisis*.

[27] Quoted in Des Forges, *Leave None to Tell the Story*, p. 85.

you are men ... who do not let themselves be invaded, who refuse to be scorned."[28]

For those authors who regard the 1994 Rwandan genocide as a mass uprising in which huge portions – perhaps a majority – of Hutu participated, the genocidal ideology and its historical narrative are key to understanding popular support for the killing campaign. Mahmood Mamdani, for example, portrays the Rwandan genocide as unique because of its mass nature and extensive popular participation.[29] He seeks in his text to "make popular agency ... thinkable,"[30] and contends that the genocide was deeply rooted in the history developed in the colonial era. What happened in Rwanda, "was a genocide by those who saw themselves as sons – and daughters – of the soil, and their mission as one of clearing the soil of a threatening *alien* presence."[31] Jean-Pierre Chrétien emphasized the role of hate radio in disseminating the message that the Hutu needed to defend themselves against Tutsi trying to re-establish feudalism.[32]

My own experience in Rwanda just prior to the genocide and my subsequent field research on the genocide (particularly the research I conducted in 1995–1996 for the book *Leave None to Tell the Story*), convince me that the level of popular participation in the genocide is commonly over-estimated and the role of ideology is exaggerated. Relatively small groups of committed (and trained) killers carried out most of the major massacres at churches, schools, and other central locations before mandatory participation in security patrols and roadblocks implicated a larger portion of the population. Many Hutu men participated in the patrols and roadblocks quite reluctantly, and most of those who participated were not involved in killing. Even those who did participate in the killing, however, were not necessarily driven by a deep hatred of Tutsi whipped up by the genocidal ideology. My own research confirms the findings of Scott Straus's interviews with confessed genocide perpetrators that people participated primarily out of fear created by the RPF invasion of the country and fear of the consequences of resisting orders by authorities to kill.[33] Lee Ann Fujii emphasizes the importance of social networks to

[28] Ibid., p. 84.
[29] Mamdani, *When Victims Become Killers*, pp. 3–7, implies that nearly every Hutu man participated. He quotes one survivor as saying, "There were about 5,000 in our *secteur*. Of the 3,500 Hutu, all the men participated," (p. 4).
[30] Ibid., p. 8.
[31] Ibid., p. 14.
[32] Jean-Pierre Chrétien, ed., *Rwanda: Les medias du genocide*, Paris: Karthala, 1995; Jean-Pierre Chrétien, *Le défie de l'Ethnisme: Rwanda et Burundi: 1990–1996*, Paris: Karthala, 1997.
[33] Scott Straus, *The Order of Genocide: Race, Power, and War in Rwanda*, Ithaca: Cornell University Press, 2006.

explaining participation in the genocide, another factor where the ideology mattered little.[34]

Nevertheless, the historical narrative about Rwanda's past and the ideology that drew upon it were significant to the genocide in several ways. Straus's conclusion that "an 'ideology of genocide' did not drive participation in the genocide"[35] seems accurate for the vast majority of Rwandans involved in the genocide, but many of the core group of committed killers and those who organized the genocide seem to have been influenced by ideas about a history of oppression and humiliation. For political and social leaders who found their authority slipping away in the early 1990s, the idea of a Tutsi conspiracy made sense. Like other African leaders, Habyarimana developed a neo-patrimonial structure in which he gained support from powerful individuals – principally Hutu from his home region in the north, but also others who were willing to back him – in exchange for opportunities, such as the chance for personal enrichment through embezzling public funds. When the democracy movement challenged this patrimonial elite, their response was not to admit to their own corruption, incompetence, and brutality but to question the motives of those who threatened their power. Because of discrimination, Tutsi were mostly excluded from the elite and widely supported the opposition. Leaders of the regime could thus dismiss the reform movement as a Tutsi conspiracy, particularly when a largely Tutsi army, the RPF, was invading the country. While some Hutu Power leaders may have embraced the ideology of genocide cynically as a tool to motivate popular support, many intensely hated Tutsi. They sincerely believed in the history of Tutsi conquest and domination and deemed themselves the defenders of Hutu interests against a malevolent power-hungry foreign presence on Rwandan soil. The anti-Tutsi ideology's historical narrative may not explain most popular participation, but it does seem to have motivated many elite participants.

The historical narrative made an even more significant contribution to the genocide, however, in defining the very identity of victims and perpetrators. For scholars, the constructed nature of identities in Rwanda is particularly obvious. Hutu and Tutsi share the same territory and have a common language and culture. Even if claims of physical distinctions between the two groups had historical merit, which they do not, the historic flexibility of group membership and the frequency of intermarriage would have eliminated the reliability of judging individuals

---

[34] Lee Ann Fujii, *Killing Neighbors: Webs of Violence in Rwanda*, Ithaca: Cornell University Press, 2011.

[35] Ibid., p. 244.

by their appearance. What distinguishes the two groups, ultimately, is the idea that they have different historical origins. The fact that historical and anthropological research disproves the assertion that the groups originated through separate migrations[36] was politically less significant than the fact that people *believed* that the two groups were distinct. Jan Vansina's claim that, "an ethnic group is a group of people who believe *erroneously* that they share a common history,"[37] is quite telling in the Rwandan case. The belief that Hutu and Tutsi had different histories ultimately served to distinguish the groups from one another. Long after any occupational differentiation had disappeared, long after Tutsi had lost the reins of power in Rwanda, what separated them from Hutu was a belief in their difference rooted in the historical narrative of separate origins. Colonialists did not invent Hutu, Tutsi, and Twa as categories, but they worked with Tutsi elites to develop a history that endowed the groups with distinct origins and made it possible to think about them as separate races. This distinction, rooted in a historical narrative, ultimately made the genocide possible by delineating the boundaries of group membership.

The Official Historical Narrative

After the RPF swept to power in July 1994, tens of thousands of Tutsi who had been living as refugees, primarily in Uganda, Zaire, and Burundi, began flooding back into Rwanda. These repatriated Tutsi, widely known in Rwanda as the *rapatriés*, or returnees, had varying experiences abroad. Many had lived in exile for more than three decades, and a large portion was born abroad and had never set foot in Rwanda. Many refugees grew up in the limited confines of camps – particularly in Uganda – but some enjoyed considerable opportunity and prospered in their adopted lands, as in Congo where many Tutsi made successful careers in trade. Despite their diverse backgrounds, most Tutsi refugees shared, to at least some extent, a common vision of Rwanda and its past that was at sharp variance with the historical narrative widely accepted within Rwandan territory at the time. As Liisa Malkki has demonstrated through her perceptive study of Burundian Hutu refugees in Tanzania, the constructed memory of their homeland can be a powerful social force among refugees.[38] In the perspective of the Tutsi refugees, the Rwandan

---

[36] David Lee Schoenbrun, *A Green Place, A Good Place: Agrarian Change, Gender, and Social Change in the Great Lakes Region to the Fifteenth Century*, Portsmouth, NH: Heinneman, 1998.

[37] Personal communication, 1993.

[38] Liisa Malkki, *Purity and Exile: Violence, Memory and Cosmology among Hutu Refugees in Tanzania*, Chicago: University of Chicago Press, 1995.

population had been unified prior to colonialism, and the colonial state and the Catholic Church were largely to blame for the persecution and exclusion of the Tutsi. Corrupt post-independence governments worked in league with foreign powers to manipulate the uneducated and gullible population to prevent the return of Tutsi to their rightful place in Rwandan society. The idea of Rwanda as homeland remained central to the refugee community's identity, and the desire to return was powerful, particularly during periods when the Tutsi faced discrimination because of their outsider status, as in the second Obote regime in Uganda in the early 1980s.[39] As Gerard Prunier wrote, "As the years passed and memories of the real Rwanda began to recede, Rwanda slowly became a mythical country in the refugees' minds."[40] For the young who had no personal experience of Rwanda, "Contrasting an idealized past life with the difficulties they were experiencing, their image of Rwanda became that of a land of milk and honey. Economic problems linked with their eventual return, such as overpopulation, overgrazing or soil erosion, were dismissed as Kigali regime propaganda."[41] As Malkki suggests, the context in which refugees live affects the degree to which they are driven by collective memory.[42] The RPF had its roots in the refugee camps of southern Uganda, where life was hard and refugees faced repression. The experience of persecution and limited opportunity shaped the refugees's view of their own past and the conditions that had forced them to flee into exile. Those who emerged to lead the RPF were motivated by a vision of the past in which the Tutsi were unjustly persecuted.

When the RPF took power in Rwanda, the returned refugees viewed Rwanda through the framework of the collective memory they had developed abroad but found a population whose understanding of the past was quite different from their own. The RPF and its supporters correctly perceived that history had been distorted and used to mobilize the population and enable the genocide.[43] To achieve a durable peace, they recognized a need to re-educate the population about the country's history and replace the previous historical narrative with a new narrative

---

[39] On the Tutsi refugees in Uganda and the formation of the RPF, see Catharine Watson, *Exile from Rwanda: Background to an Invasion*, Washington: US Committee for Refugees, February 1991; Prunier, *The Rwanda Crisis*, pp. 61–74; and Mamdani, *When Victims Become Killers*, pp. 159–184.

[40] Prunier, *The Rwanda Crisis*, p. 66.

[41] Ibid.

[42] Malkki, *Purity and Exile* found that memories of violence were a driving force for Burundian Hutu refugees living in refugee camps, but for refugees who had integrated into local communities, the memories were less important.

[43] Josias Semujonga, "Le discours scientific comme porteur du stereotypes: Le cas de l'historiographie rwandaise," in *Rapport de Synthese du Seminaire sur l'Histoire du Rwanda*, Butare, December 14–18, 1998.

in which Tutsi were not foreign invaders but sons and daughters of the Rwandan soil. Immediately after taking power, the government placed a moratorium on the teaching of history in Rwandan secondary schools, while a group of repatriated intellectuals – including government officials, professors, and other intellectuals, such as priests – began to work on revising Rwanda's formal history. Scholars with strong international reputations, such as Paul Rutayisire, Gamaliel Mbonimana, Faustin Rutembesa, Célestin Kalimba, and Déogratias Byanafashe, most of whom had been professors in Burundi or Zaire, sought to introduce their ideas to a new Rwandan audience.[44] As Jean Nizurugero Rugagi asserted, "The current and urgent task for the historian is to place before the eyes of Rwandans and before international opinion the authentic course of Rwandan history to better denounce the manipulation that it experienced."[45] Dominican Father Bernardin Muzungu founded a quarterly journal, *Lumière et Société*, focused on correcting understandings of the Rwandan past, the Center for Conflict Management at the NUR in Butare undertook research on issues such as the migration of people into Rwanda and the historic sources of ethnic conflict, and major conferences on the history of Rwanda were organized at the NUR in 1998 and 1999. Government officials in their public addresses, the national radio in both news reports and special programing, and various newspapers and magazines have regularly discussed both Rwanda's recent and more remote history, using the same historical narrative as the historians.[46] In the remainder of this chapter, I provide a brief overview of the major themes raised in both the academic historical works and official government discourse.

The Essential Unity of the Rwandan People

The fundamental unity of Rwanda's people in pre-colonial times is a major theme of the new historical narrative. The scholarship generally does not pretend that the region was entirely peaceful, as kingdoms rose and fell and various individuals and groups vied for political power,

---

[44] One could also add to this list Joseph Gahama who, though Burundian, moved to Rwanda in the late 1990s and participated in the new historiography.

[45] Jean Nizurugero Rugagi, "Decolonisation et democratization du Rwanda," *Cahiers Lumière et Société*, no. 7, October 1997, 43–54.

[46] Interestingly, until recently nearly all of the academic work was in French, since the Francophone territories of Burundi and Zaire allowed Tutsi to become professors, while discrimination in Uganda limited opportunities for educational and social advancement for Tutsi refugees. By contrast, most of the political discourse is in English or Kinyarwanda, as the RPF emerged in Anglophone Uganda and remains dominated by former Ugandan refugees.

but conflicts did not occur along lines of identity. In fact, the narrative challenges the idea that ethnic divisions have a historic basis. Scholars draw on linguistic analysis and archeology to demonstrate that patterns of migration into Rwanda were complex and do not explain the emergence of the country's ethnic groups.[47] The fact that clans cut across ethnic lines is raised as proof of the historic unity of the three groups.[48] The shared use of the Kinyarwanda language is offered as evidence of the cultural unity of the Rwandan people,[49] as is the unifying belief in a high god, Imana.[50] President Kagame has often asserted the unity of pre-colonial Rwandans, as in a 2003 speech in San Francisco, in which he stated, "The Bahutu, Batutsi, and Batwa were Banyarwanda until the colonial adventure."[51] Pre-colonial Rwanda was effectively a nation state, because it had a single national identity and clearly defined territory,[52] which is said to have been considerably larger than the boundaries of Rwanda set in colonial times, encompassing much of eastern Congo and southern Uganda, a fact used to justify modern incursions into Congo.[53]

The narrative contends that while the categories Hutu, Tutsi, and Twa existed before colonialism, they emerged within Rwanda rather than through migration. Oral sources are cited to suggest that Hutu, Tutsi, and Twa come from common descent. According to Rwandan

[47] Misago Kanimba, "Peuplement ancien du Rwanda: à la lumière de récentes recherches," *Cahiers du Centre de Gestion des Conflits*, no. 5, ND, 2003, 8–44, for example, explains that many groups migrated to Rwanda "with different languages, Khoi-san, Sudanic, Cushitic, and Bantu. This last linguistic group progressively assimilated the other linguistic groups that were part of more scattered communities and thus less bound together. They had to adopt the language of a more stable group. The long coexistence of these groups (autochthonous and immigrant) ended in the fusion of cultural and linguistic elements as well as genes" (p. 37).

[48] Bernardin Muzungu, "Ethnies et Clans," *Cahiers Centre Saint-Dominique*, no.1, August 8, 1995: "There are no clans of a single ethnic group: the three are found in each clan."

[49] Alexis Gakuba, "Le Kinyarwanda: Instrument de l'Unité Nationale," *Les Cahiers Evangile et Société*, no. 3, June 1996, 59–67.

[50] Gérard Nyirimanzi, "Les solidaritiés traditionneles," *Cahiers Lumière et Société*, no. 14, June 1999, 19–41, p. 33.

[51] President Paul Kagame, "Beyond Absolute Terror: Post-Genocide Reconstruction in Rwanda," Speech to the Commonwealth Club of California, San Francisco, March 7, 2003.

[52] Gamaliel Mbonimana, "Le Rwanda état-nation au XIXe siècle," in *Rapport de Synthese du Seminaire sur l'Histoire du Rwanda*, Butare, December 14–18, 1998.

[53] Célestin Kalimba, "Rwanda: Les frontiers," in *Rapport de Synthese du Seminaire sur l'Histoire du Rwanda*, Butare, December 14–18, 1998. The idea of a "Greater Rwanda" was a key justification for the incursions in Congo in 1996 and 1998, since it suggested that territories under threat of anti-Tutsi ethnic violence were a Rwandan concern rather than something purely internal to Congo. A map of pre-colonial Rwanda that suggests the borders included not only all of modern Rwanda but also most of North Kivu and a large section of southwestern Uganda was widely circulated in the mid and late 1990s, particularly in the period just preceding the invasion of Zaire in 1996. It appeared, for example, inside the cover of several issues of *Cahiers Lumière et Société* in 1999.

myths, the three social groups are descendants of the children of one father. Imana (God) gave them each milk to guard. Gatwa drank his milk, Gahutu spilled his, and only Gatutsi kept his milk safe, which is why Imana put Gatutsi in charge of his brothers. The story "shows that in the ancestral tradition, what we currently call ethnicities are not a question of race but of 'wealth and social rank.' In effect, the story speaks of three brothers, not of three races."[54] In pre-colonial Rwanda, the three groups lived in harmony, and their relations were not grossly unequal, with each fulfilling a defined social and economic function. In particular, the relationship between Hutu and Tutsi was not feudal, as colonial scholars purported, because relations were reciprocal and mutually beneficial.[55] Many writers argue that Rwanda was like a large extended family with diverse members nevertheless intimately tied together. "It was on this natural line that national unity was grafted as a larger extension of the family. In this way, the king was considered not only as the political chief, but above all as the 'supreme patriarch of all families.'"[56]

The idea that the monarchy served to unify Rwandans of all groups is key to the narrative. The royal Nyiginya clan gradually centralized its rule over the Rwandan population in the centuries before colonialism. "The result of this centralization and this increased uniformity of the management of the country was a consciousness of the unity of the population. One king, one law, one people – such was Rwanda in this pre-colonial 'Nyiginya' period. This step of development of the country was the supreme realization of Rwanda as a family whose members were named the Rwandans or Rwandan people."[57] The king was above ethnicity. As a presidential commission on Rwanda's national unity concluded, "The King was the crux for all Rwandans. ... [A]fter he was enthroned, people said that 'he was no umututsi anymore,' but the King for the people. ... In the programme of expanding Rwanda, there was no room for disputes between Hutus, Tutsi and Twas. The King brought all of them

<hr>

[54] Bernardin Muzungu, "Les Mythes," *Cahiers Lumière et Société*, no. 5, Mayu 1997, 23–36, citation p. 34.

[55] Faustin Rutembesa, "A propos de l'usage du concept 'féodalité' dans l'etude de la société rwandaise," in *Rapport de Synthese du Seminaire sur l'Histoire du Rwanda*, Butare, December 14–18, 1998.

[56] Nyirimanzi, "Les solidaritiés traditionneles," p. 23. Michaël Kayihura, "Composantes et relations socials au Rwanda pre-colonial, colonial, et post-colonial: Hutu, Tutsi, Twa, Lignages et Clans," in *Rapport de Synthèse du Seminaire sur l'Histoire du Rwanda*, Butare, December 14–18, 1998, provides a nice summary of all of these arguments about the historic unity of the Rwandan people.

[57] Dèogratias Byanafashe, "La famille comme principe de coherence de la société rwandaise traditionnelle" *Cahiers Lumière et Société*, no. 6, August 1997, 3–26, citation p. 21.

together."[58] In sum, "The Rwandans constitute one ethnicity, not three, and have the same origin, a common biological relationship due to the numerous intermarriages over the millenniums."[59]

The Divisive Role of Colonialism

If Rwandans were historically a unified people, the narrative clearly blames colonial rule for dividing the population, particularly along ethnic lines.[60] As Gérard Nyirimanzi writes, "The current crisis has a cause exterior to our past: the racism inculcated in our united people for centuries by the colonizer."[61] The Catholic Church began the practice of ethnic segregation by establishing schools for Tutsi,[62] and the colonial administration then adopted the idea of ethnic differentiation.[63] Missionaries and others developed a historical narrative that sought to explain the different ethnic groups but that actually created the myths that gave the divisions social meaning. "Colonial historiography not only created cleavages between three social categories but, more seriously, conferred on them an ancient existence. The differences between these entities, rather falsified and unduly important, are explained in reference to the different historical origins."[64] The colonial idea that Hutu, Tutsi, and Twa were three separate racial groups that migrated into Rwanda at different times became the basis of colonial policy, and priests, teachers, and administrators ultimately duped the Rwandan population into

[58] Republic of Rwanda, Office of the President of the Republic, *The Unity of Rwandans: Before the Colonial Period and Under Colonial Rule; Under the First Republic*, Kigali, August 1999, p. 6.

[59] Jean Nizurugero Rugagi, "Les factuers favorables à l'identité citoyenne dans l'histoire du Rwanda des origins à 1900," in *Rapport de Synthèse du Seminaire sur l'Histoire du Rwanda*, Butare, December 14–18, 1998, p. 1.

[60] According to Helen Hintjens, "Post-Genocide Identity Politics in Rwanda," *Ethnicities*, 8(1), 2008, "For the current regime, only one account of Rwandan history is acceptable, which is that all was well among Rwandans until the colonizers created pseudo-racial, later ethnic identities, in order to quite deliberately divide Rwandans against one another," (p. 15).

[61] Nyirimanzi, "Les solidarities traditionneles."

[62] Gamaliel Mbonimana, "Ethnies et Eglise Catholique: Le remodelage de la société par l'école missionaire (1900–1931)," *Cahiers Centre Saint-Dominique*, no. 1, August 8, 1995, 52–67.

[63] Rugagi, "Décolonisation et democratization du Rwanda," writes, "The Belgian administration, despite its preferences for the *Hutu*, preferred to align with the thesis of Mgr. Classe who affirmed that *the Batutsi have an innate sense of command. He affirmed at the same time that the Bahutu were only good for manual labor, because they had a base spirit*" (p. 46) (emphasis in original).

[64] Misago Kanimba, "Le peuplement du territoire rwandais: a la lumière archéologiques," *Les Cahiers Lumière et Société*, no. 5, May 1997, 68–79, citation p. 79.

believing the veracity of the racial origins of Rwanda's differences.[65] As Michaël Kayihura states, "The Western historians, ethnographers, and anthropologists accustomed us to a certain number of physical, moral, social, and cultural stereotypes, about which the least that one can say is that they have had a long life, since they still remain in the work of certain post-colonial authors."[66]

The power and benefits that came to the Tutsi during the colonial period were not due to their own actions but part of the colonial strategy of domination. Once the Tutsi began to seek to wrest control of their country, the colonial rulers switched support to the Hutu in a cynical bid to retain as much power as possible. The Europeans in Rwanda created an "exacerbation through words and acts of the differences between Hutu and Tutsi, by the colony and the mission. The Roman tactic of 'divide et impera' (divide to better manipulate) was chosen to prevent the independence of Rwanda. To do this, it was necessary to raise up the Hutu who didn't ask for it against the Tutsi who demanded it."[67] Cynical colonial manipulations cast the Tutsi as arrogant, dominating foreigners. "After the alliances were changed, the Tutsi were abandoned by the colonizers for having committed the fault of demanding the independence of their country, what were previously Tutsi qualities became faults or, more exactly, the opposite of an asset."[68]

Even well-meaning colonials, such as progressive priests, acted out of a misunderstanding of the Rwandan situation. Flemish priests saw in the Hutu a working class like the Flemish and equated the Tutsi with arrogant Walloons who had historically dominated Belgium. They saw their fight for the Hutu as a fight for justice. "In this hope for justice, these young Flemish forget the great majority of Tutsi who lived in a low social condition at the same level as the Hutu."[69]

The History of Genocide and Post-Independent Governance

According to the official narrative, the uprising of 1959 was not, as previously contended, a "revolution" but instead the first instance of genocide

---

[65] Muzungu, "Ethnies et Clans," writes, "Bantu, Hamite, and Pygmoid. These three races would be the source of our so-called three ethnic groups: Hutu, Tutsi, Twa. No one can ignore the political and colonial impact that weighed on these theories" (p. 25).

[66] Kayihura, "Composantes et relations socials," p. 1.

[67] Octave Ugirashebuja, "L'ideologie du Tutsi oppresseur," *Les Cahiers Evangile et Société*, no. 4, December 1996, 57–67.

[68] Bernardin Muzungu, "Le prejugé de race," *Les Cahiers Evangile et Société*, No. 4, December 1996, 20–29.

[69] Nizurugero, "Décolonisation et democratization," p. 48.

in Rwanda's history.[70] This first instance of ethnic violence in Rwanda's history was due directly to European manipulations, as colonial administrators, missionaries, and others feared losing their control to a radicalized Tutsi political class who would not have allowed neocolonial domination. A key idea in the narrative is that colonial and post-colonial manipulation distorted democracy in Rwanda. Majority rule came to be understood not as government by the political majority but as rule by the ethnic majority, the Hutu. "The identification of the mass as only the Hutu was the fatal error for the country. This logic culminated in negating purely and simply the nationality of all Tutsi and ignored the existence of the Twa. We already have here the premises of the genocide of 1994."[71]

The First and Second Republics are understood as pawns of neocolonial authority. The Hutu who took power were handpicked by the Europeans and betrayed the interests of the Rwandan people for their own personal benefit. "The two first republics were simply extensions of colonization by imposed 'natives.' "[72] "The Rwandan social order created by colonization endured more than 30 years in the two first republics."[73]

Violence against Tutsi began in 1959, and the governments of both Kayibanda and Habyarimana must also be understood in light of this violence. Nyirimanzi's reference to, "the catastrophe that befell our country beginning in 1959 and the culmination of which took place in 1994,"[74] is typical in regarding the period of 1959–1994 as a continuous time of violence against the Tutsi, gradually and inevitably building toward the 1994 genocide.[75] Failure to hold anyone accountable for the earlier violence made possible the genocide in 1994. The anti-Tutsi ideology and policies of the regimes completely overshadow any other policies, such

---

[70] Pierre Mungarulire, "Le revolution de 1959 au Rwanda," in *Rapport de Synthèse du Seminaire sur l'Histoire du Rwanda*, Butare, December 14–18, 1998, writes "This so-called 'Revolution of 1959,' even baptized by others as the 'Popular Revolution of 1959,' I call the 'so-called' revolution, because in my opinion … the bloody events that took place in Rwanda, as in November 1959, were not at all a revolution, much less a popular revolution." See also, Pierre Kamanzi, "Révolution ou Régression?" *Cahiers Lumière et Société*, no. 16, December 1999, 61–72.

[71] Rugagi, "Décolonisation et democratization," p. 48.

[72] Byanafashe, "La famille comme principe," p. 23.

[73] Bernardin Muzungu, "A qui profitent nos malheurs?" *Cahiers Lumière et Société*, March 1999, 35–54.

[74] Nyirimanzi, "Les solidarities traditionneles."

[75] One speaker at a conference in Butare in preparation for the national week of mourning in 2003, for example, declared, "Even if the true genocide began on April 6, 1994, just after the death of Habyarimana, the genocide really began in 1959." Quoted on Radio Rwanda, April 2, 2003.

as the focus on economic development.[76] Issues not related to ethnic violence are glossed over or entirely ignored. For example, Jean-Damascène Ndayambaje writes that, "Violence by the Parmehutu Party against the Tutsi marked the entire period 1959–1973,"[77] ignoring the actual periodic nature of the violence and the general absence of ethnic violence between 1965 and 1973. The history of both republics is reduced to the aspects relevant to ethnic discrimination and ethnic violence, as though nothing other than identity issues were politically relevant.[78] As Kagame has said, "The period of 1959 to 1994 is indeed a history of genocide in slow motion."[79]

The Centrality of the Genocide

The genocide is the focal point of Rwanda's current historical narrative. Much as the previous regimes referred endlessly to the 1959 "revolution" to justify their actions and interpreted contemporary history in light of this uprising against Tutsi and colonial oppressors, the RPF regime has identified the genocide as the key event against which all Rwandan history before and since must be considered. Colonial history is seen as laying the groundwork for genocide,[80] and the First and Second Republics are understood to have built inevitably toward the 1994 genocide. President Kagame and other politicians regularly refer to the genocide as the primary source of Rwanda's ongoing challenges and as justification for many current government policies. Kagame began his 2003 San Francisco speech with the line, "There is no greater crime than genocide,"[81] using the genocide to frame all of his subsequent remarks. The RPF claims considerable moral authority for having stopped the genocide, and the threat of renewed genocide justifies many ongoing government policies.

[76] For example, according to Radio Rwanda the participants in a 2002 meeting of former government officials in Ruhengeri, "found that the regimes that followed the colonial regime did nothing to correct these errors [of ethnic division], but rather they aggravated things to the point that the divisions launched the 1994 genocide." Radio Rwanda, Morning News, September 19, 2002.

[77] Jean-Damascène Ndayambaje, "Le genocide des Tutsi: Genese et execution," in *Rapport de Synthèse du Seminaire sur l'Histoire du Rwanda*, Butare, December 14–18, 1998.

[78] C.f., Ferdinand Kayoboke, "Le M.D.R. Parmehutu et la 1ère République," in *Rapport de Synthèse du Seminaire sur l'Histoire du Rwanda*, Butare, December 14–18, 1998; Médard Rutijanwa, "Le MRND et la IIème République Rwandaise: Essai d'Analyse critique du Système Politique et Idéologique du MRND," in *Rapport de Synthèse du Seminaire sur l'Histoire du Rwanda*, Butare, December 14–18, 1998. In addition to ethnicity, both authors discuss the relevance of regional discrimination among Hutu in the two regimes.

[79] Kagame, "Beyond Absolute Terror."

[80] Muzungu, "A qui profitent nos malheurs?" writes, "Historically speaking, the Hutu-Tutsi antagonism was created by colonization" (p. 39).

[81] Kagame, "Beyond Absolute Terror."

The historical narrative offers an interpretation of the genocide that emphasizes its mass popular nature and its brutality. The government and its supporters have consistently insisted on the largest possible number of victims – usually over one million – to emphasize the very serious nature of the genocide.[82] The editors of *Cahiers Lumière et Société* assert (without supporting evidence) that since 1959 two million people have been killed in Hutu–Tutsi violence in Rwanda.[83] Along with a large number of victims, the narrative portrays the genocide as an event in which nearly every Hutu in the country was caught up and that involved extraordinary depravity. This emphasis implies that anyone in Rwanda at the time of the genocide is tainted by the violence. Only those who lost their lives opposing the genocide can be known to have truly challenged the violence. Survival implies cooption; one has to have done something to survive. Hence, not only all Hutu who survived are suspect, even if they seemed to actively oppose the genocide, but also by implication, so are Tutsi survivors.[84]

The narrative attributes the genocide to sources both external and internal to Rwanda. International responsibility for the genocide is assigned not simply to the role that colonialism played in creating ethnic divisions, but also to ongoing failures by the international community.[85] France is singled out in particular for having supported the Habyarimana regime, cooperated with the FAR in combating the RPF, trained and armed the militia groups that carried out the genocide, and helped the Rwandan army and militia members escape into Zaire by establishing the Zone Turquoise.[86] Kagame writes, "I hold the French government, in particular, responsible

[82] Des Forges, *Leave None to Tell the Story*, p. 16, offers an interesting discussion of the conflict over numbers of victims.

[83] "Conclusion Generale," *Cahiers Lumière et Société*, December 1999, 73–76.

[84] In a speech to commemorate the Day of Heroes, a national holiday created by the RPF to focus on those who have resisted ethnic violence, President Kagame declared, "The most essential things is to remember these heroes, because they are no longer living. It is unfortunate that they are no longer living ... But their work, resting on their ideologies that they put into application, is not erased. This [commemoration] keeps them among us. We must follow their example." Paul Kagame, Speech on the Day of Heroes, Nyange, Kibuye, broadcast on Radio Rwanda, February 1, 2003. The idea that those who opposed ethnic violence, the "heroes," are all dead implies that those still living did not oppose ethnic violence. I develop the idea of collective guilt more fully in Chapter 4.

[85] Bénoit Kaboyi, representative of the survivors' group IBUKA, speaking at a "Solidarity Camp" for recently released prisoners, Nkumba, Ruhengeri, broadcast on Radio Rwanda, April 2, 2003, declared, "I don't want to speak about the role of the colonizers, the French who trained the Interahamwe, the sellers of arms, etc."

[86] The culpability of France was a point of particular emphasis for the RPF leadership, as the French government is among the only international governments to challenge the RPF's interpretation of the genocide and its moral position. The Rwandan government accused France of supporting the genocide (c.f., Jeevan Vasagar, "France Blamed as Rwanda Marks Genocide Date," *The Guardian*, April 8, 2004), while the French government has accused the RPF of inciting the genocide by assassinating Habyarimana

for helping to arm and train the militias that dispersed throughout the country to wipe out the Tutsi population."[87] The rest of the international community bears responsibility for failing to stop the genocide. Kagame asserted, "The UN and the international community as a whole abandoned Rwanda in 1994."[88] Gasana Ndoba, the president of the National Commission for Human Rights, asserted that, "the genocide was prepared and executed in the view of and with the knowledge of the international community."[89] In his speech on the ninth anniversary of the genocide, President Kagame, asked, "Fifty years ago they said, 'Never again,' but what did they do so that this would not be committed in our country?"[90]

The narrative attributes blame within the country in two distinct ways. Responsibility lies first with the elite, particularly government officials, who selfishly used their power for personal gain and served foreign interests rather than the national interest. Bad governance is a common theme in discussions of the genocide. The leaders of both the First and Second Republics are regarded as having set the stage for the genocide with their abuse of power and their ethnic discrimination. The discourse pays scant attention to the internal process of democratization from 1990 to 1994 other than to note that many politicians formerly in opposition ultimately re-aligned themselves with President Habyarimana and the Hutu-Power movement. The Democratic Republican Movement (*Mouvement Démocratique Républicain*, MDR) is particularly singled out for having maintained the anti-Tutsi values of its predecessor party Parmehutu.[91] A few Hutu, such as Prime Minister Agathe Uwilingiyimana, are recognized as martyrs, but the narrative sees most Hutu as having in fact been complicit in the genocide.

by shooting down his plane. The French ultimately issued warrants for the arrest of top RPF officials for their involvement in the assassination ("France Issues Rwanda Warrants," BBC News, November 23, 2006). The tension ultimately led to a severing of diplomatic ties between Rwanda and France in November 2006 ("Rwanda Cuts Relations with France," BBC News, November 24, 2006).

[87] Paul Kagame, "Preface," in Phil Clark and Zachary D. Kaufman, eds., *After Genocide: Transitional Justice, Post-Conflict Reconstruction and Reconciliation in Rwanda and Beyond*, London: Hurst, 2008.

[88] Ibid.

[89] Ndoba Gasana, reported on Evening News, Radio Rwanda, April 2, 2003.

[90] Paul Kagame, speech given at the national commemoration of the ninth anniversary of the 1994 genocide, Mwurire, Rwangana, Kibungo, broadcast on Radio Rwanda, April 7, 2003.

[91] Reyntjens, "Rwanda 10 Years On." In April 2003, the Transitional National Assembly voted to ban the MDR after a parliamentary commission reported that the party had supported the genocide and retained a genocidal ideology. Republique Rwandaise, Assembleé Nationale, *Rapport de la Commission Parlementaire de controle mise en place le 27 decembre 2002 pour enqueter sur les problemes du MDR*, accepted by the National Transitional Assembly, April 14, 2003.

Elites outside the government are also condemned for their complicity. Members of civil society – even human rights organizations – are said to have participated in the genocide, indicating the total bankruptcy of the intellectual class. Paul Rutayisire makes a stinging critique of the Catholic Church and its complicity in the genocide, both for its historic and contemporary role, a perspective embraced by many of the former refugee intellectuals. "In the process that led to genocide, the Catholic hierarchy was complicit, as much in its behavior as in its teachings, in broadcasting the evil that ate away at Rwandan society. Even the most unconditional defenders of the Catholic Church do not contest this fact."[92] In general, the educated in Rwanda, whether in the government or outside, are considered to have led the country down the road to genocide.

The narrative walks a fine line between blaming the Rwandan population and vindicating them by blaming the international community and the national leadership. The masses are regarded as having participated widely in the genocide, but mostly because of their severe poverty and ignorance that made them vulnerable to manipulation by ill-intentioned elites. The masses were deceived by "an ideology of discrimination,"[93] that claimed not only that the Tutsi were foreigners and that Rwanda belonged to Hutu,[94] but that all Tutsi in Rwanda were enemies of the Hutu; killing Tutsi was therefore self-defense.[95] The low level of education within the population limited the masses' capacity to critically assess the false ideas being fed to them.[96] Poverty is also considered a major cause of the genocide, as the wretched lives of the masses made them respond to promises of economic opportunity.

Given its centrality, the genocide must be highlighted and commemorated in order to prevent it from recurring. As the regional representative of the survivors' group IBUKA reported in a radio interview, "Some people have even said that remembering [the genocide] does not coincide with the process of unity and reconciliation of Rwandans. This is

[92] Paul Rutayisire, "Le catholicisme rwandais en procès," in *Rapport de Synthèse du Seminaire sur l'Histoire du Rwanda*, Butare, December 14–18, 1998, p. 16. See also, Paul Rutayisire and Bernardin Muzumgu, "L'ethnisme au Coeur de la guerre," *Cahiers Centre Saint-Dominique*, no. 1, August 8, 1995, 68–82.

[93] JB Habyarimana, president of the National Commission for Unity and Reconciliation, cited on Radio Rwanda, January 21, 2003. "The genocide is the result of several influences that come together and the points of departure are social conditions, grave economic problems, conditions that drove toward the troubles, political problems, but equally the psychological conditions that were created by an ideology of discrimination."

[94] Bernardin Muzungu, "Un Mensonge politique," *Cahiers Lumière et Société*, no. 10, May 1998, 26–46.

[95] Rutayisire and Muzungu, "L'ethnisme au Coeur de la guerre."

[96] The fact that those who *were* educated are blamed for the genocide does not diminish the degree to which ignorance is considered a key cause.

not a good idea. People holding this opinion only take account of their own interests. ... He who doesn't know where he is coming from, doesn't know where he is going."[97]

The RPF as Agent of Peace and Democracy

The narrative depicts the RPF as Rwanda's saviors who reluctantly used military force for the benefit of all Rwandan people. Rwanda was suffering under dictatorship and violence, and the Habyarimana regime was unwilling to accept real democracy or allow refugees the right to return to their homeland. "The RPF had to develop an armed wing, because the Rwandan regime did not understand the language of peace."[98] The goals of the RPF were the repatriation of refugees, the overthrow of the dictatorship, and the "elimination of the virus of divisionism."[99]

The narrative portrays the RPF as serving a noble cause and acting out of self-sacrifice, and their invasion is called the "War of Liberation." The beginning of the war in 1990 is commemorated as a national holiday annually on October 1, known as the Day of Patriotism. In a speech marking the holiday in 2002, President Kagame claimed, "[T]welve years ago to the day, Rwandans began to struggle against injustice in Rwanda and to proceed with the general reform of the bad politics that scatter the Rwandan people. ... This day ... reminds us that Rwandans who love their country whether in the interior or the exterior rose up to struggle against the bad leadership that existed in the country."[100] While the War of October, as it was known within Rwanda, was extremely unpopular within the country at the time, the RPF has attempted to use the Day of Patriotism to recast the war as a struggle not *against* the Rwandan people but *by* the Rwandan people against corrupt authoritarian governance and ethnic violence. Ignoring the pro-democracy movement that had begun months earlier, the narrative treats the RPF invasion as the beginning of efforts for reform.

The idea that the RPF stopped the genocide is a crucial element of the historical narrative. While the international community utterly failed to act on the promise of "never again," the RPF acted boldly, renewing its attack on Rwanda with the sole purpose of stopping the genocide. According to Bernardin Muzungu, "While the machete and other

---

⁹⁷ Benoit Kaboyi, representative of Ibuka, Radio Rwanda, April 2, 2003.

⁹⁸ Tito Rutaremara and Bernardin Muzungu, "Qui liberera le Rwanda de l'idéologie divisionniste?" *Les Cahiers Evangile et Société*, no. 3, June 1996, 46–56, citation p. 49.

⁹⁹ Ibid., pp. 52–53.

¹⁰⁰ Paul Kagame, "Speech on the Occasion of the Day of Patriotism," Radio Rwanda, October 1, 2002.

instruments of death made the law in Rwanda and the international community waited with arms crossed, the RPF-Inkotanyi threw its youth into the fire. The dispersal of the killers was total."[101] The attack on Rwanda that the RPF renewed in April 1994 is reinterpreted as an "anti-genocidal campaign."[102]

According to the narrative, the RPF has devoted itself since taking power to correcting the mistakes of the past and reforming Rwanda so that ethnic violence will never recur. As Kagame said, "When the RPF took over, Rwanda was in utter anarchy. … We quickly realized that our task was to restore hope to the Rwandan people and to return power to the population. We have restored trust in the judiciary and have therefore been able to avoid revenge. The long established culture of impunity, which made possible the 1994 genocide, has at last been broken. People now have complete security of life and property."[103] The RPF fought against ethnic discrimination and "divisionism," establishing a multi-party, multi-ethnic "government of transition."[104] The mention of ethnicity was removed from national identity cards, and positions in schools and government employment are now determined by the principle of merit. Many articles on the history of ethnic violence include a statement on how the current regime has broken with the practice of discrimination. For example, Kayihura writes, "Today, four years after the genocide, the Government of National Unity is striving, against winds and tides, to restore the Rwandan society in a context of beneficial national reconciliation."[105]

A corollary of the narrative depicting the RPF as noble and self-sacrificing seeks to obliterate any public memory of RPF abuses during and after the 1990–1994 war. As heroic saviors of the country, the RPF cannot also be villains. The idea that the RPF bears any responsibility for the genocide itself, for having attacked the country without regard for the consequences for Tutsi still within Rwanda, is categorically rejected.[106]

---

[101] Bernardin Muzungu, "Les signes d'espoir," *Cahiers Lumière et Société*, no. 11, August 1998, 7–20, citation p. 14.

[102] Kagame, "Preface."

[103] Kagame, "Beyond Absolute Terror."

[104] Muzungu, "Les signes d'espoir," writes, "As an antidote against ethnic exclusion and racism, a Government of all Rwandans and all political formations, except the *génocidaires*, is at work. Alas those who would combat it and want to return us to the fire of tribalism" (p. 14).

[105] Kayihura, "Composantes et Relations Sociales," p. 30.

[106] Rene Lemarchand, "Genocide in the Great Lakes: Which Genocide, Whose Genocide?" *African Studies Review*, 41, 1, April 1998, 3–16, asks, "Would the genocide have occurred if the RPF invasion had not taken place, threatening both the heritage of the 1959–62 Hutu revolution, and the state born of the revolution? Why should the genocide of the Tutsi, and their presumptive allies among the Hutu population, mask the countless atrocities committed by the RPF in the course of their military operations in Rwanda?" p. 4. Rutayisire and Muzungu, "L'ethnisme au Coeur de la guerre," completely reject this idea.

Furthermore, any apparent abuses during the war and its aftermath are either unfortunate casualties of a just war (generally seen as misunderstood or exaggerated) or the actions of rogue individuals who operated outside the approval of the RPF leadership. As Kagame said, "We acted to stop a genocide, but you cannot stop individuals from committing crimes individually."[107] His point is that any violence carried out against civilians by the RPF or its soldiers was incidental and not systematic. The idea of a "double genocide" advanced by some regime critics is vociferously rejected as a form of genocide denial; if both sides committed genocide, then blame is shared and the crime is less serious. As Kagame said in response to a question about potential indictments of RPF officials at the ICTR, "What in Rwanda we are opposed to is equating inequitable situations. ... Don't divert from the main purpose of the Tribunal, and that is to try those involved in the genocide."[108] Rwanda's two incursions into the DRC in 1996–1997 and 1998–2002 were necessary for Rwanda's security, particularly to prevent a recurrence of genocide. The troops "showed their courage and their sacrifice based on their patriotic love [of Rwanda]"[109]

Criticism of the RPF is treated as revisionist support for the "double genocide" theory. An article on the double-genocide theory equates criticism of the RPF with both genocide denial and support for the *génocidaires*.[110] Those in the international community who criticize the RPF regime are hypocrites, since they did not oppose the regime that carried out the genocide but now dare to condemn the RPF, which stopped the genocide.[111] Those Rwandans who criticize the RPF demonstrate their continuing adherence to genocidal ideologies. For example, when former President Bizimungu's political party was banned for promoting "*divisionism*," those who supported the new political party that he formed were accused of supporting genocide.[112] A few months later, the MDR was similarly criticized for having, "always supported the divisions that

---

[107] Kagame, "Beyond Absolute Terror."

[108] Ibid.

[109] Kagame, "Speech on the Occasion of the Day of Patriotism."

[110] "La nouvelle strategie du 'double genocide,'" *Cahier Lumière et Société*, no. 9, March 1998.

[111] "The humanitarian associations, many of which are linked to the churches and share their malaise, as well as organisms of the press that are close to them, believe themselves obliged to be all the more vigilant, demanding and scrupulous in the respect to human rights for the current government, when they were complaisant or passive in the past." "La nouvelle strategie du 'double genocide.'"

[112] For example, the mayor of Gikondo in Kigali held public meetings with his constituents in July 2002 to denounce the party for sowing disorder. "The first problem concerns the political party PDR-Ubuyanja that wanted to form and that was stopped after its ethnically divisive teachings." Radio Rwanda, Mid-Day News, July 28, 2002.

have beset our country,"[113] and its presidential candidate, former Prime Minister Twagiramungu was accused of having denied the genocide.[114] The parliamentary committee ultimately concluded that the MDR should be suppressed, because the ideology of the party was merely a continuation of Kayibanda's anti-Tutsi Parmehutu and the leadership was both implicated in the genocide and continued to support a genocidal ideology.[115] Critics of the regime are also commonly accused of putting their own interests first and indulging in corruption. As one governor declared in a public meeting, "The ethnic divisions that have characterized Rwanda are hidden behind people who would simply fill their stomachs – for selfish interests."[116] In short, the RPF has the best interests of the country in mind, and those who would criticize the party and government hold only selfish interests and have yet to give up the divisive racist thinking of the past.

President Kagame's forward to a book on transitional justice in Rwanda amply demonstrates the various points about the RPF that I have outlined here:

A new phenomenon has emerged in the form of individuals and groups who seek to revise history for their own gain, including many who deny outright that genocide took place in Rwanda in 1994. These revisionists, including Rwandan and non-Rwandan ideologues, academics, journalists and political leaders, now claim that the genocide was a myth; that what occurred in 1994 was simply a civil war between two equal sides or the spontaneous flaring of ancient tribal hatred. Even worse, some of these sources accuse the RPF, the force that halted the genocide, of seeking to exterminate the Hutu population. This is an absolute falsehood, sheer nonsense. While some rogue RPF elements committed crimes against civilians during the civil war after 1990, and during the anti-genocidal campaign, individuals were punished severely according to the RPF's internal procedures of the day. To try to construct a case of moral equivalency between genocide crimes and isolated crimes committed by rogue RPF members is morally bankrupt and an insult to all Rwandans, especially survivors of the genocide. Objective history illustrates the bankruptcy of this emerging revisionism. The fact that there was no mass revenge in the post-genocide period – which could have easily occurred – is evidence of the clarity of purpose of the Rwandan

---

[113] Evening News, Radio Rwanda, December 12, 2002.

[114] A dissident MDR leader declared on Radio Rwanda that Twagiramungu, "dared to say to the ICTR that there was no genocide in 1994, the very genocide that he planned and that [former MDR Prime Minister during the genocide Jean] Kambanda as well as other genocidaires have themselves recognized and have accepted to be punished for." Radio Rwanda, December 12, 2002.

[115] I discuss the suppression of the MDR in greater detail in Chapter 5. See "Rapport de la Commission Parlementaire sur les problèmes du MDR," Kigali, March 17, 2003, available at www.cnlg.gov.rw/fileadmin/templates/documents/MDR_RAPPORT_ PARLEMENT_2003.pdf.

[116] Boniface Rucagu, Governor of Kibuye, Radio Rwanda, September 19, 2002.

leadership that actively mobilized the Rwandan population for higher moral purposes than the revisionists contend.[117]

The Official Narrative and Constraints on Historical Debate

I have attempted above to provide as accurate as possible a summation of the official historical narrative advanced by the RPF and its supporters with little commentary.[118] My goal in this chapter is not to assess the accuracy of the historical discourse but rather to understand its main points in order to appreciate the major themes of the collective memory that the RPF has sought to promote. In fact, many of the points in the current official narrative diverge from or directly contradict the conclusions of most historians and other scholars outside Rwanda. The need to emphasize unity and reject the significance of ethnicity has led to distortions of historical reality. The narrative exaggerates the unifying role of the monarchy by denying the fluid nature of political boundaries in pre-colonial Rwanda, ignoring both the presence of autonomous Hutu kingdoms within the territory and the tenuous ties of peripheral areas to the central court. Placing the genocide at the center of Rwandan history treats the past hundred years as a linear progression toward that signal event, ignoring much of the actual complexity of events in both the colonial and post-colonial eras. The official interpretation of the genocide conceals the facilitating role of the RPF invasion and ignores atrocities committed by the RPF itself.

In promoting a singular narrative, Rwanda's new elite seeks to develop a unified collective memory for the Rwandan population, one they hope not only creates a propitious environment for their continuing social, economic, and political dominance but will also ultimately reshape what it means to be Rwandan in a way that will prevent future ethnic violence. If, as I have argued, the belief in distinct historical origins made the genocide possible by delineating Hutu from Tutsi and Twa, then developing a belief in a unified history, it is hoped, will eliminate the basis for

---

[117] Kagame, "Preface."

[118] My account of the RPF narrative is consistent with Thomson's summary of the post-genocide "official history" in *Whispering Truth to Power*: "The RPF-led government presents the genocide as a clear-cut affair: Hutu killed Tutsi because of ethnic divisions that were introduced during the colonial period (1890–1962) and hardened to the point of individual action during the postcolonial period (1962–1994) ... Ethnicity is a fiction created by colonial divide-and-rule policies. Ultimate blame for the 1994 genocide therefore lies with Rwanda's colonial powers, who instituted policies that made the Hutu population hate Tutsi. Divisive politics grounded in decades of bad governance resulted in deep-rooted ethnic hatred of *all* Tutsi by *all* Hutu" (pp. 81–82).

inter-group violence. Whatever their merits, the distinctly political goals of the effort to rewrite history leave little room for dissention and debate.

In the project that I helped direct to develop modules for a history curriculum for Rwandan secondary schools, we sought to encourage an alternative method of approaching history as a set of questions and problems rather than a list of facts.[119] In the course of this project, however, my American colleagues and I witnessed exactly how the official narrative serves to constrain discussions of history even among trained historians. Two small incidents serve as examples. The first involves the choice of focus for the working group on pre-colonial Rwanda. David Newbury, a prominent historian of Rwanda, participated in the project as a consultant and advised the pre-colonial group. Newbury has written extensively on clans, and in a definitive work on the topic published in 1980, he argued that clans were not, as earlier histories had maintained, the most important social identifier in pre-colonial Rwanda. While clans were significant for the organization of power in the central court, for most people in what is today Rwanda they were less significant as social identifiers than region and lineage. In fact, the expansion of the clan structure throughout Rwanda was actually part of the process of the extension of central control by the monarchy.[120]

The official post-genocide narrative, however, has treated clans as a central aspect of Rwandan history. The fact that clans in Rwanda are multi-ethnic, most including all three groups, is used in the official narrative to support the ideas that the Rwandan people were historically unified and that ethnicity was an artificial creation of the colonial state. Furthermore, clans were important to competitions for power in the Rwandan royal court, even into the colonial period. Tutsi who fled Rwanda beginning in 1959 came disproportionately from the political elite, and in exile, particularly in Uganda, clan identity remained important to them. Inside Rwanda, clans diminished even further in importance, serving little purpose other than limiting marital choices (since Rwandans marry outside their clans). The refugees who returned to Rwanda beginning in 1994 brought with them the perspective that clans were central to Rwandan society. (President Kagame is from the clan of the queen mother, the Abega, and many people have said that his rise to power represents the final victory of the Abega over the Nyiginya

---

[119] For this project, we brought in the US-based NGO Facing History and Ourselves, which develops teaching materials and trains teachers on confronting difficult histories to help students develop critical thinking skills and develop skills for responsible citizenship.

[120] David S. Newbury, "The Clans of Rwanda: An Historical Hypothesis," *Africa: Journal of the International Africa Institute*, 50, no. 4, 1980, 389–403.

clan.) Thus, despite the advice from the pre-eminent expert on clans in Rwanda that the pre-colonial working group focus on a topic less distorted by ideology, the pre-colonial group insisted on choosing clans as their focus and presented clans in a fashion consistent with the official narrative – though they did include a few references to the work of Newbury to indicate that there were divergent perspectives.

Another example from our project of how politicized history has become in Rwanda involved the working group charged with treating the post-independence period. The group included in the initial draft of their materials a section that sought to implicate one of Rwanda's most respected Hutu human rights activists, Father André Sibomana, in a notorious case of anti-Tutsi discrimination in the late-1980s, the "Muvara Affair." In 1988, the Vatican appointed as bishop Father Félicièn Muvara, a Tutsi priest, but just days before his installation, he withdrew, claiming "personal reasons." In fact, rumors quickly spread that he had been pressured to withdraw by leaders in both the government and the church after a "whispering campaign" falsely accused him of fathering a child out of wedlock.[121] The materials presented by the post-independence group asserted that Sibomana had instigated the rumors against Muvara.

I strongly believe that the accusations against Sibomana were driven not by the actual events related to Muvara but rather by a contemporary attempt to discredit Sibomana in the post-genocide context. I personally knew both Muvara and Sibomana and researched the Muvara affair during the period just prior to the genocide. Muvara was the curé of one of the Catholic parishes where I conducted research in 1992–1993, and I interviewed him several times, including an extended interview focused specifically on his abandoned appointment as bishop. The evidence that he and others provided me painted a very different picture that directly implicated the archbishop, a close ally of President Haybarimana.

Sibomana, meanwhile, had played an important role in inspiring opposition to the Habyarimana regime and encouraging support for democratic political reform as editor of the Catholic newspaper, *Kinyamateka*, beginning in 1988. He also became the founding president of the human rights group ADL in 1990, one of the most important human rights organizations in the period leading up to the genocide. During the genocide, death squads targeted Sibomana as an opponent of both the regime and the genocide, but he survived by going into hiding. After 1994, the Vatican named Sibomana acting bishop of Kabgayi, and he was widely expected to be named bishop. He earned the wrath of those in power, however, by continuing his advocacy for human rights, particularly by

---

[121] I discuss this case in Longman, *Christianity and Genocide in Rwanda*, p. 96.

publicly denouncing the terrible condition of the prison in his diocese, where prisoners were dying in large numbers from dysentery and other diseases related to the unsanitary conditions. As a result, Sibomana ironically became himself an object of a "whispering campaign" by allies of the RPF regime who accused him of being anti-Tutsi and participating in the genocide – despite the reality that he was himself targeted by it. Ultimately, the Vatican passed him over for bishop, naming a mild-mannered Hutu unlikely to challenge the government. Sibomana returned to the editorship of *Kinyamateka* and his work with ADL, but he faced harassment and intimidation, and his health fell into decline. He died in 1988 after the government denied him the right to leave Rwanda for medical treatment.[122] In response to international criticism surrounding his death, the government stepped up its campaign against him, seeking to discredit him posthumously and thereby justify their own hostility to him.

Having worked with Sibomana as director of the HRW and FIDH office in Rwanda, I was consistently impressed by his courage and principles, and I found the accusations against him poorly supported and inconsistent with widespread testimonies that I heard from Rwandans. Furthermore, the source for the section in our curriculum accusing Sibomana in the Muvara Affair was a notoriously unreliable, pro-RPF and anti-Catholic French press, Golias. Since the accusations against Sibomana were not essential to the text and seemed to serve no useful purpose, I spoke with the professor directing the project and urged that they be edited out. Nonetheless, in the final version, the accusations against Sibomana remained. These accusations served the purpose of discrediting a prominent moderate Hutu who had criticized the RPF government and had suffered as a result. Discrediting Sibomana helped to protect the image of the RPF as a supporter of human rights and democracy and also to promote the impression that Hutu elite were almost universally implicated in the genocide.

These are but two minor examples of the ways in which the official narrative constrains historical discussion, but they occurred in an academic setting that included the top Rwandan historians and education specialists in a project in which participants had committed themselves to developing more democratic approaches to the teaching of history. If even the country's best historians are unwilling to complicate their discussions of the Rwandan past and allow for alternative perspectives, how much more difficult must it be for common citizens to articulate

---

[122] André Sibomana, *Hope for Rwanda: Conversations with Laure Guilbert and Hervé Deguine*, London: Pluto Press, 1999.

divergent narratives? As I demonstrate in the next several chapters, the main themes of the historical narrative developed here are reinforced through a variety of means. Genocide memorials, trials, political reform, and other government policies support the official narrative and seek to advance a collective memory that will both promote national unity and justify RPF rule. Given these political goals, alternative perspectives cannot be tolerated. In post-genocide Rwanda, the RPF and its supporters are clearly the ones who claim the right to speak for the past, and their aggressive political agenda does not allow contests over the past to challenge their dominance of the present.

3   Symbolic Struggles

> The dead. The body count. We don't like to admit the war was even partly our fault because so many of our people died. And all the mournings veiled the truth. It's not "lest we forget," it's "lest we remember." That's what all this is about – the memorials, the cenotaph, the two minutes' silence. Because there is no better way of forgetting something than by commemorating it.
>
> – Tom Irwin in *The History Boys*

A tour of massacre sites has become an obligatory part of any business or tourist visit to post-genocide Rwanda. Both deeply affecting and also disconcerting, the genocide-site pilgrimage highlights the horrors of the genocide while at the same time revealing the crass uses for which the memory of the genocide is employed. Most genocide tours begin at the impressive Kigali Memorial Centre at Gisozi on the outskirts of the capital city. The genocide museum is a striking white stucco modernist structure perched atop a hill near the location of a major roadblock in 1994 where hundreds of Tutsi were slaughtered. It was built with foreign funds, using the latest in museum design, and informed by Holocaust museums in the United States, Europe, and Israel. The first portion of the museum traces the history of the genocide, in English, French, and Kinyarwanda, from pre-colonial times until 1994. There are sections on politics, propaganda, women, and other themes, in a presentation reminiscent of the United States Holocaust Memorial Museum in Washington, DC. The historical narrative is accompanied by a few primary documents, like the Bahutu Manifesto and photos, with appropriate interpretive commentary.

The rest of the museum uses less straightforward means to create an impression of the genocide that appeals more to the emotions than to the mind. One room is filled with abstract statues depicting the suffering of the genocide. Another room focuses on the children killed. Still another room contains photographs of people who died in the genocide, hung as if floating in space on wires that run from floor to ceiling. This image from the museum has become iconic, gracing the covers of books and appearing in discussions of genocide or violence. The museum is surrounded by a memorial garden providing beautiful views of Kigali. A wall of names lists all of the people from Kigali known to have been killed in the genocide, reminiscent of the Vietnam Veterans Memorial in Washington, DC. Finally, there is a mass grave, large slabs of concrete that line the side of the garden with the best views, and on one side an open mausoleum, where families who were able to identify the remains of their loved ones have placed the bodies in coffins, draped in purple cloth and white lace, and stacked one on the other in crowded underground rooms, accessible by concrete stairs. (See Figure 1.) The museum documentation claims that over 250,000 "victims of the genocide" killed in Kigali are buried in the mass grave. The memorial center is both informative and evocative, an effective introduction to the genocide – or at least the government's narrative of it – for those with little knowledge, not only stirring emotions but also providing careful direction as to how one should think about the events that led up to 1994.

Figure 1 Coffins exposed at the Kigali Memorial Centre (Photo by author).

After the museum, the genocide tour generally continues to one of the memorialized massacre sites, most often one or both of the churches relatively easily accessed just south of Kigali in Bugesera, a region where the government resettled many Tutsi after violence in the 1960s and 1973. In April 1994 Tutsi fearing violence in Bugesera fled to the Catholic centers of Nyamata and Ntarama, and as in churches throughout the country, thousands were killed in the parish complexes. But, in contrast to much of the country, in Bugesera the death squads fled before they had disposed of the dead as the RPF rapidly advanced on the area. The bodies were left lying where they had fallen, a gruesome spectacle for the RPF troops to discover and strong evidence for them of the purpose of their armed intervention. After taking power, the RPF-led government retained control of the Nyamata and Ntarama churches, and for several years the bodies were left in place, sprinkled with powdered lime to stop them from rotting but otherwise left as testament to the horrors of the genocide. Unlike Murambi in Gikongoro, where the bodies were carefully laid out and displayed, at Nyamata and Ntarama the corpses were left in place – withered bodies with scraps of clothing still attached, mere skeletons, or in some cases scraps of bones – an arm, a leg. These sites were shocking, appalling, but also deeply offensive to the survivors who were not allowed to give their family members proper burials but rather had to leave them on public display.

In 2000, apparently bowing to pressure from survivors, the local communities, and the Catholic Church, the government allowed the bodies to be removed and the sites to be cleaned up. At Nyamata, a small center of commerce and education, the local Catholic community was forced to build a new church building just up the road so that the church where the massacres had taken place could remain a memorial. The churchyard at Nyamata is enclosed in a fence, and visitors must wait for a guide to come lead them on a tour. As at all the massacre sites, the guides at Nyamata are survivors of the massacres who tell their stories as they lead visitors through the building. The sanctuary has been decorated with reminders of the genocide. When I visited in 2002, the sanctuary was mostly bare, but the pews and part of the floor were later covered with piles of soiled clothes from genocide victims, creating a much more haunting and moving image. The altar cloth, a white cotton covering carefully decorated with cross-stitched flowers, had large blotches of brown that the guide explains are stains of the blood of those slaughtered here. On the walls too there were dark stains that the guide pointed out as remnants of blood, and the tin roof was riddled with holes, apparently caused by shrapnel from grenades. The basement crypt in the back of the church was lined with ceramic tiles, and there were several glass cabinets where skulls and other bones of victims were displayed. "There are plans to build a museum here," the guide told me when I visited in 2002, but the museum has never been built.

The most affecting genocide memorial at Nyamata lay in the churchyard, which had been given over almost entirely to mass graves. Acceding to demands from survivors, the government agreed to clear the bodies from the church, but they did not allow a traditional burial. Under the supervision of the survivors' group Ibuka, the bodies were placed in open mausoleums that were a compromise between the survivors' desire to give their relatives a decent burial and the government's desire to use the bodies of victims to demonstrate the horrors of the genocide. Unlike the Kigali center, where only caskets were exposed to public view, at Nyamata the corpses and skeletons were placed underground on tiered platforms, reminiscent of the catacombs of ancient Rome, and they are visible from above ground through large entryways. The top tier was filled with caskets containing the remains of those whose bodies were identified by their families. Should visitors wish to enter the crypts, stairs lead down inside, and there were neat passageways along the rows of corpses.

Less than ten miles away, the chapel at Ntarama was much smaller than Nyamata, not a full parish but merely a rural outpost for weekly prayer services or occasional Eucharist for those living too far from the central parish to attend mass on a regular basis. In 1994, some 5,000 people were killed at Ntarama. Like Nyamata, the chapel of Ntarama was initially left as it was found, with bodies grotesquely scattered around the building and grounds. Around 2001, the bodies were cleared from the church, but improvements had not yet been undertaken to create of Ntarama a sleek memorial like Nyamata or Gisovu. As a result, Ntarama was much more disturbing. When I first visited the church in 2002, several burlap bags in the back of the sanctuary were filled with bones. The guide, a rural Tutsi farmer who lived just down the road from the church, said that the bones were awaiting burial but that there were no funds available for a proper mass grave. The floor of the chapel was cluttered with the detritus of the people who had sought refuge in the place but instead found death – scraps of clothing, notebooks, and bones, some identifiable as ribs and finger-bones, others mere broken fragments. (See Figure 2.) It was still impossible to walk through the building without stepping on bones, creating a horrifying crunch under foot. At the front of the church, a cross was propped against the altar, where a solitary skull had been placed, creating a haunting monument. Just outside the entrance to the chapel, a shed held hundreds of skulls placed on display on a long platform. (See Figure 3.) In the buildings behind the chapel,

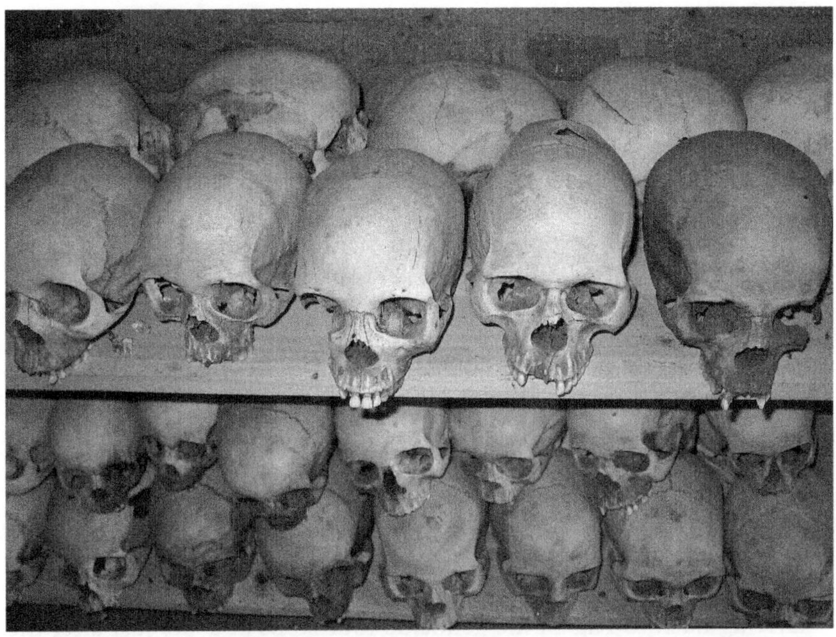

Figure 2 Skulls on display at Ntarama memorial site (Photo by author).

Figure 3 The debris-strewn floor of Ntarama memorial site (Photo by author).

there were piles of rotting clothes taken off the skeletons, and another pile of personal items – baskets, plastic basins, jerricans, and suitcases.

Returning to Ntarama in 2005 with a group of colleagues, I found that the skulls had been moved into the chapel itself, displayed on open bookshelves in the back of the sanctuary, but few other changes had taken place. The piles of personal effects remained in the back buildings, and the floor of the chapel remained scattered with bones and other fragments of life. "Have the bones been buried?" I asked the guide, the same farmer I had met a few years before. "No," he told me. "There is no money for that." Since then, some improvements were made to the site. A large open metal shed was built over the chapel to protect the structure. The bones were taken out of the sacks, but rather than being buried, they were scattered around the floor of the church once again. Visitors had to step from bench to bench to avoid stepping on the remains. More bones were placed on the floor of a room behind the chapel, where the stained clothes of genocide victims were hung from the ceiling. The effect was disturbing and macabre, and the fact that the bones had been carefully placed on display was not obvious.

Driving back to Kigali, the genocide tour stops at a site just after the southern entrance to the city. There are several large mass graves here for people killed at a nearby school and at a roadblock that was situated on the road here. There is also a brick and cement monument to members of the human rights group Kanyarwanda killed in the genocide. Most moving, however, is a field filled with simple white crosses made of painted wood. This was an art installation, part of a consortium of African writers and artists brought to Rwanda in 1998 for three months to learn about the Rwandan genocide and produce works inspired by it. After several years, the white paint had faded and some of the crosses had tipped to the side or lost an arm, but this apparent disarray added to the effect of sadness and loss.

Of all these sites, Ntarama was undoubtedly the most affecting, because its unpolished rawness gave a sense of proximity to the genocide. The Genocide Memorial Center in Kigali was modern and sophisticated and very moving, but it also left one feeling a bit manipulated, rather like the reaction to Hollywood movies where events are orchestrated carefully to force tears but where the pathos does not ultimately seem genuine. Given the very true horror of the genocide, the sense of emotional manipulation is all the more disturbing. Perhaps it is the carefully worded script that lays out a single interpretation of the past that irritates, or the very polish that somehow seems to obscure a genocide that was in many ways low tech. And yet Ntarama, with its skulls on display and bone-strewn floor, is no less manipulative. It is merely that the lack of polish seems more visceral and therefore closer to the truth. There is no obvious transcript at Ntarama, and the hand of the government in creating an image of the genocide is less obvious.

At Ntarama, as at Nyamata and Murambi, visitors were asked to sign a guest book, where they could list their names and home countries and write reactions to the memorial – "Very sad." "Never again" – and where their donations to the guide of one or two thousand francs were dutifully recorded. On my 2005 visit to Nyamata, I leafed through the book and noted the names of the visitors – mostly Europeans and Americans. The last visitors before me were United States officials – Pierre Prosper, the Special Ambassador for War Crimes, and Jendayi Frazier, the Undersecretary of State for Africa. These were the ultimate audience for these sites, it struck me.

Understanding Memorials and Memory

As the academic world has taken up the topic of memory, commemorations and memorials have become a major focus of scholarly analysis. In his comprehensive analysis of the "sites of memory" used to construct French Republican identity, Nora argued that in the past, people lived in close relationship with memory, in "*milieux de memoire*," but that in the modern world, cut off as we are from family and places of origin and traditional values, we depend on "sites of memory" to construct a historical transcript of the past that serves to create a collective memory and, thereby, a shared national identity.[1] Coming at a time when scholars were exploring the constructed nature of identities, particularly national identities,[2] Nora's work inspired many to analyze sites of memory in other contexts. Statues of prominent figures, war memorials, museums, and public holidays have all come under scrutiny for the narrative they seek to convey. As Jan-Werner Müller said, "Wherever 'national identity' seems to be in question, memory comes to be a key to national recovery through reconfiguring the past."[3]

Some scholars have taken issue with Nora's suggestion that memorials and other sites of memory create a shared transcript and instead

---

[1] Nora, *Les Lieux de Memoire*.

[2] C.f., Anderson, *Imagined Communities*; Ernest Gellner, *Nations and Nationalism*, Ithaca: Cornell University Press, 1983; Hobsbawm, *Nations and Nationalism since 1780*.

[3] Jan-Werner Müller, "Introduction: The Power of Memory, the Memory of Power, and the Power over Memory," in Jan-Werner Müller, ed., *Memory and Power in Post-War Europe: Studies in the Presence of the Past*, Cambridge: Cambridge University Press, 2002, pp. 1–35, p. 18.

emphasize the contestation that surrounds sites of memory. James Young's influential analysis of Holocaust memorials, for example, argued that they create "collected memories" rather than "collective memories," since the same space can be interpreted and experienced in vastly different ways, providing a source of pride for one, and a mark of shame for another.[4] In societies where debate is possible, the creation of a memorial or a museum can become a focus for public debate about the past, as conflicting constituencies have divergent ideas that they hope to convey through a commemorative site. The erection of the Vietnam Veterans memorial in Washington, DC, in 1982, for example, inspired a debate over the legacies of the Vietnam War.[5] The Smithsonian's planned 1995 exhibit of the Enola Gay, the airplane that dropped the atomic bomb over Hiroshima, brought to the surface controversies over the American role in the Second World War and the appropriateness of the use of nuclear weapons.[6] A memorial to victims of Peru's political violence provoked conversations over who has the right to be considered a victim and who is labeled a perpetrator.[7] In a comparative analysis, Turnbridge and Ashworth found conflicting ways in which the past was managed in different societies, often being used to exonerate perpetrators, even by blaming victims. Yet they also recognized the possibility for commemorations to provide opportunities for reconciliation between perpetrators and victims.[8] These analyses suggest that memorials allow multiple interpretations and can be important vehicles for encouraging conversation about traumatic experiences of the past – but this assumes a context where open conversation is possible.

Many other scholars focus on the coercive nature of memorialization, looking at how political leaders and other elites dominate the presentation of the past and seek to manufacture politically useful collective memories. In his comprehensive argument for the importance

[4] Young, *The Texture of Memory*.

[5] Robin Wagner-Pacifici and Barry Schwartz, "The Vietnam Veterans Memorial: Commemorating a Difficult Past," *American Journal of Sociology*, 97, no. 2, September 1991, 376–420.

[6] Otto Mayr, "The Enola Gay Fiasco: History, Politics, and the Museum," *Technology and Culture*, 39, no. 3, July 1998, 462–473; Robert C. Post, "A Narrative of Our Time: The Enola Gay 'and after that, period,'" *Technology and Culture*, 45, no. 2, April 2004, 373–395. For a different example, see Daniel J. Sherman, "Art, Commerce, and the Production of Memory in France after WWI" in John R. Gillis, ed., *Commemorations: The Politics of National Identity*. Princeton: Princeton University Press, 1994 on struggles over World War I memorials in France.

[7] Katherine Hite, "'The Eye that Cries': The Politics of Representing Victims in Contemporary Peru," *A Contra Coriente*, Fall 2007, 108–124.

[8] J. E. Tunbridge and G. J. Ashworth, *Dissonant Heritage: The Management of the Past as a Resource in Conflict*, Chichester; New York: J. Wiley, 1996.

of memory, Paul Riceour identified a number of "abuses of memory" related to commemoration and memorialization. He saw a danger in mere memorization taking the place of real historical memory, creating an "unnatural memory."[9] He decried the manipulation of memory, in which, "The heart of the problem is the mobilization of memory in the service of the quest, the appeal, the demand for identity,"[10] and warned against forcing people to remember the past, which leads to its distortion.[11] Forest and Johnson found that in Moscow after the fall of communism, political elites sought to reinterpret Soviet-era monuments in their efforts to build symbolic capital. Their research on popular reactions to the memorials found that elites were responsive to popular sentiment but that in critical periods where symbols are open for reinterpretation, "powerful political actors ... impress their conceptions of the national character onto the public landscape."[12] In a study quite relevant for the analysis of memorials in Rwanda, Claudia Koonz compared memorialization and amnesia in East and West Germany following the Second World War. She asserted that "imposed official history ... bears little resemblance to what people remember," resulting in an "organized oblivion" that "vindicates leaders and vilifies enemies," leaving "average citizens cynical and alienated."[13] After the fall of the Berlin wall, East German museums went under renovation, seeking to integrate the Jews into the history of the concentration camps. Jews remained nevertheless unrecognized in popular memory, illustrating a disconnect between official attempts at consensus and popular sentiment.[14]

Some scholars have analyzed the lacunae in official memorialization, the issues and events that are left out of memorials, that are – sometimes quite intentionally – excluded from the official historical narrative. Henry Roussou, for example, analyzed how in the aftermath of the Second World War, the French sought to exonerate themselves by emphasizing the heroism of the resistance while ignoring the collaboration of the Vichy regime and the fact that more people were involved in

---

[9] Paul Ricouer, *Memory, History, Forgetting*, Chicago and London: University of Chicago Press, 2004, p. 58.

[10] Ibid., p. 81.

[11] Ibid., p. 87.

[12] Benjamin Forest and Juliet Johnson, "Unraveling the Threads of History: Soviet-Era Monuments and Post-Soviet National Identity in Moscow," *Annals of the Association of American Geographers*, 92, no. 3, 2002, 534–547, quote p. 527.

[13] Claudia Koonz, "Between Memory and Oblivion: Concentration Camps in German Memory," in John R. Gillis, ed., *Commemorations: The Politics of National Identity*, Princeton: Princeton University Press, 1994, citation p. 258.

[14] Ibid.

the Vichy regime than in the resistance.[15] Anne Pitcher argued that in Mozambique, even as the government's official narrative sought to erase memory of past Marxist-Leninist policies, a process she called "organized forgetting," urban workers kept alive this memory as a basis for making demands for rights.[16] The experiences of women have often been excluded from sites of memory. In particular, sexual violence against women is often a taboo subject and is sublimated in favor of narratives that highlight the heroics of men.[17]

The growing literature on the connections between official commemoration and collective memory raises a number of questions to consider in relation to the commemorations of the Rwandan genocide. In this chapter, I review the various sites of memory in Rwanda – massacre sites, museums, holidays, and other official commemorations established by the Rwandan government. I contend that the government used memorialization to promote the historical narrative described in the previous chapter as collective memory. I argue that the government also used what I term Rwanda's "sites of forgetting," pointedly excluding from public commemoration particular events, people, and experiences that it hopes the population will forget or disavow. This review of the government's agenda lays the groundwork for my consideration in Chapter 7 of how the Rwandan population itself interprets the past.

Manufacturing Memory: Genocide Memorials and Commemorations

In the years immediately after 1994, the scars of war remained visible throughout the Rwandan countryside. Bodies lay unburied in some genocide massacre sites, and in many places, hard rains washed away soils and exposed bodies tossed carelessly in shallow graves either during the genocide or in the violence that surrounded the RPF's accession to power. Primarily local governments took up the task of organizing the cleanup of genocide sites, burying bodies left exposed, and exhuming and reburying bodies unceremoniously dumped in latrines and hastily dug shallow tombs. Marked mass graves quickly became ubiquitous on the Rwandan landscape, many of them slabs of cement with flowers

---

[15] Henry Rousso, *The Vichy Syndrome*, Cambridge: Harvard University Press, 1991.

[16] M. Anne Pitcher, "Forgetting from Above and Memory from Below: Strategies of Legitimation and Struggle in Postsocialist Mozambique," *Africa*, Winter 2006, 88–112.

[17] For example, Marlene Epp, "The Memory of Violence: Soviet and East European Mennonite Refugees and Rape in the Second World War," *Journal of Women's History*, 9, no. 1, Spring 1997, 58–88, looks at the various ways in which memory of sexual violence against Mennonite women in Eastern Europe is suppressed.

planted around, others merely covered in earth, with a stone marker
or small garden. Reburials were usually accompanied by a solemn service that included both religious prayers and statements by government
officials.

Many other reminders of the genocide could be seen throughout the
country. Much of Rwanda's infrastructure was destroyed by the war –
bridges, water systems, power lines, roads. With substantial support from
the international community, the government set about rebuilding. The
remains of many demolished homes were more poignant reminders of
the genocide. Those who carried out the genocide sought not merely
to kill the country's Tutsi minority but to eradicate their very memory,
so they symbolically demolished Tutsi homes, distributing as looted
goods the roof tiles and windows and doors as well as household items
like furniture and cooking pots. In at least a few cases, the RPF itself
sought to match the symbolic attempt to eradicate the Tutsi by demol-
ishing the homes or businesses of genocide leaders.[18] Post-1994 Rwanda
was thus scattered with the carcasses of buildings, crumbling mud walls
with weeds and brush growing in what had once been family homes and
businesses.

Buildings also bore reminders of the war and genocide in other ways.
The walls of homes and businesses in many of Rwanda's cities were
pocked by bullet holes and windows smashed or cracked. Most dramat-
ically, the Parliament building perched atop a high hill in the administrative area of Kigali bore huge craters from bombs. The Parliament
served as RPF headquarters during the failed transition begun under
the Arusha Accords, and in April 1994 five hundred RPF troops fought
their way out of the building to join the main force of RPF soldiers who
advanced from the north as the FAR rained bombs on their encamp-
ment. Even as most buildings in Rwanda were repaired or torn down to
make way for the massive building boom that swept the capital, and even
as much of the Parliament building itself was refurbished, the tall office
tower was left for years with its great bombed-out holes as a testament to
the heroism of the grossly outnumbered RPF troops.

At the same time that the RPF oversaw the rebuilding of the country – the rehabilitation of the infrastructure, the return of people to their
homes – they also sought to preserve at least some symbols of the events
of 1994. The government established an Office of Memorials in the

---

[18] On the main road in the city of Butare, several businesses were in ruins even a decade
after the genocide. When I asked local residents why they had not been rebuilt considering their prime locations, I was consistently told that the buildings had been destroyed
by the RPF as a warning. Such demolitions, however, were much less common than the
systematic destruction of Tutsi homes undertaken during the genocide.

Ministry of Youth, Sports, and Culture to monitor the process of geno-cide memorialization. The government initially attempted to retain control of most of the dozens of churches that served as massacre sites, but under objections from church leaders, they relented, ultimately focusing on only a few church buildings geographically distributed throughout the country. In most cases, the bodies of victims had been removed and the churches repaired and scrubbed clean long before the arrival of the RPF in July, since the massacres occurred primarily in April. In the handful of cases where the RPF nonetheless sought to convert the churches into memorial spaces, some compromise was reached. The sanctuary in Kibeho was reconfigured and a portion walled off to create a memorial chamber. After a protracted struggle, the Catholic cathedral at Kibuye was returned to the church, but a large mass grave, memorial garden, and cenotaph were placed in front of the entrance. Nyamata was ultimately the only parish church not resacralized and returned to religious purposes, along with the chapel at Ntarama and the convent of Nyarabuye.

A late addition to the pantheon of memorials was a lonely hill high above the shores of Lake Kivu in the province of Kibuye. While most massacres took place in churches or other public buildings, survivors of the initial massacres in some communities fled to forested hillsides, where they hoped to hide.[19] Bisesero was an open hillside where the Tutsi of Kibuye Prefecture made a valiant last stand against their attackers. The Tutsi, most of whom had fled from massacres at places both nearby, like the Kibuye Stadium and Catholic cathedral, as well as further afield, such as Kibeho, gathered at this site because of its isolation and strategic position. Some 40,000 Tutsi are estimated to have taken shelter in the thick brush on this steep hill, and for six weeks, they successfully fought off the civilian militia with stones and rough-hewn spears and other improvised weapons. They organized themselves into a defense force and stood their ground against the better-armed militia groups. Yet with virtually all the other major massacres in Rwanda already complete, the militia, joined by soldiers and police, mounted a major assault on May 13 in which thousands were killed, but several thousand survived in hiding. Under repeated subsequent attacks, however, the numbers of Tutsi here were relentlessly whittled away until French soldiers arrived in late June 1994 as part of Operation Turquoise. When they arrived, the French found only about 1,000 survivors, bedraggled and starving, who emerged gradually from the bush, believing that the French had come to

---

[19] In Nyakizu, for example, many people who fled from the attack on Cyahinda Church took refuge on Nyakizu and Gasasa Hills. See the chapters I wrote on Nyakizu in Des Forges, *Leave None to Tell the Story*.

save them. In fact, after visiting the site, the French left, and the killing continued for several more days until the French sent another contingent to protect the few survivors.[20]

The government raised up Bisesero as a symbol both of Tutsi resistance and also the incompetence and complicity of the international community. An official biography of Kagame discusses Bisesero in a typical fashion, "One major exception to the pattern of defenselessness and desperation stands out in the annals of the grisly period of the genocide ... The resistance put up by thousands of mostly unarmed Tutsi at Bisesero in Kibuye Province in the west of Rwanda constitutes a memorial in itself to the determination of one major group of the population to not become victims."[21] While at the conclusion of the genocide corpses lay scattered across the hillside at Bisesero, shortly after the RPF victory, the bodies were buried in mass graves, and bodies of genocide victims from throughout the local area were brought to this location for interment. Around 2001, the government constructed a monument at Bisesero and renamed the site "The Hill of Resistance." The monument consists of a path that mounts the hill with nine buildings representing the nine communes of Kibuye Prefecture at the time of the genocide. Each building contains bones said to be those of victims from each commune, though as in other sites, the exact source of these bones is unclear, since those killed at the site were buried a number of years before. As a website explaining the memorial stated, "These images of human remains ... are a powerful reminder of the concept of 'Never Again.'"[22]

In addition to the major genocide memorials, the central government encouraged local governments to develop their own memorials. The annual commemoration of the genocide in April became a popular time to rebury remains of genocide victims and dedicate mass graves as memorials. The sheer number of mass graves, however, challenged the ability of governments with limited resources to develop and maintain memorial sites. While some sites were developed with attractive gardens, statues, and other features, many mass graves were little more than a large

---

[20] Siméon Karamaga, Testimony gathered by the Survivors' Fund UK, available at www .survivors-fund.org.uk/assets/docs/testimonies/simeon_karamaga.pdf.

[21] Colin M. Waugh, *Paul Kagame and Rwanda: Power, Genocide and the Rwandan Patriotic Front*, London: McFarland and Co., 2004, p. 74.

[22] According to a website about this memorial, "In 1996 soon after the genocide, survivors gathered together with members of a survivors' association called 'Kibuye Solidarity' and came up with the idea of gathering all the victims who were scattered over different hills and valleys into one place in order to bury them with dignity. Today, a large number of those remains have been buried. However, a small number have been conserved in order to be placed in the memorial where they will be displayed in order to preserve the memory of what happened in Bisesero." www.museum.gov.rw/2_museums/kibuye/ bisesero/pages/bisesero.htm.

cement slab. At the time of our research, other mass graves were merely marked with crosses, though the government was working to gather bodies from these dispersed sites and rebury them in central memorials. In Kigali, for example, bodies had been brought from throughout the municipality to be buried at the Genocide Museum at Gisozi.

The construction of memorials was not the only means Rwanda used to commemorate the genocide. A year after the onset of the genocide, the government organized a Week of Mourning that has since become a major annual holiday for Rwanda. The first week of remembrance was scheduled from April 7 through April 14, with a national commemoration taking place on April 7 in Kigali, where a formal burial of the moderate Hutu Prime Minister Agathe Uwilingiyimana took place as well as the reburial of about 200 Tutsi killed at the Kigali Hospital. Local communities throughout the country also organized their own commemorations at massacre sites, many of them taking the opportunity to dedicate mass graves. In the years since, the government has declared a Week of Mourning annually, with a national ceremony of commemoration taking place at a different massacre site each year and many local communities organizing their own ceremonies of commemoration. The activities during the week are overseen by both the Office of Memorials and the National Unity and Reconciliation Commission, which organizes seminars and educational workshops. The commemoration ceremonies are accompanied by political speeches in which leaders such as President Kagame expound on the ongoing significance of the genocide and the need to remain vigilant lest genocide against Tutsi recur in Rwanda. Several times Kagame used the occasion of the annual commemoration to launch a harsh attack on those he claims promote a "genocidal ideology" that threatens the stability of Rwanda.[23] While the first annual commemoration included a focus on moderate Hutus who were also killed in the genocide,[24] subsequent commemorations focused increasingly on Tutsi victims and the heroism of the RPF in bringing the genocide to an end. These commemorations were an opportunity to reiterate the lessons that the government hopes the population takes from the memorials and the historical events that they memorialize. An address by President

[23] In the 1999 commemoration held at Kibeho, President Bizimungu accused Catholic Bishop Augustin Misago, who was in attendance, of participation in the genocide. In 2002, Kagame denounced Bizimungu himself for criticizing the RPF and forming a new political party. Lars Waldorf, "A Justice 'Trickle Down': Rwanda's First Post-Genocide President on Trial," in Ellen Lutz and Caitlin Reiger, eds., *Prosecuting Heads of State*, Cambridge: Cambridge University Press, 2009, pp. 151–175.

[24] Chris McGreal, "Survivors Condemn Tribute to Top Hutus: Rwanda's Government 'Wants to Forget the Genocide,'" *The Guardian*, April 5, 1995.

Kagame at the commemoration of the eighth anniversary of the genocide in 2002 held at the Catholic seminary at Nyakibanda in southern Rwanda gives a good idea of the sort of political messages pronounced at these events. Kagame explained that in 1994, even churches were not sanctuaries for those fleeing the violence:

This is what made the 1994 atrocities different from the horrors of the past, but there were also similarities. The similarities are that all those things that we are in the process of doing, for example the dignified burial of the dead, speaking about the massacres that took place, but also in trying to distinguish them by their size or people choosing to call them by another name, and this makes people want to forget the roots of the killings. All this finds its origins in bad politics and bad governance ...

A professor of history has written about Africans, because of the many African problems, saying that Africans who studied or read history in books, read it only to pass their exams. They did not read history to learn something from it. It is useful to read history to understand something that can change life and leave behind the bad in moving toward the good ... There are Rwandans who have read history without learning anything from it. If you look at the present, the astonishing thing ... is that there are Rwandans who try to tell us their predictions that in five years, in ten years, it will not be surprising if there is again a genocide, and saying this in a manner that they think is political! These people who say this were the authorities. They stand here and speak about extraordinary things. These people, I ask myself what history they have read? ... They say these things, but they say it is just politics! But it is politics that sows division among Rwandans. And after this they run to the embassies saying that they were just engaging in politics, and these embassies welcome them, these people who consider themselves very intelligent. They share tea saying that they are just engaging in politics. But this is the politics that kills people like the people who are dead here. It is not just machetes that killed; they were merely carrying out the program. People were killed first by politics.[25]

The message of this and other commemorations is clear: without the leadership of the RPF, Rwanda would once again experience genocide.

In addition to the Week of Mourning, the RPF government decreed several other holidays related to the genocide. Liberation Day on July 4 celebrates the day that the RPF took control of Kigali in 1994. Although the genocidal government had fled Kigali weeks before and fighting continued for two more weeks before the FAR were routed from the country, the capture of Kigali after a three-month battle symbolically represented the effective seizure of power. Even as the Week of Mourning commemorates the beginning of the genocide, Liberation Day celebrates the end of

---

[25] Paul Kagame, Speech by the President of the Republic for the commemoration of the Eighth Anniversary of the 1994 Genocide, broadcast on Radio Rwanda, April 7, 2000.

the genocide and clearly links this to the RPF victory. The Day of Heroes held in February recognizes Rwandan heroes, mostly Hutu killed resisting the genocide or other instances of anti-Tutsi ethnic violence, such as Prime Minister Uwilingiyimana.

The Kigali Memorial Centre

In 2004, on the tenth anniversary of the genocide, the annual national ceremony of commemoration took place in conjunction with the dedication of the new Kigali Genocide Memorial Centre, which has since become an important tool for conveying interpretations of the 1994 violence. (See Figure 4.) The center was built in cooperation with the Kigali municipality under the direction of the Aegis Trust, an NGO based in the United Kingdom. The Aegis Trust is the initiative of two English brothers, Stephen and James Smith, who initially built a Holocaust center in London in 1995 and then became interested in the Rwandan genocide and founded the Aegis Trust in 2000, seeking to memorialize the Rwandan genocide and use the Rwandan example as a means of preventing further genocides in Rwanda and elsewhere. As the center's website explains:

Aegis observed that if [Rwanda] is to make a sustainable recovery, *memory* and *education* are critical factors. *Memory*, because survivors need time and space. They need to be heard within their own society and further afield. So too, Rwandan society needs to reckon with its collective conscience, to be clear about what it is remembering and why. *Education*, because new and emerging generations, on all sides of the genocidal divide, need to feel comfortable confronting the country's past and absorbing its demanding lessons.[26]

While formally working with the municipality of Kigali, the Aegis Trust put their clear imprint on the Kigali Memorial Centre, which they, "modeled on the Beth Shalom Holocaust Centre"[27] that they had earlier built in the United Kingdom. As Stephen Smith, director of Aegis Trust, said in a 2004 press release, "We do not create museums for the sake of museums. We create museums to dignify the past, to ensure the historical record and to provide an educational tool for future generations."[28] The center's website claimed that in 2000, "The Aegis Trust then began to collect data from across the world to create the three graphical exhibits. The text for all three exhibitions was printed in three languages, designed

---

[26] www.aegistrust.org/index.php?option=content&task=view&id=37&Itemid=68, accessed on October 20, 2007.

[27] Aegis Trust, "10 Years On."

[28] Ibid.

Figure 4 The room of victim photos at the Kigali Memorial Centre (Photo by author).

in the UK at the Aegis head office by their design team, and shipped to Rwanda to be installed."[29]

Despite this international origin, the text in the exhibitions clearly reflected the historical narrative promoted by the RPF regime. A panel printed on a sepia-toned photograph of Rwandan children highlighted the significance of clans in pre-colonial Rwanda and argued that Rwandans lived in peace before colonial rule and that colonialism introduced ethnic differentiation:

The primary identity of all Rwandans was originally associated with eighteen different clans. The categories Hutu, Tutsi and Twa were socio-economic classifications within the clans, which could change with personal circumstances. Under colonial rule, the distinctions were made racial, particularly with the introduction of the identity card in 1932. In creating these distinctions, the colonial power identified anyone with ten cows in 1932 as a Tutsi and anyone with less than ten cows as Hutu, and this also applied to his descendants. We had lived in peace for many centuries, but now the divide between us had begun ...

[29] www.kigalimemorialcentre.org/centre/, accessed on October 20, 2007.

Another panel had a photo of Rwanda's first president, Kayibanda, with an unattributed quote, perhaps from one of his speeches:

The Hutu and the Tutsi communities are two nations in a single state. Two nations between whom there is no intercourse and no sympathy, who are ignorant of each other's habits, thoughts and feelings as if they were the inhabitants of different zones of planets.

Yet another panel stated:

Over 700,000 Tutsis were exiled from our country between 1959–1973 as a result of the ethnic cleansing encouraged by the Belgian colonialists. The refugees were prevented from returning, despite many peaceful efforts to do so. Some then joined the Rwandan Patriotic Front (RPF) who, on 1 October 1990, invaded Rwanda. Civil war followed, which resulted in the internal displacement of Rwandans, many of whom were held in internal refugees camps by the Government of Rwanda. Times were tense.

Here, not only is colonialism blamed for the genocide, but the idea is put forward that the RPF was motivated by noble purposes, founded only after the failure of "many peaceful efforts" to allow repatriation of refugees. The unfounded claim that those internally displaced by the RPF's attacks on the country "were *held* in internal refugee camps" deflects negative criticism away from the RPF's attacks and onto the government that was forced to house and provision more than a million people affected by the war.[30] The next panel continues the exoneration of the RPF, building on the reality that President Habyarimana exploited social divisions:

The RPF were intent on establishing equal rights and the rule of law, as well as the opportunity for the refugees to return. Habyarimana used the tension to exploit divisions in the population, launching campaigns of persecution and fuelling fear among the people. The war on the Tutsi minority was going largely unnoticed, even though many Tutsi and Hutu opponents of the divisive ideology were in prison, tortured or murdered.

The terminology used in the museum reflects the shift in public discourse about the events of 1994. In the years immediately after 1994, the government, media, and other sources referred to the genocide as *itsemba bwoko*, literally meaning "ethnic killing," a new term created

---

[30] Living in Rwanda in 1992–1993, I can personally attest to the extraordinary disruption created by the RPF invasions. People in Ruhengeri and Byumba who had been able to return to their homes after the August 1, 1992, ceasefire were again displaced by the February 7, 1993, attack, along with thousands of others. Visiting these camps for the internally displaced and interviewing people whose families were being housed in schools and other facilities, public anger was clearly directed against the RPF and not the government.

out of existing Kinyarwandan words. When referring to *itsemba bwoko* officials and others often made reference as well to *itsemba-tsemba*, an established Kinyarwanda term for massacres, acknowledging that while genocide had taken place against the Tutsi because of their ethnicity, many Rwandans were killed by the armed forces because of their moderate political views or caught in the war or in RPF attacks on civilians. The Kigali Genocide Memorial Centre, however, used the term *jenoside*, a Kinyarwanda transliteration of the word genocide that officials began actively promoting several years before the tenth anniversary. Officials argued that *itsemba bwoko* was not an accurate term to describe what happened in 1994, because the killing was not merely an ethnic massacre but genocide. At the same time, the discussion of *itsemba-tsemba* was dropped from public rhetoric. A few years later, the regime began to promote another more specific term, *jenoside y'Abatutsi*, genocide of the Tutsi. This terminology was added to the constitution in 2008 and incorporated into the Memorial Centre.[31] The Memorial Centre exhibits did mention the killing of moderate Hutu but made no reference at all to massacres carried out by the RPF.

In addition to the museum, with its educational purpose, the center also is a memorial to those killed in the genocide. The municipal government decided to gather together the remains of all those killed in Kigali in 1994. Bodies were exhumed from mass graves throughout the city and brought to Gisozi to be placed in the large crypts built in the gardens surrounding the museum. As the website for the center explained, "The Center provided an opportunity to offer a place in which the bereaved could bury their families and friends, and over 250,000 victims of the genocide are now buried at the site – a clear reminder of the cost of ignorance."[32] The clear implication is that the bodies buried at Gisozi are those of genocide victims, but in fact Kigali was the site of protracted battles between the Rwandan Armed Forces and the RPF from April through June 1994, and many civilians were caught in the crossfire. In addition, a large portion of Kigali was under RPF control, where Tutsi enjoyed safe haven but many Hutu faced arbitrary execution or other attacks.[33] In other words, while 250,000 bodies may be buried at Gisozi, there is no evidence that they are in fact "victims of the genocide." If this claim were true, then Kigali would have suffered at least a quarter of the casualties in the genocide (if one even accepts the inflated figure of one million dead). Yet the population

[31] Lars Waldorf, "Revisiting *Hotel Rwanda*: Genocide Ideology, Reconciliation, and Rescuers," *Journal of Genocide Research*, 11, no. 1, 2009, 101–125.
[32] www.kigalimemorialcentre.org/centre/
[33] Des Forges, *Leave None to Tell the Story*.

of Kigali according to the 1991 census was 235,664, and only a minority of that number was Tutsi.[34] Furthermore, when the genocide began and the civil war renewed, much of the population fled the city. Hence, the basis for the claim of 250,000 genocide victims buried at Gisozi remains entirely unclear.

Sites of Forgetting

A few miles south of the important Catholic center of Kabgayi, near the former regional capital Gitarama in the central part of the country, a house perched prominently on a small hill just off the main highway was left to fall to ruins. Though only one story, the house was spacious by Rwandan standards, and modern looking, spreading in a large U-shape around an open flat lawn. While not demolished, in contrast to many of the homes touched by the genocide, this house was neglected, with many windows broken out and the roof collapsing in some places. No plaque marked the spot, but most Rwandans knew this house, because it was the home of Rwanda's first president, Grégoire Kayibanda. After being deposed from office in 1973, Kayibanda lived out his last few years here, and this is where in 1976 he died a quiet death.

In the mythology of the current Rwandan regime, Kayibanda holds a special vilified place. He is regarded as the father of the country's anti-Tutsi ideology, having helped write the Bahutu Manifesto in 1957 and led the Party of the Hutu Emancipation Movement (*Parti du Mouvement de l'Emancipation Hutu*, Parmehutu) that championed Hutu majority rule and dominated the country from 1960 to 1973. He is blamed for inspiring the "first genocide" of Tutsi in 1959 with his anti-Tutsi ideas. Kayibanda is also regarded as a stooge of the Europeans, a puppet of the Catholic missionaries who promoted his political ascendancy and the leader who allowed Belgium and other foreign powers to retain their neo-colonial control over Rwanda.

While President Habyarimana justified his removal of Kayibanda as necessary to restore order and promote development, his own rhetoric spoke of "finishing the revolution," building on the legacy that Kayibanda had begun, but focusing on economic development rather than ethnic exclusion. Habyarimana did not execute Kayibanda but kept him under house rest and, despite rumors that the former president died of starvation and neglect, after his death the house was maintained, the

---

[34] National Census Service, "The General Census of Population and Housing, Rwanda: 16–30 August 2002: Report on the Preliminary Results," Kigali: Ministry of Finance and Economic Planning, February 2003, p. 16.

walls kept painted, the gardens tended. Until 1994, travelers along the Kigali–Butare road saw a prosperous, well-kept, but unoccupied home whose upkeep seemed to signal a concession to the First Republic. After the RPF took power, however, the Kayibanda home was abandoned – not destroyed or taken over by an official of the current regime, but left to fall into disrepair, serving as a symbol of the rejection of the ideas that Kayibanda represented.

Just as the landscape of Rwanda is scattered with mass graves and memorials that serve as reminders of the 1994 genocide and highlight its centrality to Rwandan society and politics, the countryside is full of sites, like the Kayibanda home, that have been conspicuously neglected and send an equally powerful message about what the current regime rejects. While mass graves associated with the genocide were carefully marked and tended, mass graves of those killed by the RPF were pointedly ignored and neglected. While genocide massacre sites were marked by plaques and memorials, sites of other massacres were ignored. Kibeho, for example, was a religious pilgrimage site prior to the genocide, where the Virgin Mary was believed to have appeared to several schoolgirls and local peasant farmers.[35] During the genocide, the Kibeho church was the site of a major massacre early in the genocide, where an estimated 17,500 people were killed.[36] Both of these events are commemorated at Kibeho. The Catholic Church has constructed a new chapel at the site of the apparitions, while both the church and the government have built memorials – one inside the church building and another at the mass grave in the church yard. (See Figure 5.) Yet Kibeho was also the site of the most publicized RPF massacre in post-genocide Rwanda. Following the RPF rise to power, thousands of internally displaced people (IDP) camped at Kibeho, which was part of the French area of occupation, the Zone Turquoise. When the French left in August 1994, the RPF called upon the IDPs to leave the camps and return to their homes. When people refused, the RPF forcibly closed the camps. RPF soldiers opened fire on the IDPs at Kibeho in April 1995, killing an estimated 2,000–4,000.[37] Yet Kibeho today has no sign whatsoever of those killed by the RPF. There is no mass grave, no plaque, nor any other indication that a massacre took place at this location.

[35] Gabriel Maindron, *Des Apparitions à Kibeho: Annonce de Marie au Coeur de l'Afrique*, Paris: O.E.I.L., 1984; Augustin Misago, *Les Apparitions de Kibeho au Rwanda*, Kinshasa: Faculté Catholique de Kinshasa, 1991.

[36] ICTR, "Judgement and Sentence," *The Prosecutor versus Aloys Simba*, Case No. ICTR-01-76-T, p. 16.

[37] Human Rights Watch, "Human Rights Watch and FIDH Commend Peaceful End to Kibeho Crisis but Warn Rwandan Judicial System Needs Immediate Action," New York: Human Rights Watch, May 11, 1995.

Figure 5 Kibeho genocide memorial and church (Photo by author).

Kibeho, like every other location where the RPF massacred people, serves as a site of forgetting, a site where leaders have pointedly
ignored past events and removed their traces in an effort to obliterate their memory. Like "disavowed" memorials to a deposed regime,
where traces "are literally or symbolically erased from the landscape
either through active destruction or through neglect by the state,"[38]
mass graves of RPF victims are allowed to disappear from public view,
growing over with weeds and brush until they are indistinguishable
from the surrounding landscape. In many cases, the bodies have simply
been disinterred and added to those at genocide mass graves, under the
pretense that they too were killed in the genocide rather than victims
of the RPF. The RPF regime is certainly not exceptional in avoiding
commemorating its own abuses and failures, but in a regime obsessed
with memorialization, the choice *not* to memorialize significant events
must be regarded as intentional and politically significant. Considering
the brutal dictatorships of Latin America, Elizabeth Jelin noted that,
"Erasures and voids can ... be the result of explicit policies furthering
forgetting and silence, promoted by actors who seek to hide and destroy
evidence and traces of the past in order to impede their retrieval in the

[38] Forest and Johnson, "Unraveling the Threads of History," p. 525.

future ... In these cases, there is a willful political act of destruction of evidence and traces, with the goal of promoting selective memory loss through the elimination of documentary evidence."[39] Visiting Kibeho or sites of other RPF massacres, one cannot help but note "the presence of an absence,"[40] the pointed decision to erase the memory of the events that took place there. Jennie Burnet calls this practice of chosen forgetting "amplified silence" and argues that, "While amplified silence has served the RPF regime in the short term, in the long term it has undermined the state's legitimacy and perpetuated divisions in Rwandan society. Amplified silence prevented Rwandans from discussing the past openly."[41]

Memorials as Narrative

Just as the official narrative discussed in the previous chapter promotes a particular version of the past, the choice of what to memorialize and what to ignore in post-genocide Rwanda sends a clear message. In contrast to many cases discussed by scholars of memory and memorialization, Rwanda has not been a place where open debate has been tolerated. Political repression has limited the level of public participation in the process of memorial conceptualization. The government has built the vast majority of memorials, and even those built by churches or other groups received strict oversight and had to accord with government expectations. Hence, memorials represent a means for the government to articulate its narrative of the past. They complement the government's efforts to revise public thinking about Rwandan history, particularly the events of 1994.

The Kigali Genocide Memorial Centre at Gisozi, with its texts and photos presenting Rwandan history, comes closest to presenting a traditional historical narrative. The main points of the narrative are quite consistent with the official discourse: Rwanda's people historically got along, colonialism divided the country by creating the division between Hutu, Tutsi, and Twa, the post-colonial national leaders bought into the colonial definition of ethnicity and betrayed the interests of the Rwandan people, and the RPF waged war only reluctantly and with the noblest of

---

[39] Elizabeth Jelin, *State Repression and the Labors of Memory*, Minneapolis: University of Minnesota Press, 2003, p. 18.
[40] Richard S. Esbenshade, "Remembering to Forget: Memory, History, National Identity in Postwar East-Central Europe," *Representations*, no. 49, Winter 1995, 72–79, citation p. 73.
[41] Burnet, *Genocide Lives In Us*, p. 216.

intentions. Yet in addition to this written narrative, the museum seeks to touch the emotions with the haunting display of photos, abstract art, and open graves. Like the other large memorials at Murambi, Nyarabuye, Nyamata, and Ntarama, Gisozi seeks to demonstrate the horror of the genocide. The display of bodies and bones at most of the sites is meant to shock and offend. The presentation of skulls with machete wounds and women's bodies with legs spread and a branch inserted seeks to define the nature of the genocide for those who visit, to express the extreme brutality of the crimes. The shock of row upon row of skulls or room after room of ghostly bodies is meant to show the extraordinary numbers of people killed. Bisesero, with its large white monument high above Lake Kivu sends a different message, the fact of Tutsi resistance intended to dispel the idea that Tutsi were merely passive victims of the violence.[42]

To understand these sites fully, though, requires understanding their audience. Average Rwandans rarely visit the sites; the local communities avoid them. As the guides at Nyamata, Ntarama, and Murambi told me – and their visitors books backed them up – only two groups of people came to the genocide memorials: foreigners and repatriated Tutsi. While local people might have questioned the authenticity of the display of bodies and bones, to those unfamiliar with the community, they served as clear evidence of the genocide. As my interview with the Director of Memorials made clear, a primary purpose of these memorials is to serve as proof of the genocide, to refute those who would deny the genocide.[43] In "proving" the genocide and highlighting its magnitude and brutality, these memorials serve to justify not only the RPF's leadership of the country but also its tactics. These memorials serve as a backdrop to politicians who seek to explain the need to rein in criticism, to limit civil society and political parties, since they demonstrate the continuing legacies of genocide that might not otherwise be obvious.

Rwanda's memorialization also has a message for the Rwandan population as a whole. The ubiquity of smaller genocide memorials reminds Rwandans that the genocide occurred throughout the country and keeps the genocide always in mind. Almost every community now has a mass grave or monument commemorating the genocide. One cannot drive

---

[42] Sabine Marschall, "Gestures of Compensation: Post-Apartheid Monuments and Memorials," *Transformation* 2004, 78–95, writes that, "By emphasising resistance and triumph, post-apartheid South African identity transcends the mould of eternal victim. The focus on resistance and triumph functions as a powerful and affirmative counterpoint to the narrative of oppression, sadness and reproach" (p. 88).

[43] Interview in Kigali, June 2003.

far along Rwanda's highways without passing a memorial site. On the
short road from Butare to Gitarama alone includes memorials at the
Institute for Scientific and Technical Research at Rubona, the Institute
for Agronomic Sciences in Rwanda at Songa, the former royal capital of
Nyanza, the market town of Ruhango, and the entrance to the Catholic
complex at Kabgayi. During the Week of Mourning, officials pressure
the general public to attend ceremonies held at each of these sites, compelling people not only to come to a genocide memorial that they might
otherwise avoid but also to participate in a public ritual acknowledging
and condemning the genocide.[44]

A crucial purpose of the genocide memorials and commemorations
is to reinforce the centrality of the genocide to Rwandan history. With
memorials present in most communities, people are regularly reminded
of the genocide. Tutsi, particularly *rapatriés*, are reminded of the peril
that they face as a minority group, while Hutu are reminded of the
atrocities for which they are responsible and that explain their need to
remain silent and accept RPF rule. The pointed refusal publicly to commemorate those killed by the RPF sends a message that these deaths,
while perhaps unfortunate, are not socially meaningful. The erasure of
the physical traces of RPF massacres underlines the government's rhetoric about the historical insignificance of deaths outside the genocide as
accidental and non-systematic, and thus not worth remembering.

The Director of the Office for Genocide Memorials expressed many
of these goals:

There are some people who deny that there was a genocide. But we must not forget, because if we forget it can be very dangerous, not just for Rwanda but for all
humanity... We don't keep memory alive for vengeance but to show people what
happened. It is important that future generations know what happened and why.
There are those who deny the genocide... You can't have justice without proofs.
We must demonstrate who did what... When you lose someone in a war, it is war.
It is not the same thing as genocide.[45]

For the government, then, the memorials serve as proof of the genocide
and maintain its centrality. Those who died at the hands of the RPF are
merely the unfortunate collateral damage from a war whose deaths do
not warrant commemoration.

As I discuss in Chapter 7, the message that the government intends
to send through memorials and commemorations does not necessarily dictate how the public itself "reads" them. Mass graves and public
remembrances seek to shape popular interpretations of the events of

<hr>

[44] See Chapter 7.
[45] Interview in Kigali, June 18, 2002.

1994, but individuals' own experiences affect how they understand the past. Some people do accept the government's message, but others reject it as inconsistent with their own experience, while still others reinterpret the memorials according to their own needs and ideas. What is clear to nearly everyone, however, is that the government regards the genocide as definitive and a justification for its actions.

Closure is not possible. Even if it were, any closure would insult those whose lives are forever ruptured. Even to speak, to grope for words to describe horrific events, is to pretend to negate their unspeakable qualities and effects. Yet silence is also an unacceptable offense, a shocking implication that the perpetrators in fact succeeded, a stunning indictment that the present audience is simply the current incarnation of the silent bystanders complicit with oppressive regimes. Legal responses are inevitably frail and insufficient... But inaction by legal institutions means that the perpetrators prevailed in paralyzing the instruments of justice. Even new waves of massive violence turned upon the oppressors would offer more hope than inaction for the resurgence of ideals, of justice, of humanity. Yet new cycles of revenge and violence in the name of justice kill even that hope.

– Martha Minow, Between Vengeance and Forgiveness

The Prison on a Hill

Gisovu Prison lies on a high mountain along the continental divide between the Nile and Congo River basins several hours' drive from the capital of the former Kibuye Province. The prison is in a beautiful setting, surrounded by tea plantations and perched high above the banks of Lake Kivu, but also remote, on steep gravel and dirt roads that become impassible after heavy rains. Built with international funds after the genocide as a second prison for Kibuye to help solve problems of overcrowding, Gisovu became the province's only prison when government officials determined that the Kibuye Central Prison's position in the center of town detracted from plans to develop Kibuye, with its breathtaking lake views, as a major tourist site.

In my years as a human rights worker and researcher, I have visited many prisons. In 1995, I walked through the squalor of the Butare Prison that had been built for 1,000 prisoners but was housing more than 8,000 individuals, with people forced to sleep on the roof and in the bathrooms and showers. I have seen the fresh scars of prisoners who have been whipped and beaten. I have searched prisons for individuals arrested secretly and now missing. I have interviewed many prisoners, some of whom I was convinced were innocent, others I was sure were murderers. But I approached Gisovu Prison with particular trepidation and excitement. I had been told that this was the prison where the people who had murdered my friends were being kept, people I had known before the genocide but who had turned on their own neighbors and friends. I wanted to find them, and I wanted to confront them.

I lived in Rwanda shortly before the genocide, conducting research for my dissertation on religion and politics. During a yearlong period of fieldwork, I studied in several communities in various parts of the country, but Kirinda, a small village in Kibuye, was where I made a home in Rwanda. Kirinda, the site of the first Protestant parish in the country, housed two secondary schools, a hospital, and several national offices for the Presbyterian Church. I spent my first months in Rwanda there, studying Kinyarwanda, getting to know the population, and making good friends, and I came back there often during my fieldwork. Kirinda and the neighboring village of Biguhu became the center of my analysis and ultimately my first book.[1] In Kirinda, I most clearly saw the rise of ethnic and political tensions in the country and the way that ethnic politics became entwined with struggles to preserve individual power and privilege. Local leaders of the church and schools allied themselves with the increasingly racist anti-Tutsi Habyarimana regime, while the general population of all ethnicities joined parties in opposition to Habyarimana. Tensions in the community rose with every RPF attack on Rwanda, and Tutsi students came to me expressing their fear at the changing climate in Rwanda.

During the genocide, the Tutsi of both Biguhu and Kirinda gathered at one of the Kirinda schools, and a few gathered at the parish itself, where community leaders promised that they would be protected. Instead, these same leaders organized a gang of mostly unemployed and disenfranchised local youths into a militia group to attack and kill the Tutsi. The gang attacked the school and later the church and killed Tito, the former hospital chauffeur, and his wife and children. They killed the Biguhu pastor's wife and all seven of his children, though he himself managed to escape and flee into hiding. Géras, the agronomist I worked with closely in Biguhu, paid the head of the hospital to save him, but as he and his wife and daughters were led away, they were betrayed and killed anyway. His youngest daughter, who was born while I was staying in Biguhu,

---

[1] Longman, *Christianity and Genocide in Rwanda*.

survived for a while until she was murdered in her hospital bed during a campaign in May to finish off the survivors. The local government organized a security committee, composed of the principal of one of the high schools, the head of the hospital, and Musa, a local businessman, and they organized the local community to work barricades and carry out patrols that helped to root out survivors of the first massacres. Church leaders supported these efforts, urging their parishioners to defend the country from the RPF menace. In the end, only four or five of Kirinda's Tutsi survived, while all the rest were slaughtered by their neighbors. One close Tutsi friend survived, but was gang raped. Another friend lost his entire family.

When I returned to Rwanda in 1995 as head of the HRW office, I researched what happened in this community where I had found a home. I located the Tutsi survivors, most of whom lived outside Kirinda, and they told me their stories of murder, rape, and torture. I went back to Kirinda and interviewed other people in the community and searched through the records at the communal office. The leaders of the communal government clearly worked closely with the leaders of the church, its school and hospital, and the local business community to organize the genocide in Kirinda. As the RPF arrived, the community fled en masse to Zaire, where the village gathered in a single refugee camp and the leaders maintained their hold over the population. When the RPF bombed and closed the camps in 1996, most of the leaders of Kirinda returned to the community, and many were arrested and eventually ended up in Gisovu. Amani, the young businessman who had led the militia death squad, escaped into Congo and was never found, but Fidèle, the high school principal, Léonidas, the regional church president, Musa, the businessman who supplied the killers with machetes, and Antoine, the hospital chief, were all imprisoned in Kibuye and then moved to Gisovu. These were people I knew before the genocide. Both eyewitness testimonies and written records proved them responsible for the murder of my friends, for the rape of my friends, for using the genocide as a tool to build their personal power and wealth at the expense of everyone else. I wanted to see these people, to confront them, to hear directly from them what happened in Kirinda and why they did what they did.

In January 2005, I traveled to Gisovu with a research team and film crew from the Internews Newsreel Project, a program to raise consciousness on justice issues and the judicial process and to develop journalistic skills by producing and showing films about gacaca, the ICTR, and Rwandan courts. The Internews group was scheduled to screen a film for the prison population and interview several prisoners for a future film. My research team was to conduct focus group interviews with prisoners after the screening for an assessment of Internews that I had been hired to undertake.[2] The film screening was set for the early afternoon, and my research team and I planned to meet the Internews crew at the prison. We left Kibuye town just after lunch and set off going south along the shores of Lake Kivu, on the poorly kept rocky road that linked Kibuye with Cyangugu. Even with a four-wheel-drive Landcruiser, our progress on the rocky road was slow. After some distance along the lake, we turned inland off the main road and began to climb up toward the continental divide. We passed Bisesero, where Tutsi had resisted the genocide and a monument now stood, and kept going. As the road went on and on, we stopped periodically to ask directions, to make sure we were not lost. Eventually, more than three hours after leaving Kibuye, we arrived at a tea plantation in the high mountains, and there in the middle of the beautiful verdant tea fields sat, incongruously, the Gisovu prison.

While we waited for the Internews film crew to arrive, I arranged the focus groups and explored the prison. I struck up a conversation with the assistant warden, who, it turned out, had attended high school in Kirinda before the genocide. We compared notes on people we knew in common and where they were today, and we talked about what had happened in Kirinda in 1994. I told him that I would like to interview some of the leaders of Kirinda, those I held responsible for the genocide there, and he just shook his head. "There are only peasants here now. All the important people, all those with influence, they have been released. People have intervened for them, and they are now free. So it is only the poor and powerless who are left." He confirmed that Léonidas and Musa and Fidèle had all been imprisoned in Gisovu at one point, but they had used their wealth and connections to gain their freedom. Now it was only the minor actors, those who had followed their orders, who were left in prison.

When the Internews team arrived, the entire prison population of over 3,000 gathered in the central prison courtyard, crowded together on small wooden benches, or looking in from the windows of the surrounding buildings. My research team and I were seated in the front of the crowd, and the warden introduced us, along with the Internews workers. He mentioned that I had lived in Kirinda before the war and asked those from Kirinda to stand. A few young men in bright pink prison uniforms stood shyly here and there in the crowd, and I saw that the assistant warden had been right. These were not the pastors and teachers and doctors

[2] On the work of Internews in Rwanda, see www.internews.org/regions/africa/default .shtm#rwanda. Their documentary films on justice in post-genocide Rwanda are available in a number of US and international libraries and provide an excellent overview of the ICTR and Rwandan national trials.

and businessmen who had overseen the killing in Kirinda. These were the poor, unemployed youths who had been the mere foot soldiers of the genocide. Promised opportunity and power in exchange for their cooperation, they were now abandoned to undefined terms in prison awaiting trial, while those who had led them astray walked free. My vision of confronting the people who killed my friends was not to be, at least not here at Gisovu Prison on this day.

Justice and the Rwandan Genocide

The Rwandan genocide has become the most heavily adjudicated mass atrocity in history. In the aftermath of the 1994 genocide, the United Nations established the International Criminal Tribunal for Rwanda (ICTR) to try the genocide's organizers, while Belgium, Finland, France, Sweden, Canada, and Switzerland have tried Rwandan citizens in their national courts for genocide offenses. In Rwanda itself, more than 125,000 people were imprisoned on genocide charges in the years immediately after the RPF took power.[3] The Rwandan courts began to try cases in 1996, but the extraordinary caseload overwhelmed the system, that would, it was predicted, need 100 years to try all of the accused. To speed up the prosecutions, Rwandan officials developed an innovative popular form of justice based loosely on a traditional dispute resolution mechanism. Set up throughout the country, gacaca courts had popularly elected panels of non-professional judges charged with determining how the genocide occurred in their community and sitting in judgment over the majority of those accused. The gacaca courts represented a massive undertaking, involving over 170,000 judges in more than 9,000 jurisdictions.[4]

For both the international community and the Government of Rwanda, judicial action has become the most significant and far reaching means of seeking to promote the reconstruction of Rwandan society. Yet the motives for holding trials have been mixed, and their actual impact on Rwandan society is poorly understood. Like the memorials reviewed in the last chapter, trials contribute to public discourse about the past and attempt to shape public perceptions. In Chapter 8, I explore the public

---

[3] Alison Des Forges and Timothy Longman, "Legal Responses to Genocide in Rwanda," in Harvey Weinstein and Eric Stover, eds., *My Neighbor, My Enemy: Justice and Social Reconstruction in Rwanda and the Former Yugoslavia*, Cambridge: Cambridge University Press, 2004, pp. 49–68.

[4] On the gacaca courts see Phil Clark, *The Gacaca Courts, Post-Genocide Justice and Reconciliation in Rwanda: Justice without Lawyers*, New York: Cambridge University Press, 2011; Lars Waldorf, "Mass Justice for Mass Atrocity: Transitional Justice and Illiberal Peace-Building in Rwanda," PhD Dissertation, National University of Ireland, Galway, November 2013; and Chakravarty, *Investing in Authoritarian Rule*.

reaction to the many trials held in Rwanda and discuss their impact. In this chapter, I review the scholarly analysis of trials in the aftermath of mass atrocity then explain the various judicial processes that have been undertaken in response to the Rwandan genocide. I explore the motives of various parties for holding trials and argue that for the Rwandan government, the goal of "seeking justice" was less important than securing the authority of the regime and controlling the population. The rhetoric from government officials about the trials and the extraordinary reach of the prosecution implied collective guilt for the Hutu population that effectively disempowered them politically and socially.[5]

Trials after Mass Atrocity

The military tribunals held in Germany and Japan following the Second World War set an important precedent for holding individuals, particularly national leaders, accountable to international standards of propriety.[6] Although they represent the classic cases of victors' justice, carried out by the victorious armies at the conclusion of war, these trials established several important principles that have become foundations for modern international law. In the most famous of these trials, the Trial of Major War Criminals held in Nuremberg from November 1945 to October 1946, the Allies prosecuted twenty-four prominent German leaders on four charges: conspiracy to "crimes against peace"; "waging wars of aggression" in violation of various peace treaties; "war crimes," the violation of the Geneva Convention's protections of prisoners of war and injured soldiers; and a newly developed category of "crimes against humanity," for their treatment of civilians, particularly in occupied territories. This last category of crimes allowed the prosecution to enter evidence about the massacres of Jews, Roma, and other groups the Germans deemed undesirable, but the legal basis for these charges was questionable, since there were no treaties that defined the offenses, and there was no precedent for holding national leaders accountable for their treatment of their own citizens.[7]

---

[5] Eltringham, *Accounting for Horror*, pp. 69–99 explores how post-genocide language has served to imply collective guilt for Hutu and collective victimization for Tutsi.

[6] Although commonly known as the Nuremberg and Tokyo Military Tribunals, the United States and other allied powers actually organized a number of military tribunals in a number of locations in Germany and Japan.

[7] Donald Bloxham, *Genocide on Trial: The War Crimes Trials and the Formation of Holocaust History and Memory*, Oxford: Oxford University Press, 2001; Drexel A. Sprecher, *Inside the Nuremberg Trial: A Prosecutor's Comprehensive Account*, Lanham, MD: University Press of America, 1999.

The limitation in international law highlighted by the Nuremberg Trials and the international reaction against the horrors of the Holocaust inspired the adoption of a series of human rights declarations and treaties in the next several decades – the Universal Declaration of Human Rights (1948), Convention on the Prevention and Punishment of the Crime of Genocide (1948), International Covenant on Economic, Social, and Cultural Rights (1966), International Covenant on Civil and Political Rights (1966), and a growing list of additional human rights documents. Despite the growth in international human rights law, the precedent of the Nuremberg and Tokyo trials lay fallow for more than four decades. Genocides in Indonesia, Cambodia, and Iraq were largely overlooked by the international community, as were mass atrocities in places such as China, Congo, and Biafra. Yet the creation in May 1993 of the International Criminal Tribunal for the Former Yugoslavia (ICTY) inspired a new wave of prosecutions, both national and international, that has quickly transformed judicial action into an essential part of post-authoritarian and post-conflict transition. Following the creation of the International Criminal Tribunal for Rwanda (ICTR) in 1994, the international community helped organize trials in Sierra Leone, Kosovo, Timor Leste, and Cambodia. Countries such as Ethiopia, Argentina, and Peru have prosecuted members of former regimes for abuses during their tenure. Charges were brought against the former presidents of Chile, Chad, and Liberia. Following the Rome Convention in 1998, the International Criminal Court (ICC) came into existence in 2002, and the ICC has investigated cases in the Democratic Republic of Congo, northern Uganda, the Central African Republic, the Darfur region of Sudan, Libya, Kenya, and Côte d'Ivoire.[8] Trials have become the cornerstone of transitional justice, the now ubiquitous approach to promoting peace and reconciliation through accountability for the past that also includes truth commissions, memorialization, reparations, and historical revision.[9]

Despite the widespread use of trials as a response to mass atrocity, little agreement exists over what exact purpose holding perpetrators of

---

[8] Kathryin Sikkink, *The Justice Cascade: How Human Rights Prosecutions are Changing World Politics*, New York: WW Norton, 2011, explores the development of the idea of putting perpetrators of mass atrocities on trial.

[9] For other useful reviews of the legal initiatives in the area of transitional justice, see Teitel, *Transitional Justice*; Naomi Roht-Arriaza and Javier Mariezcurrena, eds., *Transitional Justice in the 21st Century and Beyond*, Cambridge University Press, 2006; Steven R. Ratner and Jason S. Abrahams, *Accountability for Human Rights Atrocities in International Law: Beyond the Nuremberg Legacy*, Oxford: Oxford University Press, 2001; and Melissa Williams, Rosemary Nagy, and Jon Elster, eds., *Transitional Justice*, New York: New York University Press, 2012.

atrocities accountable for their actions serves in the aftermath of violence. In her celebrated work on the trial of Adolf Eichman, Hannah Arendt wrote that, "The purpose of a trial is to render justice, and nothing else; even the noblest of ulterior purposes ... can only detract from the law's main business: to weigh the charges brought against the accused, to render judgment, and to mete out due punishment."[10] Leaving aside the question of what "rendering justice" means,[11] many scholars agree with Arendt that justice is a good in and of itself. Many human rights activists and legal scholars claim that people should be held accountable for violating human rights, because allowing impunity is unjust. For example, Aryeh Neier, head of the Open Society Institute, criticized societies that do not hold trials after mass atrocities for failing to "do justice."[12] The leading international human rights organizations Human Rights Watch and Amnesty International regularly call for accountability following massive human rights abuses and denounce attempts to grant amnesties to offenders.[13]

Yet the pure interest in "rendering justice" is not the primary purpose driving the recent wave of transitional justice. Even the most ardent supporters of justice as a motive in and of itself see other important reasons for holding trials. Neier, for example, touched on another reason for holding trials, probably the primary reason they have been implemented so widely after mass violence, the idea that accountability helps to fight impunity and establish rule of law. He argued that, "A retributive theory of justice turns on the arguments that society punishes to restore equilibrium of benefits and burdens in a society unfairly disrupted by crime and that it needs to demonstrate the seriousness with which it regards its laws against criminality, its condemnation of transgressions, and its respect for victims."[14] If people are allowed to get away with human rights violations, then the law itself loses value, and people will not respect it. In the

---

[10] Hannah Arendt, *Eichman in Jerusalem: A Report on the Banality of Evil*, New York: Penguin, 1991, 1992, p. 253.

[11] For example, Brad R. Roth, "Peaceful Transition and Retrospective Justice: Some Reservations: A Response to Juan Méndez," *Ethics and International Affairs*, 15, no. 1, 2001, 45–50, critiques human rights lawyer and activist Juan Méndez for assuming that the content of "justice ... derived by reference to established international human rights standards, is taken to be unproblematic."

[12] Aryeh Neier, *War Crimes: Brutality, Genocide, Terror, and the Struggle for Justice*, New York: Random House, 1998, writes critically in an overview of political transitions that, "For the most part, civilian governments in the other Latin American countries that underwent transitions from military rule in the 1980s also failed to do justice" because they did not hold trials (p. 85).

[13] The reports available at HRW.org and Amnesty.org regularly call for trials as part of their recommendations.

[14] Neier, *War Crimes*, p. 83.

aftermath of conflict, fighting impunity and establishing rule of law can contribute to building a peaceful society, since if there is accountability, people who might otherwise want to carry out crimes will be deterred from doing so, while building the rule of law encourages people to settle disputes through legal means rather than through violence. Martha Minow argued that trials can help to stop cycles of revenge, because they take the role of seeking vengeance out of the hands of individuals. According to Minow, "A trial in the aftermath of mass atrocity ... transfers the individuals' desires for revenge to the state or official bodies. The transfer cools vengeance into retribution, slows judgment with procedure, and interrupts, with documents, cross-examination, and the presumption of innocence, the vicious cycle of blame and feud."[15]

Another major reason that people advocate for trials after mass atrocity is to promote reconciliation. The idea that trials contribute to reconciliation is based on several results that many advocates assume trials produce. By identifying specific perpetrators guilty of specific crimes, trials are thought to help avoid collective guilt, thus allowing those not found guilty – even if they are from the same ethnic or religious community as the perpetrators – to be reintegrated into their communities. As Antonio Cassese, first president of the ICTY, wrote, "trials establish individual responsibility over collective assignation of guilt, i.e., they establish that not all Germans were responsible for the Holocaust, nor all Turks for the Armenian genocide, nor all Serbs, Muslims, Croats or Hutus but individual perpetrators."[16]

Many advocates of trials contend that trials help victims by allowing them to move on with their lives. Some advocates argue that trials demonstrate that society takes the crimes committed seriously, recognize the suffering of the victims, and provide valuable information, such as how people died, who is responsible, and where bodies are buried.[17] Some claim that after trials, "victims are prepared to be reconciled with their

---

[15] Minow, *Between Vengeance and Forgiveness*, p. 26. While recognizing that trials can add to reconciliation in certain circumstances, Minow sees serious limitations in the ability of trials to rebuild social relations.

[16] Antonio Cassese, "Reflections on International Criminal Justice," *Modern Law Review*, January 1998, 1–10, citation p. 7.

[17] See Jose Zalaquett, "Confronting Human Rights Violations Committed by Former Governments: Principles Applicable and Political Constraints," in Neil J. Kritz, ed., *Transitional Justice*, Washington, DC: United States Institute of Peace Press, 1995, pp. 3–31; Naomi Roht-Arriaza, "State Responsibility to Investigate and Prosecute Grave Human Rights Violations in International Law," *California Law Review*, March 1990, 449–513, argues, "Investigation of past violations is essential to provide victims' families with some relief, especially in cases of disappearance where the victim's fate may still be unknown" (p. 508).

erstwhile tormentors, because they know that the latter have now paid for their crimes."[18]

Another way that trials are seen as supporting reconciliation is in encouraging dialogue within a society over the nature of the violence they experienced. Mark Osiel is a strong advocate of trials as a means of getting a society to talk about what went wrong. He argued that trials of key leaders of mass atrocities may be used effectively after conflicts to, "stimulate public discussion in ways that foster the liberal virtues of toleration, moderation, and civil respect."[19] While many other scholars feel that Osiel goes too far in arguing that post-conflict trials should focus on their didactic purposes, even at the expense of fair trial standards, many advocates do believe, like Osiel, that trials help to open a conversation about social conflict.[20]

Finally, advocates urge trials after mass atrocity to help establish a collective understanding of the truth surrounding human rights violations. Juan Mendez, UN Special Advisor for the Prevention of Genocide, has argued that because trials allow confrontation and cross-examination and ultimately end in a verdict, "the truth thus established has a 'tested' quality that makes it all the more persuasive."[21] Some advocates of trials believe that developing an official transcript about past crimes can allow societies to move forward and avoid future atrocities. Naomi Roht-Arriaza, for example, argued that investigation of abuses for trials, "allows the 'air to be cleared' of the rumors, fear, and mutual suspicion created by years of repression, so that the country may move forward on a firm footing."[22]

Other writers and activists have challenged the decision for trials in the aftermath of mass violence and human rights abuses. The Truth and Reconciliation Commission (TRC), implemented by South Africa in 1996, has inspired considerable focus on forms of transitional justice that are less confrontational than trials.[23] Truth commissions have

---

[18] Cassese, "Reflections on International Criminal Justice," p. 7. Laurel E. Fletcher and Harvey M. Weinstein, "Violence and Social Repair: Rethinking the Contribution of Justice to Reconciliation," *Human Rights Quarterly*, 2002, 573–639 and Minow, *Between Vengeance and Forgiveness*, p. 5, strongly criticize the idea that trials bring closure for victims.

[19] Mark Osiel, *Mass Atrocity, Collective Memory and the Law*, New Brunswick and London: Transaction Publishers, 1997, citation p. 2.

[20] See review of Osiel by Samantha Power, "The Stages of Justice," *The New Republic*, March 2, 1998, 32–38.

[21] Juan Mendez, "Accountability for Past Abuses," *Human Rights Quarterly*, 19, no. 2, 1997, 255–282, citation p. 278.

[22] Roht-Arriaza, "State Responsibility to Investigate and Prosecute," pp. 508–509.

[23] Lyn S. Graybill, *Truth and Reconciliation in South Africa: Miracle or Model?*, Boulder and London: Lynne Rienner Publishers, 2002; Martin Meredith, *Coming to Terms: South Africa's Search for Truth*, Washington: Public Affairs, 19; Beth Lyons, "Between

been chosen generally in cases of negotiated transition, where those who committed atrocities retain considerable power, but some claim they are a more effective means of encouraging public dialogue without exacerbating social divisions.[24] Truth commissions are promoted as a form of restorative, rather than retributive, justice, a more effective means of rebuilding community bonds and promoting reconciliation. In Guatemala, Sierra Leone, Peru, and elsewhere, often with the assistance of the international community, truth commissions have sought to establish a public record of atrocities that have taken place, hoping that this will allow societies to build a collective memory of the past that can become a basis for a more peaceful and just future.[25] While truth commissions are sometimes portrayed as opting for truth over justice,[26] initiatives in Sierra Leone, Timor Leste, and Peru have challenged this dichotomy by combining truth commissions and trials.[27] Other tools of transitional justice have also been attempted as alternatives to trials. Following the fall of communism in Eastern Europe, the primary form of accountability for past human rights abuses was lustration, a policy that forbids former communist officials or others implicated by files from the secret police from holding public office.[28] In other cases, reparations for victims of abuse have been a means of seeking accountability,[29] in some cases including symbolic reparations.[30]

Nuremberg and Amnesia: The Truth and Reconciliation Commission in South Africa," *Monthly Review*, 49, no. 4, September 1997, 5–23.

[24] Minow, *Between Vengeance and Forgiveness*.

[25] Priscilla B. Hayner, *Unspeakable Truths: Confronting State Terror and Atrocity: How Truth Commissions Around the World are Challenging the Past and Shaping the Future*, New York and London: Routledge, 2001; Tina Rosenberg, "Recovering from Apartheid," *The New Yorker*, November 18, 1996, 86–95; Desmond Tutu, "Healing a Nation", interview, *Index on Censorship*, 5, 1996, 39–51.

[26] Reed Brody, "Justice: The First Casualty of Truth? The Global Movement to End Impunity for Human Rights Abuses Faces a Daunting Question," *The Nation*, April 30, 2001; Heribert Adam, "Trading Justice for Truth," *The World Today*, January 1998, 11–13; Adeale Maja-Pearce, "Binding the Wounds: Resentment, Anger and the Desire for Revenge Threaten to Undermine the Truth Commission's Attempt to Reconcile Victims and Oppressors," *Index on Censorship*, 5, 1996, 48–53.

[27] Roht-Arriaza and Mariezcurrena, *Transitional Justice in the 21st Century and Beyond*.

[28] Vojtech Cepl and Mark Gillis, "Making Amends After Communism," *Journal of Democracy*, October 1996, 118–124; Roman David and Susanne Choi Yuk-ping, "Victims on Transitional Justice: Lessons from the Reparation of Human Rights Abuses in the Czech Republic," *Human Rights Quarterly*, May 2005, 392–435; Adam Michnik, "Reflections on the Collapse of Communism," *Journal of Democracy*, January 2000, 119–126.

[29] Naomi Roht-Arriaza, "Reparations in the Aftermath of Mass Violence," in Eric Stover and Harvey Weinstein, eds., *My Neighbor, My Enemy: Justice and Community in the Aftermath of Mass Atrocity*, Cambridge: Cambridge University Press, 2004, pp. 121–139; Christian Pross, *Paying for the Past: The Struggle over Reparations for Surviving Victims of the Nazi Terror*, Baltimore: Johns Hopkins University Press, 1998.

[30] Hite, "The Eye that Cries."

Some scholars challenge the effectiveness and fairness of all forms of transitional justice, whether trials or other means. Reviewing the array of recent trials and truth commissions across the globe, Charles T. Call argued that, "New international tribunals, truth-telling mechanisms, and post-transition hybrid courts have recurrent, structural problems. These problems range from a lack of resources to politicization to virtual impunity for rich countries."[31] Call in particular decried the selective application of transitional justice, its use against those groups and individuals who lose armed conflicts while the winners enjoy impunity and the reality that, "Individuals from powerful or wealthy countries, particularly the United States, enjoy significantly more immunity from international criminal prosecution."[32] Bronwyn Anne Leebaw argued that transitional justice mechanisms, whether trials or truth commissions, are hampered by their conflicting interests in simultaneously trying to promote rule of law and political transformation. She wrote that, "in evaluating the political role of transitional justice institutions, more attention should be given to the ways in which their efforts to expose, remember, and understand political violence are in tension with their role as tools for establishing stability and legitimating transitional compromises."[33] She went on to note the political purposes for which legal mechanisms are often employed. "While law can be a tool for regulating violence and exposing abuses of power, law is also utilized to obfuscate and legitimate abuses of power."[34]

A review of the decision to opt for prosecution in the Rwandan case reveals a multiplicity of motives. The apparently noble purposes of "rendering justice," promoting rule of law, acknowledging the suffering of victims, encouraging dialogue, and promoting reconciliation lauded by advocates of trials are tempered in the Rwandan case by a desire to divert attention from negligence and human rights abuses. In addition, for the Rwandan government, trials have served as an important means of exerting control over the population. While gacaca may have been influenced by ideas of restorative justice, the decision to prosecute Hutu for even the most minor genocide-related offenses while completely excluding the prosecution of offenses *against* Hutu has effectively intimidated and silenced the Hutu population. Some observers have described the use of legal mechanisms to dominate Rwanda's population as "lawfare," the use

---

[31] Charles T. Call, "Is Transitional Justice Really Just?" *Brown Journal of International Affairs*, Summer/Fall 2004, 101–111, citation p. 102.

[32] Ibid, p. 109.

[33] Bronwyn Anne Leebaw, "The Irreconcilable Goals of Transitional Justice," *Human Rights Quarterly*, January 2008, 95–118.

[34] Ibid.

of law as a tool of war.[35] In this chapter I contend that, like memorialization and commemoration, trials have served the government of Rwanda as another means of promoting a narrative that stresses the centrality of the genocide and obliterates memory of RPF abuses. In Rwanda, trials have more to do with promoting a particular national narrative and reinforcing the authority of the state and regime than in promoting justice or accountability.

The International Criminal Tribunal for Rwanda

In the aftermath of the 1994 war and genocide, the Rwandan judicial system lay shattered. Not only were many judicial buildings literally in ruins, but the vast majority of judges, magistrates, and lawyers had either been killed or were in exile, some of them implicated in the genocide. Both the international community and leaders of the RPF felt that the genocide was a sufficiently serious atrocity that perpetrators had to be held accountable, yet the Rwandan judicial system was incapable of organizing trials at the time. Furthermore, the vast majority of perpetrators had fled Rwanda as the RPF advanced and were now outside the country and thus outside the reach of Rwandan law. As a result, after the RPF took control of the country, the UN ambassador from Rwanda, which had a seat on the Security Council at the time, formally requested that the Security Council create an international criminal tribunal, like the one recently created for the former Yugoslavia. In August 1994, the Security Council mandated a commission of experts to investigate the case that found that "there exists overwhelming evidence to prove that acts of genocide against the Tutsi group were perpetrated by Hutu elements in a concerted, planned, systematic, and methodical way."[36] On November 8, 1994, the Security Council voted 14 to 1 to amend the statute creating the ICTY to expand its jurisdiction to include crime committed in Rwanda from January 1 to December 31, 1994.[37]

---

[35] Jens Meierhenrich, *Lawfare: Gacaca Jurisdictions in Rwanda*, unpublished manuscript; Constance Morrill, "Show Business and 'Lawfare' in Rwanda: Twelve Years after the Genocide," *Dissent*, Summer 2006, 14–20.

[36] UN Document S/1994/1125 cited in Payam Akhavan, "The International Criminal Tribunal for Rwanda: The Politics and Pragmatics of Punishment," *American Journal of International Law*, 90, no. 3, July 1996, 501–510, citation p. 502.

[37] The official name of the ICTR is "the International Criminal Tribunal for the Prosecution of Persons Responsible for Genocide and Other Serious Violations of International Humanitarian Law Committed in the Territory of Rwanda and Rwandan Citizens Responsible for Genocide and Other Such Violations Committed in the Territory of Neighbouring States, Between 1 January 1994 and 31 December 1994." Akhavan, "The International Criminal Tribunal for Rwanda," p. 502.

In Chapter 8, I consider how successful the ICTR has been at influencing the process of reconciliation within Rwanda. In this chapter, however, my interest is in how the ICTR contributes to public discourses on justice and history. To approach this topic, considering the motives for creating the ICTR is useful. The Preamble of the Security Council resolution creating the ICTR suggests several of the motives for holding trials discussed above:

Determining that this situation continues to constitute a threat to international peace and security,

Determined to put an end to such crimes and to take effective measures to bring to justice the persons who are responsible for them,

Convinced that in the particular circumstances of Rwanda, the prosecution of persons responsible for serious violations of international humanitarian law would enable this aim to be achieved and would contribute to the process of national reconciliation and to the restoration and maintenance of peace,

Believing that the establishment of an international tribunal for the prosecution of persons responsible for genocide and the other above-mentioned violations of international humanitarian law will contribute to ensuring that such violations are halted and effectively redressed.[38]

The resolution indicates goals for the tribunal both in the international community and within Rwanda. At one level, the resolution suggests that the ICTR is needed by the international community to protect against the "threat to international peace and security." In stating a desire "to put an end to such crimes" and to see that "such violations are halted and effectively redressed," the resolution seems to refer not only to the specific crimes in Rwanda but to the same sorts of crimes in other contexts, that is, to serve a deterrent function internationally by showing that crimes like those committed in Rwanda will not go unpunished and thereby to fight impunity internationally. At another level, however, the ICTR was clearly intended to assist Rwanda in its rebuilding, as the resolution claims that the Tribunal can, "contribute to the process of national reconciliation and to the restoration and maintenance of peace." The Rwandan ambassador to the United Nations himself argued during the Security Council debate in favor of the creation of the Tribunal as a means of combating impunity in Rwanda, stating that people "who were taught that it was acceptable to kill as long as the victim was from a different ethnic group or from an opposition party, cannot arrive at national reconciliation unless they learn new values." This could only occur, he argued, "if equitable justice is established and if the survivors are assured that what has happened will never happen again."[39]

---

[38] United Nations Security Council Resolution 955 (1994), adopted November 8, 1994, available at www.un.org/ictr/english/Resolutions/955e.htm, accessed November 7, 2007.
[39] Quoted in Akhavan, "The International Criminal Tribunal for Rwanda."

In addition to the ostensibly noble purposes of fighting impunity internationally and promoting peace and reconciliation within Rwanda, scholars have noted several less laudable goals behind the Security Council's decision to create the ICTR. Having not simply failed to end the genocide but empowered the perpetrators through mischaracterization of and disregard for the violence in international diplomatic contexts and through the withdrawal of both most foreign nationals from Rwanda and the majority of United Nations troops stationed in the country at the time of the genocide, the world powers – particularly the United States – felt the need to atone for their previous failures. Having sent troops initially only to evacuate non-Rwandans from the country, France – which Samantha Power correctly called, "perhaps the least appropriate country to intervene because of its warm relationship with the genocidal Hutu regime"[40] – sent a contingent of troops into southwest Rwanda in late June 1994 to create a "safe zone," supposedly to protect the civilian population but in actual fact facilitating the safe withdrawal into Zaire of the genocidal government and army. The United States joined other countries to deploy troops to Eastern Zaire in response to the terrible humanitarian crisis created by the flight of over a million Rwandan refugees across the border in advance of the RPF seizure of power.[41] These interventions, however, merely reinforced the perception of the international community's failure to protect Rwanda's Tutsi minority during the genocide. In supporting the creation of the ICTR, the United States and other international actors could appear to be taking the strong action that they had failed to take when the genocide was actually underway. Support for the ICTR seems to have been motivated both by sincere remorse over the failure to stop the genocide and by a political interest in concealing this major policy failure.[42]

Despite having initially called for the creation of the ICTR, Rwanda ultimately cast the sole dissenting vote in the Security Council against the ICTR resolution, and relations between the ICTR and the Government of Rwanda were publicly antagonistic ever after. The Rwandan government objected to the primacy given to the tribunal over Rwandan courts, the decision to locate the tribunal outside Rwanda, and the absence of the death penalty in the ICTR statute. More broadly, however, as Victor

---

[40] Samantha Power, *A Problem from Hell: The United States in the Age of Genocide*, New York: Basic Books, 2002, p. 380.

[41] Des Forges, *Leave None to Tell the Story*, pp. 668–690; Power, *A Problem from Hell*, p. 381.

[42] My own conversations in November 2001 with officials who were in the State Department at the time of the Rwandan genocide confirms Power's assessment of the Clinton administration's failed policy process but also indicates a widespread awareness on the part of both foreign service officers and politicians of the Rwandan genocide representing a major policy failure.

Peskin stated, "The central political dispute concerns the United Nations' failure to intervene to stop the genocide."[43] Since the international community had failed to stop the genocide, the Government of Rwanda resented their intervention, even as they needed substantial financial and logistical support not just to rebuild their country, but also to guarantee that those responsible for the genocide would be held accountable. The fact that most of the main perpetrators of the genocide were outside Rwanda made the ICTR necessary, but despite having called for the ICTR's creation, the RPF leadership begrudged what they perceived as the arrogance of the international community, particularly in claiming judicial primacy over Rwandan courts.[44] After the ICTR's creation, President Kagame and others regularly criticized the court in public settings, particularly over the amount of money being expended on the ICTR given its relatively small number of cases when compared to the national courts of Rwanda.[45] Gerald Gahima, then the Attorney General, told me in an interview, "When we look at the resources the international community provides to the Tribunal, and that money is intended to promote rule of law in Rwanda, they are not getting their money's worth."[46]

Certainly many of the criticisms leveled by the Rwandan government have merit. I have elsewhere discussed the substantial problems that plagued the operations of the ICTR – ranging from inadequate finances and personnel to bad management to the lack of a prosecutorial strategy.[47] Nevertheless, I would contend that the government's public condemnations of the ICTR were a form of political theater. In practice, the government allowed the ICTR to operate freely within Rwanda and generally cooperated on the

[43] Victor Peskin, "International Justice and Domestic Rebuilding: An Analysis of the Role of the International Tribunal for Rwanda," *The Journal of Humanitarian Assistance*, October 1999.

[44] On the issue of primacy, see Madeleine H. Morris, "The Trials of Concurrent Jurisdiction: The Case of Rwanda," Special Symposium on Justice in Cataclysm: Criminal Trials in the Wake of Mass Violence, *Duke Journal of Comparative and International Law*, Spring 1997, 349–374.

[45] C.f., Government of Rwanda, "The position of the government of the Republic of Rwanda on the International Criminal Tribunal for Rwanda (ICTR)," With: originally published on the website of the Rwandan Embassy to the US, now available at www.metafro.be/grandslacs/grandslacsdir600/0608.pdf, 1997. The ICTR was also regularly criticized on the official radio station, Radio Rwanda, in the Evening News on Radio Rwanda, July 24, 2002; August 15, 2002; August 20, 2002; November 20, 2002; December 13, 2002. On December 4, 2002 Evening News on Radio Rwanda reported that the government representative at the ICTR, Martin Ngoga, "said that the government of Rwanda has always criticized the fashion in which Madame [Chief Prosecutor] Karla Del Ponte has worked."

[46] Interview in Kigali, August 27, 2002.

[47] Des Forges and Longman, "Legal Responses to Genocide in Rwanda."

prosecution of cases. The public hostility was calculated to play on guilt in the international community for its failures in the genocide and thereby to shame donors into continuing to provide financial assistance to the Rwandan judicial system and other government programs. Highlighting the failures of the ICTR undermined the legitimacy of the international community in criticizing the Rwandan government for its ongoing human rights abuses. Finally, significantly, the antagonism from the RPF effectively prevented the ICTR from pursuing criminal cases against the RPF.

Despite the tensions between the Government of Rwanda and the ICTR – in fact, in part because of them – by avoiding pursuing cases against the RPF, the ICTR actually contributed to the vision of justice promulgated by the RPF. The mandate of the ICTR was to prosecute those responsible for "genocide and other serious violations of humanitarian law." This mandate included crimes committed by the RPF. While the attacks on Kibeho in early 1995 and on the refugee camps in Zaire in 1996 fell outside the timeframe of the ICTR mandate, RPF attacks on civilians as the troops advanced across Rwanda during the genocide and summary executions, revenge attacks, and other violations immediately after the RPF took power fell clearly within the mandate. Nevertheless, no charges were ever brought by the ICTR prosecutors against any figures in the RPF. The RPF leadership strongly condemned suggestions that its members should face prosecution at the ICTR as an attempt to equate the behavior of those who orchestrated the genocide with the RPF. The first two Chief Prosecutors, Richard Goldstone and Louise Arbour, both discussed bringing charges against the RPF but left office before any indictments were announced. When the third Chief Prosecutor, Carla Del Ponte, sought to initiate investigations of RPF officials in 2003, the Government of Rwanda pressured the United Nations into reorganizing the ICTR, removing Del Ponte's responsibility over the ICTR and setting up a separate prosecutor. President Kagame argued forcefully at the time against the ICTR pursuing cases against the RPF. "What's done in this Tribunal is politics, rather than rendering justice. It is unimaginable to compare crimes of vengeance and reprisal committed by individual members of the RPF, who have faced severe punishment, with the genocide."[48] Del Ponte's replacement, the Gambian judge Hassan Jallow, showed no interest in pursuing prosecution of RPF officials.[49]

---

[48] President Paul Kagame, Press Conference broadcast on Radio Rwanda, July 2, 2002.

[49] "Prosecutor Loses Rwanda Role," London: BBC News, August 28, 2003, http://news .bbc.co.uk/2/hi/africa/3189045.stm; "New Rwandan Prosecutor Named," London: BBC News, August 29, 2003, www.newsvote.bbc.uk/mpapps/pagetools/print/news.bbc.co.uk/ 1/hi/world/af/3190833.stm; Integrated Regional Information Networks, "Rwanda: Focus on UN Tribunal," OCHA, Dar es Salaam, February 3, 2004.

Despite its weak beginning, the initially very slow pace of trials, and the flaws in the prosecution of many of the cases,[50] the ICTR ultimately built an impressive judicial record. In contrast to the ICTY, where few of the chief organizers of the violence were available for prosecution, countries around the world apprehended most of those sought by the ICTR, allowing the tribunal to pursue cases against a wide range of those responsible for the genocide – military leaders, government ministers, the media, businesspeople, religious leaders, and officials from the various regions of the country. The ICTR made important contributions to international law, bringing the first conviction of an individual for genocide and the first conviction of sexual violence as a form of genocide. The ICTR indictments and prosecutions also contributed to the international isolation of Rwanda's deposed government, preventing the former leaders from establishing an effective government in exile to mount a serious challenge to the new regime.[51]

Yet in failing to bring any indictments against RPF officials, the ICTR contributed to an unbalanced application of justice. While the RPF has vociferously rejected parallels between their own actions and those of the *genocidaires*, they did use extensive violence against the civilian population, particularly as they took control of the country and in the first years of their rule. The RPF has deflected criticism by characterizing their own violence as the result of rogue agents or as necessary to establish order and understandable *because of the genocide*. In fact, while the RPF did not engage in killings as systematic or as extensive as the genocide, as HRW asserted, "The Rwandan Patriotic Army murdered thousands in 1994, committing war crimes and crimes against humanity,"[52] for which they have not been held accountable. ICTR and ICTY adviser Payam Akhavan argued that in addition to isolating the perpetrators of the genocide:

The ICTR's other key role in postconflict peace building is in moderating Tutsi revenge killings against Hutu. Although the fighting in the DRC has claimed many more civilian lives, international accountability has made the Tutsi government more cautious about violent anti-Hutu reprisals. In effect, the international recognition of the Tutsi's status as victims of genocide has made moral credibility

---

[50] For critiques of the ICTR, see International Crisis Group, "International Criminal Tribunal for Rwanda: Justice Delayed," Brussels: International Crisis Group, June 7, 2001; International Crisis Group, "Tribunal Penal International pour le Rwanda: Pragmatisme de Rigueur," Brussels: International Crisis Group, September 26, 2003.

[51] Payam Akhavan, "Beyond Impunity: Can International Criminal Justice Prevent Future Atrocities?" *The American Journal of International Law*, 95, no. 7, January 2001, 7–31.

[52] Human Rights Watch, "Rwanda: Deliver Justice for Victims of Both Sides," New York: Human Rights Watch, August 12, 2002.

a valuable political asset for the present regime and increased the costs of anti-Hutu revanchism. The interests of the Tutsi government are clearly served by distinguishing itself from the previous rulers of Rwanda and avoiding any suggestion of moral parity.[53]

I find no evidence for Akhavan's assertion that the ICTR prosecutions have constrained the RPF. Instead, as Thierry Cruvellier effectively argues, the RPF actively used and manipulated the ICTR for its own political purposes.[54] The lack of accountability for RPF crimes seems to have promoted impunity. My own research confirmed RPF involvement in massacres of thousands in the DRC in both Congolese civil wars. In 1996, the RPF bombed the Rwandan refugee camps along the border, ordered the refugees to return to Rwanda, then systematically hunted down those who fled further into Congo.[55] The RPF also participated in attacks on civilians and other war crimes and crimes against humanity during the second war in Congo, which began in 1998.[56] Further, by failing to hold RPF soldiers accountable for any human rights abuses, the ICTR has contributed to the discourse that regards the genocide as the only politically and legally important crime and uses the genocide to excuse other abuses. For serious crimes other than genocide, the ICTR actually promoted impunity. Drawing on the lessons of Rwanda, activists working on Darfur spent much energy trying to prove that the violence there was genocide precisely because genocide has become the only crime that the international community seems committed to ending.[57]

Trials as Tools of Reconciliation

While the ICTR prosecuted the most important leaders of the genocide, it tried fewer than 100 individuals by the time it officially closed in 2015. By contrast, courts inside Rwanda have tried tens of thousands

---

[53] Akhavan, "Beyond Impunity," p. 25.

[54] Thierry Cruvellier, *Court of Remorse: Inside the International Criminal Tribunal for Rwanda*, Madison, University of Wisconsin Press, 2006.

[55] Timothy Longman and Alison Des Forges, "Attacked by All Sides: Civilians and the War in Eastern Zaire," New York: Human Rights Watch; Paris: FIDH, March 1997.

[56] Timothy Longman, "Eastern Congo Ravaged," New York: Human Rights Watch, May 2000; Timothy Longman, "The Complex Reasons for Rwanda's Engagement in Congo," in John F. Clark, ed., *The Continental Stakes in the Congo War*, New York: Palgrave, 2002, pp. 129–144.

[57] Although a number of scholars – such as Gerard Prunier, *Darfur: The Ambiguous Genocide*, Ithaca: Cornell University Press, 2005, as well as Amnesty International and Human Rights Watch – have not found that the violence in Darfur constitutes genocide, even though they say it represents serious violations of human rights and must be stopped, at conferences and advocacy meetings on Darfur, anyone who challenges the idea that the violence is genocide is denounced, because of the recognition that only genocide gains sufficient international attention.

of cases. Within five years after taking power, the Rwandan authorities had detained over 120,000 individuals on genocide charges. Both the Rwandan government and the international community committed considerable attention and resources to rebuilding the domestic judicial system, building new court facilities and expanding prisons, training judges, lawyers, and other judicial personnel, and revising the legal codes, including adopting a genocide law to serve as a basis for prosecution and establishing special genocide courts.[58] The first genocide trials began in December 1996, amid considerable criticism for their failure to respect fair trial standards.[59] Groups were tried together, many defendants lacked access to defense attorneys, trials were sometimes carried out in a language that defendants did not understand without translation, and defense witnesses were sometimes intimidated into withholding testimony.[60] The Rwandan government gained additional criticism when, on April 24, 1998, Rwanda carried out the public execution of twenty-three people in several stadiums around the country.[61]

Over time, however, some of the human rights concerns related to Rwanda's legal system were mitigated. Observers reported that trial standards did improve, in part because judges, magistrates, and others gained experience.[62] Furthermore, no additional executions took place, and in 2007, in response to negotiations with the ICTR on extradition of suspects, Rwanda adopted a law abolishing the death penalty.[63] However, the extraordinary number of people detained on genocide charges created a massive backlog of cases that posed a major challenge to the right to a speedy trial.[64] Maintaining such a large number of people in prison drained government resources, and even after the construction and expansion of prisons, facilities were not adequate to the needs, creating overcrowding and sanitation problems. Most of the

---

[58] Human Rights Watch, "Rwanda," *World Report 1999*, New York: Human Rights Watch, 1998, reports that the international community gave $30 million for development of Rwanda's judicial sector by 1999.

[59] "First Trial in Rwanda of Suspects of '94 Killing," *New York Times*, December 28, 1996.

[60] Lawyers Committee for Human Rights, "Prosecuting Genocide in Rwanda: A Lawyers Committee report on the ICTR and National Trials," New York, 1997.

[61] Amnesty International, "Rwanda: 23 Public Executions Will Harm Hope of Reconciliation," London, April 23, 1998.

[62] Centre de Documentation et d'Information sur les Procès de Génocide (CDIPG), *Quatre Ans de Proccés de Genocide: Quelle Base pour les "Juridictions Gacaca?"* Kigali: LIPRODHOR: July 2001, pp. 36–38.

[63] Amnesty International, "Rwanda Abolishes the Death Penalty," London: Amnesty International, August 2, 2007.

[64] The right to a speedy trial is guaranteed in the International Covenant on Civil and Political Rights, available online at www2.ohchr.org/english/law/ccpr.htm. Article 14c states that all people accused of a crime have a right, "To be tried without undue delay."

prisoners were men who might otherwise be working their farms or otherwise contributing to the national economy, and their detention created a burden on their families, with thousands of women left as head of household and thousands of families deprived of their main income earner.

The idea to adapt gacaca, Rwanda's historic local conflict resolution mechanism, into a modern judicial instrument to try genocide suspects within their communities was first discussed immediately after the genocide.[65] The specific proposal to create the gacaca court system, however, emerged from the 1998–1999 Village Urugwiro meetings. The prime initial motivation for creating gacaca was the interest in speeding up the prosecution and release of the prisoners, though other justifications were subsequently promoted as well.[66] The official website for the gacaca courts stated that, "The classic justice didn't meet expectations because after approximately a five years period only 6,000 files out of 120,000 detenees [*sic*] were tried. At this working speed, it would take more than a century (+ 100 years) to try these detenees."[67]

Gacaca literally means "small grass," after the lawns where community elders historically gathered to settle conflicts in their communities. In contrast to more official dispute resolution mechanisms, like the *Bashingantahe* system in neighboring Burundi, in which the position of judges was more permanent and more formally integrated into the legal structure of the court,[68] the position of gacaca judges, *Inyangamugayo*, literally "those who detest dishonesty," was less established and the institution itself less formal. In gacaca, respected elders in a community came together when necessary to settle disputes over stolen property, contested dowries, and other issues. When the colonial regime established formal Western-style courts, gacaca continued but was limited to settling smaller disputes within families or between community members. In the 1980s, Filip Reyntjens observed gacaca meetings in southern Rwanda and found that they received informal support from both public authorities and the formal courts.[69]

---

[65] As early as 1995, when I was based in Butare, my colleague at Human Rights Watch, historian Michelle Wagner, was in conversations with professors at the university there about the possibilities of adapting gacaca.

[66] Alice Karekezi, "Juridictions Gacaca: Lutte contre l'Impunité et Promotion de la Réconciliation Nationale," *Cahiers du Centre de Gestion des Conflits*, no. 3, May 2001, 9–96.

[67] www.inkiko-gacaca.gov.rw/En/Generaties.htm.

[68] Philemone Ntahombaye, A. Ntabona, Joseph Gahama, and L. Kagabo, *L'Institution des Bashingantahe au Burundi: Etudes Pluridisciplinaire*, Bujumbura, 1999.

[69] Filip Reyntjens, "Le *gacaca* ou la justice du gazon au Rwanda," *Politique Africaine*, no. 40, December 1990, 31–41.

The new system of gacaca courts represented a compromise between traditional gacaca and modern Western courts. As a justice of the Sixth Chamber of the Supreme Court charged with overseeing gacaca told me, "Gacaca is composed of traditional [Rwandan] ways, but also classical judicial ways, of solving social problems. Before, gacaca was never written down, but now we have a law governing gacaca jurisdictions in place."[70] Like traditional gacaca, the new gacaca courts were made up of non-professional jurists, but in the new system, the *Inyangamugayo* were formally elected and could include women and young people. Whereas traditional gacaca was a grassroots institution organized by the community, the new gacaca courts were created by the national government and charged with enforcing national law. The rules that governed the gacaca courts themselves were spelled out by law.[71] Recognizing the differences with traditional gacaca, the new system was known as *Inkiko gacaca*, "gacaca courts."[72]

An ad hoc committee under the direction of the Minister of Justice developed the formal proposal for gacaca courts for the Village Urugwiro meetings, where it gained approval from the entire gathering. Within a year, on October 12, 2000, the Transitional National Assembly adopted a new organic law for gacaca, and in October 2001, each of the country's smallest political units, the cell, of which there were 9,001, elected nineteen *Inyangamugayo*. Judges from the cell level selected representatives for the next highest level, the country's 1,545 sectors, who in turn selected judges for the 106 districts. In total, more than 250,000 judges were selected for the gacaca courts throughout Rwanda.[73] The genocide law of August 30, 1996, established four categories of genocide crimes, and the gacaca law gave gacaca courts jurisdiction over all but the most serious cases, category one crimes – those accused of organizing the genocide, participating with particular vigor, or participating in rape. Reacting to pressure from human rights groups and the international community, the government launched the gacaca process in a trial phase in one sector

---

[70] Interview in Kigali, May 31, 2002.

[71] The October 2000 law creating gacaca was known as the "Organic Law concerning the creation of Gacaca Courts and organization of pursuit of infractions constituting genocide or crimes against humanity, committed between 1 October 1990 and 31 December 1994." In response to criticisms from human rights organizations and others, a law modifying the original law was adopted in June 2001. Numerous additional revisions were subsequently adopted.

[72] Karekezi, "Juridictions Gacaca."

[73] The organization of the courts was revised several times, with district-level gacaca courts replaced by courts of appeal. After the trial phase of gacaca, the number of judges was reduced to seven, with two alternates. See the Organic Laws numbers 28/2006 of June 27, 2006, 10/2007 of March 1, 2007, and 13/2008, May 19, 2008.

in each of the eleven provinces in June 2002. Gacaca was then revised and expanded to one sector in each district in the country in November 2002.[74] The government suspended gacaca proceedings in 2003 during the electoral process. The suspension continued throughout 2004, while revisions to the gacaca law were undertaken, then, on January 15, 2005, gacaca was formally launched throughout the country.[75]

The gacaca courts were established as a participatory system, involving weekly community meetings to process genocide cases. Attendance was initially optional, with a quorum of one hundred in each community, but after problems with low participation arose in the test phase, the revised gacaca law required attendance and the quorum requirements were dropped but attendance was required. The Gacaca court proceedings involved several stages. In the first part of the process, the information gathering stage, the community drew up a list of all of the crimes that occurred in the community and a list of all those who died in the genocide. People had an opportunity to confess to having committed genocide crimes, and the community then put together a list of those accused of participating in the genocide, categorizing their alleged crimes into one of the four categories. The cell-level gacaca then moved into the trial phase, adjudicating category four cases, property crimes, while the sector-level gacaca courts dealt with category three cases, bodily injury, and district-level gacaca courts dealt with category two cases, participating in killing but not organizing the genocide. Subsequent revisions to the gacaca law reorganized and consolidated the courts, expanding the jurisdiction of the lower-level bodies.[76]

The explicit reasons that leaders of the RPF opted to make trials the centerpiece of the country's social reconstruction reflect the diverse goals for trials articulated in the transitional justice literature. The theme of preventing ethnic violence by fighting impunity and building rule of law has been central to official discussions of post-genocide justice. In a 2002 *Washington Post* editorial, the Rwandan ambassador to Washington made this point clear:

[74] Marco Domeniconi, "Gacaca Takes off Slowly," Foundation Hirondelle, October 14, 2002.

[75] Timothy Longman, "Justice at the Grassroots? Gacaca Trials in Rwanda," in Naomi Roht-Arriaza and Javier Mariezcurrena, eds., *Beyond Truth Versus Justice: Transitional Justice in the New Millenium*, Cambridge University Press, 2006.

[76] Allison Corey and Sandra F. Joireman, "Retributive Justice: The *Gacaca* Courts in Rwanda," *African Affairs*, 2004, no. 103, 73–89; Bert Ingelaere, "'Does the Truth Pass Across the Fire Without Burning?' Locating the Short Circuit in Rwanda's *Gacaca* Courts," *Journal of Modern African Studies*, 2009; Peter Uvin and Charles Mironko, "Western and Local Approaches to Justice in Rwanda," *Global Governance*, April–Jun 2003, 9, no. 2, 219–231, on gacaca see 226–228.

To say we faced moral dilemmas in our quest for justice would be the ultimate understatement. On the one hand, Rwandan President Paul Kagame had made clear that revenge killings were not an option. On the other, the justice system had been completely destroyed in 1994... Furthermore, during Rwanda's history, successive regimes had promoted people, even in the justice system, who had been the most zealous during the anti-Tutsi pogroms of 1959, 1963, 1967, 1973, and 1992. To prevent a repeat of the genocide, we had to eradicate the idea that people could kill with impunity.[77]

In his editorial, the ambassador endorsed trials for two main reasons. First he saw trials as a means of fighting impunity – of creating negative consequences for engaging in ethnic violence that will dissuade people from participating in the future. Second, like Minow, the ambassador argued that using trials "cools vengeance into retribution,"[78] allowing the targets of the violence – Tutsi – to feel that justice had been done so that they would not feel a need to seek revenge and take justice into their own hands in ways that might undermine rule of law and perpetuate a cycle of violence.[79] Kagame himself has made similar arguments about the need to fight impunity, build rule of law, and divert vengeance into justice. In a 2004 speech at the Woodrow Wilson Center, he saw the failure to punish perpetrators of ethnic violence in the past as one of the key causes of the genocide. "[T]here was a culture of impunity to the extent that the criminals who killed were rewarded."[80] He went on to claim that promoting justice helped to establish rule of law in Rwanda. "After genocide, law and order had completely broken down, but we have managed to restore peace and stability in the whole country. We not only reformed our legal system, we have also restored public trust in it, and the Rwandan people now know and enjoy their fundamental rights."[81] Holding trials, he suggests, has not simply helped to prevent future ethnic violence but has also built respect for the law and for legal institutions more generally. In his speech at the inauguration of the trial phase of gacaca, Kagame similarly argued that gacaca is intended, "to uproot the culture of impunity."[82] The official gacaca

---

[77] Richard Sezibera, "The Only Way to Bring Justice to Rwanda," *Washington Post*, April 7, 2002.

[78] Minow, *Between Vengeance and Forgiveness*, p. 26.

[79] According to news reports, a similar argument was made in 1997 by the minister of justice. "Rwanda will never see real peace until the guilty are punished for the genocide of 1994, the country's Justice Minister Faustin Nteziryayo told the U.N. Human Rights Commission..." "Rwanda Minister: No Peace Until the Guilty are Punished," Deutsche Presse-Agentur, March 12, 1997.

[80] Paul Kagame, "Speech to the Woodrow Wilson International Center for Scholars," Washington, DC, April 21, 2004.

[81] Ibid.

[82] Paul Kagame, speech given on the occasion of the official launching of the gacaca process, Kigali, June 18, 2002. Printed in Penal Reform International, Klaas de Jonge,

court website also lists eradicating the culture of impunity as one of the five objectives of gacaca:

In their cells, the citizens will play an important role in the reconstruction of the facts and in the accusation of those who perpetrated them. None of those who took part in them will escape punishment. Thus, people will understand that the infringement implies the punishment for the criminal without exception.[83]

In addition to building rule of law, Rwanda's leaders believed that trials could contribute to reconciliation by helping to demonstrate that justice had been done and by establishing the truth about the genocide. They regarded gacaca as even more effective for promoting reconciliation than courtroom trials. In a speech officially inaugurating the gacaca courts, Kagame argued that gacaca would, "unify Rwandans on a basis of justice while reinforcing unity and reconciliation" and would "demonstrate the capacity of the Rwandan family to resolve its own problems."[84] Then Attorney General Gahima told me that, "Gacaca is a process to promote rule of law but also to promote reconciliation and bringing people together... Our justice is not justice for the sake of implementing the law alone but is a justice that is intended to accomplish certain political goals as well."[85] The National Authority for Gacaca Jurisdictions asserted that, "In relation to genocide, the gacaca process is a cornerstone for reconciliation among Rwandans."[86]

While gacaca was initially viewed as an expedient solution to the problems of prison overcrowding, delayed justice, and economic costs,[87] many officials and other advocates of gacaca came to regard it as providing a different type of justice than classic trials, one more adapted to promoting reconciliation. Whereas courtroom trials provide retributive justice, focused on punishing people for offenses, gacaca was regarded as providing restorative justice, an increasingly popular approach to justice that brings victims, perpetrators, and

"PRI Research Team on *Gacaca* Report III: April–June 2002," Kigali: Penal Reform International, July 2002.

[83] National Service of Gacaca Jurisdictions, www.inkiko-gacaca.gov.rw/En/EnObjectives.htm.

[84] Kagame, speech on the occasion of the official launching of gacaca.

[85] Interview in Kigali, August 27, 2002.

[86] National Service of Gacaca Jurisdictions, "Gacaca Jurisdictions: Achievements, Problems, and Future Prospects," www.inkiko-gacaca.gov.rw/En/EnObjectives.htm.

[87] The second purpose for gacaca listed by the National Service of Gacaca Jurisdictions is "To speed up the genocide trials." National Service of Gacaca Jurisdictions, www.inkiko-gacaca.gov.rw/En/EnObjectives.htm.

communities together to resolve criminal issues rather than leaving justice exclusively to the state.[88] The work of South Africa's TRC raised the profile of alternative means of seeking justice, often called restorative justice. Rwandan leaders initially rejected the idea of a TRC because of the need to provide justice in the face of the genocide,[89] but as gacaca was being developed, many pointed out resemblances to South Africa's TRC. In early discussions in 1996 about the possibility of adapting gacaca to deal with the genocide, the Minister of Justice reportedly told members of parliament that the new courts could help in "establishing the truth on the number and identity of the victims as well as their lost possessions."[90] The first purpose that President Kagame listed for gacaca was, "To make known the truth about what happened."[91] The National Service of the Gacaca Jurisdictions directly linked establishing truth to the process of reconciliation. "The unity and reconciliation of the Rwandans that are targetted [*sic*] are based on justice for all. But, this justice can become true only if the truth about the events is established."[92]

Like the TRC, gacaca trials also involved large public community gatherings where victims and perpetrators had an opportunity to confront one another. As in the TRC, where perpetrators of human rights abuses were granted immunity in exchange for their testimonies,[93] gacaca relied heavily on confession, offering reduced sentences and the possibility of community service replacing prison time to lower-level perpetrators who would admit their participation in the genocide, testify in gacaca hearings, and implicate others. For early advocates of gacaca, the benefits of public confrontation and conversation about the genocide were closely tied with the elimination of collective guilt made possible by identifying

---

[88] On restorative justice, see Gordon Brazemore, "Restorative Justice and Earned Redemption: Communities, Victims, and Offender Reintegration," *American Behavioral Scientist* 41, no. 6, 1998, 768–814; 34, no. 3 1995, 228–249; M. Umbreit, *Victim Meets Offender: The Impact of Restorative Justice and Mediation*, Monsey, NY: Criminal Justice Press, 1994; Howard Zehr, "Restorative Justice: The Concept: Movement Sweeping Criminal Justice Field Focuses on Harm and Responsibility," *Corrections Today*, December 1997, 68–70.

[89] Jeremy Sarkin, "The Necessity and Challenges of Establishing a Truth and Reconciliation Commission in Rwanda," *Human Rights Quarterly*, 21, no. 3, 1999, 767–823.

[90] Reported in Jacques Fierens, "*Gacaca* Courts: Between Fantasy and Reality," *Journal of International Criminal Justice*, 2005, no. 3, 896–919, citation p. 901.

[91] Kagame, speech on the occasion of the official launching of gacaca, Radio Rwanda, January 2005.

[92] National Service of Gacaca Jurisdictions, www.inkiko-gacaca.gov.rw/En/EnObjectives .htm.

[93] On the TRC see Graybill, *Truth and Reconciliation in South Africa;* Richard A. Wilson, *The Politics of Truth and Reconciliation in South Africa: Legitimizing the Post-Apartheid State*, Cambridge: Cambridge University Press, 2001.

those who were actually culpable in the genocide. As the National Service of Gacaca Jurisdictions claimed:

The Gacaca Courts system will allow the population of the same Cell, the same Sector to work together in order to judge those who have participated in the genocide, identify the victims and rehabilitate the innocents. The Gacaca Courts system will thus become the basis of collaboration and unity, mainly because when the truth will be known, there will be no more suspicion, the author will be punished, justice will be done to the victim and to the innocent prisoner who will be reintegrated in the Rwandan society.[94]

The Tyranny of False Accusations

"Aloysie" came to me for help when I was the head of the Rwanda office for HRW and FIDH in Butare. Before the genocide, Aloysie had been a teacher, and one of her former primary school students sent her to me. Aloysie came to ask for assistance in negotiating a delicate situation where she needed support from government officials. In July 1994, as the RPF approached her community, she and her family had fled to the "Zone Turquoise." Along with thousands of others, Aloysie and her family gathered at the camp for the displaced at Kibeho until RPF soldiers forcibly closed the camp in April 1995. In the violence that surrounded the camp closure, the family became divided. Aloysie's husband made it back to their home community just across the border from Burundi before his wife, but he found that the family house had been taken over by a neighboring family of Tutsi genocide survivors. He went to stay with a relative, but when word came of his return, the new occupant of his home went to the police to accuse him of being involved in the genocide. He decided to flee across the border into Burundi, but he never returned. According to reports that Aloysie heard, he was arrested across the border, returned to Rwanda, and turned over to RPF soldiers who summarily executed him. When news came of her husband's disappearance, Aloysie chose not to return to her community. Her home had been occupied by the family of survivors ever since.

Before 1994, Aloysie and her husband had built a nice home and acquired a sizable amount of land. For over a year, Aloysie had been living in another part of Butare Province with a friend. She had found employment and had no intentions of returning permanently to her home, but now she was faced with a problem. Her adult daughter had returned to their home commune and needed land to cultivate. Realizing that she

[94] National Service of Gacaca Jurisdictions, www.inkiko-gacaca.gov.rw/En/EnObjectives .htm.

could not lay claim to her old home without facing retribution, Aloysie hoped that she could at least secure the right for her daughter to once again farm the family's land – even a small portion of it. The family of survivors occupying the house and land had no legal right to it. They were not, as was the case in some property disputes at the time, former refugees who had abandoned the land when they fled the country and were reclaiming it upon their return. In fact, the family had never had claims to this land, but had merely taken advantage of the owners' absence in the months after the genocide to grab their land and their home. While they had no legal right to the land, as survivors, they enjoyed a certain moral authority in the community that discouraged authorities from intervening. More significantly, the father in the family of survivors held a political office, having been named the councilor for the sector. Because of his position, Aloysie did not feel that she could ask him to vacate the house, despite her legal right to do so. Instead, she had met with the man to ask whether he would allow her daughter to farm some of the land. He had refused outright.

Aloysie came to me hoping that I could help her to intervene on this matter. She wanted to meet with the burgomaster, the top political leader of the commune, to ask him to grant her rights to the land. But she was afraid of returning to the community, fearing what might happen to her. She wanted me to accompany her, to help add weight to her claims with the burgomaster, but also to provide protection, so that nothing bad could befall her. While I was reluctant, doubting that I could be of much use, she insisted, and my interpreter – her former student – asked that I go as a favor to him.

The three of us thus set out late on a Friday morning to drive down to her community, about forty-five minutes from Butare. We stopped first at the office of the commune to meet with the burgomaster. Aloysie had scheduled an appointment, but the burgomaster was not in the office when we arrived, so we went to a nearby parish to speak with the priest to see whether he could use his influence in the case. A Hutu who himself felt vulnerable, he was polite but demurred that there was little he could do. After stopping for sodas at a small kiosk not far from the communal office, we finally saw the burgomaster's car returning to the office, so we headed there for a meeting. Aloysie filled him in on her situation and her request to gain access to some of her land. After listening to her story, the burgomaster told her that she had to go through the appropriate channels. She needed an official request signed by the councilor of her sector – who was, of course, the man occupying her home and land. The burgomaster said that she needed to at least attempt to get his signature and that, if she was not successful, she should come back to make a formal appeal to him, and he would then grant the request. It was, however, important, he told us, to go through the appropriate steps so that no one could challenge the final decision.

Aloysie's former home was some distance from the office of the burgomaster on poorly maintained roads, so the afternoon was already late by the time we arrived at her house. We parked in front of the house and sent for the counselor. He had been a poor farmer before the genocide, poorer certainly than Aloysie and her family. As Aloysie explained, because of the proximity of the community to Burundi, he and all of his family had been able to flee into Burundi before the violence spread into their commune. As a Tutsi who had lived in Rwanda at the time of the genocide, he was known by the term "survivor," but his experience was much more fortunate than that of most survivors. The man arrived a short time later. A tall, thin man in a shabby suit jacket with graying hair, he looked quite old but was probably only in his fifties. When he arrived, it was obvious that he was quite drunk, his gait unsteady, his eyes deeply bloodshot. Aloysie demurely approached him and greeted him. He did not greet us, nor invite us into his compound, nor offer us anywhere to sit, as Rwandan custom would dictate. Aloysie began to explain her request and her need for his signature. He interrupted her and began to shout. He condemned her for coming to harass him. Pointing at me, he accused her of bringing foreign spies into the community. He demanded that we leave and then went into his house.

We got back into the truck and headed back to Butare. By this time, it was too late to go back to the communal office. Aloysie said that she would return the next week and speak to the burgomaster. I offered to go with her again, but she said that she would be fine. Unfortunately, she was mistaken. As my interpreter later told me, when Aloysie returned to the communal office the next Tuesday, she was promptly arrested. The councilor, who was in Burundi when the violence in his community began, had lodged charges against her for participating in the genocide, so she was thrown into the communal jail. I returned to the commune and spoke to the burgomaster a week later, but he said that there was nothing that he could do; the justice system would simply have to sort it out. He would not even allow us to visit her, since our government authorization to visit prisons did not specify that we could visit communal jails. When I left Rwanda five months later, Aloysie was still sitting in the jail awaiting formal charges but with no prospect of a trial in the near future, one of thousands imprisoned in Rwanda on false charges.

Trials as Instruments of Control

The objectives that officials in Rwanda publicly articulated for holding genocide trials are laudable. Building rule of law, promoting justice, advancing reconciliation, establishing a truthful account of the past, encouraging dialogue, and avoiding collective guilt by identifying specific guilty individuals are all goals described in the literature on transitional justice. Yet these widely lauded goals, as much as they may have sincerely motivated Rwanda's leaders, have not been the only factors driving the policy of genocide prosecutions. Other less openly articulated objectives have been at least as influential in shaping judicial policy. They have little to do with justice and much more to do with political power and control.

After coming to power in July 1994, the RPF opted to pursue a policy of aggressively arresting and prosecuting individuals facing genocide accusations. By their nature, the trials that were undertaken in Rwanda were punitive. Like trials everywhere, they were part of a legal system that exercised the coercive force of the state. Even the gacaca courts were ultimately part of a retributive judicial system, since despite the discussion of restorative justice, gacaca courts were able to sentence those found guilty to prison terms as long as life in prison.[95] Setting aside arguments that challenge the ability of trials to contribute to reconciliation,[96] the punitive nature of the trials in Rwanda would not, in itself, raise concerns about their ability to contribute to social reconstruction. After all, many advocates of trials argue that punishment of perpetrators of atrocities is essential to achieving justice, fighting impunity, and building rule of law in the aftermath of mass violence, factors considered essential as a basis for sustained peace and reconciliation.[97] Yet the transitional justice literature pays little attention to the authority overseeing trials, assuming that trials are conducted from a position of neutrality with a goal of promoting recovery from conflict. In post-genocide Rwanda, however, such neutrality cannot be assumed. As I discuss in the next chapter, despite government rhetoric that denied the significance of ethnicity and embraced democracy, Rwanda remained an authoritarian state where identity politics were highly salient. The judicial system was used to promote both the control of those in power and the interests of a specific social group. The point that I want to demonstrate in the remainder of this chapter is that the ability of genocide trials in Rwandan to contribute to reconciliation was tempered by the fact that the judicial system was an important tool of political domination by a specific social group.

The political use of the judicial system was most obvious in the first years of RPF rule. When the RPF took power in 1994, much of the

---

[95] Corey and Joireman, "Retributive Justice."

[96] Fletcher and Weinstein, "Violence and Social Repair"; Call, "Is Transitional Justice Really Just?"

[97] C.f., Neier, *War Crimes*; Roht-Arriaza, "State Responsibility to Investigate and Prosecute"; Mendez, "Accountability for Past Abuses."

population remaining in Rwanda was open to supporting the new regime. The RPF leadership, however, decided to impose their authority with force. Arresting large numbers of people on genocide charges was one way that the RPF established its authority. The RPF opted for large-scale arrests even though the majority of *genocidaires* had fled the country as the RPF advanced and those left in Rwanda were a few low-level perpetrators and many people who had not participated in the genocide. The decision to begin widespread arrests was particularly troubling because of the sad state of Rwanda's judicial system. Much of the judicial personnel was killed in the genocide or fled the country, with one government source reporting that by November 1994, the number of prosecutors in Rwanda had declined from 70 before the genocide to 12, while the number of judges had dropped from 758 to 244.[98] As a result, arrest on a genocide charge was tantamount to a conviction to a long prison term, since the first trials did not begin until two years after the RPF came to power, and the pace of trials remained extremely slow. Those accused had no opportunity to defend themselves, even when the charges against them were extremely weak. When I visited a number of prisons for HRW and FIDH in 1995 and 1996, police investigators and prison officials openly admitted that a majority of prisoners had no formal case files; in some instances, even the formal charges that had led to the arrest of an individual were not known. Thousands of people were, thus, in prison indefinitely, often not knowing the charges against them, with no opportunity to defend themselves in a court of law or to otherwise gain release.

Between July 1994 and October 1996, when RPF attacks on the camps in the DRC forced thousands of people back into Rwanda, including many of the *genocidaires*, the government arrested over 83,000 people.[99] During 1995, the rate of incarceration was 1,500 people per week.[100] Since most of the *genocidaires* were outside Rwanda and most of those arrested would not stand trial in the foreseeable future, arresting such large numbers of people in the immediate aftermath of the genocide had little to do with a sincere desire to see justice done. The massive number

[98] National Service of Gacaca Jurisdictions, "Gacaca Jurisdictions: Achievements, Problems, and Future Prospects," p. 4.

[99] Human Rights Watch, "Rwanda," *World Report 1997*, New York: Human Rights Watch, December 1996. James C. McKinley, "76,000 Still in Jail in Rwanda Awaiting Trial in '94 Slayings," *New York Times*, June 24, 1996, put the figure of those in jail in June 1996 at 76,000, though he concurs with the rate of new arrests at 4,000 per month. His slightly lower figure seems to include only those in the country's fourteen prisons and does not include the thousands detained in jails and other smaller facilities.

[100] Human Rights Watch reported in its annual report that the number of people detained on genocide charges had increased from 15,000 at the beginning of 1995 to more than 57,000 at the end of the year. Human Rights Watch, "Rwanda," *World Report 1996*, New York: Human Rights Watch, December 1995.

of arrests had much more to do with the new regime's desire to consolidate its control over the Rwandan population. The regime used arrest in part as a means of eliminating those who challenged its authority. Furthermore, with little possibility of a trial and with extraordinary overcrowding contributing to terrible prison conditions, the mere threat of imprisonment was enough to pressure individuals to cease political activities or even flee the country.[101]

In the office of Human Rights Watch and the International Federation of Human Rights where I worked from 1995 to 1996, I found myself dealing on a weekly basis with people facing accusations that they claimed were false. In many cases, the evidence suggested that they were being sincere. A prosecutor in Nyanza who had ordered the release of prisoners who lacked charges against them was himself arrested on genocide charges that my investigations in his home community in Gitarama proved could not be true. A judge on the Supreme Court in Kigali who had criticized fair trial standards was denounced on the radio as a *genocidaire* and contacted me worried not simply about arrest but fearing for his life after several attacks on his home. The moderate leader of a human rights group was accused of participation in the genocide; fearing arrest and with no means to defend himself, he and his wife eventually fled the country. While the cases like these that I encountered in my work are only impressionistic, they are consistent with findings by other observers and suggest a troubling pattern of using genocide accusations for political purposes.[102]

The government was not alone in using accusations of participation in the genocide for purposes other than promoting justice. There were numerous cases like that of Aloysie Niyonshuti where individuals were imprisoned under false accusations because someone wanted their house or wanted to eliminate them as a business rival or merely wanted to settle an old score. When I worked for HRW and FIDH, I learned of several individuals blackmailing others by threatening to lodge genocide charges against them; the victims of the extortion scheme paid handsomely to

[101] There were numerous reports in 1995–1996 about the terrible conditions in Rwanda's prisons. As early as November 1994, Robert M. Press, "In Rwanda's 'Slave Ship' Prisons, Life Is Grim for Suspected Killers," *The Christian Science Monitor*, November 18, 1994, reported, "More than 15,000 adults and children accused by the Tutsi-led government of genocide languish in overcrowded cells. EXCEPT for lack of chains, the tightly packed prison cell, with three tiers of wooden bunks, looks like the hold of an 18th-century slave ship."

[102] Roland Siegloff, "Rwanda's Legal System Facing Paralysis over Backlog of Genocide Trials," Deutsche Presse-Agentur, March 8, 1997, writes that, "The innocent in Kigali's central jail are locked up along with the condemned … 8,024 have been waiting in the brick building for almost three years since the massacres to face trial on genocide charges. Many could be innocent, as government officials acknowledge."

avoid being condemned to prison. There were also stories in a number of cities of individual genocide survivors who sent hundreds of Hutu to prison on false accusations not for personal gain but as a means of exacting vengeance on Hutu as a group, particularly those who emerged from the genocide relatively unscathed and still benefited from family and employment while the survivors themselves had lost their families and their homes and lived in poverty.

While no statistics are available on the number of people imprisoned under false charges,[103] the evidence shows that RPF officials used arrest as a means to demonstrate their power. They kept people in prison despite the efforts of some civilian authorities to apply human rights standards. A human rights report in early 1995 documented efforts by prosecutors and others to seek the release of individuals against whom there were no formal charges but reported that "the military blocks the release of detainees."[104] The government chose to begin its prosecutions by starting not with the people who seemed to be most likely falsely detained but with "the worst cases," prominent *genocidaires* who were more easily proven guilty.[105] The government itself ultimately seemed to acknowledge the problem with a growing emphasis on speeding the release of prisoners beginning in early 1997, when a few thousand children, elderly, and sick prisoners were released from detention.[106] The problem of prisoners unjustly in prison was one of the reasons that Village Urugwiro participants supported the idea of gacaca courts to speed up trials. In fact, the first action in the gacaca process was a "pre-gacaca" exercise, where prisoners without case files were presented to their communities and, if no one had any accusations against them, released on the spot.[107] Prisoners who confessed to all but the most serious crimes were also eligible for provisional release.

Despite the emphasis on using gacaca to release prisoners and the discussion of gacaca as a type of restorative justice, in practice, gacaca was

---

[103] In a conversation in March 1996 with two friends who were Tutsi genocide survivors, they estimated that as many as 80 percent of those in prison at the time were innocent. Conversations I had with several human rights activists at the time concurred with this estimation.

[104] Alison Des Forges and Eric Gillet, "Rwanda: The Crisis Continues," New York: Human Rights Watch, 7, no. 1, and Paris: FIDH, April 1995. This report was published before I began working for the two organizations.

[105] Siegleff, "Rwanda's Legal System Facing Paralysis," reports that, "The legal system, itself bled dry by the civil war, has started with the worst cases. The Justice Minister estimates that around 1,500 people guilty of crimes against humanity fall into this category."

[106] "Protests as Rwandan Government Frees Detainees," *Business Day*, February 12, 1997.

[107] George S. Yacoubian, "Releasing Accused Genocidal Perpetrators in Rwanda: The Displacement of Preventive Justice," *Loyola University Chicago International Law Review*, Fall–Winter 2005, 3, no. 21, 21–39.

an even more effective and far-reaching instrument for exercising state power than classical courtroom trials. Gacaca had elements of restorative justice, in that it engaged the community and allowed confrontation between victims and perpetrators, but it also involved harsh sentencing guidelines that included long prison terms. Only prisoners who confessed were eligible for provisional release and community service in place of prison time; those who wanted to prove their innocence had to languish in prison until they could defend themselves in front of a gacaca trial. Furthermore, community service was available only for people who had already served time in prison. Mere confession was also not sufficient to gain provisional release; gacaca courts had the discretion to reject confessions that were too limited or implicated too few individuals. The more new names that prisoners could add to the list of the accused, the more likely they would be granted a reduced sentence.[108]

One important aspect of both the courtroom trials and gacaca courts was the strict limitation of their focus on genocide crimes. When challenged on whether RPF soldiers would be tried for war crimes or other abuses, government officials denied any equivalency between RPF abuses and the genocide, asserting that offenses by the RPF were not the result of policy but the action of rogue soldiers, and that they were rare and not systematic. They also claimed that, since they were not extraordinary, such cases could be dealt with in regular courts or military courts – and that all reported abuses had in fact been dealt with.[109] If it is true that RPF soldiers have been tried for human rights abuses, then their cases have been kept very quiet indeed and are little known by the Rwandan public.[110] In one of the few cases of this sort, the commander of RPF troops that opened fire in April 1995 in the camp Kibeho, killing as many as 8,000, was tried in a military court and acquitted of personal responsibility but found guilty of failure to stop the violence; he was released for time supposedly already served after paying a $30 fine.[111]

Gacaca has also been focused exclusively on crimes related to the genocide. The law defining gacaca courts asserts that they are "charged with prosecuting and trying the perpetrators of the crime of genocide *and other crimes against humanity* committed between October 1, 1990 and

[108] Ingelaere, "'Does the Truth Pass Across the Fire Without Burning?'"

[109] See, for example, President Kagame's response to a question about RPF abuses raised at his Commonwealth Club speech in 2003.

[110] Human Rights Watch, *World Report 1999*, mentions that a number of soldiers were tried in military courts for common criminality, but "few of the accused were brought to trial or seriously punished for human rights abuses in the course of military operations."

[111] Human Rights Watch, "Rwanda," *World Report 1998*, New York: Human Rights Watch, December 1997.

December 31, 1994."[112] This left open the possibility of trying Rwandan Patriotic Army (RPA) soldiers or others involved in massacres of civilians, summary executions, and other crimes perpetrated during the RPF advance and in the first months of RPF rule. Yet the government made clear as it initiated the gacaca system that the trials would focus solely on the genocide and would exclude crimes committed by the RPF. The specific focus of gacaca was made clear in the training of the *Inyangamugayo* and reiterated regularly by officials overseeing gacaca. The manual used for training gacaca judges in 2002 explains that those who confess must be asked whether they killed victims because of their ethnic identity or political party. Only *itsemba bwoko* and *itsemba tsemba* were included.[113] As one lawyer who served as a gacaca trainer explained, "Those killed not for ethnicity or ideology would be judged in regular courts. The local population doesn't know the [RPF] soldiers [who carried out massacres]."[114] The first phase of gacaca called on communities to make lists of those killed in 1994, but when people attempted to list community members killed by the RPF either in the community or later during the 1996 RPF invasion of Congo, officials intervened to insist that those deaths were not germane to gacaca. Since many people were killed away from their homes, sorting out who died in the genocide and who died at the hands of the RPF was not always easy.

Given the one-sided nature of the trials since 1994, they have, I contend, been less concerned with making "known the truth about what happened," as President Kagame asserted, than promoting a particular version of the past that serves the interests of those in power. The rhetorical and institutional strategies utilized by the regime have sought to promote a specific narrative about the genocide and war. Like the memorials and commemorations, legal processes have sought to emphasize the centrality and importance of the genocide and to negate the significance of RPF crimes. The national leadership used trials to develop as complete an account as possible of crimes related to the genocide, bolstering their claims of the extent and brutality of the crimes committed. At the same time, the strict refusal to allow any discussion of crimes committed by the RPF reinforced the idea that these crimes were

---

[112] Government of Rwanda, "Organic Law no. 13/2008 of 19/05/2008 modifying and complementing Organic Law no. 16/2004 of 19/06/2004, Establishing the Organization, Competence and Functioning of Gacaca Courts Charged with Prosecuting and Trying the Perpetrators of the Crime of Genocide and other Crimes Against Humanity Committed between October 1, 1990 and December 31, 1994 as Modified and Complemented to Date," *Official Gazette of the Republic of Rwanda*, 47, no. 11, June 1, 2008. Emphasis added.

[113] Official Training Manual for Gacaca Judges, consulted in 2002.

[114] Interview in Kigali, June 16, 2002.

rare and insignificant, making trials sites of forgetting. Government officials were swift to condemn any efforts to call for accountability for RPF
crimes as an attempt to diminish or deny the genocide by equating it
with other violence. A circular logic prevails: officials deny the need for
trials for RPF crimes because of their supposedly limited extent and historically insignificant nature, while the absence of trials for RPF crimes
reinforces the idea that these crimes were limited and insignificant.

The framing of the various trials not only added to the erasure of RPF
crimes, but also helped to shape perceptions of the genocide itself by
obscuring the degree to which RPF action influenced the conduct of
anti-Tutsi violence in Rwanda. The 1994 genocide is best understood as
the culmination of a process of ethnic exclusion and violence that began
in 1990. The first massacres of Tutsi in nearly twenty years occurred in
Rwanda after the RPF attack in October 1990, and massacres occurred
repeatedly in 1991–1993. These attacks were organized with government support,[115] and they served as a blueprint for how to carry out
the genocide, innovating, for example, on the use of radio to incite violence.[116] Including the entire 1990–1994 period in genocide prosecutions would thus make sense, and officially the genocide laws, including
the gacaca laws, gave the courts jurisdiction over crimes committed
from 1990 through 1994.[117] To approach the genocide in this fashion,
however, would have drawn attention to the role the RPF's invasion of
Rwanda played in inciting the population to anti-Tutsi violence. The War
of October was a primary feature of the anti-Tutsi ideology promoted
by supporters of the Habyarimana regime beginning after the 1990
attack. Habyarimana had lost considerable popularity among Hutu, but
the repeated and increasingly successful RPF attacks on Rwanda fanned
popular anti-Tutsi sentiments. Reports of RPF attacks on civilians created substantial anger in the population.[118] The idea that Tutsi were seeking to re-establish dominance over the Hutu masses was only credible
in the context of the RPF invasion. This is not to blame the RPF for
the genocide, since clearly members of the regime then in power bear
responsibility, but it does raise questions about the RPF's decision to

[115] A 1993 international human rights mission to Rwanda uncovered convincing evidence of government complicity in the 1990–1992 attacks. Africa Watch, FIDH, et al.,
"Rapport de la Commission Internationale."

[116] Des Forges, *Leave None to Tell the Story*, pp. 87–91.

[117] Alice Karekezi, "Juridictions Gacaca: Lutte contre l'Impunité et Promotion de la
Réconciliation Nationale." *Cahiers du Centre de Gestion des Conflits*, 3, May 2001: 9-96.

[118] Living in Rwanda at the time, I can attest to the impact on the population of the
February 1993 attack that drove more than one million people from their homes, which
was filled with fear over what the RPF would do if they took power. I remember students whose families were displaced struggling to find news of their loved ones and
fearing that they might have been killed by the RPF.

pursue combat in a context where they knew the impact it could have on Tutsi within Rwanda. Some critics of the RPF, including some survivors I have interviewed, believe that, contrary to the way they portray themselves, the RPF leaders were not primarily interested in saving Rwanda's Tutsi or bringing democracy but instead were greedy for power. Yet by limiting the focus of the special genocide courts and gacaca courts to the period from April to July 1994, the relationship of RPF attacks on Rwanda to anti-Tutsi violence within Rwanda from 1990 to 1993 was suppressed. The RPF thereby preserved its image as the savior of the Tutsi within Rwanda rather than having crassly determined to ignore the fate of their Tutsi brethren and pursue war no matter the cost.[119]

Rwanda's genocide trials contradicted the public rhetoric of the regime in another important way. Although the rejection of ethnicity was a central component of the RPF's public rhetoric, the genocide trials actually served to reinforce the centrality of ethnicity within Rwandan public life. The crime of genocide is defined as an attacked on individuals because of their perceived membership in an identity group.[120] In the Rwandan case, the victims of the genocide were Tutsi, defined by their perceived ethnic identity. By contrast, most of the victims of RPF violence were Hutu. The regime claimed that these victims were not targeted because of their ethnic identity but rather were killed in revenge attacks or because they were seen as a security threat, and my research provides no reason to doubt these claims. To be clear, I reject the assertions that some people have made of a "double genocide."[121] However, excluding RPF attacks from judicial consideration and focusing solely on crimes of genocide made ethnicity the defining characteristic for determining which crimes were to be adjudicated and which were to be excluded. In effect, Hutu who committed crimes against Tutsi were to be held accountable, while Tutsi who committed crimes against Hutu were unlikely ever to face judgment. The crimes related to the genocide were

<hr>

[119] Alan J. Kuperman, "Provoking Genocide: A Revised History of the Rwandan Patriotic Front," *Journal of Genocide Research*, 6, no. 1, 2004.

[120] United Nations, "Convention on the Prevention and Punishment of the Crime of Genocide," Office of the High Commissioner of Human Rights, approved 1948, www2 .ohchr.org/english/law/genocide.htm; Frank Chalk and Kurt Jonassohn, *The History and Sociology of Genocide: Analyses and Case Studies*, New Haven: Yale University Press, 1990, 8–32; and Helen Fein, *Genocide: A Sociological Perspective*, London and Newbury Park: SAGE, 1993, 8–31.

[121] Christian Davenport and Allan Stam, "What Really Happened in Rwanda," *Truthout*, October 6, 2009, www.truthout.org/10070911, present a highly controversial academic defense of the double genocide hypothesis, while Philip Verwimp, "Testing the Double-Genocide Thesis for Central and Southern Rwanda," *The Journal of Conflict Resolution*, 47, no. 4, August 2003, 423–442 convincingly disproves the hypothesis. See also Lemarchand, "Genocide in the Great Lakes."

not merely considered more important and more demanding of judicial action – a reasonable assertion, given the brutal nature of the genocide and its extent. Instead, since there was no effort whatsoever to seek justice for Hutu who suffered at the hands of the RPF, the trials served to broadcast a clear message that these crimes did not matter, at least not to the current regime. The decision to ignore RPF crimes was not dictated by any principles of justice and could not be justified on the basis of human rights law. Instead, the exclusion of RPF crimes from judicial consideration seems to be a political decision driven by the interests of those in power with preserving their own authority and with dominating the population.[122] The claims that trials served to build rule of law and fight impunity were undermined by the reality that military officers and government officials then in power faced no consequences for their own actions during the war, no matter how many civilians were killed.

The reality that trials in post-genocide Rwanda focused only on some crimes – those committed against Tutsi – committed by one ethnic group – Hutu – undermined the ability of trials to promote justice and reconciliation. While advocates of trials after mass atrocity claim that they help to individualize guilt and thereby prevent the imputation of collective guilt,[123] the organization of Rwandan trials in fact helped to promote a generalization of guilt for the Hutu population. The regime has regularly maintained that participation in the genocide was extremely widespread, a line that many scholars sympathetic to the RPF regime embraced.[124] Focused as they were exclusively on Hutu attacks on Tutsi, gacaca courts were organized in every community in the country, even in communities that were occupied by the RPF, where the only massacres that occurred were carried out by the RPF against Hutu. The gacaca trials pushed communities to identify as many suspects as possible. Prisoners were offered diminished sentences if they confessed to crimes, but those who confessed were required to name others who participated to gain the preferential treatment. Over time, accusations were made against more and more people. In some cases long-detained prisoners

---

[122] Corey and Joireman, "Retributive Justice," 89.

[123] Nicole Fritz and Alison Smith, "Current Apathy for Coming Anarchy: Building the Special Court for Sierra Leone," *Fordham International Law Journal*, 25, December 2001, 391, arguing for the Special Court in Sierra Leone, claimed that, "Criminal trials in the wake of mass atrocity are valuable, not least because they individualize guilt and militate against demonization of whole groups." See also, Michael P. Scharf, "The Prosecutor v. Dusko Tadic: An Appraisal of the First International War Crimes Trial Since Nuremberg," Paper presented on the panel, "Conceptualizing Violence: Present and Future Developments in International Law," Adjudicating Violence: Problems Confronting International Law and Policy on War Crimes and Crimes Against Humanity, *Albany Law Review*, 1997, 60, 861, 874.

[124] C.f., Gourevitch, *We Wish to Inform You*, and Mamdani, *When Victims Become Killers*.

were angry with those on the outside who had remained free and used gacaca to get revenge and get others imprisoned.

The government encouraged widespread accusations not only through their exhortations for confession, but in public speculations about the massive numbers involved in genocide crimes.[125] Attorney General Gahima told me, "If one million people died, easily another two or three million were involved in the crimes. If you implement the law strictly, hundreds of thousands of people would be harmed and shot." He went on to assert that gacaca provided an alternative to retributive justice, claiming that, "A genocide in which a large number of people participated is not something you can deal with just through trials."[126] In practice, gacaca was used to reinforce his initial point about the massive number of guilty Hutu. At the time of the genocide, Rwanda had 7.7 million people, around 7 million of whom were Hutu. Since over half were too young to be criminally culpable and half of those remaining were women, and thus rarely the focus of genocide charges, the claim that one million would be tried suggested that more than half of Hutu men who were adults at the time would face judgment in gacaca courts. Gahima's claim that as many as three million participated suggested that virtually all adult Hutu women and men participated.[127]

Having carefully studied the development of the genocide in a number of communes in Butare, Gikongoro, Kibuye, and Byumba prefectures for the HRW/FIDH book, *Leave None to Tell the Story*, and for my own research, I find the widely held argument of mass participation to be exaggerated. In fact, the vast majority of Tutsi were killed in the initial massacres, which were carried out by relatively small groups of militia members, soldiers, and police.[128] Although the government forced nearly all adult men to participate in patrols and manning barricades, and these patrols and barricades finished off many of the survivors of the initial attacks, the mere fact of participating in the patrols and barricades did not mean that all participants joined in killings. Since every community had militia groups under government control, thousands of people were certainly involved in the killing, but the implication that one million were involved is simply baseless, while the claim that two-to-three million

---

[125] Andrew Meldrum, "One Million Rwandans to Face Killing Charges in Village Courts," *The Manchester Guardian*, January 15, 2005, reported that the executive secretary of the gacaca courts, Domatila Mukantanganzwa, asserted the claim that one million could be tried in gacaca.

[126] Interview in Kigali, August 27, 2002.

[127] Scott Straus, "How Many Perpetrators Were There in the Rwandan Genocide: An Estimate," *Journal of Genocide Research*, 6, no 1, March 2004 estimate 175,000 to 210,000 participants in the Rwandan genocide.

[128] Des Forges, *Leave None to Tell the Story*, clearly explains the modalities of the genocide.

were involved borders on the ludicrous – though it serves the government effort to generalize guilt to all Hutu (or at least all Hutu men). Yet whatever the realities of participation in the genocide, in the end, nearly two million cases were tried in gacaca courts against more than one million individuals.[129]

While generalizing Hutu guilt, the gacaca courts still allowed the RPF to promote the image of itself as a populist, multi-ethnic movement, while securing government control over the population. By requiring the entire population to participate in the gacaca meetings, every Rwandan citizen became implicated in the process of judging those who participated in the genocide – and also ignoring RPF abuses. The RPF, meanwhile, gained credit for offering provisional release to prisoners, giving diminished sentences, and involving the population in the process of dealing with the genocide (something which is, in fact, worthy of praise!).[130] Yet at the same time, the RPF maintained strict control over what is discussed in gacaca sessions and quickly quashed anything that incriminated the RPF. Participants in gacaca became vested in the government's project – regardless of what their personal opinions may have been before their participation. Meanwhile, the accused were offered incentive to buy into the RPF's project by admitting guilt (whether or not they were guilty) in exchange for the opportunity to leave prison and rejoin their communities. Without ever discussing ethnicity explicitly, the gacaca process encouraged people to admit their fault in embracing an ethnic ideology and instead to buy into a nationalist ideology where ethnicity has no significance – though the trials themselves were defined by ethnicity. By seeking to implicate the largest number of Hutu possible for even the most minor offenses committed against Tutsi – the looting of property, for example – while completely ignoring even the most serious of crimes committed by Tutsi against Hutu – the RPF slaughter of tens of thousands of unarmed civilians in eastern Congo[131] – the genocide courts, gacaca courts in particular, effectively defined all Tutsi as victims and all Hutu as genocidaires. If, as I contended earlier, nearly all positions in the administration, business, higher education, civil society groups, and other areas of social and economic advancement are occupied by Tutsi

---

[129] Integrated Regional Information Networks, "Jury Still Out on Effectiveness of 'Gacaca' Courts," United Nations Office for the Coordination of Humanitarian Affairs, June 23, 2009; Faith Karimi, "Rwandan Genocide Survivor Finds Solace in Gacacas," CNN.com, July 27, 2009.

[130] In Longman, "Justice at the Grassroots," I explain why I think gacaca in principle had much potential, while I was worried about the degree to which it may be susceptible to political manipulation.

[131] Longman and Des Forges, "Attacked by All Sides"; Longman, "Eastern Congo Ravaged."

returnees today, this is not, according to the logic of the regime, directly because of ethnic discrimination but rather because the entire generation of Hutu adults disqualified themselves from social advancement through their implication in the genocide.

As I learned at Gisovu Prison, the interest of the regime in preserving its power was certainly not the only factor undermining the administration of justice in post-genocide Rwanda. As the assistant warden at the prison told me, "All the important people, all those with influence, they have been released ... So it is only the poor and powerless who are left." By the end of the first decade after the genocide, most of those who could afford to pay a bribe or who had the right connections had gained their release, while the poor languished in prison. Even the Attorney General admitted that corruption in courts was a problem. As he told me, "Just because you've changed the law, you do not translate the intent of the law into the values of the judges. Important people try to influence the process."[132] Those Hutu who had been powerful individuals before the genocide and gained their release through bribery or other means were tainted and diminished by their time in prison and no longer posed a threat to the regime. Because of their association with the genocide and the reality that they could be imprisoned again at any time, they must be careful to keep a low profile. They cannot aspire to positions of prominence in the new Rwanda but might hope to occupy more modest positions as a teacher rather than a principle, a doctor rather than a hospital director, an assistant pastor rather than a regional minister. The justice system was used effectively to neutralize them as community leaders, which allowed Tutsi, particularly the former refugee population, to occupy their posts.

Corruption is not generally as serious a challenge in Rwanda as in other countries in the region, such as Kenya and the DRC, but the cases that I encountered of false accusation and arrest at the front end of the judicial process and of purchased release at the back end of the process are sufficiently abundant to raise serious concerns about the degree to which corruption may have compromised the judicial process. People like Aloysie, having lost her husband at the hands of the RPF, having herself been imprisoned on obviously invented charges, are unlikely to feel that the genocide courts in Rwanda have anything to do with justice. As I discuss in Chapter 8, the plan for gacaca courts was initially popular with the population, because it implied that they could take justice away from political intrigue and into their own hands. In practice, however, as gacaca was manipulated by those who sought to use gacaca to implicate

---

[132] Interview in Kigali, August 27, 2002.

the largest possible number of people, popular support waned. Nearly every Hutu I have ever worked with in Rwanda – human rights activists, university professors, civil society organizers, church workers, students, most of them moderate people, supportive of democracy and opposed to ethnic discrimination, having been critics of the pre-genocide government (often at the risk of their lives) and appalled by the genocide – was charged in gacaca courts for participating in the genocide. Many of these Hutu now live in exile, having been harassed and threatened by the current regime. Most of the others who remained in Rwanda were imprisoned.

Some cases of miscarried justice were so egregiously unreasonable that they gained international attention. Guy Theunis, a priest from the White Father order, had been an outspoken critic of the Habyarimana regime and a founding member of a major Rwandan human rights organization, having used his position with the Catholic monthly *Dialogue* to promote democracy and condemn ethnic violence. On a return visit to Rwanda in 2005, he was charged in a gacaca court and detained in a Rwandan prison for several months before being released into Belgian custody for a review of his case.[133] François-Xavier Byuma, longtime leader of the Rwandan League for the Promotion and Defense of Human Rights (*Ligue Rwandaise pour la Promotion et la Défense des Droits de l'Homme*, LIPRODHOR), gained condemnation from many for supporting the government effort in 2004 to purge the membership of LIPRODHOR, Rwandan's last independent human rights organization, by accusing its members of either having participated in the genocide or supporting a "genocidal ideology."[134] A list of accused LIPRODHOR activists was published, and most fled abroad. Several of those accused told me at the time that Byuma was only trying to protect his own skin. Yet ironically, he was himself accused in 2007 and convicted of genocide crimes in a gacaca court in the district where he lived during the genocide in Kigali. The case was so obviously fabricated and the publicity surrounding it so negative that the National Service of Gacaca Jurisdictions felt it necessary to issue a press release defending the case.[135]

Over time, the punitive possibilities of the gacaca courts became more prominent, while their potential to promote reconciliation was de-emphasized. Rhetoric claiming that many gacaca judges themselves were guilty of genocide crimes created a climate of intimidation in which the

---

[133]   Reporters without Borders, "Rwanda, the Arrest of Father Guy Theunis: An Investigation of the Charges, the Legal Action, and Possible Reasons," Brussels: Reporters without Borders, November 2005.

[134]   I discuss this attack on LIPRODHOR in greater detail in Chapter 5. See Lars Waldorf, "Censorship and Propaganda in Post-Genocide Rwanda," International Development Research Center, 2006.

[135]   Domatilla Mutakaganzwa, "Byuma Francois Xavier's Case," Kigali: National Service of Gacaca Jurisdictions, June 12, 2007.

judges worried that leniency against the accused might be taken as evidence of their own complicity.[136] Even the goal of using gacaca to speed up prosecutions became secondary, as the regime introduced numerous delays, particularly surrounding the 2003 elections that solidified the RPF hold on power. Before being allowed to return to their communities, confessed genocidaires released provisionally from prison were required to attend *ingando* re-education camps in which the RPF combined lessons in its official historical narrative with paramilitary training intended to integrate the former prisoners into a pro-RPF reserve militia. The entire judicial process, thus, contributed to a climate of intimidation and fear in which people did not feel free to openly discuss the past but rather felt constrained to repeat the official rhetoric and to participate in the conviction of their neighbors, regardless of the actual dictates of justice.

Bonaventure Bizumuremyi, a Tutsi genocide survivor who edited the paper *Umuco*, expressed disappointment with gacaca in late 2005:

I was hoping to finally understand why people had attacked my poor family. Above all, I was hoping that these people would express their regrets and I wanted to be reassured that the same thing would never happen to us again. I am not so optimistic anymore. Gacaca has become a very repressive form of justice. For the accused, it's a matter of defending themselves through all means possible in order to get the minimum sentence or be acquitted. At the same time, there has been a major push to get people to turn in suspects, and people are being encouraged, sometimes even forced, to plead guilty and to testify against as many neighbors as possible. So much for the truth![137]

As if to reinforce the point that judicial processes in Rwanda were used more for social control than for promoting rule of law and justice, Bizumuremyi was charged with defamation in 2008 and forced to flee Rwanda.

Conclusion

Institutions, including states, are never fully coherent, since whatever their relative autonomy and whatever constraints they place on officeholders, they are composed of individuals with diverse perceptions, abilities, and motivations. To suggest that trials have been used to exercise

---

[136] Speeches on the eighth anniversary of the genocide in 2002 by the head of the survivors' organization Ibuka and by President Kagame. Paul Kagame, "Discourse of the President of the Republic on the 8th Anniversary in the Memory of the Genocide and the Massacres of 1994," Nyakibanda, April 7, 2002.

[137] International Justice Tribune, "Questions Pile up for Swamped Gacaca," Radio Netherlands Worldwide, www.rnw.nl, October 23, 2005.

the power of the regime and to promote a particular narrative of the past is not to deny that officials who have supported trials have also been motivated by the desire to see justice done and promote reconciliation. The leaders of the country are driven by varied and competing – often contradictory – concerns, and different leaders are driven by different concerns to varying degrees. The desires to build rule of law, to avoid future ethnic violence by reforming the mentality of the population, and to stay in power by intimidating the population into submission all function simultaneously.

The contradictions in the post-genocide judicial initiatives in Rwanda are the central contradictions at the heart of the Government of Rwanda's project of social reconstruction. In post-genocide Rwanda, justice in the face of atrocities was demanded – but only a selective justice was implemented and only for some atrocities. The truth about the past was required, but only a partial accounting of the past was allowed, while other truths were suppressed. The reality of ethnicity was denied even as in practice the impact of ethnicity as a lived reality was reinforced. To understand what impact the contradictory programs of the regime have had on the population requires looking in depth at the processes of social reconstruction within Rwandan communities. In the final part of the book, I turn to this task, focusing on three communities in different parts of the country. Looking at how the population in these communities has reacted to political reform, memorialization, trials, and other programs, I find that the regime has effectively asserted control, pushing the population into compliance, and their policies have shaped popular discourse to an extent. At the same time, the government has not been able to dictate a collective memory and create a unified national Rwandan identity. The inconsistencies between the official narrative and people's lived experience have left "average citizens cynical and alienated."[138] As the review of their impact will demonstrate, the extensive transitional justice initiatives implemented in Rwanda have actually exacerbated social divisions and increased tensions. Rwanda stands as a warning about the limitations – or even the dangers – of transitional justice.

---

[138] Koonz, "Between Memory and Oblivion," p. 258.

5 From Violent Repression to Political Domination: Transitional Justice, Political Reform, and Development

> Today's dictators understand that in a globalized world the more brutal forms of intimidation – mass arrests, firing squads, and violent crackdowns – are best replaced with more subtle forms of coercion. Rather than forcibly arrest members of a human rights group, today's most effective despots deploy tax collectors or health inspectors to shut down dissident groups. Laws are written broadly, then used like a scalpel to target the groups the government deems a threat. Rather than shutter all media, modern-day despots make exceptions for small outlets – usually newspapers – that allow for a limited public discussion. Today's dictators pepper their speeches with references to liberty, justice, and the rule of law ... Modern dictators understand it is better to appear to win a contested election than to openly steal it.
>
> – William J. Dobson, *The Dictator's Learning Curve*

Breakfast with the Secretary General

The headquarters of the Rwandan Patriotic Front were housed in a building that previously served as a large private residence. Situated on the edge of Kimihurura, long one of Kigali's most fashionable neighborhoods, the office was located conveniently between downtown and Kacyiru, home to many government ministries. We arrived very early on a Friday morning – just 7 a.m. – because the Secretary General of the RPF, Charles Murigande, had granted us an interview and insisted that we not be late. He had a very busy day, his secretary had told us, and he could only accord us forty-five minutes.

We arrived early and parked our car on the dirt and gravel street in front of the RPF offices. An armed soldier opened the front gate, and we were invited inside and up the grand staircase to a hallway that had been furnished with chairs to serve as a waiting room. The house was quiet, with only a few people present, but Murigande was already hard at work in his office. After a few minutes of waiting, we were ushered inside a room that had once served as a bedroom, now furnished with a dark wooden desk and heavy curtains. Murigande rose from behind the desk, greeted us, and offered us seats on the hard wooden upright chairs situated in front of his desk. I explained our purpose: The three of us – I, another American scholar, and a Rwandan political scientist – were conducting an assessment of the political situation in Rwanda for the United States Agency for International Development to help the US Government determine how to support democratic consolidation in Rwanda. "We are hoping that as the leader of the dominant political party in the country, you can provide some insight into the role of parties and how democracy can be strengthened here." When I paused, without offering us an opportunity to pose our first question, the Secretary General of the RPF launched into a discourse about politics in Rwanda and the role of the RPF:

Since 1994, when the RPF was able to stop the genocide and drive out of power the government that was carrying out the genocide, it did something contrary to human nature. And perhaps that is why people have refused to accept it. It isn't natural for a party to win power and then invite other parties to share it. The RPF having as a primary goal the unity of the country, the RPF refused to be bound by human nature. Rwanda had a history of non-representative government. We put into place a broad-based government made of six political parties and put into place a transitional parliament of eight parties. It is difficult to understand why people refer to the RPF as the party in power, when you consider that in the government, all decisions are taken by consensus.[1]

Murigande spoke in deliberate and forceful English. Like many of the leaders of the RPF, Murigande was born in Rwanda but fled the country with his family when anti-Tutsi ethnic violence broke out in 1959. Unlike most of the top RPF brass, however, Murigande did not flee to Uganda. Since his family was from southern Rwanda, from Butare, they fled to neighboring Burundi. Murigande grew up in Bujumbura, the capital, and he began his university education at the National University of Burundi. He continued his studies at the University of Namur in Belgium, where he earned a Masters and PhD in mathematics, then returned to Burundi. While few Tutsi refugees from Burundi have held prominent positions in the RPF, Murigande had the advantage of having excelled at his studies of English in addition to his fluent French. In 1989, he assumed a position at Howard University in Washington, DC, placing him in a key position for representing the position of the RPF when their invasion of Rwanda began the following year. His loyalty to the RPF and his political stridency eventually earned him a position

---

[1] All quotes in this section from interview with Charles Murigande in Kigali, September 2002.

as a trusted confidant of Paul Kagame, who was himself in the United States – receiving military training at Ft. Leavenworth, Kansas – at the time the war began in October 1990:

Anyone who states that a society that experienced genocide can be totally healed in just eight years is probably not a sane human being. That is my answer to anyone who claims that this society is not still fragile. How can you think that yesterday people who were being hunted down like deer can today be totally at peace? Or even those who were hunting human beings as though they were deer can be at peace. No they are not at peace. If the tragedy had stopped in 1994, then eight years could be sufficient time for healing, but don't forget that we have continued to confront those who want to carry out genocide ...

Murigande had a reputation for being serious and severe. He was widely known to be an *umurokore*, a strict born-again Christian, who eschews alcohol, cigarettes, and other vices, including corruption. In 1998–1999, he served for a year as the rector of the National University of Rwanda in Butare, but his rigid approach to discipline clashed sharply with the inevitable youthful tendency for rebellion among university students. When I taught at the NUR in 2001, students still told stories about the swiftness with which Murigande had expelled students who protested against the poor conditions of student housing. Yet Murigande's seriousness of purpose and strict probity are exactly the qualities that impress outsiders who praise the RPF for its good management and clear purpose. In fact, Kagame moved Murigande into the leadership of the RPF in 1998, when he was seeking to root out growing corruption in the party. Murigande's unwavering attention to rules also made him an excellent choice for maintaining party discipline under the guise of democratic governance:

One of the basic principles of working in the RPF is discussion, sometimes endless discussion. Usually all decisions are taken by consensus. We debate until consensus is achieved ... If you feel strongly about an issue, you can always ask that it be re-debated. That is something that distinguishes the RPF from other parties. But once the party decides on an issue, you can't go out and oppose it. Once your arguments are defeated, you must go along.

Having lived in both Europe and the United States, Murigande understood well the Western mindset, and like many in the RPF, he pointedly rejected the West as a model for Rwanda. The roots of the RPF can be traced back to the anti-colonial struggles of the late 1950s and 1960s. Like elites in many African countries, young Tutsi in Rwanda in the 1950s developed a strong anti-European and politically radical ideology and began a movement for independence from Belgium.[2] But an emerging

---

[2] Lemarchand, *Rwanda and Burundi*.

Hutu "counter-elite," cultivated by Catholic missionaries and Belgian colonial authorities, raised concerns about the prospect of independence under Tutsi dominance.[3] When a 1959 attack on a Hutu sub-chief led to a wave of attacks on Tutsi leaders and counter-attacks on Hutu, Belgian authorities moved quickly to calm the situation by shifting Hutu into political offices. Many Tutsi, particularly those from elite families, fled into exile. The exiled Tutsi blamed the Belgians for the violence against them, and armed bands of Tutsi exiles sought to retake power from the new Hutu government in a series of attacks in the 1960s. Violent reprisals against Tutsi still in Rwanda killed hundreds and drove thousands more to flee the country.[4] Although the Hutu-dominated governments of independent Rwanda characterized the uprising in 1959 as a revolution, since the Hutu majority displaced the Tutsi elite, the Tutsi exiles in Burundi, Congo, and Uganda regarded the governments of Kayibanda and Habyarimana as reactionary puppets of Western interests.

Like many of the rebellions that arose in Africa after 1960, Uganda's National Resistance Movement (NRM) was influenced by revolutionary principles drawn from Marx, Lenin, and Mao. Led by Yoweri Museveni, the rebel group that took to the bush in 1980 and fought its way to power in 1986 characterized its struggle as a "revolution" and implemented a Maoist structure of revolutionary councils that linked people from the most local level to the party leaders at the top.[5] Rwandan refugees Paul Kagame and Fred Rwigyema were among the twenty-six individuals who originally joined Museveni's rebellion, and they modeled the RPF after the NRM. Even as the RPF leadership, like Museveni before them, jettisoned Marxist economic rhetoric and strongly embraced capitalism, the RPF leaders retained not only the Leninist principles of party organization and democratic centralism[6] – what Murigande described as allowing debate until a party decision had been made[7] – but also the

---

[3] Ian Linden with Jane Linden, *Church and Revolution in Rwanda*, New York: Africana Publishing Company, 1977.

[4] Lemarchand, *Rwanda and Burundi*; Prunier, *The Rwanda Crisis*, pp. 61–74, 90–92.

[5] Dan M. Mudoola, "Institution Building: The Case of the NRM and the Military in Uganda, 1986–9," in Holger Bernt Hansen and Michael Twaddle, eds., *Changing Uganda*, Athens, OH: Ohio University Press, 1991, pp. 230–246; J. Oloku-Onyanga, "The National Resistance Movement, 'Grassroots Democracy,' and Dictatorship in Uganda," in Robin Cohen and Harry Goulbourne, eds., *Democracy and Socialism in Africa*, Boulder: Westview Press, 1991.

[6] V. I. Lenin, "Report on the Unity Congress of the R.S.D.L.P.," 1906, available at www.marxists.org/archive/lenin/works/1906/rucong/viii.htm, writes "Freedom of discussion, unity of action. That is what we must strive to achieve." See also Michael Waller, *Democratic Centralism: An Historical Commentary*, New York: St. Martin's Press, 1981.

[7] Gerald Gahima, *Transitional Justice in Rwanda: Accountability for Atrocity*, Routledge, 2013, confirms this approach to decision-making in the RPF, with extensive debate until a decision is made then expected conformity.

strong anti-imperialist and anti-Western attitudes typical of revolutionary movements.[8] The failure of Western states to intervene to stop the genocide – even the complicity of some states such as France – only reinforced an already powerful sense within the RPF leadership of the moral bankruptcy of the West. Murigande and other RPF leaders felt that Western countries had utterly failed to acknowledge their role in the genocide, using the ICTR as a smokescreen to cover their own complicity, and lacked authority to criticize the human rights abuses of the RPF, which, after all, stopped the genocide. Although RPF leaders actively courted Western political support and investment, they felt the West's attempts to interfere in Rwandan affairs were selfishly motivated forms of neo-colonialism that served only to reinforce those same ideas and individuals that had promoted the genocide:

Thanks to the VOA Kinyarwanda language programs and the BBC Kinyarwanda language programs, we continue to receive poison. I don't think the country is healed. I don't know any country that has more debate than in Rwanda … You should go to the solidarity camps. No subject is taboo. People talk about everything.

At the end of forty-five minutes, at precisely ten minutes before 8 a.m., Murigande suddenly stopped, looked at his watch, thanked us, and offered us the door. The time was up, and our interview was concluded. As we left the office, we encountered a large line of people now seated in the waiting area hoping to ask Murigande for help with family problems or assistance in getting a job. Despite Murigande's protestations, many Rwandans believed that the RPF – not the government – was the real seat of power in Rwanda.

In the introduction to this section of the book, I presented two sharply contrasting perspectives on the RPF. While some observers consider Rwanda's ruling party a model of political leadership that promotes peace, stability, and development, others regard the RPF as a brutal, authoritarian regime, aggressively imposing its will on an oppressed population. In this chapter, I attempt to reconcile these contrasting perspectives. In this chapter, I do not offer a comprehensive analysis of the political developments and policy changes since 1994 nor catalog the human rights abuses that have informed my skeptical view of the RPF-led regime.[9] I instead focus on analyzing how the RPF has exercised

---

[8] In *The Rwanda Crisis*, Prunier writes that Rwigyema and Kagame shared with Museveni "the same left-leaning nationalist views, distrust of the West, hatred of dictatorship and belief in the redemptive powers of 'popular warfare'" (p. 68).

[9] For just such a detailed overview, see Filip Reyntjens, *Political Governance in Post-Genocide Rwanda*, New York: Cambridge University Press, 2014.

power. I first review the history of RPF repression in the years immediately after taking power and contend that violence was more extensive than is usually acknowledged today and set a foundation of intimidation and obedience that shaped how the population has responded to the extensive reform programs implemented after the RPF shifted to less violent means of rule around 2000. I also argue that efforts to promote political reform and economic development are driven by contradictory motivations. On the one hand, reform efforts are inspired by a compelling vision of societal purification and social uplift, closely tied to ideas of transitional justice. On the other hand, RPF leaders and the repatriated Tutsi who are their main supporters regard the general Rwandan population with suspicion and disdain, seeing them as either willing perpetrators or shameful victims of the 1994 genocide. Preventing future violence while transforming Rwanda according to the RPF's grand vision requires that they hold tightly onto power rather than ceding power to the majority. The ruling elite's strong belief in their right to rule and suspicion of the general population makes their policies particularly prone to top-down, heavy-handed implementation that requires active compliance regardless of the negative consequences of policy initiatives.

Establishing Control and the Road Not Taken: 1994–1995

Immediately after the RPF took power in Rwanda in 1994, a tangible possibility existed for a broadly popular multi-ethnic effort to establish peace, rebuild Rwanda, and return the country rapidly to democracy.[10] As the RPF troops advanced across the country, many of the Hutu who stayed in their communities rather than fleeing with their neighbors to Tanzania, the DRC, or the French-controlled Zone Turquoise, chose to remain because they had opposed the Hutu Power regime that perpetrated the genocide and hoped that the RPF could bring peace and democracy to the country. Many welcomed the RPF victory and cautiously embraced its leadership and effort to reconstruct the country.[11]

---

[10] While emphasizing the public's caution more than I do, Sibomana made a similar point about the opportunity that the RPF squandered: "When the RPF took control of Kigali in July 1994, everything was still possible. ... The vast majority of the population mistrusted the RPF, because of the propaganda of Hutu extremists or because of the crimes it had committed. But it could prove itself: by taking power, it could stop being a minority armed rebellion movement and commit itself to promoting a new Rwandan state." Sibomana, *Hope for Rwanda*, p. 138.

[11] This point was emphasized to me repeatedly during the year that I lived in Rwanda prior to the October 1996 closure of the refugee camps in the DRC, particularly in the south, where opposition to Habyarimana had been strong, but also among many Hutu with whom I interacted in Kigali.

Some early RPF actions gave cause for optimism. The RPF leaders promised to move rapidly toward democratic elections, and on July 19, 1994, the day after taking the last outpost of the genocidal regime, they named a government of national unity.[12] Based loosely on the 1993 Arusha Peace Accords, the government included nearly equal numbers of Hutu and Tutsi ministers drawn not only from the RPF but also from the main parties that had opposed the Habyarimana regime – the MDR, Social Democratic Party (*Parti Social Démocrat*, PSD), and Liberal Party. The RPF installed Hutu RPF official Pasteur Bizimungu as president and moderate Hutu leader Faustin Twagiramungu of the MDR as prime minister. Other well-respected Hutu in the government included human rights activist Alphonse Marie-Nkubito as Justice Minister and the RPF's Seth Sendashonga as Interior Minister.[13] When the government named new prefects in October 1994, the majority was Hutu, and only four of the eleven were from the RPF.[14] The RPF leaders decried revenge attacks and advocated national unity. They also tackled the difficult job of rebuilding the country's devastated infrastructure. International aid poured into Rwanda along with large numbers of international humanitarian workers, and the RPF quickly gained a reputation for competence and probity.[15]

Yet by the time I returned to Rwanda in late 1995, deep disappointment with the new regime had set in among many Rwandans. Within weeks of taking control, the RPF established a method of rule that combined eloquent rhetoric in support of a unified and peaceful country with an attitude of deep distrust and condescension for the populace. For all the talk of national unity and reconciliation, the population experienced RPF rule as highly oppressive. Rwandans swiftly learned that the best way to avoid becoming a target of violence or arrest was not only to show compliance with RPF directives but also to parrot RPF rhetoric, at least in public. Those who engaged in civil society or political party activity risked being seen by the regime as a threat, particularly if they were not

---

[12] Prunier, *The Rwanda Crisis*, pp. 268–273, 295–305.

[13] The government named by Bizimungu in July 1994 included nine ministers from the RPF and nine from other parties. Ten were Tutsi and eight Hutu. In September and October, three more ministers were named, all Hutu. André Guichaoua, *Les crises politiques au Burundi et au Rwanda (1993–1994)*, Lille: Université des Sciences et Technologies de Lille, 1995, pp. 759–761.

[14] Ibid., pp. 772–773.

[15] According to the World Bank, net official development assistance to Rwanda rose from $353.91 million in 1993 to $711.75 million in 1994 and $694.7 million in 1995. Foreign investment tapered off for a few years while Rwanda was involved in military interventions in the DRC, but climbed sharply again beginning in 2004 to reach a peak of $1.264 billion in 2011. World Bank, "Net Official Development Assistance Received (Current US$)," www.data.worldbank.org/indicator/DT.ODA.ODAT.CD.

from the repatriated Tutsi community. As one Hutu civil society activist told me in 1996, "Those of us [Hutu] who stayed in the country, we had supported the RPF. But we were mistaken. Now we are all being harassed."[16]

The RPF used substantial violence in gaining power and establishing its initial authority. According to HRW, between April and July 1994, "The RPF killed thousands of civilians both during the course of combat ... and in the more lengthy process of establishing its control throughout the country."[17] In some places, as the RPF troops advanced, they opened fire on anyone they encountered.[18] In many communities, after seizing control, the RPF called a public meeting where they separated out a portion of the population – sometimes all men of fighting age, sometimes only those accused by their fellow citizens of having participated in the genocide – and took them away for summary execution.[19] In my research in Butare, Gikongoro, Kibuye, Kibungo, and Byumba from 1995 to 2006, individuals regularly pointed out the location of mass graves of victims of RPF violence, though the bodies from these graves were in some cases subsequently exhumed and reburied in mass graves for victims of the genocide. While these RPF killings were less systematic and not based on identity and thus cannot be equated with the genocide, they nevertheless represent serious war crimes and crimes against humanity.[20]

By September 1994, the RPF replaced the extensive use of violence with a strategy of dominating the population through widespread arrest and detention coupled with more selective disappearances and killings. As discussed in Chapter 4, the RPF used judicial action to intimidate and control the population, an approach made particularly effective because the lack of formal charges and absence of trials meant that unsubstantiated accusations could indefinitely remove from public life those viewed as threats to the regime, while their detention was easily justified as part of the effort to seek accountability for genocide crimes and to strengthen

---

[16] Interview in Kigali, May 14, 1996.

[17] Des Forges, *Leave None to Tell the Story*, p. 702.

[18] One Tutsi man in Butare told me his family was killed in Kibungo by the RPF, who assumed anyone they found alive was a combatant. Interview in Butare, February 1995. Burnet, *Genocide Lives in Us*, reports similar cases.

[19] Des Forges, *Leave None to Tell the Story*, pp. 705–722. See also, Amnesty International, "Rwanda: Reports of Killings and Abductions," pp. 1–9.

[20] A Hutu civil society activist who was threatened by Hutu Power during the genocide and sought refuge behind RPF lines told me that at the camp for IDPs in Byumba where he spent several months, the RPF regularly took away individuals, particularly those suspected of having connections to the Habyarimana government; most were never heard from again. Interview in Kigali, April 1996. Judi Rever, "Rwanda's Memory Hole," *Foreign Policy Journal*, April 14, 2015, documents a massacre in Byumba Stadium in April 1994 and RPF efforts to suppress memory of the killings.

security in a still fragile post-conflict society. The threat of indefinite detention became a powerful weapon to silence would-be regime critics. By the end of 1994, 15,000 people were imprisoned on genocide charges, while by the end of 1995, the number had risen to 57,000, at a time before the closure of the camps in the DRC that presumably housed the majority of perpetrators.[21]

At the same time, the RPF continued to use violence in a limited and selective fashion. In early 1995, the RPF forcibly closed camps for IDPs that had been formed in southwest Rwanda when the region was under French control, including the camp at Kibeho where as many as 8,000 died.[22] During my work with HRW in Rwanda in 1995–1996, numerous witnesses told me about individuals killed, attacked, or disappeared, including government officials, journalists, and civil society activists as well as average Hutu killed after they returned home from the IDP camps.[23] Human rights activist Father Sibomana observed in this period:

It's always the same scenario: men, women, children, priests, and magistrates are killed, in the daytime or at night, with knives or with firearms. Witnesses accuse armed men wearing military uniforms who, strangely, move about freely without fear of being arrested. How can we fail to conclude that they are soldiers of the Rwandan Patriotic Army?[24]

When massacres and violent attacks on individuals were made public, the RPF responded wherever possible by denying connection to the violence, attributing it to remnants of the genocidal militias or to mere criminality. Where RPF involvement was obvious, as in the massacres at Kibeho, where international observers witnessed RPF soldiers firing

---

[21] Human Rights Watch, *World Report 1996*.

[22] Medecines Sans Frontiers, "Report on Events in Kibeho Camp, April 1995," Paris: MSF, May 25, 1995; Amnesty International, "Rwanda: Independent forensic inquiry and urgent protection needed for internally displaced persons following the massacre of several thousands," AFR 47/09/95, London: Amnesty International, April 24, 1995. Other large-scale massacres took place in 1995 in Kanama in Gisenyi Prefecture and in the Nyungwe Forest, Amnesty International, "Rwanda, Two Years After the Genocide: An Open Letter to President Pasteur Bizimungu," AFR 47/42/96, London: Amnesty International, April 4, 1996.

[23] In 1995 alone, assassinations of government officials included the Butare prefect in March, the deputy prefect of Gisenyi in July, and a judge and the deputy prefect of Gitarama in Butare in August. Human Rights Watch, *World Report 1996*.

[24] Sibomana, *Hope for Rwanda*, p. 140. Amnesty International, "Two Years After the Genocide," reported in April 1996, "a pattern of killings and 'disappearances' of unarmed civilians by members of the Rwandese Patriotic Army (RPA) has developed over the last year ... [I]ndividuals – unarmed civilians, including women, young children and the elderly – have been mysteriously murdered by members of the RPA or 'disappeared' without trace, in various parts of the country ... Although there is no evidence that the government directly ordered each of these killings, there has been little official action to break the pattern." (p. 5).

on unarmed civilians, RPF leaders claimed that troops who perpetrated violence were rogue agents seeking revenge for the murder of their fellow Tutsi or driven unavoidably to unfortunate actions because of the horrible legacy of insecurity left by the genocide. The regime sometimes made a public show of investigating and even occasionally prosecuting RPF members accused of abuses, but real accountability was almost entirely lacking.[25]

National Unity Through Repression: Securing RPF Dominance 1995–1999

The pattern established in the first year of RPF rule of combining moderate rhetoric and ostensibly positive policy initiatives with intolerance of criticism and strict control of social and political life, backed up by a willingness to use coercive force where necessary, continued over the next five years and set the context for the post-2000 political agenda, when overt repression was replaced by popular mobilization and less violent means of control. The RPF's most widespread use of force after 1995 was across Rwanda's borders in the Democratic Republic of Congo (called Zaire until 1997). In 1996, the RPF organized a Congolese rebel movement and joined them in invading Eastern DRC. The RPF bombed and forcibly closed the refugee camps, demanding that Rwandan refugees return to Rwanda, then systematically hunted down those who chose instead to flee into the Congolese rainforest.[26] Gaining support from local ethnic militias, the Ugandan and Burundian armies, and numerous deserters from the Congolese army, they swiftly advanced across the DRC, ultimately driving long-time dictator Mobutu Sese Seko out of power in May 1997 and installing rebel leader Laurent Kabila as president.[27] For

[25] The commander of troops at Kibeho, Fred Ibingira, was found guilty of non-assistance to persons in danger but acquitted of murder. Although sentenced to eighteen months in prison, he was immediately released and subsequently promoted to brigadier general. Filip Reyntjens and Steff Vandeginste, "Rwanda: An Atypical Transition," in Elin Skaar, Siri Gloppen, and Astri Suhrke, eds., *Roads to Reconciliation*, Lanham MD: Lexington Books, 2005. Similarly, four officers tried in a military court for a massacre of more than 100 civilians in Kanama, Gisenyi, in August 1995 were ultimately sentenced only for non-assistance to persons in danger. Sibomana, *Hope for Rwanda*, p. 142.

[26] The Rwandan camps did include armed elements who were legitimate targets and were preventing refugees from returning to Rwanda, but as I wrote for Human Rights Watch at the time, the AFDL and RPF forces "went beyond simply opening a path for those who wanted to return; they also fired on camps where there were no more soldiers present to force people in the camps to return to Rwanda." Longman and Des Forges, "Attacked by All Sides."

[27] There is a rich and growing literature on the two wars in Congo. C.f., Georges Nzongola-Ntalaja, *Congo: From Leopold to Kabila*, London: Zed Books, 2002; Séverine Autesserre, *The Trouble with the Congo: Local Violence and the Failure of International Peacebuilding*, Cambridge: Cambridge University Press, 2010; Thomas Turner, *The*

many of the Rwandans interviewed in my research, the experience of violence in Congo shaped how they viewed the RPF and its initiatives. As I discuss in the next section of this book, the complete lack of accountability for this violence and its erasure from public memory affect how people experience transitional justice programs focused exclusively on the genocide.[28]

Ironically, in driving the Hutu militia away from the Rwandan border, the intervention in Congo forced many militia members back into Rwanda, actually adding to insecurity. Following the closure of the camps, insurgent attacks in Rwanda increased, particularly in the northwest. Seeking to contain the insurgency, the RPF attacked Hutu civilians in the northwest, carrying out summary executions of suspected militants and in several cases massacring civilians, particularly in communities where insurgents killed RPF soldiers in attacks. As many as 10,000 civilians were killed between October 1997 and January 1998.[29] Combat, threats from the insurgents, and RPF counterattacks drove thousands to flee their homes, with nearly half a million in IDP camps by mid-1998. The RPF began to move people forcibly out of their homes in a regroupment policy that sought to separate the civilian population from the insurgents by creating new concentrated settlements, primarily along roadsides, where they could be closely monitored.[30]

Growing tension between the Rwandan leadership and the Kabila government led the RPF to support a second rebellion in Congo. Rwandan and Ugandan troops re-entered Congo in August 1998 to support a new rebel group comprised primarily of Banyamulenge defectors from the Congolese army. Although initially highly successful, the intervention of

Congo Wars: Conflict, Myth, and Reality, London: Zed Books, 2007; Stearns, *Dancing in the Glory of Monsters*; Lemarchand, *The Dynamics of Violence in Central Africa*; Reyntjens, *The Great African War.*

[28] The best account of the violence against Hutu refugees in Congo is Marie Béatrice Umutesi, *Surviving the Slaughter: The Ordeal of a Rwandan Refugee in Zaire,* Madison: University of Wisconsin Press, 2000. See also Amnesty International, "Rwanda: Human Rights Overlooked in Mass Repatriation," AFR 47/02/97, London: Amnesty International, January 1997; Human Rights Watch, "Zaire: Transition, War and Human Rights," New York: Human Rights Watch/Africa, April 1997; United Nations High Commission for Human Rights, "Democratic Republic of the Congo, 1993–2003: Report of the Mapping Exercise documenting the most serious violations of human rights and international humanitarian law committed within the territory of the Democratic Republic of the Congo between March 1993 and June 2003," Geneva: UNHCHR, August 2010.

[29] Filip Reyntjens, "Rwanda, Ten Years On: From Genocide to Dictatorship," *African Affairs* 103, 2004, p. 195; Amnesty International, "Rwanda: Ending the Silence," AFR 47/32/97, London: Amnesty International, September 25, 1997; Amnesty International, "Rwanda: Civilians trapped in armed conflict. 'The dead can no longer be counted,'" AFR 47/044/1997, London: Amnesty International, December 19, 1997.

[30] Human Rights Watch, *World Report 1999*; Human Rights Watch, "Rwanda: Uprooting the Rural Poor," New York: Human Rights Watch, May 1, 2001.

Angola, Zimbabwe, and other African countries on behalf of Kabila produced a stalemate on the battlefield and fracturing of the rebel movement, including a rupture between erstwhile allies Rwanda and Uganda. A humanitarian and human rights disaster ensued, in which all sides engaged in attacks on civilians.[31] The second Congo war pushed the Hutu militias deeper into Congo and put them on the defensive. Since late 1999, the RPF has experienced no organized armed resistance, and the RPF has engaged in no large-scale attacks on civilians within Rwanda.

In most of Rwanda, after the initial wave of violence in 1994 and 1995, the RPF shifted to subtler means of control. By appearing moderate and inclusive in their governance, quickly and effectively rebuilding the infrastructure, and promoting rapid economic growth, they hoped to build legitimacy and gain support from as much of the Rwandan population as possible – not only genocide survivors and repatriated Tutsi, but sympathetic Hutu as well. The RPF leadership appealed to the international community for financial assistance, playing on the diplomatic community's guilt over the failure to stop the genocide and promising that resources would not be squandered on corruption and inefficiency. International inputs focused at first on emergency assistance but shifted to development of the infrastructure and social services, allowing the government to provide direct benefits to the population.[32] Education was an early major policy focus, as the RPF sought to expand the number of schools, increase the percentage of children matriculating, and improve the quality of education. The government shifted to a merit-based system of advancement, both eliminating the ethnic quota system that limited opportunities for Tutsi and demonstrating a willingness to provide opportunities to Hutu.[33]

Contradictions in RPF policy ultimately undermined efforts to promote legitimacy. On ethnicity, for example, the RPF discouraged open discussion of ethnic identities and issued new identity cards that eliminated mention of ethnicity, but at the same time, the calculated

---

[31] Research that I conducted in Goma and Bukavu in March 2000 confirmed that the RPF was directly involved in major human rights violations during the second war. Longman, "Eastern Congo Ravaged." See also, John F. Clark, ed., *The African Stakes of the Congo War*, New York: Palgrave MacMillan, 2002; Reyntjens, *The Great African War*; Autesserre, *The Trouble with the Congo*.

[32] Organization for Economic Cooperation and Development (OECD), *Geographical Distribution of Financial Flows to Aid Recipients: Disbursements, Commitments, Country Indicators*, Paris: OECD, 2001, 2006, 2011; World Bank, "Net Official Development Assistance Received."

[33] King, *From Classrooms to Conflict in Rwanda*; Freedman et al., "Confronting the Past in Rwandan Schools." The policies to expand education were motivated both by the presumed economic benefits of a more educated population and a belief that ignorance was a major reason the population participated in the genocide.

appointment of Hutu to top government posts in the effort to appear inclusive demonstrated a continuing consciousness of ethnicity. Despite a façade of inclusivity, in practice RPF leaders feared relinquishing real control to anyone outside their immediate constituency, and real power remained in the hands of Tutsi from the RPF, mostly former refugees from Uganda. In ministries and other offices led by Hutu, the second- or third-ranked position was always held by a Tutsi RPF officer, usually Anglophone, who retained real control.[34] Rwandans widely believed that Paul Kagame, the Tutsi RPF leader who served as vice-president and minister of defense, was more powerful than President Bizimungu and actually called the shots.[35] In August 1995, five Hutu ministers – including Nkubito, Twagiramungu, and Sendashonga – resigned from the Government of National Unity, complaining about their lack of real power and the continuing violence perpetrated by RPF soldiers.[36]

The approach to civil society and the press similarly undermined efforts to promote legitimacy, as they contradicted claims about the irrelevance of ethnicity and demonstrated the RPF's willingness to use force. The RPF allowed civil society groups to proliferate but sought to rein them in, ensuring that people they could trust were in leadership positions – generally repatriated Tutsi, but also sometimes genocide survivors.[37] Where necessary, the RPF used coercion to force groups to change their leadership to preferred candidates. For example, churches faced pressures to appoint leaders trusted by the RPF. In the Free Methodist Church, RPF troops reportedly encircled a national church board meeting in 1995 until it selected the RPF's preferred candidate, while the regime froze the bank accounts of the Episcopal and Pentecostal churches until they agreed to leadership changes.[38] Among human rights organizations, two largely Tutsi groups received strong RPF backing, as did the main umbrella group for human rights organizations, after they selected as

---

[34] Gahima, *Transitional Justice in Rwanda*, confirms this as the RPF's method of control.

[35] Joseph Sebarenzi, with Laura Ann Mullane, *God Sleeps in Rwanda: A Journey of Transformation*, New York: Atria Books, 2009, National Assembly Speaker from 1997 to 2000, wrote, "[I]t was no secret that Kagame held the reins of government and that Bizimungu had little power ... Because Bizimungu was a Hutu and member of the RPF, his presidency gave the government a diverse face and made the international community think it was inclusive, not a Tutsi-dominated government. In reality, Bizimungu's presidency was window-dressing, not a commitment to reconciliation" (p. 139).

[36] Reyntjens, "Rwanda, Ten Years On."

[37] For example, the Iwacu Center was a development group that was important in fostering civil society opposition to Habyarimana. After the war pro-RPF official Antoine Mugesera took over and ensured the group provided no resistance to the new regime. A group of returnees from Congo relaunched Pro-Femmes Twesehamwe, an umbrella organization for women's groups that successfully pushed for important advancements on women's rights without fundamentally challenging the RPF.

[38] Interviews in Kigali, April 1996 and October 2002.

president a Tutsi genocide survivor with close ties to the regime who discouraged the group and its member organizations from researching RPF abuses.[39] By contrast, groups headed by Father Sibomana and former Justice Minister Nkubito faced considerable harassment. After Nkubito died in 1997, the RPF exploited his group's status as a voluntary organization by flooding its membership roles with RPF supporters who redirected the group away from investigating RPF abuses. The executive secretary, Richard Nsanzabaganwa, himself a Tutsi genocide survivor, fled Rwanda in 1998.[40] While ostensibly allowing newspapers to publish freely, in practice, journalists who criticized the RPF or challenged its vision for Rwanda were routinely harassed. As Allan Thompson writes, "Shortly after coming to power, the RPF began to censor independent journals and persecute independent journalists."[41]

Selective use of violence also helped the regime keep the population in line. Although relatively rare, assassinations remained a tool to silence political opponents and send a message to other would-be dissidents. Two Hutu RPF members who fled Rwanda and became regime critics, Sendashonga and member of parliament Théoneste Lizinde, were assassinated in Nairobi in 1997 and 1998. Occasional attacks on journalists and civil society activists had a chilling effect on others who might speak out against the government.[42] The general Hutu population also faced periodic disappearances and summary executions, helping to keep ordinary citizens in line, though large-scale violence was limited to Congo and northwest Rwanda.[43]

[39] Interview in Kigali June 2001.

[40] Personal communication with Alison Des Forges, December 1998.

[41] Allan Thompson, *The Media and the Rwandan Genocide*, London: Pluto Press, 2007, p. 407. Cases of journalists beaten or killed, like Edouard Mutsinzi, the editor of *Le Messager-Intumwa* and Manasse Mugabo, director of the Kinyarwanda service for the United Nations radio station, who disappeared in August 1995, had a chilling effect. Sibomana, *Hope for Rwanda*, p. 143; Amnesty International, "Rwanda: Jean RUBADUKA, magistrate and human rights activist Abbé André SIBOMANA, acting bishop and human rights activist and other human rights activists," AFR 47/23/95, London: Amnesty International, November 30, 1995.

[42] In April 1997, after the journal *Umuravumba* published descriptions of RPF massacres, it was seized by the government and its editor was assassinated. A deputy chief justice, Vincent Nsanzabaganwa, was killed at his home in Kigali in 1997. Thompson, *The Media and the Rwandan Genocide*, p. 408. A former judge in Cyangugu working with the NGO *Avocats sans Frontières* on defense for genocide cases was strangled in January 1998, and a few days later, a Croatian priest, Vjeko Curic, a close associate of Abbé Sibomana, was shot dead in the middle of the day in downtown Kigali. Amnesty International, "The Hidden Violence."

[43] During the insurgency in the northwest, a number of people originating in Gisenyi and Ruhengeri disappeared in Kigali and elsewhere, apparently taken by soldiers who believed that they were connected with the insurgency. In Umutara at least a hundred people, nearly all Hutu returned from refugee camps in Tanzania, disappeared in December 1997 and January 1998, apparently linked to conflicts over land. At least

The threat of arrest and detention ultimately became more common than the actual use of violence to control both Hutu elites and the general population.[44] The number of Hutu arrested on genocide charges continued to mount. In 1996, the government adopted new laws governing genocide crimes, and in December they began the first genocide trials. A 1996 policy requiring all Rwandans to return to their communes of origin to receive new identity cards forced genocide suspects living in Kigali and elsewhere to return to their home communities, where many were arrested. Thousands of Hutu who returned from Congo in 1996 were also arrested. By the end of 1998, 126,000 people were in prison on genocide charges.[45]

While initial RPF efforts to maintain control focused on Hutu, beginning in 1999, Tutsi critics of the government faced increasing threat of reprisal, something that has remained a factor in Rwandan politics, belying the effort to explain Rwandan politics in simple ethnic terms. In November 1999, the RPF arrested around 200 people in Kigali and charged them with supporting a supposed new security threat, "The Army of the King." Although a Tutsi, the Rwandan King, living in exile since 1961, by custom represented interests of all Rwandans. Some Rwandans hoped for his return, believing that he could provide a rallying point for a multi-ethnic alternative to Kagame and the RPF. The idea of the king's return gained support not only among Hutu, but among some Tutsi genocide survivors frustrated with the post-genocide government and even among repatriated Tutsi from Burundi and Congo, frustrated at the dominance of Tutsi repatriated from Uganda. As HRW explained at the time, "The multi-ethnic nature of the monarchist group poses a major challenge to authorities who previously could discredit opposition groups for being composed only of Hutu and for including persons implicated in the genocide."[46] The willingness to target Tutsi became an important element in Kagame and the RPF's move to further consolidate control.

Toward a New Political Order

The *imidugudu* program was an early RPF attempt to radically reconstruct Rwandan society and drive development. It served as a forerunner to the more extensive programs for social engineering implemented after

thirty bodies were later found. Also in 1998, several dozen people were killed in parts of Gitarama. Amnesty International, "The Hidden Violence," pp. 5–9; Human Rights Watch, *World Report 1999*.

[44] Waldorf, "Mass Justice for Mass Atrocity."

[45] Human Rights Watch, *World Report 1999*.

[46] Human Rights Watch, "Rwanda: The Search for Security and Human Rights Abuses," New York: Human Rights Watch, April 1, 2000.

2000. In December 1996, the government adopted a National Habitat Policy in which they proposed to move all Rwandans in rural areas out of their traditional scattered homesteads and into villages, known as *imidugudu* (singular, *umudugudu*). The immediate impetus for the policy was the conflict over housing arising from the mass return of refugees from Tanzania and Congo, since many of the repatriated Tutsi who had returned to Rwanda beginning in 1994 had occupied homes abandoned by Hutu who had gone into exile and now had returned, seeking to reclaim their property. However, the RPF had been talking about the need for reorganizing rural life since the 1993 Arusha Accords, and housing built by the government, UNHCR, and other international agencies since 1994 for genocide survivors and repatriated refugees was entirely in concentrated settlements. The primary justification stated in the law for moving rural people into concentrated settlements was economic development – to facilitate the provision of public services and allow land redistribution. A January 1997 law banned building new homes outside designated sites, and in February the government began implementing the villagization policy in the eastern prefectures of Umutara, Kibungo, and Kigali-Rural. Authorities ordered residents to abandon their homes and build new houses in designated locations. At the same time, they also redistributed land in many areas to repatriated Tutsi. The *imidugudu* policy was expanded into in Gisenyi and Ruhengeri as order was restored in 1998 and 1999, with displaced families in many areas required to move into newly constructed villages rather than returning to their homes.[47]

Not surprisingly, the attempt to force people to leave their homes and move into the new settlements met with considerable resistance. By tradition, Rwandans did not live in villages but in scattered homesteads, and the smallest unit of social organization was the hill (*umusozi*). The traditional pattern of habitation throughout Rwanda consisted of families living in an enclosed compound surrounded by banana groves and fields, with adult children and other relatives often living in close proximity in their own compounds. The new *imidugudu* were often quite far from fields, requiring farmers to walk long distances to cultivate and making

---

[47] Human Rights Watch, "Uprooting the Rural Poor"; Saskia Van Hoyweghen, "The Urgency of Land and Agrarian Reform in Rwanda," *African Affairs*, 98, 392, July 1999, 353–372; Herman Musahara and Chris Huggins, "Land Reform, Land Scarcity, and Post-Conflict Reconstruction: A Case Study of Rwanda," in Chris Huggins and Jenny Clover, eds., *From the Ground Up: Land Rights, Conflict, and Peace in Sub-Saharan Africa*, Pretoria: Institute for Security Studies, June 2005; Ansoms, "Re-engineering Rural Society"; Catharine Newbury, "High Modernism at the Ground Level: The *Imidugudu* Policy at the Ground Level," in *Remaking Rwanda: State Building and Human Rights After Mass Violence*, Madison: University of Wisconsin Press, 2011, pp. 223–239.

protecting fields from theft difficult. Despite the claim that a major goal of the program was to improve the quality of rural life, services arrived slowly to most *imidugudu*. Although foreign donors supported construction in some areas, the new houses were often inferior to those that families were forced to abandon. In many cases individuals had to build new homes without any assistance or resources. Because of resistance, government officials employed threats and sometimes fined individuals who refused to move, though little violence was reported. Many people were also required to destroy their existing homes even before the new homes were constructed.[48]

Although the program of forced villagization was put on hold in 1999 because of strong resistance from donors, the government made clear that it intended eventually to pursue villagization,[49] and the land reform policies adopted a few years later continued to call for villagization of most rural residents. Discussing agrarian and land reform, Saskia van Hoyweghen contended that the repatriated Tutsi, "have not only brought with them different experiences but most of all a vision of what their home country ought to be like and a strong will to re-shape it to fit the mould."[50] While part of an ostensibly well-intentioned program to promote development and improve rural life, popular resistance required the government to force compliance. As many of those who resisted expected, the final result of the program was actually to make conditions worse for most of those affected. As with many later policies in Rwanda, good intentions were tempered by security concerns that ended up dominating much of the *imidugudu* policy's implementation. HRW's research indicates that Tutsi genocide survivors were particularly affected by the policy, many of them resisted, and many faced government coercion forcing them to relocate.[51]

The year 2000 marked a major shift in the RPF's governance of Rwanda, as the party assumed overt control of public institutions, Paul Kagame assumed more direct control of the party, and the government launched a much broader and more ambitious program of social and political transformation. A series of weekly meetings held at Village Urugwiro, the presidential residence, from May 1998 through March

---

[48] Human Rights Watch, "Uprooting the Rural Poor"; Musahara and Huggins, "Land Reform, Land Scarcity, and Post-Conflict Reconstruction."

[49] The Ministry of Land said in July 1999 that, "Imidugudu will [be] the only recommended and promoted form of settlement in rural areas. The ultimate objective of the government is to enable the *entire* rural population to live in grouped settlements." Quoted in Human Rights Watch, "Uprooting the Rural Poor."

[50] Van Hoyweghen, "The Urgency of Land and Agrarian Reform," p. 365.

[51] Human Rights Watch, "Uprooting the Rural Poor."

1999, brought together Rwanda's key political leaders to discuss the country's future.[52] The proposals that emerged from the meetings set the agenda for aggressive political reform and popular mobilization in the following decade – the promotion of national unity and fight against "sectarianism," adoption of new national symbols, transition to a democratic system "suitable for Rwanda," adoption of gacaca to speed the prosecution of genocide crimes, fighting corruption, land reform, promoting rapid economic development, and, above all, the need for popular participation.[53] Transitional justice programs were thus embedded in a broader reform agenda, and the ethos of transitional justice, the idea of reshaping memory and identity through popular mobilization, pervaded other programs not obviously tied to truth-telling and accountability.

The consolidation of political power in the hands of the RPF began around 1998. While previously the RPF strove to be the dominant party in a coalition of independent political parties, in the late 1990s RPF leaders became increasingly intolerant of political independence and sought to establish more complete hegemonic control over Rwanda's political life. The RPF sought to weaken and co-opt other political parties. While continuing to name ministers from other parties, the RPF stopped consulting party leaders on whom from their parties to appoint.[54] Within the National Assembly, the RPF pushed through the creation of a Forum of Political Parties, a supra-parliamentary committee with the power to vet members and refuse to seat or remove those deemed unfit to hold office – allegedly those involved in corruption or promoting ethnic division, but in practice, those who challenged the supremacy of the RPF. The RPF dominated the Forum, giving them a veto over other parties' members, thus creating a de facto one-party state.[55]

At the same time that the RPF acted to control other parties more thoroughly, Kagame moved to consolidate both the power of the executive

---

[52] The Village Urugwiro process was somewhat like the national conferences held in much of francophone Africa earlier in the decade, but under more direct control of the regime. John F. Clark and David E. Gardinier, eds., *Political Reform in Francophone Africa*, Boulder: Westview Press, 1996.

[53] Republic of Rwanda, "Report on the Reflection Meetings Held in the Office of the President of the Republic from May 1998 to March 1999," Kigali: Office of the President of the Republic, August 1999.

[54] As Joseph Sebarenzi, Speaker of the National Assembly during this period, pointed out, "This shifted appointees' allegiance from their political parties to the RPF. After all, if the RPF put them in office, keeping the RPF happy would be their priority." Sebarenzi, *God Sleeps in Rwanda*, p. 141.

[55] Sebarenzi, *God Sleeps in Rwanda*, writes that, "The forum is unconstitutional and unjust. It also works against the very principle of separation of powers ..." (p. 149). It was written into the 2003 constitution as a permanent and official feature of the Rwandan system.

branch and his own personal power. Although his role
was usually well hidden, Kagame sought to strengthen his h...
ing the replacement of a number of ministers and other official...
executive branch, including Alexis Kanyarengwe, a Hutu defector fro...
the Habyarimana regime who served as chairman of the RPF during the
1990–1994 war and was vice prime minister and minister of the interior
after 1994. Several individuals were driven out under charges of corruption, sometimes after parliamentary investigations; some Hutu were
accused of having hidden their involvement in the genocide.[56] Several
prominent military officials were sent overseas as ambassadors or for
military training, which served to neutralize their political influence as
well as allowing Kagame to root out corruption that had been growing since the RPF's intervention in mineral-rich DRC.[57] Kagame also
moved to rein in the independence of the judiciary. In 1998 and 1999,
the RPF leadership pushed out five of the six supreme court justices.
While two were Hutu, three were repatriated Tutsi members of the RPF,
but they were not part of Kagame's trusted inner circle; all were replaced
by Kagame loyalists.[58]

Having laid the groundwork in 1998 and 1999, Kagame dramati-
cally changed Rwanda's political landscape in early 2000 by replacing
the country's three top officials, personally assuming the presidency,
and making clear that his regime would not tolerate dissent or insub-
ordination even from Tutsi genocide survivors. The first national leader
to be forced out was the speaker of the National Assembly, Joseph
Sebarenzi. Although he was not in Rwanda in 1994, having fled after
being arrested in the sweep of Tutsi following the October 1990 RPF
invasion, Sebarenzi was closely identified with the survivors' community. A well-respected man of high integrity from the Liberal Party that

---

[56] Sebarenzi, who was involved in the investigation and removal of several ministers, wrote, "I later learned that Kagame supported our investigation of these ministers because he wanted many of them out of office himself. His support was tactical, not principled" (p. 155). Among those removed were Hutu from other parties, like Minister in the Presidency Anastase Gasana (MDR) and Minister of Communications Charles Ntakirutinka (PSD), but also some within the RPF whom Kagame saw as threats.

[57] One highly placed individual in the Kagame regime explained to me a few years later his observation that at this time Kagame's inner circle – those people with real decision-making power – shrank as he moved to eliminate his rivals, while at the same time the RPF's outer circle – those people with important positions that gave them a degree of influence over national policy – was expanded with the creation of the national commissions and other institutions to include more women, new members of the RPF, and Hutu, giving an impression of inclusivity. Personal communication, Kigali, September 2002. While other observers challenge the idea that any expansion took place, since repatriated Tutsi, particularly from Uganda, continued to occupy most positions, the observation on the consolidation around Kagame is clearly well founded.

[58] Sebarenzi, *God Sleeps in Rwanda*, pp. 142–146, 151–152.

drew its primary support from genocide survivors, Sebarenzi attempted to build the independence of the legislative branch and provide oversight on executive action, which brought him into regular disagreement with Kagame. As a Tutsi who had been outside the country in 1994, he could not be slandered with accusations of genocide complicity; instead, he was falsely accused of working with the deposed king to overthrow the government and of misusing public funds. Under pressure from the RPF – ultimately including direct pressure from Kagame – Sebarenzi resigned his position in early January 2000 and secretly fled the country, fearing for his safety.[59]

Pierre-Célestin Rwigema, a Hutu from the MDR who had succeeded Twagiramungu as prime minister, was forced to resign in February, under accusations of corruption and fled to the United States.[60] The RPF ultimately brought genocide charges against him and sought his extradition from the United States, which was rejected.[61] Bernard Makuza, another Hutu from the MDR became prime minister, but unlike Rwigema, he was handpicked by Kagame, lacked a constituency within the party, and ultimately left the MDR to join the RPF. Kagame's next target was President Bizimungu, who had found himself increasingly at odds with Kagame. After Théoneste Lizinde's and Sendashonga's departures (and assassinations) and Kanyarengwe's resignation in 1997, Bizimungu was the last leading Hutu in the RPF leadership. Along with appointing Hutu to important government posts, allowing a few parties to operate with limited freedom, and portraying the image of a balance of powers between the executive, legislature, and judiciary, placing Hutu in prominent roles in the RPF leadership was part of the strategy used until 2000 to disguise the real nature of power in Rwanda. With an official transition to democratic government and planned elections, it became important both for the RPF's supremacy to be more firmly established and for Kagame to situate himself more clearly as national leader. The removal of Sebarenzi and Rwigema, along with the creation of the Forum of Political Parties, helped to weaken the independence of the other parties. Although few Rwandans believed Bizimungu was ever at the center of RPF power, he had become an obstacle to Kagame's ambitions. He resigned under

---

[59] Reyntjens, "Rwanda, Ten Years On," p. 181; Sebarenzi, *God Sleeps in Rwanda*, pp. 166–182.

[60] Reyntjens, "Rwanda, Ten Years On," p. 181.

[61] Rwigema returned to Rwanda in October 2011, amid reports that he had been provided cash and promises that his genocide case was to be dropped. He joined the RPF and was named a representative in the East African Parliament. "Pierre Celestin Rwigema, the Rwandan exiled prime minister returns as revealed before," *Umuvugizi*, October 24, 2011. Sebarenzi, *God Sleeps in Rwanda*, p. 159.

pressure in March 2000 and immediately faced charges of tax fraud and other forms of corruption.[62]

With Bizimungu's resignation, Kagame assumed the presidency, stepping from behind the curtain that had obscured his power to situate himself publicly as the key player in Rwandan politics. Yet the actual organization of power within the RPF remained concealed. Sebarenzi wrote that, "Kagame controlled people through secrecy. No one ever knew what he really thought about anything until it was too late."[63] Kagame was at the center of a shifting group of powerful RPF officials that grew progressively smaller as he concentrated control increasingly in his own hands and those of a few people that he trusted but did not view as serious contenders for his power. As four powerful members of the RPF's inner circle who broke with Kagame and fled Rwanda in the late 2000s wrote in 2010:

The RPF has, over time, been transformed into a vehicle to serve the political and economic interests of one person – the party president. President Kagame does not tolerate dissenting views within the RPF … All major decisions affecting the organization are made by the party leader, President Paul Kagame. Organs of the party are merely rubber stamps that serve to legitimize decisions already made by the party leader and his very few close advisers behind the scenes. The party, like the rest of the country, is engulfed by fear, held hostage to President Kagame's arbitrary and repressive rule.[64]

Control Through Co-optation and Intimidation: RPF Rule 2000–2015

After taking direct power in 2000, Kagame and the RPF shifted further away from general use of violence and increasingly sought to exercise authority over the population through implicating them in a wide range of mass mobilization programs. The government required the general public to mobilize for gacaca courts, constitutional reform, elections, *umuganda* community labor, *ingando* re-education camps, land reform, and other programs. Failure to participate led not only to reprimands and fines but to heightened official scrutiny that

---

[62] Reyntjens, "Rwanda, Ten Years On," p. 181. As Sebarenzi explained, "When Kagame decided that he didn't like someone, they weren't just removed from power, they were ruined. Smear campaigns would begin from which the victims hardly ever recovered. 'Everyone ignores a dead dog in the road until it begins to smell – then they want it removed,' Kagame was supposedly fond of saying." Sebarenzi, *God Sleeps in Rwanda*, p. 159.

[63] Sebarenzi, *God Sleeps in Rwanda*, p. 169.

[64] Kayumba Nyamwasa, Patrick Karegeya, Theogene Rudasingwa, and Gerald Gahima, "Rwanda Briefing," unpublished document, August 2010.

made government services harder to access and exposed noncompliant individuals to the possibility of harassment, arrest, and even violence. Those people willing to embrace the RPF and its initiatives overtly and enthusiastically received preferential treatment, political positions, and other incentives. This created a system of punishments and rewards that pushed those outside the RPF's main constituency to adapt their behavior, strengthening RPF control and undercutting potential opposition. As Anuradha Chakravarty pointed out, "Under conditions of the unrivaled dominance of the RPF, elite political actors learned over time to regulate themselves in anticipation of benefits and protections, and to avoid targeted punishments."[65] The system of incentives and punishments pressured not just the elite but ordinary Rwandans as well.

The programs for popular mobilization were part of a broad agenda of social, political, and economic transformation launched in 2000 that, taken together, marked a sweeping effort to reorganize public life and ultimately change the character of Rwandan society. Many of the RPF's reform initiatives seemed motivated by a sincere desire to improve the lives of the Rwandan people. Yet the population experienced the numerous new regulations, repeated popular mobilizations, and ongoing institutional and spatial restructuring as heavy-handed and intrusive exercise of state power. As several scholars of post-genocide Rwanda have already noted,[66] James Scott's study of failed state-sponsored social engineering, *Seeing Like a State*, sheds light on how the RPF program for Rwanda can combine apparently well-intentioned ambitions for social improvement with disturbingly authoritarian tactics. According to Scott, many centralized modern states, directed by a vision of social improvement and technocratic expertise, have implemented plans for social reform that failed because they were imposed in a top-down fashion and did not adequately consult the populations most directly affected.[67] A "high modernist" ideology, "involving uncritical belief in the possibilities for the comprehensive planning of human settlement and production" and implemented by a bureaucratic

---

[65] Chakravarty, *Investing in Authoritarian Rule*, p. 74.

[66] On "high modernism" in Rwanda, see Scott Straus and Lars Waldorf, "Introduction: Seeing Like a Post-Conflict State," in Scott Straus and Lars Waldorf, eds., *Remaking Rwanda: State Building and Human Rights After Mass Violence*, Madison: University of Wisconsin Press, 2011, pp. 3–21; Newbury, "High Modernism at the Ground Level; Purdeková, *Making Ubumwe*; and Huggins, "Seeing Like a Neoliberal State?"

[67] James C. Scott, *Seeing Like a State: How Certain Schemes to Improve the Human Condition Have Failed*, New Haven: Yale University Press, 1998.

and authoritarian state unconstrained by an independent civil society, has driven programs like *ujamaa* villagization in Nyerere's Tanzania or the construction of planned cities like Brasilia.[68]

Yet in Rwandan, the RPF's authoritarian implementation of programs was driven not only by technocratic arrogance but also by the beliefs that most of the Rwandan people were "willing executioners"[69] of their neighbors and that genocide ideology remained deeply rooted within the population.[70] Hence, the RPF's agenda sought not simply to improve society according to a technocratic ideal but to transform Rwanda comprehensively and completely. The RPF regarded the population as not only ignorant but also flawed and morally deficient. Programs for political reform and economic development, thus, were linked directly to the ideas of transitional justice. Policies for urban renewal and agricultural restructuring sought to create a new prosperous country, rooted in a transformed unified national Rwandan identity. To resist the new Rwanda – for example, to object to being forced out of your home into a new suburban development or to oppose the requirements that you grow specified crops – was to hold onto the old Rwanda, the Rwanda of ignorance and genocide. Criticizing the government or challenging reforms demonstrated a genocidal ideology that had to be eliminated. To fail to buy into the narrative of the RPF as a progressive force for change was to embrace the narratives of the previous regime and to justify your exclusion from public life.

For much of the population, the supposedly benevolent initiatives to promote economic development, political participation, reconciliation, national unity, and accountability were built on a foundation of violent and repressive rule that prevailed between 1994 and 1999. As I will develop in the second half of the book, although the regime's use of violence diminished after 2000, the experiences of losing family members to RPF violence, being driven violently from an IDP or refugee camp, or being imprisoned for years without the possibility of a trial remained in many people's memories and shaped how they reacted to efforts to promote accountability, reconciliation, national unity, political participation, and economic development. Attempts to erase RPF oppression

[68] Ibid., pp. 4–5.

[69] This from the title of Daniel Jonah Goldhagen's controversial text asserting that Germans were much more actively supportive of the Holocaust than most scholarship indicates. *Hitler's Willing Executioners: Ordinary Germans and the Holocaust*, New York: Vintage Books, 1997.

[70] Recall Secretary General Murigande's assertion that the tragedy did not stop in 1994 but that, "we have continued to confront those who want to carry out genocide." Interview with Charles Murigande in Kigali, September 2002.

from popular memory ran up against people's lived experiences and encouraged cynicism.

Confronting the Past and Envisioning the Future through Political Reform

The 1998–1999 Village Urugwiro meetings provided the starting point for many of the post-2000 political programs and reforms. The government created the National Human Rights Commission and National Unity and Reconciliation Commission (NURC) (both mentioned in the Arusha Accords) in 1999. While the Human Rights Commission has maintained a low public profile, the NURC launched an extensive, highly visible program to promote national unity, influenced by the idea drawn from transitional justice of confronting the past to move forward. Under the leadership of dynamic executive secretaries – Aloysia Inyumba, then from 2002 Fatuma Ndangiza, who as a Muslim woman in an key leadership post embodied the very sort of inclusivity that the NURC and the RPF claimed to promote – the NURC initiated programs in civic education and conflict mediation. Intentionally multi-ethnic in its work, the NURC regularly referenced the genocide but focused more on building current community relations.[71]

Among the most important NURC initiatives was *ingando* reeducation camps, organized to teach the RPF's ideas on national unity to returned refugees, released prisoners, entering university students, and others. With roots in secret training camps for Tutsi held during the 1990–1993 civil war,[72] the Ministry of Youth Culture and Sports sponsored *ingando* within Rwanda as early as 1996, primarily for repatriated Tutsi. The idea to expand the program for more of the population came from the Village Urugwiro meetings. In 1999, the NURC began to sponsor *ingando* for ex-combatants returning from the DRC and Hutu militia members demobilized after the uprising in the northwest. The program was later required for prisoners released from detention, then expanded to include those perceived as future leaders – university students and newly elected government officials.[73] The NURC official in

---

[71] Paul Nantulya, Karin Alexander, Didace Kanyugu, et al., "Evaluation and Impact Assessment of the National Unity and Reconciliation Commission (NURC)," Kigali: Institute for Justice and Reconciliation, November 2005.

[72] Chi Mgbako, "*Ingando* Solidarity Camps: Reconciliation and Political Indoctrination in Post-Genocide Rwanda," *Harvard Human Rights Journal*, 201, 2005, 201–224, citation p. 208. Several survivors that I knew from before 1994 confirmed after the war that they had attended these camps and then returned to Rwanda.

[73] Purdeková, *Making Ubumwe*, offers the most complete consideration of the *ingando*.

charge of the *ingando* program told me that they had, "three objectives in civic education: to dispense education that will help inform the population, to help the population know their rights, and to help the population arrive at social unity."[74] He stated that the schedule included analysis of Rwanda's history, with a focus on "the origins and nature of divisions ... and the role of the community in the struggle against these divisions."[75] He and other officials insisted that the *ingando* held open discussion in which people were free to air their perspectives on Rwandan history.

My own interviews with *ingando* participants confirmed Chi Mgbako's conclusion that "political indoctrination is a dominant part of the *ingando* experience."[76] While defenders of *ingando* claimed that they used a Socratic teaching method, in which students were challenged through questioning to determine their own basic ideas, the method was actually closer to a Maoist struggle session, in which students were pushed to engage in self-criticism and led to a pre-determined set of ideas about history, politics, and society. Participants in the *ingando* were indoctrinated in the historical narrative described in Chapter 2, with emphasis on cultural unity and what Andrea Purdeková calls "de-ethnicization," the attempt to deconstruct and discredit ethnic identities.[77] Susan Thomson concluded that despite this focus, "The graduates of these *ingando* camps that I met do not believe in the national unity of the re-imagined past or in the reconciliation of a re-engineered future. Rather, they see the camps and their ideological discourse as efforts to exercise social control over adult Hutu men."[78]

In 2007, the NURC adapted *ingando* into a new program called *itorero*, referencing the historic training at the royal court of *intore*, the sons of chiefs destined to lead the Rwandan kingdom. The *itorero* now trains civil servants and other community leaders into a new class of *intore*, elites with a commitment to building the country "due to a change of

---

[74] Interview with Edouard Nkurayija, Director of Civic Education at the NURC in Kigali, May 30, 2001.

[75] Ibid.

[76] Mgbako, "*Ingando* Solidarity Camps," p. 211.

[77] Andrea Purdeková, "Repatriation and Reconciliation in Divided Society: The Case of Rwanda's 'Ingando,'" Refugee Studies Center Working Paper 43, Oxford University, January 2008. For the most extensive discussion of *ingando*, see Purdeková, *Making Ubumwe*, especially pp. 174–202.

[78] Having been detained and forced to attend an *ingando*, Susan Thomson, "Reeducation for Reconciliation: Participant Observation on *Ingando*," in Scott Straus and Lars Waldorf, *Remaking Rwanda: State Building and Human Rights after Mass Violence*, Madison: University of Wisconsin Press, 2011, pp. 331–339, provides a particularly interesting perspective. Citation p. 338.

Figure 6 Rwanda's new national flag (Photo by author).

the mindset, behavior and efficiency [*sic*] in work" who could serve as catalysts for national development.[79]

In another political reform seeking to reject Rwanda's past and create a new Rwandan identity, in 2001 the government announced plans to change the country's national symbols. Officials argued that the national anthem was divisive, because it contained references to the three ethnic groups, and that the flag and the national seal brought back hurtful memories to genocide survivors because the seal included an image of a machete (meant to symbolize Rwanda's agricultural nature) while the flag included red, which some said represented the blood of the Tutsi. The general population was invited to submit designs for the new symbols, and much was made of the fact that the winning entry for national anthem was composed by a Hutu man in prison on genocide charges. The reform thus allowed the regime to wipe away vestiges of previous regimes while appearing to be responsive to the public will. (See Figure 6.)[80]

Reforms of state structures also combined efforts to confront the past and reshape Rwandan political identities for the future. Beginning in

[79] National Unity and Reconciliation Commission, "Itorero Ry'gihugu," Kigali: NURC, January 12, 2010. Also Penal Reform International, "From Camp to Hill: The Reintegration of Released Prisoners," Research Report on the *Gacaca* VI, Paris: May 2004, 111; and Government of Rwanda, "National Itorero Commission (Strategy)," Kigali, November 2011.

[80] "Rwanda Adopts New Flag, Anthem in Effort to Heal," *Los Angeles Times*, January 1, 2002.

2000, the RPF made substantial reforms to state institutions that directly affected how people organized themselves and related to the state. The government adopted a program of political decentralization that claimed to give greater autonomy to local communities. As part of decentralization, 154 communes governed by burgomasters were consolidated into 91 districts and 15 municipalities governed by mayors and executive committees.[81] The government reordered political geography even more radically in 2006 by consolidating the country's twelve prefectures (already renamed provinces in 2001, with prefects renamed governors in 2003) into five large provinces with reduced authority, while consolidating districts from 106 into 30. Sectors, the level below districts, were vested with increased responsibilities.[82] The reordering of political space sought to reorient political loyalties and shape popular memory by – twice in five years – changing the names and boundaries of the units of government and the names of all government offices that people encountered most regularly and directly in their daily lives.

The RPF implemented the decentralization program of which the redrawn boundaries was the most visible part, "on the assumption that if decision making is undertaken at the local level where the problems are felt, there will be increased effectiveness, efficiency in service delivery, empowerment of citizens, and maximum participation of communities."[83] In practice, decentralization policies did more to streamline central state control than to transfer power to the local level.[84] The first administrative reorganization showed promise of transferring greater

[81] Pierre Munyura, "Rwanda Decentralization Assessment," Kigali: Strategies 2000 SARL, for USAID, July 2002, pp. 13–22; Jean-Paul Kimonyo, Noël Twagiramungu, and Christophe Kayumba, "Supporting the Post-Genocide Transition in Rwanda: The Role of the International Community," Democratic Transitions in Post-Conflict Societies Project, Working Paper 32, The Hague: The Netherlands Institute of International Relations Clingendael, 2004.

[82] "Rwanda: Government Said Planning to Redraw Provincial Boundaries," *The East African*, September 6, 2005; Oscar Kimanuka, "Rwanda: Giving Power to the People," *The East African*, January 10, 2006; "What Happens after Re-Demarcation?" *The New Times*, September 12, 2005.

[83] Munyura, "Rwanda Decentralization Assessment," p. 1.

[84] Comparative research demonstrates that decentralization has often involved the lack of a real shift of power to the local level. More substantial decentralization has generally been carried out by leaders who believe that it furthers their strategic interests. C.f., Richard Stren, "Decentralization: False Start or New Dawn?" United Nations Human Settlement Program, *Habitat Debate*, 8, no. 1, March 2002, 1–2; Kent Eaton, "Risky Business: Decentralization from Above in Chile and Uruguay," *Comparative Politics*, 37, no. 1, October 2004, 1–22; Kent Eaton, "Decentralization's Undemocratic Roots: Authoritarianism and Subnational Reform in Latin America," *Latin American Politics and Society*, 48, no. 1, 2006, 1–26; Kent Eaton, Kai Kaiser, and Paul Smoke, *The Political Economy of Decentralization Reforms: Implications for Aid Effectiveness*, Washington: World Bank, 2010; James Manor, *The Political Economy of Democratic Decentralization*, Washington: World Bank, 1999.

power to the local level by vesting local governance in elected executive committees. At the district level, the councils included a mayor and several vice-mayors, each with a distinct portfolio. The 2006 reform, however, eliminated much of the power (and salaries) of the executive committees and councils and transferred most responsibilities to paid administrators appointed by the central government. The appointed executive secretaries became the most important leader in each sector, and they were not beholden to the local population.[85]

Central control over these executive secretaries was strengthened through a required annual performance contract with the president, in which each executive secretary agreed to specific targets for how his or her district will work toward national goals in the coming year. These contracts were called *imihigo*, referring to an oath that warriors made with the king in pre-colonial Rwanda.[86] As Bert Ingelaere stated, the nature of the *imihigo* "implies that the chain of accountability goes upwards toward higher authorities and not downwards toward the population; the most powerful person is appointed, not elected."[87] While each district now established its own development plan, these were based directly on national goals set by the central government.[88] Continuing control over financing for districts and sectors reinforced central power. The result of all this, according to Purdeková, is that the new structure "effectively 'dispatches' rather than 'decentralises' control. The latter would suggest that the centre loses some of its hold, but what we witness is not devolution of power to conceive and decide, just the devolution of implementation."[89] State restructuring thus combines a rejection of the previous political system (in throwing out the political lines drawn by Habyarimana), a nod to pre-colonial Rwanda (in naming the *imihigo* system), and a contradictory approach to reshaping the Rwandan future

[85] Bert Ingelaere, "Living the Transition: A Bottom Up Perspective on Rwanda's Political Transition," Discussion Paper 2007.06, Institute of Development Policy and Management, University of Antwerp, November 2007 provides an excellent overview of the reformed local administrative structure.

[86] David Booth and Frederick Golooba-Mutebi, "Developmental Patrimonialism? The Case of Rwanda," *African Affairs*, 111, no. 444, May 2012, 379–403; Ansoms, "Re-engineering Rural Society," p. 306; Ingelaere, "Peasants, Power, and Ethnicity," pp. 228–289.

[87] Ingelaere, "Peasants, Power, and Ethnicity," pp. 288–289.

[88] Ansoms, "Re-engineering Rural Society," p. 306.

[89] Andrea Purdeková, "'Even If I am Not Here, There are So Many Eyes': Surveillance and State Reach in Rwanda," *Journal of Modern African Studies*, 49, no. 3, 2011, 475–497, citation p. 486. Malin Hasselskog and Isabell Schierenbeck, "National Policy in Local Practice: the Case of Rwanda," *Third World Quarterly*, 36, no. 5, 2015, 950–966 similarly found that in decentralization "neither local participation nor downward accountability was enhanced," p. 962.

(purported devolution of power to the population that actually increases the power of the central government).

The transition to a supposedly democratic political system was another example of the inherent contradictions in RPF initiatives. Kagame's ascension to the presidency took place at the beginning of a political process that the government characterized as a democracy transition. Elections for public offices were phased in beginning in 1999 at the level of the smallest administrative units, the cell and sector, expanding to the district level in 2001. The RPF leaders hoped that shifting to elected leaders would increase public connection to the government and improve domestic and international legitimacy. At the same time, they lacked confidence that the population was ready for a fully free electoral process. The actual transition, thus, sought to address legacies of authoritarian governance but actually consolidated authoritarian rule.

In 2001, the government launched a constitutional reform process that involved popular consultation but was tightly controlled by the RPF. Former head of the RPF's political wing and member of the RPF inner circle, Tito Rutaremara, chaired the Legal and Constitutional Reform Commission. They presented proposed constitutional principles at public meetings around the country ostensibly seeking feedback, but the setting was not conducive to honest exchange. As one civil society leader told me, "The Constitutional Commission has a consultation process, but the population is skeptical. People doubt that their ideas will be taken into account. They say that they are going to consider the opinions of the majority, but how will this be determined?"[90] The constitution was put up for a vote in May 2003 and passed with 90 percent support. Although the constitution guaranteed human rights and democracy, many Rwandans questioned the degree of democracy that the RPF would allow. The leader of a national civil society group told me:

Democracy and good governance are good principles, but they need to be put into action. That is always the problem, to put them into action. I don't personally see much democratic opening. It is true that just after the war, all of life was militarized. That has diminished. But as for democratic opening, I don't really see it. According to some testimonies, there were cases where the authorities elected were not the ones who won. There were candidates that the RPF absolutely wanted elected, and in most cases, they were elected.[91]

The transition culminated in 2003 with presidential elections in August and parliamentary elections in September and October. While the RPF claimed that the 2003 elections marked a transition to full democracy,

<hr>

[90] Interview in Kigali, August 29, 2002.
[91] Interview in Kigali, August 27, 2002.

in fact the RPF leadership tightly controlled the elections and the results allowed the party to assume an even more dominant hold on government. In the 2003 elections, only parties in close alliance with the RPF were allowed to operate freely, while parties that sought to remain independent of the RPF were suppressed. The Forum of Political Parties was written into the 2003 constitution, allowing the RPF to veto parties and candidates, yet at the same time the regime continued to aggressively suppress parties it deemed as presenting a potential threat. In May 2001, former President Pasteur Bizimungu announced the formation of a new party, the Party for Democratic Renewal-Ubuyanja (PDR-Ubuyanja). As he asserted at the time, "If you do not share the ideas of those in power, you are threatened and put in jail."[92] As if to prove his point, the government immediately banned the party, and the organizers were arrested, beaten, killed, or disappeared. Bizimungu was himself arrested, tried, and sentenced in 2004 to fifteen years in prison, though Kagame pardoned him in 2007.[93]

Even more extensive actions were taken to subdue the RPF's most persistent rival, the MDR. In March 2003, a parliamentary commission issued an official report charging the MDR with encouraging "divisionism" and "genocide ideology," and in April, the parliament voted unanimously to ban the MDR. The report accused forty-seven individuals by name of supporting divisionism; one disappeared shortly before the party was banned and several others fled the country.[94] The MDR presidential candidate, former Prime Minister Twagiramungu, was allowed to appear on the ballot as an independent, but the government forbade him from organizing rallies and confiscated his campaign literature, while the pro-RPF press attacked and threatened him. According to official results, Kagame won the 2003 elections with 95.1 percent of the vote, compared to Twagiramungu's 3.6 percent, but outside observers widely condemned the elections as fraudulent, both because of the pressure on the population to vote for Kagame and the manipulation of the results.[95] In the parliamentary elections, the RPF and its official allies won 73.8 percent of the vote. The rest of the vote went to

---

[92] Quoted in Reyntjens, "Rwanda, Ten Years On," p. 193.

[93] Ibid.

[94] Human Rights Watch, "Preparing for Elections: Tightening Control in the Name of Unity," New York: Human Rights Watch, May 8, 2003; Amnesty International, "Rwanda: Escalating Repression Against Political Opposition, AFR 47/004/2003, April 22, 2003; Republic of Rwanda, *Rapport de la Commission Parlementaire*, 2003.

[95] The observer team from the Norwegian Center for Human Rights noted that, "even though the presidential elections were conducted in a technically good manner, the degree of pressure to vote for the incumbent candidate cannot be underestimated." Ingrid Samset and Orrvar Dalby, "Rwanda: Presidential and Parliamentary Elections

parties allied with the RPF.[96] The Rwandan population experienced the elections not as a transition to democracy but as a series of forced mobilizations that ultimately helped to consolidate RPF rule.

Subsequent elections have been no more free or fair. After the 2003 vote, rumors spread that districts that voted too heavily for the opposition were punished by cuts in funding and projects, while their administrators were sacked. People also claimed that despite a supposedly secret ballot, individuals who voted for Twagiramungu were harassed and intimidated.[97] In subsequent elections the population thus feared the consequences of voting against the RPF, and administrators worked to ensure that their communities provided the RPF with maximum votes possible. In 2008 parliamentary elections, official results gave the RPF coalition only 78.8 percent of the vote, but a European Union Election Observation Mission found that actual support for the RPF was 98.4 percent,[98] suggesting that the RPF artificially inflated results for other parties to make the elections appear more legitimate.

Blatant intimidation marred the 2010 presidential elections. A group of dissident RPF members, mostly Anglophone Tutsi returnees from Uganda, formed the Democratic Green Party of Rwanda (DGPR) in 2009 but were prevented from holding an official foundational convention. Both the DGPR and another new party, the United Democratic Forces-Inkingi (*Forces démocratiques unifiées Inkingi*, FDU-Inkingi), were prevented from officially registering and so could not field presidential candidates. Victoire Ingabire, the FDU-Inkingi's leader, was physically attacked, then later arrested for "genocide ideology" after she spoke publicly at a genocide memorial about the need to commemorate both the Tutsi victims of the genocide and Hutu victims of crimes against humanity. She was released on bail then re-arrested just after the elections and ultimately tried and sentenced to eight years in prison. The Social Party-Imberakuri was allowed to register in 2009, but its president and general secretary were arrested, preventing the party from fielding a presidential

2003," Oslo: Norwegian Center for Human Rights, 2003, www.cmi.no/publications/file/1770-rwanda-presidential-and-parliamentary-elections.pdf. Chakravarty quotes a respondent as saying, "We were ordered to elect Kagame because he was the only candidate…we could not refuse to elect a King who came back" (p. 248). Anuradha Chakravarty, "Navigating the Middle Ground: The Political Values of Ordinary Hutu in Post-Genocide Rwanda," *African Affairs*, 113, no. 451, 2014, 232–253.

[96] European Union Election Observation Mission, *Rwanda: Élection presidentielle 25 Aôut 2003; Élections legislatives 29 et 30 Septembre, 2 Octobre 2003* (final report), Brussels: European Union, 2003.

[97] Begley, "'Resolved to Fight the Ideology of Genocide.'"

[98] European Union Election Observation Mission, "Final Report: Legislative Elections to the Chamber of Deputies," 15–18 September 2008, Brussels: European Union, September 2008, www.euromrwanda.org/EN/Final_Report.html.

candidate. On July 13, 2010, the vice-president of the DGPR was assassinated. Without any serious opposition and in a climate of intimidation, Kagame won re-election with 93.8 percent of the vote.[99]

The RPF's use of elections confuses many outside observers, who feel either that the RPF's high election numbers serve as evidence of its popularity or reveal the regime's authoritarian nature, leading them to ask why the regime bothers with elections at all.[100] In fact, the use of elections has long been a standard feature of authoritarian regimes seeking to mobilize and distract their populations and build international legitimacy.[101] What distinguishes the form of elections practiced by the RPF from elections sponsored by past authoritarian regimes is the inclusion of other political parties and candidates that give a greater appearance of competition, even though the final result is pre-determined. Yet this practice – what Steven Levitsky and Lucan A. Way term "competitive authoritarianism"[102] – is common to many post–Cold War authoritarian regimes. As William Dobson points out from a comparison of Russia, Venezuela, Malaysia, and Egypt, allowing highly constrained competition can bolster regimes by appeasing the international community and distracting and enervating potential opponents.[103]

[99] Amnesty International, "Pre-Election Attacks on Rwandan Politicians and Journalists Condemned," London: Amnesty International, August 4, 2010, www.amnesty.org/en/news-and-updates/pre-election-attacks-rwandan-politicians-and-journalists-condemned-2010-08-05; Eric Brown, "Rwandan Genocide: Is Rwanda Gearing up for Another Genocide," New York: Human Rights First, February 23, 2010; "'Disturbing Events' Marred Rwandan Leader's Re-Election, US Says," *New York Times*, August 15, 2010; Sudarsan Raghavan, "Rwanda's Success Story Fails to Silence Concerns about Rights: Slayings and Censorship Mar Campaign Season, Top Opponents Barred," *Washington Post*, August 9, 2010.

[100] In an interview for a syndicated public radio program surrounding the 2010 presidential elections, after I had described the ongoing political repression in Rwanda, the interviewer asked, "Well why is Kagame so popular?" When I asked her basis for believing that he was popular, she said, "He's expected to win the elections by a wide margin," as though that proved his popularity.

[101] Rejecting the idea that autocracies use elections to promote domestic legitimacy, Jillian Schwedler and Laryssa Chomiak, "And the Winner Is ... Authoritarian Elections in the Arab World," *Middle East Report*, Spring 2006, argues that, "The explanation for why authoritarian regimes hold elections is more likely to be found among these five reasons: to carry out a real commitment to democratization; to distract citizens from other crises; to respond to foreign pressure; to display state power; and simply because they have held them in the past," 13. See also, Fred M. Hayward, ed., *Elections in Independent Africa*, Boulder: Westview Press, 1987.

[102] Steven Levitsky and Lucan A. Way, *Competitive Authoritarianism*, New York: Cambridge University Press, 2010.

[103] William Dobson, *The Dictator's Learning Curve: Inside the Global Battle for Democracy*, New York: Random House, 2012. See also, Jason Brownlee, *Authoritarianism in an Age of Democratization*, New York: Cambridge University Press, 2007; Dan Slater, *Ordering Power: Contentious Politics and Authoritarian Leviathans in Southeast Asia*, New York: Cambridge University Press, 2010.

The organization of elections is important in mobilizing the population and integrating them into the state,[104] but the RPF does not trust Rwandans to use democracy wisely. As Tito Rutaremara, then head of the Legal and Constitutional Reform Commission, told me:

If you give freedom to someone who is ignorant and incompetent, he will not know how to use it … Here in Rwanda, democracy doesn't mean democracy; it means majority. Officials and others hide behind ethnicity and call it democracy. But when you go to the population, they tell you something different: 'The problems come from the middle class. You people from political parties, you people from Kigali, come to consensus.' We need a period of building consensus before we come to a more confrontational democracy.[105]

The 2003 constitution included a two-term limit for the presidency, a principle President Kagame claimed at the time to accept. Yet in advance of 2017 elections, calls for term limits to be eliminated proliferated. Kagame supporters organized a campaign to collect signatures in favor of amending the constitution and delivered thousands of petitions to parliament. Yet as I discuss in Chapter 6, this did not reflect the popular will, as people were coerced into signing the petitions. Though he claimed to be reluctant to stay on, Kagame apparently dismissed two senior members of the RPF leadership from ministerial posts because they opposed his bid for a third term.[106] Parliament adopted the proposed constitutional amendment unanimously, and 98 percent of the population voted in favor of the change in a December 2015 referendum.[107]

One aspect of the RPF's program of political reform deserves particular praise – the promotion of women's political participation. Women have served in a number of influential national positions, including as president of the Supreme Court, president of the gacaca courts, leader of the NURC, Mayor of Kigali, and Ombudsman. The post-genocide governments regularly included a number of women in the cabinet. Women were well represented at other level as well. The RPF ensured that the new electoral system adopted in 2003 would guarantee significant representation for women, setting aside 30 percent of seats in the lower house for women while also requiring parties to include women in their party lists. As a result, in the 2003 parliamentary elections, women won

[104] Murray Edelman, *The Symbolic Uses of Politics*, Urbana: University of Illinois Press, 1964.
[105] Tito Rutaremara, Head of Legal and Constitutional Reform Commission, Interview in Kigali, August 29, 2002.
[106] Edmund Kagire, "Kagame drops last two RPF 'historicals,'" *The East African*, June 1, 2013.
[107] "Rwandan Senate Votes to Allow Third Term for Kagame," Aljazeera, November 17, 2015; Tracy McVeigh, "Rwanda Votes to Give President Kagame Right to Rule until 2034," *The Guardian*, December 19, 2015.

48.8 percent of seats, giving Rwanda the highest percentage of women in any legislature. In the 2008 elections, Rwanda became the first country in the world where women constituted a legislative majority. While the authoritarian nature of the Rwandan state limits the influence of the parliament, including for women representatives, significant legal reforms to benefit women have been adopted, such as increasing women's inheritance rights.[108] The RPF created opportunities for other marginalized groups as well, such as handicapped and youth, who were also guaranteed representation in government institutions.

Limiting Dissent, Manufacturing Support

Just as the RPF gradually extended control over all formal political society by co-opting, threatening, or banning every competing political party, they also systematically subdued civil society and the media. They initially used extralegal means – attacks, illegal detentions, and assassinations – to silence critics, but after 2000 the RPF used the law itself as an effective tool to hobble groups that they believed threaten their hegemony. The RPF drew on the legacy of the genocide and laudable goal of preventing future ethnic violence to adopt a legal framework that allowed them to crack down on critics in the name of accountability and genocide prevention. Charges of genocide complicity continued to be used to disqualify some Hutu politicians and activists, but a series of other laws proved very effective tools for suppressing potential dissent. In 2001, Rwanda's parliament adopted a Law on Prevention, Suppression, and Punishment of the Crimes of Discrimination and Sectarianism that included language criminalizing the undefined crime of "divisionism." This law made the growing taboo on discussing ethnic identity formally illegal. This law effectively precludes complaints of discrimination against Hutu and also allows those who would criticize the government to be accused of fomenting division. The government cracked down on Bizimungu's PDR-Ubuyanja with accusations

---

[108] Longman, "Rwanda: Achieving Equality or Serving an Authoritarian State?"; Jennie E. Burnet, "Gender Balance and the Meanings of Women in Governance in Post-Genocide Rwanda," *African Affairs*, 107, no. 428, May 2008, 361–386. Jennie E. Burnet, "Women Have Found Respect: Gender Quotas, Symbolic Representation, and Female Empowerment in Rwanda," *Politics and Gender*, 7, no. 3, September 2011, 303–334, finds that the increasing political representation of women in Rwanda has produced tangible benefits, including a greater willingness for women to speak out in public, greater access to education, more women involved in business, and more equity in marital relations. Yet she also notes that women's involvement in politics has done little to improve the perceptions of a political system that many see as corrupt and undemocratic.

of divisionism. Other groups and individuals were accused of association with PDR-Ubuyanja and by extension of promoting divisionism. Laurien Ntezimana was a long-time organizer of Catholic reconciliation programs whose organization, Association Modeste et Innocent (AMI) included the word "ubuyanja," a term meaning rebirth or renewal, in the masthead of their journal, *Ubuntu.* In January 2002, Ntezimana and two others from his organization were arrested. Though released after a month, their organization was banned and *Ubuntu* was forced to cease publication.[109]

Laws banning negation of the genocide and "genocide ideology" have been used to similar effect. Article 13 of the 2003 constitution declared that, "Revisionism, negationism and trivialisation of genocide are punishable by the law."[110] The constitution also sets as the state's first "fundamental principle," "fighting the ideology of genocide and all its manifestations; – eradication of ethnic, regional and other divisions and promotion of national unity."[111] Banning the denial that the killing of Tutsi in 1994 was genocide resembles European laws banning Holocaust denial, but as Lars Waldorf explained, in Rwanda genocide denial has been conflated with genocide ideology in a way that "has made it much harder to distinguish true negationism from unwanted political criticism."[112] In 2004, a process similar to the one used to ban the MDR was directed against Rwanda's last remaining independent human rights organization, the LIPRODHOR, which had faced growing harassment for several years. A parliamentary report claimed that some members of LIPRODHOR had been involved in the 1994 genocide and that others were guilty of promoting genocide ideology. The report linked LIPRODHOR to recent attacks on Tutsi genocide survivors and urged that the organization be banned.[113] A list was leaked of LIPRODHOR activists to be arrested, leading a number to flee the country. The parliamentary report also named several international non-governmental

---

[109] Interview with Laurien Ntezimana, Butare, September 3, 2002. See also Human Rights Watch, "Preparing for Elections."

[110] Government of Rwanda, "Constitution of the Republic of Rwanda," June 4, 2003.

[111] Ibid., Article 9.

[112] Lars Waldorf, "Instrumentalizing Genocide: The RPF's Campaign against 'Genocide Ideology,'" in Scott Straus and Lars Waldorf, eds., *Remaking Rwanda: State Building and Human Rights after Mass Violence*, Madison: University of Wisconsin Press, 2011, pp. 48–66.

[113] Parliament of Rwanda, "La où l'Idéologie Génocidaire se fair Observer au Rwanda," Kigali, June 2004, available at www.grandslacs.net/doc/3301.pdf.

organizations, including Care, Norwegian People's Aid, and Trocaire, as purveyors of genocide ideology.[114]

A 2006 Senate commission issued a lengthy report on genocide ideology that "conflates genocide ideology with any ethnic discourse, political criticism, revisionism, and negationism."[115] A fourth parliamentary commission issued a report in 2007 focused on genocide ideology in schools, accusing some school administrators, teachers, and students of manifesting genocide ideology, leading a number to flee the country. Parliament adopted a law in 2008 against genocide ideology that included only a vague definition of the term, allowing considerable discretion in enforcement.[116] The desire to prevent genocide ideology and stop people from promoting social divisions is understandable, but in practice accusations of divisionism and genocide ideology have been used mostly to silence government critics.

Other strategies allowing the RPF to assert control over civil society and the media included a 2001 civil society law that required non-governmental groups officially to register, allowing considerable control over their organization, financing, and activities. Following the model of the Forum of Political Parties, the regime used self-regulation to enforce its will, with the four leading civil society umbrella groups establishing a Civil Society Platform in 2004 that regulated relations between civil society and the government, while the Media High Council regulated the content of the media. In 2009, a new media law regulated journalists by setting educational and other standards that are selectively enforced.[117] The RPF also continued to use co-optation to take control of organizations. In 2013, the government again targeted LIPRODHOR – weak but still functioning – to install a sympathetic board of directors.[118] Even the organization of genocide widows, Association of Genocide Widows Agahozo (Association des Veuves du Génocide Agahozo, AVEGA), was led by a repatriated Tutsi rather than a survivor. When necessary to assert control, the RPF remained willing to use coercive force. The government seized and suspended newspapers and shut down radio stations.

<hr>

[114] Amnesty International, "Rwanda: Deeper into the Abyss – Waging War on Civil Society," AFR 47/013/2004, London: Amnesty International, July 6, 2004; Amnesty International, "Safer to Stay Silent: The Chilling Effects of Rwanda's Laws on 'Genocide Ideology' and 'Sectarianism,'" AFR 47/005/2010, London: Amnesty International, August 2010, p. 32.

[115] Waldorf, "Instrumentalizing Genocide," p. 54.

[116] Ibid.

[117] Amnesty International, "Safer to Stay Silent."

[118] Amnesty International, "Rwanda: Official Interference in Affairs of Human Rights NGO Places Independent Human Rights Work in Peril," London: Amnesty International, August 16, 2013.

The BBC's Kinyarwanda-language broadcasts were twice suspended.[119] Anjan Sundaram, who ran a training program for journalists in Kigali for five years, listed sixty journalists killed, attacked, arrested, or otherwise harassed in Rwanda between 1995 and 2014. The government's efforts to control journalists, he argued, forced them to self-censor and silenced journalists with fear and paranoia.[120]

RPF efforts to rein in civil society and the media have targeted all ethnic groups. The umbrella survivors organization, Ibuka, became increasingly critical of the government in the late 1990s, decrying the government's failure to provide financial compensation to genocide survivors. Leaders of the community of genocide survivors saw the 2000 assassination of Assiel Kabera, former prefect of Kibuye Prefecture and advisor to President Bizimungu, as a warning, since one of his brothers was vice-president of Ibuka and the other was executive secretary of the National Fund for Genocide Survivors (FARG). Both fled the country, as did founding Ibuka member Bosco Rutagengwa and Secretary General Anastase Murumba.[121] The board of Ibuka then appointed Antoine Mugesera, a member of the RPF Central Committee who was outside Rwanda in 1994, as new executive secretary. The observations of Janvier Kanyamashuli, Director of FARG, effectively revealed the government's perspective on the affair:

The original [Ibuka] founders are out of the country, they have fled. They were very hot, but they were not close to the members of Ibuka. They wanted a war with the government. Their confrontational approach was not advantageous to the government. Ibuka today works closely with the NURC. They have taken a major role in gacaca. They have opted for a method of consensus and compromise.[122]

RPF efforts to quash dissent have extended to every corner of society. In 2014, Kizito Mihigo, a genocide survivor and popular gospel singer, fell afoul of the regime when he released a song, "The Significance of Death," in which he called for honoring the memory not only of victims

---

[119] Timothy Longman, "The Uses and Abuses of the Media: Rwanda Before and After the Genocide," in Clara Ramirez-Barat, ed., *Transitional Justice, Culture, and Society: Beyond Outreach*, New York: Social Science Research Council, 2014.

[120] Anjan Sundaram, *Bad News: Last Journalists in a Dictatorship*, New York: Doubleday, 2016.

[121] Interview with Noel Twagiramungu, Executive Director of LDGL, Kigali, August 28, 2002; International Crisis Group, "Rwanda at the End of Transition: A Necessary Political Liberalization," Brussels: ICG, November 13, 2002; Human Rights Watch, "The Search for Security." Kabera himself was outside Rwanda in 1994, but his two brothers were considered survivors. Kayijabo was also head of the human rights collective CLADHO.

[122] Interview with Janvier Kanyamashuli, Director of the National Fund for Genocide Survivors, Kigali, August 31, 2002.

of the genocide but also of victims of massacres, presumably meaning Hutu. He was arrested and charged with conspiring against the regime then confessed in a public press conference where he was handcuffed and appeared to show signs of torture.[123]

Rwanda today boasts numerous civil society organizations, but almost none are independent of the state. Rwanda has moved toward a corporatist structure, in which civil society groups help to implement government policy rather than serving as vehicles for interest groups to express their ideas to the state. A journalist close to the regime reflected the attitude of RPF supporters that civil society and the media were more a threat than a resource. "We have been able to contain the elites who might otherwise do bad. We need to continue to limit elite society."[124] Human rights leader Noel Twagiramungu told me that after Bizimungu launched his political party, President Kagame made clear to civil society that they needed to stop relying on international support and instead ally with the government: "At a speech a few weeks later, Kagame said 'The international community is not ready to help us, just to use us. There is no free lunch ... You in civil society, you have to make a choice: working with your government hand in hand or remaining beggars ... Neither for the government nor for civil society, there is no free lunch.'"[125] The head of a leading civil society group said that his organization:

still works, but we have troubles. Many of the founders have left the country ... There is a general impression that civil society has lost its weight. Since 1997, we have seen a weakening of groups due to the infiltration of some of them and the intimidation of others ... There are no longer any activists. Some have left the groups, many have fled the country, a few have been brought into government. The press merely plays a role in diffusion of information from the government. They just read what they are given.[126]

No obvious options exist for those unhappy with the government and its policies to express their discontent. The RPF even showed its willingness to pursue Rwandans who would try to criticize the regime from abroad. A former close Kagame ally turned dissident, Kayumba Nyamwasa, survived two assassination attempts in exile in South Africa, while former intelligence chief Patrick Karegeya was killed in Johannesburg in 2014.[127]

<hr>

[123] Jonathan W. Rosen, "Dissident 'Choirboy': Rwandan Gospel Star on Trial," Al Jazeera English, December 11, 2014; Emmanuel Hakizimana and Gallican Gasana, "Le Président Kagame Vient de Révéler sa Plus Grande Peur," *L'Aut' Journal*, April 17, 2014.

[124] Interview in Kigali, September 5, 2002.

[125] Noel Twagiramungu, Executive Director of LDGL, August 28, 2002.

[126] Interview in Kigali, August 27, 2002.

[127] David Smith, "Rwanda's Former Spy Chief 'Murdered' in South Africa," *The Guardian*, January 2, 2014.

Not content to limit the ability of Rwandans to dissent, the regime has sought to mobilize the population to display active support. After the 2000 transition to direct RPF rule, the regime began to require popular mobilization for a variety of public programs. People were required to attend numerous public meetings held to discuss the transition, the proposed constitution, and elections, and people were mobilized to vote in a series of elections between 1999 and 2003. The gacaca courts involved extensive and regular popular mobilization beginning in 2001. Once the courts were launched nationally in 2005, communities had to gather weekly for much of a day to deliberate on genocide cases. A program of collective public labor called *umuganda*, originally implemented by the Habyarimana regime to bring communities together to repair roads, build bridges, terrace fields, and do other community improvement projects, was gradually reinstituted in communities across Rwanda as early as 1998. In 2007, the parliament adopted a law mandating *umuganda* throughout the country, with all adults required to join their communities in service programs on the last Saturday of each month (though in many communities, particularly in rural areas, *umuganda* occurs more often).[128]

Some of these public programs, such as *umuganda* and gacaca, levied fines against those who failed to attend. Others, such as public meetings or the annual genocide commemorations, do not legally require attendance, but participation is expected. Officials note those who do not participate and identify them as potential troublemakers who need to receive increased scrutiny. Thus, when RPF party leaders or government officials call, most people show up because they fear the consequences of failing to do so.

Vision 2020: An Ambitious Development Agenda

The restrictions on political and civil life described above were premised in part on mistrust of the population and an assumption that security remained fragile, but limitations on free expression and political participation were also justified on the assumption that what most Rwandans ultimately really wanted was peace and prosperity. As one NURC official told me:

I don't think that the Rwandan population is ready for a democracy of one-man-one-vote. There are prerequisites. The population is not ready for multiparty

---

[128] On a variety of these community mobilization programs, see Huggins, "Seeing Like a Neoliberal State?"

government. We need to teach them more. They first need to eat. We need to fight poverty. We need to teach people about their rights. We need to train the population to respect diversity. The elections next year will be really hot. What the peasants want is not that but security. The intellectuals want elections. But for peasants, hunger is a greater concern.[129]

Peace was regarded as a necessary precondition for economic development, and dissent was regarded as disruptive and destabilizing. Kagame held up Singapore as a model for rapid economic development – a small densely populated country without natural resources where strict government control and good governance pushed the population into prosperity that gained the government popular support despite its authoritarian practices.[130]

RPF leaders had a strong commitment to modernization as an engine for economic growth. The six pillars of Vision 2020[131] that have guided much of Rwanda's policy program since 2000 reflect a technocratic approach to governance that places great faith in economists and other experts.[132] The flip side of the faith in expertise and modernization is a distrust and disdain for ordinary Rwandans, particularly rural farmers. The approach Rwandan leaders take to policy development and implementation reflects a belief that most Rwandans are backward and must be pushed to embrace new modes of behavior, social structures, and economic practices they are likely to resist but that will ultimately benefit them. According to An Ansoms:

The social engineering ambitions of the Rwandan government officials reveal a very top-down developmentalist agenda without much room for grassroots participation or for bottom-up feedback. Instead, the elite approaches law and policy as tools for 'shaping' society, and often neglects to consider the institutional and environmental conditions in which the new law(s) will operate … The elite believes in a rapid modernization and professionalization of the agricultural

---

[129] Interview in Kigali, August 31, 2002.

[130] Christina Caryl, "Africa's Singapore Dream: Why Rwanda's Leader Styles Himself as the Heir to Lee Kuan Yew," *Foreign Policy*, April 2, 2015.

[131] The six pillars are, "Good governance and a capable state"; a shift to a knowledge-based economy; promotion of free-market private enterprise; development of the infrastructure; commercialization of agriculture; and regional and international integration. Ministry of Finance and Economic Planning, "Rwanda Vision 2020," pp. 11–19. For useful discussions of Vision 2020, see An Ansoms and Donatella Rostagno, "Rwanda's Vision 2020 Halfway Through: What the Eye Does Not See," *Review of African Political Economy*, 39, no. 133, September 2012, 427–450 and Sterling Recker, "Vision 2020: An Analysis of Policy Implementation and Agrarian Change in Rural Rwanda," PhD Dissertation, University of Missouri-St. Louis, July 2014.

[132] On technocratic governance, see Beverly H. Burris, *Technocracy at Work*, Albany: SUNY Press, 1993 and William Easterly, *Tyranny of Experts: Economists, Dictators, and the Forgotten Rights of the Poor*. New York: Basic Books, 2015.

sector, and strongly rejects subsistence-based agriculture, although it remains the way of life for the majority of the rural population.[133]

Christopher Huggins notes, "The 'good governance' concept in Rwanda [one of the pillars of Vision 2020] has greater emphasis on efficiency and anti-corruption principles, and less on citizen empowerment, than elsewhere."[134]

The *imidugudu* program was a first major attempt to restructure Rwandan society. Motivated by the ideas that villages make greater economic sense and are more sustainable and that concentrating settlement facilitates service delivery, the villagization program, which remains official policy, represents a major reordering of Rwanda's rural social structure.[135] Since 2000, the government has implemented a variety of additional rural economic programs, many of them also highly disruptive to traditional social structures and practices. As a group of scholars of rural development in Rwanda has written:

[T]he government's vision for a professional, market-driven and efficient agricultural sector appears incompatible with traditional Rwandan habitat and cultivation patterns as well as landownership arrangements ... and risk-averse agricultural practices, common among Rwandan peasants. Therefore, Rwandan authorities believe that a profound reorganization of rural space is required.[136]

Land reform has been a major government initiative. As families have grown and fields have been divided and subdivided over the generations, an increasing number of Rwandan households farm land that is simply too limited to produce the food necessary for subsistence. Since families cannot allow fields to lie fallow but must keep them in constant cultivation, the soil has become increasingly infertile.[137]

---

[133] Ansoms, "Re-Engineering Rural Society," pp. 308–309.

[134] Christopher Huggins, "'Control Grabbing' and Small Scale Agricultural Intensification: Emerging Patterns of State-facilitated 'Agricultural Investment' in Rwanda." *The Journal of Peasant Studies*, May 14, 2014, 368.

[135] Saskia Van Hoyweghen, "The Rwandan Villagisation Programme: Resettlement for Reconstruction?" in Didier Goyvaerts, ed., *Conflict and Ethnicity in Central Africa*, Tokyo: Institute for the Study of Languages and Cultures of Asia and Africa, 2000, pp. 209–224. These ideas are surprisingly similar to the justifications for the *ujamaa* villagization policy in Tanzania in the 1970s, a policy almost universally recognized as a major failure in both social and economic terms. See Goran Hyden, *Beyond Ujamaa in Tanzania: Underdevelopment and an Uncaptured Peasantry*, Berkeley: University of California Press, 1980.

[136] An Ansoms, Giuseppe Cioffo, Chris Huggins, and Jude Murison, "The Reorganization of Rural Space in Rwanda: Habitat Concentration, Land Consolidation and Collective Marshland Cultivation," in An Ansoms and Thea Hilhorst, eds., *Losing Your Land: Dispossession in the Great Lakes*, Suffolk: James Currey, 2014, pp. 163–185.

[137] Catherine André and Jean-Philippe Platteau, "Land Relations Under Unbearable Stress: Rwanda Caught in the Malthusian Trap," *Journal of Economic Behavior and Organization*, 34, no. 1, 1998, 1–47.

Land distribution and use are thus very serious problems, and to address them, the government has adopted several land reform programs. The government began to develop a new land policy in 2000, which culminated in the 2005 Organic Land Law and 2013 Land Law that required all land to be officially registered and all land sales to be regulated by the state. The idea of providing poor farmers with formal titles to their land and then regulating land sales within a market system, popularized by Peruvian economist Hernando de Soto, has become a key idea promoted by international development agencies and embraced by the RPF regime to fight poverty and promote rural development.[138]

While the land reform laws make economic sense on their surface, in practice like other well-meaning government policies, they take little account of local realities and have been implemented in a heavy-handed fashion. Rwanda's policy encourages land consolidation, even though "small family farms make up over 90 percent of all production units."[139] Rwandan farmers have traditionally maintained a number of dispersed fields as a risk aversion strategy, since fields on drier high hillsides produce in years with heavy rains, while fields in valleys produce in dry years. Pushing for consolidation thus exposes farmers to greater risk. In an attempt to prevent land from being subdivided into unsustainably small plots, the law forbids families from passing on holdings smaller than one hectare. Yet "three quarters of all households have landholdings below one hectare."[140] A number of factors in the land policy favor wealthy farmers. The land registration process required farmers to pay small fees that many poorer farmers did not feel that they could pay; meanwhile, wealthier farmers paid the fees and received land titles.[141] According to Huggins, while Rwanda has prevented large-scale land acquisition by foreign investors and has less illegal land grabbing than many African countries, because policies favor land consolidation, land dispossession and consolidation have continued to occur.[142]

Until fairly recently, marshlands in much of Rwanda were considered public land and not cultivated. Many marshes began to be cleared in the

---

[138] Hernando de Soto, *The Mystery of Capital: Why Capitalism Triumphs in the West and Fails Everywhere Else*, New York: Basic Books, 2000.

[139] Ansoms, "Re-engineering Rural Society," p. 299.

[140] Ansoms et al., "The Reorganization of Rural Space in Rwanda," p. 169.

[141] An Ansoms and Jude Murison, "De 'Saoudi' au 'Darfur': L'Histoire d'un Marais au Rwanda," in Filip Reyntjens, Stef Vandeginste, and M Verpoorten, eds., *L'Afrique des Grands Lacs: Annuaire 2011–2012*, Paris: L'Harmattan, 2012.

[142] Christopher Huggins, "Land Grabbing and Land Tenure Security in Post-Genocide Rwanda," in An Ansoms and Thea Hilhorst, eds., *Losing Your Land: Dispossession in the Great Lakes*, Suffolk: James Currey, 2014, pp. 141–162.

1970s, with small farmers setting up new fields that could augment food sources available to families but were unreliable because of flooding. One government strategy to encourage land consolidation and commercialization has been to establish greater control of these marshlands. The land law does not allow private claims to the fields in marshlands and requires that they only be cultivated by cooperatives. As research by Ansoms and Jude Murison indicates, however, in practice organizations presented as cooperatives have been controlled by powerful individuals who regulate what is cultivated and charge high fees for access to the fields. These fees prevent many poor farmers from farming these lands that were previously an important resource for them.[143]

A major element of the government's strategy to commercialize agriculture has been to promote mono-cropping. Rwandan farmers have traditionally planted a diversity of crops in their fields, often interspersing crops like corn, manioc, beans, coffee and bananas in the same plot. The approach promoted by recent agriculture policies in Rwanda pushes farmers to plant a single crop in a field, planted in straight rows and supplied with fertilizer to increase production. Local government officials promote the crop that the central government has determined to be best for their region. While the strategies of mono-cropping and regional specialization expose farmers to greater risk, the government pressures farmers to adopt them by making seeds and fertilizer available only for the specified crop and providing extension support only for this crop.[144]

Approaches to urban development, particularly focused on Kigali, have been similarly driven by a technocratic approach, with outside experts lacking local cultural knowledge brought in to develop grandiose plans whose effect will be highly disruptive to many people. Before 1994, Kigali was a small, sleepy town of 236,000, more of an administrative center than a real metropolitan area. Rwanda had a distinctly rural identity, with 94 percent of the population living in the countryside, among the lowest rates of urbanization in the world.[145] But over the past two

---

[143] Ansoms and Murison, "De 'Saoudi' au 'Darfur'"; Ansoms et al., "The Reorganization of Rural Space in Rwanda."

[144] Ansoms, "The Re-organization of Rural Space in Rwanda," pp. 435–436. Catherine Newbury, "Rwanda: Recent Debates over Governance and Rural Development," in Goran Hyden and Michael Bratton, *Governance and Politics in Africa*, Boulder: Lynne Reinner, 1992, pp. 193–219 noted similar policies were implemented under Habyarimana.

[145] World Bank, "Rwanda Urban Infrastructure and City Management Project," www.documents.worldbank.org/curated/en/895731468106440461/Rwanda-Urban-Infrastructure-and-City-Management-Project; Pierre Sirven, *La Sous-urbanization et les Villes du Rwanda et du Burundi*, Published by the author, 1984.

decades, the population of Kigali skyrocketed, as a large portion of the repatriated Tutsi settled in the city, genocide survivors left the hillsides where their families were slaughtered to seek a new beginning in the capital or one of the country's smaller cities, and tens of thousands of Hutu also migrated to Kigali, seeking opportunity in the city because of growing land scarcity or fleeing the increasingly oppressive exercise of control at the local level.

While in many cities around the world, rapid urbanization has compromised the quality of life, as crime, pollution, and squalid slums proliferate, Kigali has become more attractive as it has grown. Kigali's streets were newly paved and lined with sidewalks of elegant interlocking brick. Gardens with fountains and statues at the center were placed in the middle of major intersections. New shopping and entertainment areas emerged, with cinemas, supermarkets, and nightclubs. Attractive new residential districts included housing that ranged from large apartment complexes to imposing single-family homes. Shiny new glass towers gave Kigali an impressive skyline. The recent changes in Kigali are only the beginning of a more radical reorganization of the city envisioned in the Kigali Conceptual Master Plan (KCMP), adopted by parliament in 2008 as part of the government's Vision 2020.

The development of Kigali epitomizes the social transformations that the RPF has propelled in Rwanda since 2000, involving a grand and compelling vision for the future, partnerships between the government and its allies in business and society, crucial support from the international community, coupled with a dark underside of coercive implementation and the sacrificed interests of powerless and marginalized individuals in the name of the interests of the society. According to the Rwanda Development Board, the KCMP was "initiated as a vision by President Kagame"[146] then developed by a high-powered American team that included OZ Architecture, the engineering firms AECOM and Tetra Tech, and the non-governmental organization Engineers without Borders. The 160-page KCMP has won awards from the American Planning Association and the American Academy of Landscape Architects.[147]

The KCMP involves a radical reconceptualization of Kigali as a carefully planned city along the lines of Brasilia, Dubai, or Abu Dhabi and includes drawings of gleaming glass towers and pristine shopping

---

[146] Rwanda Development Board, "Kigali Conceptual Master Plan," brochure, www.kcps .gov.rw/index.php/?id=21#Master%20plan, p. 1.

[147] The Master Plan Team (OZ architecture, EDAW, Tetra Tech, ERA, and Engineers without Borders), "Kigali Conceptual Master Plan," prepared for the Rwanda Ministry of Infrastructure, November 2007.

districts along tree-lined boulevards.[148] The comprehensiveness of the plan is breathtaking, a fantastic example of Scott's high modernist vision. The plan recognizes the challenges posed by the fact that many of the areas slated for development are already occupied, yet suggests a process of community involvement in "redevelopment and upgrading in the existing urban area,"[149] including "informal settlements," the crowded districts where migrants from rural areas have built small homes, usually without authorization:

The transformation of informal urban settlements to achieve the goals and objectives … depends on a clear understanding of existing conditions, development opportunities and constraints, and incorporating the vision and capabilities of the residents. This plan proposes a prototype for the transformation of informal settlements based on three planning principles: the inclusion of local knowledge, the strategic allocation and retrofitting of infrastructure, and the consolidation of basic services into community venues.[150]

Such a benign process may be possible in democratic societies, but in a country like Rwanda where public discourse is highly constrained, the implementation of a grand vision of this sort will almost unavoidably involve considerable coercion. The rehabilitation of Kigali began several years before the KCMP was drafted. Beginning as early as 2001, the Kigali city government oversaw the laying of sidewalks and planting of gardens. The work often employed prisoners, who could be seen participating in works crews in their bright pink prison uniforms. The use of prisoners expanded substantially after the *gacaca* process was reformed in 2005 so that most confessed *genocidaires* would not conduct community service within their local neighborhood as originally envisioned but would instead serve a period of community service in labor camps, a large number of which were built encircling Kigali.[151] While the plan to reduce prison sentences through public service requirements had merit, the use of prison labor to rebuild Kigali certainly lay beyond the naïve vision of the KCMP.

[148] The Master Plan Team, "Kigali Conceptual Master Plan."
[149] The Master Plan, Kigali Conceptual Master Plan, Chapter 4, Section 4.4, p. 84.
[150] The Master Plan, Kigali Conceptual Master Plan, Chapter 4, Section 4.4.1, p. 86.
[151] Penal Reform International, "Monitoring and Research Report on the Gacaca Community Service, Areas of Reflection," London: PRI, March 2007. According to the website of the Rwanda Correctional Service, "TIG [the acronym for community service in Rwanda] is aimed at punishing, strengthening Unity and Reconciliation of Rwandans and impacting on national development. Some of the activities under TIG include speeding up the construction of classrooms under the nine and twelve (9 & 12) Years Basic Education programme, environment protection through terracing, building and repair of roads, land consolidation, construction of houses for vulnerable genocide survivors, paving stones, planting cassava, coffee/tea among others." www.rcs .gov.rw/camps

The implementation of policies seeking "the transformation of informal urban settlements" was particularly troubling. In the name of urban renewal, the government of Kigali bulldozed homes in poor neighborhoods such as Kimisagara, Kimicanga, and Gacuriro. The authorities justified the demolitions because of the unsafe conditions of the homes due to poor quality construction, lack of water, sewage, and electricity, overcrowding, and dangers of flood and landslide. While the government has generally provided limited compensation to residents and homeowners, the construction of new housing for people has lagged, creating demand that has drastically driven up the price of both land and housing. Much of the new affordable housing is being built in areas far removed from the city center, such as the largely rural Gasabo district.[152] As Vincent Manirakiza and An Ansoms stated:

The stringent conditions for urban settlements in line with the city master plan are unrealistic for a large majority of the urban poor. In practice, the implementation of such urbanization policies therefore leads to geographic dualisation, characterized by a rising gap between the living quality in planned urban quarters and living conditions in spontaneous or peri-urban areas.[153]

The destruction of part of Kiyovu reinforced the idea that Kigali's redevelopment is disproportionately benefitting the elite. A neighborhood in central Kigali, Kiyovu is divided in two by a main road. The upper area boasts nice single-family homes, including the new presidential estate, while the lower area, known as "Poor Kiyovu," had crowded housing, including many informal buildings. Lower Kiyovu was largely demolished in 2008, while the upper area was left untouched. Residents complained that they received too little compensation to cover the expense of new housing, were moved to areas far from the city center, and had no choice in their new housing.[154] According to one press report:

After claims from residents that bulldozers were arriving without warning to demolish homes and that the compensation given was not enough, the mayor

---

[152] James Munyaneza, "City Authorities Need to Review Strategy on 'Illegal' Houses," *The New Times*, January 10, 2011; Alex Mugisha and Frances Rwema, "In Rwanda, Rapid Urbanization Chases the Poor Out of Town," *Inyenyeri News*, March 6, 2012; Alexandra Topping, "Kigali's Future, or Costly Fantasy? Plan to Reshape Rwandan City Divides Opinion," *The Guardian*, April 4, 2014.

[153] Vincent Manirakazi and An Ansoms, "'Modernizing Kigali': The Struggle for Space, in the Rwandan Urban Context," in An Ansoms and Thea Hilhorst, eds., *Losing Your Land: Dispossession in the Great Lakes*, Suffolk: James Currey, 2014, p. 187.

[154] Jenny Ford, "Rethinking Relocation in Rwanda," *The Chronicles*, May 30, 2012; "Kiyovu Residents Decry Demolitions," *The Rwanda Focus*, July 29, 2008.

responded in July 2008 by calling on "Rwandans who love their country to embrace positive change" … The authorities expropriated poor Kiyovu's inhabitants in order to place them in better housing, but also so they could build fashionable new apartments on the former shantytown. The families were moved to houses which aren't central and are expensive.[155]

The KCMP may have been motivated by laudable concerns over challenges created by rapid urbanization, such as water supplies, sanitation and sewage, and the dangers of building on steep hillsides, and the plan's recommendations are reasonable enough, attempting to account for Rwanda's modest means.[156] In practice, however, the KCMP – like other parts of Vision 2020 – provided justification for the government to implement policies that officials regarded as serving the public good but that might not have gained popular support through democratic processes. Technocratic governance was undertaken with the ostensible best interests of the population in mind, and the good intentions and grand vision of policymakers and civil servants impress many observers.[157] Yet even with the best of intentions, high modernist policies like these, implemented in a context in which residents were not free to share their "vision and capabilities," nor even free publicly to complain without facing potential dire consequences, contributed to the sense of oppressive rule that has come to dominate Rwandan politics.

Even relatively simple efforts to improve the orderliness and sanitation of the city were implemented in a heavy-handed fashion that reinforced an impression that reforms were not for the good of the general public but to serve the interests of the country's new elite. In 2006, for example, Kigali's city government identified a need to better regulate the numerous kiosks that had popped up around the city, often selling sodas and sundry items like soap and batteries. The Kigali City Council implemented a regulation allowing only approved, standardized, and licensed kiosks. The city then summarily demolished existing kiosks, without compensation. Kigali residents told me at the time that the licenses were prohibitively expensive for most previous kiosk owners – around US$500 – and that, at any rate, they were only being issued to people with connections

---

[155] François D. and Maurice M., "The Ones that Got Left Behind in Kigali's Demolished Shantytown," *Les Observateurs*, March 12, 2010.

[156] The urban population in 2012 was estimated at 19.4 percent (compared to 6 percent in 1994), with a 7.9 percent annual growth rate. UNICEF, "Rwanda: Statistics," www .unicef.org/infobycountry/rwanda_statistics.html.

[157] An economist who visited Rwanda briefly in 2014 (at the express invitation of President Kagame) told me that "They're really trying to help the people!" Notes from meeting, Boston, June 30, 2014.

to the government.[158] Enterprising individuals eventually ignored regulations and constructed new kiosks. When the city acted again in 2008 to demolish the kiosks and take possession of the goods they contained, the newspaper reported that the action was taken, "as required by the new Kigali Master Plan."[159]

Apparently taking Singapore as a model, the regime has instituted a large number of laws in both urban and rural areas that, like the demolition of kiosks, are ostensibly in the interests of public order, public health, and environmental protection. Since 2000, the government has banned public urination and spitting, required people to wear shoes in public, banned the use of plastic bags, required motorcyclists to wear helmets and forbid women from sitting side saddle on a motorbike, forbid people from baking bricks and roof tiles in traditional ovens, banned the use of reed straws for drinking sorghum and banana beers, required circumcision of all male babies, banned traditional thatched roofs and traditional charcoal production, required every home to have a compost bin, required people to dry dishes on a table rather than on the grass, and banned churches from meeting outside formal church buildings.[160]

Each of these regulations could be justified as sound policy choices, yet they have significant social and economic impacts. For example, using communal straws can spread germs, so banning their use made public health sense. Yet sharing reed straws in a calabash or bottle passed from person to person was a core social practice in Rwanda, a way of demonstrating trust and friendship. Forbidding people from sharing straws eliminated a meaningful cultural practice, and though the ban made good technocratic sense, it did not make cultural sense.[161] The central government decreed these quality of life laws with no public consultation, and their enforcement was often draconian. For example, banning the use of plastic bags made good environmental sense, but the law that went into effect in 2005 did not simply ban stores

---

[158] Interviews in Kigali, June 2006.

[159] Godfrey Ntagungira, "Rwanda: KCC Evicts Kiyovu Kiosk Owners," *The New Times*, June 21, 2008. Also Godfrey Ntagungira, "Demolished Kiosk Owners Drag KCC to Court," *The New Times*, July 14, 2008.

[160] Ingelaere, "Living the Transition," p. 37; Ansoms, "Re-engineering Rural Life," pp. 303–304.

[161] As Olivier Nyirubugara, *Complexities and Dangers of Remembering and Forgetting in Rwanda*, Sidestone Press, 2013, explains, "Until the last decade, one straw was used to pass from one mouth to the other, and that was a sign of friendship and brotherliness. Wiping or cleaning the straw before introducing it to one's mouth was the most unacceptable insult. Due to the threat such a practice posed to public health, the entire cultural, and friendship-building philosophy behind the straw was sacrificed for the good of the people, who have to *invent* new cultural ways of exteriorizing friendship" (p. 160).

from giving out plastic bags, as ordinances in some cities around the world have done, but made possession of plastic bags illegal in Rwanda. Even though Rwandans used plastic bags for a variety of purposes and rarely discarded them, plastic bags disappeared from Rwanda overnight.[162]

Many of the quality of life laws have significant economic implications. Most are enforced with fines. Ingelaere provides a long list of twenty-nine "measures improving general well being" for which people can be fined. Many of the laws require individuals to spend money, so the poor are left with a choice of, for example, buying shoes or paying a fine. Ansoms stated that in her research, "Several people reported that when arriving at the market without shoes, their food money was taken from them forcibly by the local authorities to buy them shoes."[163] Other measures have added to the cost of living. The ban on baking bricks and roof tiles in the traditional way has driven up the cost of building and maintaining a home. The added costs and fines happen alongside a variety of new fees, such as registering land and paying the annual fee for Rwanda's new national health insurance program.[164] Together, these policies have affected the poor disproportionately while creating opportunities for those with more means. Traditional brickmaking, for example, has historically been a method for people to earn off-farm income and for some to establish themselves as small-scale entrepreneurs.[165] But the costs associated with the "modern" brickmaking equipment have pushed out small-scale brickmakers in favor of wealthier businesspeople who can afford approved brick-making ovens.[166] Marc Sommers has demonstrated that the rising costs of building a home has created a housing crisis that prevents poor young men from being able to marry and settle down, keeping them from attaining social adulthood and driving youth to flee from the countryside to the city.[167]

---

[162] Flying into Kigali, airlines now advise passengers to remove duty free items from plastic bags before disembarking. Personal observation, Kigali, May 2016.

[163] Ansoms, "Re-Engineering Rural Life," p. 304.

[164] Ansoms and Rostagno, "Rwanda's Vision 2020 Halfway Through," write that farmers are confronted with a multitude of financial obligations (mutuelle de santé, costs to register landholdings, cost for young households to build houses in the agglomeration) and fines (fines for not keeping cows in stables, fines for not reaching targets from local authorities, fines for not having decent roofing, etc.), pp. 441–442.

[165] Villia Jefermovas, *Brickyards to Graveyards in Rwanda: From Production to Genocide in Rwanda*, Albany: SUNY Press, 2002.

[166] An Ansoms, "Views from Below on the Pro-Poor Growth Challenge: The Case of Rural Rwanda." *African Studies Review*, September 2010, citation p. 102.

[167] Sommers, *Stuck*.

Governance, Development, and Inequality

Although the Rwandan government asserts that the policies implemented under Vision 2020 are working, using their own statistics to tout a decline in the overall poverty rate, the severe poverty rate, and the rate of inequality since 2006,[168] fieldwork by a variety of scholars challenges the claims of policy success.[169] The research by these scholars indicates that not only have policies involved coercive enforcement and significant social disruption, but also their economic impact on the majority of the population has been less favorable than reported. Ansoms and Donatella Rostagno, for example, wrote with some irony that, "The recently reported spectacular decrease in poverty is surprising. Not least because many of Rwanda's poverty and inequality issues are inherent in the growth model applied ... In practice, the concentration of strong economic growth in the hands of a small elite results in a highly skewed developmental path with limited trickle-down potential."[170]

Yet even if the benefits of the government's development policies are in fact trickling down to the common people, even if education and healthcare are more widely available and poverty rates are declining, the implementation and enforcement of these policies severely undermines their ability to add to the regime's legitimacy. Policy decisions are made by the central government with little to no popular consultation then enforced in a draconian fashion. Those making and enforcing the policies come from a different social background from the vast majority of Rwandans, who live in rural areas and have deep roots in farming, and they approach the population with a highly condescending attitude that common Rwandans find insulting.[171] People obey the regulations out of fear, but they also feel resentful and angry.

Average Rwandans today still struggle just to survive, much less to get ahead. Having conducted extensive interviews in 2006–2007 with Rwandan young people about their life circumstances and hopes, Sommers asserted that, "the collective story they described was persistently discouraging ... [M]any youth in Kigali face circumstances ... that

---

[168] Ansoms and Rostagno, "Rwanda's Vision 2020 Halfway Through," p. 428.

[169] See Ansoms, "Striving for Growth, Bypassing the Poor"; Ansoms, "Re-engineering Rural Society"; Ansoms et al., "The Reorganization of Rural Space in Rwanda"; Ansoms and Rostagno, "Rwanda's Vision 2020 Halfway Through"; Ansoms and Murison, "De 'Saoudi' au 'Darfur'"; Huggins, "Seeing Like a Neoliberal State?"; Huggins, " 'Control Grabbing' and Small Scale Agricultural Intensification"; Ingelaere, "Peasants, Power, and Ethnicity"; Sommers, *Stuck*.

[170] Ansoms and Rostagno, "Rwanda's Vision 2020 Halfway Through," p. 441.

[171] Ansoms, "Re-engineering Rural Society."

have made them fatalistic in the extreme."[172] Unfortunately, as a result of the government's authoritarian practices, common people like those that Sommers interviewed regard the state as a problem to be avoided rather than as an ally in the struggle to improve their lives.

The popular impression that development is not being done for the good of the general population but for the good of the elite is a major political problem in Rwanda today. As Ted Gurr has argued, poverty alone does not cause people to rebel. Instead, people rebel because of frustrated expectations.[173] As I explore in greater depth in the next chapters, many average Rwandans feel that the constant mobilization they face serves to enrich a limited group of those who are already rich and powerful. They chafe at the condescending attitudes and lack of cultural understanding of those with authority over them, and they resent the coercion used to force them to follow government mandates. Particularly problematic, given Rwanda's history, is a belief that those in charge and those benefiting from post-genocide government policies are from a specific social group – repatriated Tutsi, particularly Anglophone returnees from Uganda. As Ansoms writes, "The current Rwandan elite is mostly Tutsi, urban-based and often born outside Rwanda, while the Rwandan peasantry is mostly Hutu, rural-based and born in the country."[174] Significantly, the relevant social divisions cannot be understood exclusively in ethnic terms. Ethnicity is a factor, but so are the division between those who were inside Rwanda in 1994 and those who were outside and the class divisions between the urban elite and the rural poor.

The social, economic, and political context that I have described here – both the more obvious authoritarian practices of the years immediately after the genocide and the less violent but equally oppressive authoritarian practices used since 2000 – set the context within which transitional justice initiatives in Rwanda must be understood. Rewriting history, memorializing and commemorating the past, and organizing trials for perpetrators of genocide have all occurred in an environment in which the government severely limits free speech, the ruling elite mistrusts and underestimates the population, and the common people believe that the government is being used to advance the interests of its supporters rather than the general interest. The various official initiatives for memory and transitional justice described in this book are part of a larger program of radical social engineering in which the population is constantly mobilized in a sort of permanent revolution

---

[172] Sommers, *Stuck*.
[173] Ted Robert Gurr, *Why Men Rebel*, Princeton: Princeton University Press, 1971.
[174] Ansoms, "Re-engineering Rural Society," p. 308.

intended to create "new Rwandan citizens."[175] As my research with average Rwandans shows, despite widespread popular belief in justice and accountability and support for the idea of reconciliation, the context of authoritarian rule and social and economic inequality have undermined the tools of transitional justice that have been employed in Rwanda. In fact, from the perspective of most Rwandans, rather than promoting justice, accountability, and reconciliation, transitional justice in Rwanda has been a tool of domination used by a small group to secure their power and increase their wealth.

---

[175] This terminology from Huggins, "Seeing Like a Neo-Liberal State?"

Part II

Popular Narratives

The struggle of man against power is the struggle of memory against forgetting.

– Milan Kundera, The Book of Laughter and Forgetting

6 Political Reform in Three Rwandan Communities

> As for the vote, they do their mobilization of the population, they name [the officials], and then it is announced that we voted for them.
>
> – Hutu farmer in Mabanza, Kibuye, 2015

The previous part of this book explained the extensive programs for political reform and transitional justice undertaken by the post-genocide government of Rwanda to promote national unity and secure political control. Using memorialization, commemorations, education, and judicial processes, the RPF-led government and its supporters promoted a unified narrative about Rwanda's history – encompassing both the recent and more distant past – in an effort to create a collective memory, thereby forging a cohesive national identity and legitimizing its rule. Both institutional and symbolic political reforms sought to situate the government in this national narrative, tying the present government to Rwanda's rich history and demonstrating its commitment to break with the country's destructive recent past and propel Rwanda into a new progressive future. At the same time, the government demonstrated its suspicion of the population, firm control, and intent to maintain political power.

The final section of this book explores how the population has responded to official efforts to shape the national consciousness. Drawing on four brief life histories, I first make the point that the receptiveness of a public to efforts to construct a collective memory depends not simply on the collectivity but on individual experience as well. Individuals accept the collective memory as their own based on how much it conforms to and helps make sense of their own lived experience in both the past and the ongoing political context in which the national narrative is being promulgated. The stories of four individuals from the university town Butare suggest ways that experiences in Rwanda during and after the genocide diverge widely, even for individuals from similar backgrounds living in the same community, and create very different reactions to attempts to shape a collective narrative.[1]

"Agnes" was a high school student in 1994, studying in Bukavu, Zaire, but home for the Easter holiday when President Habyarimana was killed. For the first week after Habyarimana's death, life in Butare remained relatively normal, and Agnes and her family continued to circulate through the town without trouble, even though a few additional roadblocks had been set up. The situation deteriorated rapidly after the interim president and prime minister led a meeting in Butare on April 19 introducing a new prefect and instructing all of the Butare government officials that, "the government would no longer tolerate those who sympathized with the enemy."[2] The next day, the family heard that a Tutsi university professor was killed at a roadblock only a few blocks from their home. The following day, they heard that the elderly former queen, Rosalie Gicanda, along with members of her family, had been taken from her home and shot. Agnes and her family decided to go into hiding, first staying together in a garage owned by a family friend, then splitting up to hide in various locations. She moved several times, at one point being smuggled to a new location by a Muslim friend who hid her beneath a veil pretending she was his wife, and another time bribing a worker to help her evade capture.

In June, as the RPF was approaching, the people who hid her fled Rwanda. After waiting alone for three days, Agnes went out to discover what had happened. Tired from hunger and thirst and imagining that all of her friends and family were dead, she took little precaution and was stopped at a roadblock still maintained by the army at the entrance to the city. The officer in charge told her he was going to kill her, then put her in a trench beside the roadblock. Defeated, expecting to be raped, and awaiting death, Agnes made no attempt to escape but awaited her fate. But before the officer came back for her, a group of French soldiers arrived and told the soldiers that the RPF was on its way and they should flee. The French soldiers found Agnes and took her to a nearby bus filled with children being transported to safety in Burundi. As the bus pulled away, Agnes could see the RPF troops arriving up the road and government troops falling back. At the Burundi border, Agnes was reunited with one of her sisters. After a few weeks in Bujumbura, she and her sister returned to Butare and found that most of their direct family had survived.

---

[1] The four personal stories related here are drawn from both formal interviews and informal conversations that took place during research in Rwanda in 1995–1996 and 2000–2006. I have given each of the four a pseudonym to protect their identity.

[2] Des Forges, *Leave None to Tell the Story*, p. 458.

For Agnes, whose imminent violation and death was stopped by the arrival of RPF troops, the RPF appeared as a liberator that saved her from the unspeakable horrors of the genocide, and at first Agnes was a strong supporter of the new government. Yet in the years that followed, Agnes's attitudes toward the RPF and its policies continued to evolve based on her experience living under RPF rule. Like many genocide survivors, Agnes became increasingly frustrated at the relative powerlessness of survivors in the post-genocide society. Because of the university and numerous government jobs, many repatriated Tutsi from Uganda, Congo, and Burundi came to Butare after 1994. Agnes felt that these *rapatriés* treated her with suspicion and scorn, questioning what she had done to survive the genocide, assuming that she had prostituted herself or otherwise betrayed the Tutsi to protect her life. After she took a position as a translator and interpreter for a Western NGO, Agnes faced increasing questions about her loyalties because of the strong anti-Western attitudes shared by many of the *rapatriés*. Agnes's relations with Hutu caused her further problems. Like most Rwandans who lived in the country prior to the genocide, Agnes had an ethnically mixed family, and because many of her Tutsi relatives had been killed in 1994, most of Agnes's closest living relatives were Hutu. Agnes's mother did not return from Europe after the war, so she lived with her Hutu stepfather, who was a university professor and, as a prominent moderate Hutu, faced regular charges of complicity in the genocide. Though unlike many of his associates, he managed to stay out of prison, he became increasingly isolated and lost his position of authority. Her younger half-brother, with whom she was quite close, faced harassment as well. He was briefly imprisoned under genocide charges and thus could not finish school and was subsequently unable to find employment.

Other members of Agnes's family also faced problems in post-genocide Rwanda that soured their attitude toward the regime. Shortly after the genocide, Agnes began dating a Tutsi survivor who had joined the RPF during the 1994 hostilities, and they married a few years later. Her husband's experience in the RPF, however, mirrored that of many survivors who joined the rebel army in 1994. Since seniority was based on when individuals joined, the Tutsi refugees who joined the RPF before the 1990 invasion or just after dominated the officer ranks. The thousands who joined during the 1994 conflict remained permanently in low positions, comprising the everyday foot soldiers, despite the personal losses that they suffered during the genocide. Agnes's husband, who lost most of his family, grew increasingly frustrated at the lack of respect he felt from his superiors who had lost few if any close relatives (since their families were in Uganda or Congo) and whom he felt little understood

Rwanda. He began to drink heavily and became increasingly abusive and increasingly negative toward the RPF regime.

Like many survivors, Agnes turned to religion in an attempt to find meaning. Agnes had been raised Catholic but had never been particularly observant. After she moved with her husband to Kigali in 1997, she got involved in one of the many new charismatic churches that had sprung up in the capital since 1994. The church that Agnes joined urged intense religious devotion and insisted on a strict code of conduct for members. They held loud, emotional prayer sessions until late at night, that ultimately led to conflict with the state, which sought to rein in what it perceived as religious excesses. When Agnes and her husband participated in 2002 in a prayer session that was held in defiance of a local government ban, they were arrested along with other members of their church and briefly detained. Despite his church membership, after the arrest, Agnes's husband began drinking again and once more became abusive. Ultimately, Agnes used her NGO connections to seek exile outside Rwanda, fleeing both a violent husband and a regime from which she felt increasingly alienated.

My friend "David" had an experience that was almost the reverse. I had known David before the genocide when he was a secondary school student. At the school, he had watched as tensions gradually rose after the Arusha Accords, as students and some teachers who were sympathetic to the Hutu Power movement harassed the Tutsi students as RPF spies. When President Habyarimana was killed, David was at home for Easter holiday in a commune in eastern Butare just across from Burundi. Sensing that Butare Prefecture would not remain a safe haven, David encouraged his entire family to flee early across the border, and so only his elderly grandfather who was too feeble to travel was killed in the genocide, though his family home was burned and systematically leveled to the ground. After the genocide, David completed his final year of secondary school then enrolled at the National University of Rwanda. Having lost little and faced limited direct threat in the genocide, David did not view the RPF as liberators in the way that Agnes did. Instead, David often shared with me his frustrations about life in post-genocide Rwanda, feeling that genocide survivors like his family had little place in the new country, dominated as it was by returned Tutsi refugees. As one of the few Tutsi families left in their isolated rural community, his family lived in fear of continuing violence and considered moving across the country to the new prefecture of Umutara, the only prefecture in the country where Tutsi were the majority. Once when we went together to a club near the university, David became angry at the young couples slow dancing together, the women dressed in revealing outfits with elaborate hairstyles like those worn in Kinshasa or Kampala, all of which would have been impossible in pre-genocide Rwanda's puritanical society. "This isn't Rwanda," he said through gritted teeth. "These people are like colonizers." He insisted that we leave.

Feeling increasingly frustrated and alienated and believing that he could help his impoverished family by getting a job and earning an income, David left the university before receiving a degree and secured employment as an accountant in a business. Yet his frustrations continued to build in the private sector. When money turned up missing, a repatriated Tutsi colleague who had actually embezzled the funds pointed the finger at David, so he was arrested and spent several weeks in prison. As the only Tutsi in a prison populated overwhelmingly by Hutu accused of participation in the genocide, David initially met hostility, but since his fellow prisoners feared he might be a spy, they decided it was best to treat him well, so that he would send out positive reports. He was jokingly labeled "Little Kagame" and given good access to food and a comfortable place to sleep in the severely overcrowded prison. After the charges were dropped, David left prison with a grudging respect for the *genocidaires* he had met there, yet he also left prison convinced of the sharp ethnic divide that continued to split Rwandan society. Still feeling that genocide survivors were second-class citizens, he nevertheless found himself increasingly supportive of the RPF. David came to believe that, given another opportunity, Rwandan Hutu would again slaughter Tutsi. He regarded Kagame as a Machiavellian leader who would do whatever it took to protect the Tutsi. "We're much better dictators than Habyarimana ever was," he told me in 2003. Although he still did not like Kagame on a personal level, he regarded his strict rule as necessary for the interests of the Tutsi minority.

Just as the experiences of Tutsi genocide survivors diverged, the experience of Hutu diverged as well. "Eugene" was a small, energetic man who worked before the genocide for a Dutch family that lived near me. He was a kind-hearted man, and a proud father who took me to his modest home and introduced me to his wife and children. He was very enthusiastic about the democratic reform that the country was undergoing in the early 1990s. He proudly showed me his membership card in the PSD, a party he told me he supported because it was opposed to ethnic division and supported Rwanda's poor. When I saw Eugene again in 2001, however, he was completely changed. He was gaunt and agitated, with a frightened look in his eyes. I never fully understood the details of what had happened to Eugene, because he was barely coherent in his paranoid rant about how "they," meaning the RPF, were "going to get everyone." His family had been in a refugee camp in Congo until 1996, and he told me that many of his friends and family had been killed there or after their return. As we spoke, he looked suspiciously around, as though afraid that he had been followed or that someone was listening in.

By contrast, "Patrick" was in some ways flourishing in the new Rwanda. Before the genocide, he had been the domestic worker for a group of students who lived near me. Barely eighteen at the time, he was a charming young man who was curious to meet an American and learn about American culture and ideas. Despite his limited French and my imperfect Kinyarwanda, we became fast friends. When I was ill with malaria, it was Patrick who came to stay in my house to make sure that I was okay. After the genocide, he fled like Eugene and so many others to Congo. When the RPF bombed his refugee camp, he fled into the bush, because, he explained to me, the authorities at the camp told them that the RPF was killing all Hutu who returned. He spent the next several years walking through the rainforests of Congo until he reached Mbandaka nearly a thousand miles away. He met his wife along the way, and they married there in the bush. When UNHCR finally repatriated Eugene to Rwanda in 1997, he returned to his home village just outside Butare, bought a bicycle with UNHCR assistance, and became a bicycle taxi-man. He became active in his local community and was ultimately elected president of his local gacaca court. "I feel like I wasted three years of my life in Congo," he told me. "They [the former leaders] lied to us. Life here is hard, but still … We're making do. Things are moving on."

Analysis of politics at the national level ultimately tells very little about the actual impact that government policies have on the population of a country. As these four stories indicate, individual experiences shape how people react to government initiatives. Communities in different parts of Rwanda experienced the war and genocide very differently, and even people from similar backgrounds in the same community endured very different life experiences. The effort to promote a collective memory and build reconciliation and national unity confronts the real differences in individual experience and perception. Ongoing experiences continue to shape how people view the regime and how they receive its message. In these stories, for example, while Agnes started out regarding the RPF positively, she became increasingly critical as she experienced limitations in post-genocide society. In contrast, David's initial opposition ultimately gave way to a grudging respect for the RPF's exercise of power.

In an effort to explore the local-level dynamics of post-genocide social and political life, I directed a series of linked research projects from 2001 to 2005 focused on three local communities in different regions of Rwanda. This was the period of official political transition, in which a new constitution was adopted and elections were held at all levels of government. It was also a period in which transitional justice programs were at their most intense, with genocide memorials being constructed all over the country, gacaca being launched, and the ICTR active. The case-study communes were chosen to reflect differences in levels of urbanization, divergent experiences with the genocide and violence by the RPF, historic regional differences, and different exposures to national and international judicial initiatives. Ngoma, Butare's commune, was a place I knew well, having lived and worked there both before and after the genocide. Mabanza Commune in Kibuye was somewhere I had visited a number of times over the years and the home commune of the leader of my research team. I selected Buyoga Commune in Byumba as an additional case because it was in the country's north and had a very different experience in 1994, with little genocide but extensive RPF violence.[3] In each commune, my research team and I conducted numerous one-on-one interviews with a wide range of individuals, carried out focus-group interviews with women, youth, elders, and genocide survivors, and observed the conduct of elections, gacaca trials, and other community activities. In addition, these communes were part of a survey of 2,071 households conducted in February 2002. The research focused on attitudes toward justice and reconciliation, popular narratives about the genocide, and perceptions of identity in post-genocide Rwanda. In 2015, a decade after the majority of my initial research, one of my research assistants returned to two of the case study communes for follow up interviews with a range of individuals.[4] While less extensive than my previous research, these more recent interviews allow me to track changes in attitudes, particularly since the completion of gacaca.

In this chapter, I provide an introduction to each of the case-study communes. I present an overview of each commune's geography and demographics and briefly summarize the history of the war and genocide in the commune. I then look at the commune's experience in post-genocide Rwanda, with particular attention to political events and the impact of decentralization as the communes were reorganized into districts. Finally, I look at popular reaction to the political changes in Rwanda since 1994. Despite the ostensible shift to democratic governance,

---

[3] The study focused at the commune level, because communes (roughly equivalent to a county) were the dominant sub-national political unit and because the genocide was organized by commune. As described in Chapter 5, during the course of the research project, the Government of Rwanda replaced communes with larger political units known as districts.

[4] Unfortunately, security concerns for researcher and subjects precluded conducting interviews in Buyoga.

Table 6.1 *Comparison of case-study communes in 2001–2005*

	Ngoma	Mabanza	Buyoga
Region	South	Central	North
Experience in Genocide	Extensive exposure to genocide	Extensive exposure to genocide	Limited exposure to genocide
Ethnic Composition	Very high Tutsi population	High Tutsi population	Low Tutsi population
RPF Violence	Extensive exposure to RPF violence	Limited exposure to RPF violence	Extensive exposure to RPF violence
International Justice in 2001–2003	ICTR cases underway	ICTR cases completed	No relevant ICTR cases
Gacaca in 2001–2003	No gacaca underway	Pilot phase underway	Pilot phase underway

political manipulation – including intervention by the central government – directly constrained and reshaped local governments in each of the communes. In all three communes, just during the most focused period of research in 2001–2003, one or more top political officials were arrested on politicized charges. The image emerged not of vibrant civic life and growing democratic engagement but rather of increasingly constrained and intimidated communities where the population struggled merely to survive but had to comply with increasingly onerous government demands. The lived experience of authoritarian rule and economic struggle described in this chapter directly affects popular attitudes toward accountability, justice, and reconciliation and limits the ability of leaders to promote an officially sanctioned collective memory. Government action clearly affects how individuals conceive of their group identities, but those identities develop as much in reaction *against* government initiatives as they do in response to them.

Ngoma Commune

Ngoma Commune was the home to Butare, Rwanda's third-largest city. Though Butare had fewer than 30,000 residents in 1994, Ngoma Commune was nevertheless an urban area, where the vast majority of people earned their living primarily through non-farm employment. The city, originally named Astrida, in honor of Belgian Queen Astrid, was founded in 1928 as the administrative center for the Belgian colony of Ruanda-Urundi. The colonial administration selected the site because of its strategic location near Rwanda's first Catholic mission, Save, and near the border between Rwanda and Burundi, which the Belgians administered jointly. The neighborhood that lies west of the town center and gave the commune its name, Ngoma, was the indigenous quarter in the colonial period and still has many small colonial brick houses built to lodge Rwandan civil servants and other workers. Butare has long been Rwanda's intellectual center. In 1932 the colonial administration established a secondary school here, the Groupe Scolaire d'Astrida, under the direction of the Catholic Brothers of Charity. The colonial authorities intended the school to train the country's future leaders, and Groupe Scolaire quickly emerged as a prestigious institution where Rwanda's elite families, nearly all Tutsi at that time, sent their children.[5] In the 1950s, the colonial administration founded a scientific research center (the precursor to the Rwandan Institute for Scientific Research, IRST) as well as a veterinary center and a second high school focused on the social sciences.

Because of the presence of scholarly and research centers, Butare was the natural place for the newly independent government to found a national university in 1963, and the various scholarly establishments collectively remained the largest employers in Butare at the time of the genocide. Although the Habyarimana regime created satellite campuses in Kigali and Ruhengeri, the Butare campus of the National University of Rwanda remained the most prominent, and Groupe Scolaire was still Rwanda's most prestigious secondary school. Butare had several other secondary schools in 1994, giving the city among the largest populations of high school students in the country. In addition, the Protestant Council of Rwanda had a seminary to train pastors, and the Catholic Church had a center for training catechists from throughout Central Africa. In addition to the IRST, the National Agricultural Research Institute (ISAR) was based in Butare, with major agricultural research posts in nearby communities. The university also maintained a large teaching hospital that was one of the best medical establishments in Rwanda.

Ngoma Commune was also an important administrative and religious center. Butare was the seat of Butare Prefecture, among Rwanda's most populous provinces, and the town hosted many regional government offices and institutions. The Armed Forces of Rwanda maintained a base in Ngoma sector prior to the genocide, and the School for Junior Officers (ESO) was here as well. Both the Catholic and Episcopal churches had cathedrals in Butare, and the Union of Baptist Churches in Rwanda maintained their national headquarters in the town. In addition, the

---

[5] Newbury, *Cohesion of Oppression*, p. 116.

National Museum of Rwanda was located in Butare, and maintained not only an impressive ethnographic and historical exhibit area but also an active research center.

Finally, Ngoma Commune was an important commercial hub. Butare lay on the main highway between Kigali and Bujumbura and was a major transit center for goods flowing between Rwanda and Burundi. Butare was also on the road that led from Cyangugu and Gikongoro to the rest of the country. The Butare central market was among the most active in the country, providing produce from the regions' fertile farmland to both Butare's urban population and other parts of the country. Several small manufacturing firms were based in Butare, but trade was a more important part of the economy than production of goods.

Butare lay on a long, flat ridge, spreading out on either side of the Kigali-Bujumbura highway. Entering Butare from Kigali, the road passed through a broad marshy valley used on one side for making bricks, while the other side was intensively cultivated. Before the genocide, the Loiret-Butare development partnership controlled the valley and paid farmers during the winter season to produced green beans for the French market. During the rest of the year, farmers were allowed to cultivate crops of their choosing. After the genocide, given the chilly relations between France and Rwanda, the project was discontinued and the residence and offices of the project became a *maison de passage* for the NUR. Mounting the highway into Butare, the National Museum, a taxi rank, and prefecture offices lay on the right-hand side of the road. Spreading out to the east of the highway lay the prosperous residential neighborhoods of Buye and Taba, home to several of Ngoma's educational establishments and the residence of many university professors, teachers, and businessmen. To the west, off the highway leading to Gikongoro and Cyangugu, were the Butare prison and the modest residential neighborhoods of Ngoma and Matyazo. In the center of town lay the humble downtown. The brightly painted Hotel Ibis, with its broad terrace overlooking the main road, was long the preferred venue for community elite to sit and drink bottled beers in the afternoons and weekends. The Ibis had been owned by the same Belgian family since the 1930s and had about a dozen hotel rooms and the city's best restaurant. The dilapidated red stucco Hotel Faucon just a few doors down was always a less tony gathering place for university students and others to meet to drink. The road was otherwise lined with shops and banks and commercial establishments.

To the west of downtown lay the central market and the main commercial district, known as the Swahili Quarter, because of the presence of many Muslim businessmen, whose shops sold an eclectic mix of items ranging from imported cloth to canned goods to bicycles. The market itself, housed since the 1980s under three large metal canopies in the center of the quarter, sold food items and second-hand clothing. Along the highway just past downtown was Kabutare, the neighborhood dominated by the Catholic Church, home to Groupe Scolaire, the Catholic cathedral, the offices of the Butare Catholic diocese, several monasteries and convents, and a Catholic hospital, as well as a veterinary school. Just beyond the Catholic complex along the highway lay the much smaller Episcopal Cathedral and a few related church buildings. Going south, the highway skirted a large valley to the left, where the university farmed a few fields, while the University Hospital lay on a hill to the right, with the ESO beside. The entrance to the main NUR campus lay just beyond, up a hill on the left through a wooded area, while the IRST lay across the highway, behind the University Hospital. Shortly beyond the university, before the highway headed south toward Burundi, a dirt road turned off into the two most populous neighborhoods of Butare, Cyarwa and Tumba. In contrast to Buye and Taba, where the homes were solid and large, surrounded by lush gardens and high walls, most of the houses in Cyarwa and Tumba were more humble. Close to the highway, a few large houses were owned by government officials and professors, but most of the houses further off the road were small and crowded close together. Further out, the houses were farther apart, surrounded by small fields where poor families supplemented the income they made as laborers in the city by growing beans, sweet potatoes, and vegetables, and just beyond Tumba the neighborhoods of Nkubi and Sahera, still technically within Ngoma, were mostly rural.

As an intellectual center, Butare had a reputation for being politically progressive and, in particular, a center of ethnic tolerance. With an economy dominated by schools, churches, and commerce, Ngoma Commune had a much higher percentage of Tutsi than most other communities in Rwanda. Since the ethnic quota system established by the Habyarimana regime limited the number of Tutsi who could work for schools and in government to 10 percent, many Tutsi focused on private business, while churches also offered employment opportunities for Tutsi. During the late colonial era, Butare was home to a progressive political party that sought a more multi-ethnic path to independence than Kayibanda's Parmehutu.[6] In the democratic opening in the 1990s, Butare served as the main base for the PSD, the only truly ethnically diverse political party. In 1992, President Habyarimana appointed Jean-Baptiste Habyalimana, a Tutsi from the Liberal Party, as prefect of Butare.

[6] Lemarchand, *Rwanda and Burundi*.

Given its multi-ethnic and progressive traditions, Butare Prefecture did not experience the ethnic violence that occurred in many other prefectures in the country in the years prior to the genocide. Even after Habyarimana's death in April 1994, the political and military leadership of Butare, under Prefect Habyalimana and moderate Hutu military officials Marcel Gatzinsi and Cyriaque Habyarabatuma, resisted the implementation of the genocide. During the first week after President Habyarimana's death, Nyakizu Commune, led by a burgomaster from the Hutu Power faction of the MDR, was the only Butare commune where massacres took place. The population in the rest of the prefecture turned back attacks from Nyakizu and neighboring Gikongoro, as Habyalimana and Habyarabatuma actively worked to contain violence as it began in Butare communes bordering Gikongoro.[7]

However, the central government acted aggressively to ensure that Butare would fall in line and join in the genocide. In the interim government named on April 8, both President Théodore Sindikubwabo and Prime Minister Jean Kambanda were from Butare Prefecture and maintained homes in Butare. The cabinet charged the one minister who was both from Butare and a loyal MRND member, Pauline Nyiramasuhuko, with overseeing the "pacification" of the prefecture. On April 17, the government announced that Prefect Habyalimana was being replaced (he was subsequently murdered), while Major Habyarabatuma was transferred to the frontline in Kigali. Two days later, the president and prime minister organized a meeting of Butare burgomasters in which he made clear that all the burgomasters needed to fall in line with the government's program of "self defense" or face removal. The next day a Presidential Guard contingent landed in Butare to help oversee the massacres. Nyiramasuhuko, along with military officers, including ESO commander Tharcisse Muvunyi and Lieutenant Colonel Aloys Simba, helped ensure that the genocide was carried out in each of Butare's twenty communes. In Ngoma itself, Pauline's son, Shalom Ntahobali, a student at the NUR and leader of the local MRND militia group, the *Interahamwe*, "Those Who Fight Together," played a key role in organizing civilian participation in the genocide in Butare. Shalom established a roadblock in front of his home, near the entrance to the university, and his militia executed hundreds of people in a nearby grove of woods. Massacres took place at the prefecture office, the University Hospital, the Catholic parish in Ngoma sector, the Benebekire convent, Group Scolaire, and elsewhere in the commune. Hundreds of Tutsi were killed

---

[7] Des Forges, *Leave None to Tell the Story*, pp. 438–446; André Guichaoua, *Rwanda 1994: Les politiques du génocide à Butare*, Paris: Karthala, 2005.

at the numerous roadblocks established throughout the city. Despite having resisted the genocide initially, Butare became one of the bloodiest sites in the country once the violence began, and thousands of Tutsi were slaughtered.[8]

Post-genocide Butare demonstrated well the manner in which the RPF first used military force to control the population then shifted toward political domination. As the RPF approached Ngoma Commune in early July, many people fled, some to Burundi, but most heading west to the French Zone Turquoise in Gikongoro or into the DRC. Others, many of whom had opposed the genocide or participated only reluctantly, chose to stay and welcome the RPF. On July 3, a group of about one hundred French troops arrived in Butare to evacuate people, including several hundred orphans, Tutsi who had survived in hiding, and some Hutu government officials.[9] As the RPF approached Butare, the members of civilian militias who had not already fled offered very little resistance. Nevertheless, the RPF used considerable firepower as they advanced, and a number of noncombatant civilians were killed either in crossfire or as they tried to flee. As HRW reported, "In some cases, RPF soldiers simply assumed that any people still alive in a community had killed Tutsi."[10] As one witness in Butare reported, "The first day, they killed in turn. The militia killed those who came out of hiding to flee, and when the RPF arrived here and found the bodies, they killed the others who were still alive on the spot."[11] When I was living in Butare in 1995 and 1996, I spoke with several witnesses, including both Hutu and genocide survivors, who said that as the RPF arrived in communities around Butare, they opened fire on the population, killing many, including Tutsi genocide survivors who had come out to greet them.[12]

When the RPF arrived in Ngoma shortly after the departure of the French troops on July 3, they began a program of pacification of the population. Many Tutsi who had been in hiding came out to greet the RPF as liberators, and many Hutu in fact joined them. In the city of Butare, the RPF gathered the people in places such as Groupe Scolaire for several days, apparently wanting to establish control over the population. They separated women and children from the men and gradually released most individuals once they had been registered. Whether driven

---

[8] Des Forges, *Leave None to Tell the Story*, pp. 446–553; Guichaoua, *Rwanda 1994*. See also the public records from the ICTR Butare case (Nyiramasuhuko, et al, Butare, ICTR-98-42) at www.unictr.unmict.org/en/cases/ictr-98-42.

[9] Des Forges, *Leave None to Tell the Story*, pp. 587–591.

[10] Ibid., p. 716.

[11] Quoted in ibid.

[12] Interviews in Butare, 1995–1996.

by the desire for revenge, sincerely believing that genocide perpetrators were among the detained (failing to understand that the vast majority of perpetrators had fled before their arrival), or merely seeking to establish their control and eliminate potential threats, the RPF soldiers took a number of the men into the wooded valley next to Groupe Scolaire and summarily executed them.[13] While this operation of detention and registration was ongoing, other RPF troops spread throughout Ngoma in search of people who had avoided coming to the central gathering places. They opened fire freely on those they encountered, killing hundreds. The RPF organized community gatherings in the next days in various parts of Ngoma for both local residents and displaced people from which some men were taken away and "disappeared." For example, meetings were held in Rango, at the southern edge of Tumba sector, on July 8 and 11 in which names of people that RPF investigations had determined were involved in the genocide were read off, and the men who came forward were taken away and allegedly executed.[14]

After the initial wave of killings, people were allowed to return to their homes. For several weeks, RPF soldiers continued to carry out summary executions of people they suspected of involvement in the genocide, sometimes based on testimony from genocide survivors. In other cases, violence seems to have been disconnected from summary justice and seems to have served more to intimidate the population. Intellectuals and other prominent Hutu in particular appear to have been singled out for elimination. As groups of displaced people arrived in Ngoma, including both Ngoma residents returning home and people who had fled from other communes, often passing through on their way to refuge in Burundi, RPF soldiers interrogated them and sometimes executed individuals. An investigation by a team from the UN High Commissioner for Refugees estimated that RPF troops killed 25,000 to 45,000 people between April and August 1994, particularly in Kibungo, the Bugesera region of Kigali-Rural, and Butare.[15]

[13] Interviews in Butare, March and April 1996, and Des Forges, *Leave None to Tell the Story*, p. 720.

[14] Ibid., p. 718.

[15] The "Gersony Report" was never made public and has been the source of intense controversy. Genocide deniers have claimed that the report was covered up in an attempt to hide evidence that the violence in Rwanda was a civil war rather than genocide. Apologists for the RPF regime claim that the team conducted faulty research and was intended merely to discredit the RPF. The most likely explanation seems to be that advanced by Alison Des Forges that the research team led by Gersony reported its findings of RPF abuses orally to High Commissioner for Refugees Sadako Ogato and others but never formally wrote up a report because of political pressure from countries sympathetic to the RPF. Des Forges, *Leave None to Tell the Story*, pp. 726–731.

By mid-August 1994, life in Ngoma began to return to normal – at least as normal as was possible under conditions of occupation, with thousands of residents dead (primarily killed in the genocide) and the majority of those alive having fled. Following their claims to be respecting the terms of the Arusha Accords by building a broad-based government, the RPF-named government in Kigali appointed new political leaders for the prefecture and commune. Dr. Pierre-Claver Rwangabo, a moderate Hutu and top PSD leader, was named prefect. Yet the RPF remained the real power in the region. They began to arrest and imprison large numbers of individuals, and disappearances and assassinations continued, though on a smaller scale than in the immediate aftermath of the RPF's arrival.[16] Prefect Rwangabo antagonized the RPF leadership by criticizing prison conditions and calling for the release of prisoners against whom there was no evidence. In March 1995, he was shot to death along with his son and driver returning from a meeting with Interior Minister Seth Sendashonga where he had discussed the problem of continuing ethnic tensions in Butare Prefecture.[17] Judge Bernard Nikuze, the acting president of the Butare high court, was shot in late August 1995 in front of his home just outside Butare, apparently for speaking out against human rights abuses.[18]

When I arrived in Butare in 1995, life seemed ordinary on the surface. The university had reopened, shops were well stocked, and the population was going about their daily business. The presence of many foreign relief and development workers helped bring money into the economy and supported several new restaurants and hotels. Yet tensions in the community remained high. The NUR was overwhelmingly Tutsi, and the student body was deeply divided, with Hutu, Tutsi genocide survivors, and former Tutsi from Uganda, Congo, and Burundi each socializing mostly with people from their own group. The arrival of numerous Anglophone students who had grown up in Uganda led to tensions over the appropriate language of instruction. In the non-student population, business and other opportunities were dominated by Hutu with long roots in the community and strong family connections and by the country's new elite, former Tutsi refugees returned from Uganda, Congo, and elsewhere, who benefitted from connections to the RPF and government. The genocide survivors in the community often struggled financially and felt angry and neglected. Some of them became involved in denouncing

---

[16] Human Rights Watch field notes, August 30, 1995, and October 1995.
[17] "Senior Aid in Rwanda Coalition is Killed," *New York Times*, March 5, 1995; Human Rights Watch, *World Report 1996*; Amnesty International, "Amnesty International Report 1996," London: Amnesty International, January 1, 1996.
[18] Human Rights Watch field notes, August and October 1995.

Hutu for genocide crimes, leading to the arrest of some who were genuinely guilty but also many innocent people.

The Butare prison was built to accommodate less than 2,000 prisoners, but hundreds of people were arrested each month. By late 1995, the prison held nearly 8,000 in squalid conditions. Prisoners had to sleep in shifts, with people sleeping on the roofs and on the floor of the showers and bathrooms. When I visited during a rain shower, the stench and mud and misery were extraordinary, with many men merely standing outside holding plastic bags over their heads to ward off the rain, because it was not possible to fit all of the prisoners inside. Since people could be imprisoned without any evidence and the legal system was not functioning, an accusation to the judicial police was tantamount to condemnation to years in prison. As a result, Hutu lived in fear of imprisonment, and denunciation became a means of settling scores with enemies, while the threat of denunciation became a source for blackmail.[19] Disappearances and assassinations were less common than previously but continued, particularly in rural areas outside Butare town. In my capacity as director of the HRW/FIDH office, I received regular reports of people who had been threatened, imprisoned on false charges, beaten, or disappeared. After RPF attacks closed the camps in the DRC in 1996, thousands of refugees returned to Butare, and a massive wave of arrests and some disappearances took place. Conflicts broke out over land and housing, as many refugees came back to find their homes occupied.

When I returned to Ngoma Commune in 2001 to conduct research for this book, the situation had evolved significantly. Violence had become rare, and the rate of new arrests had declined markedly. The university was more integrated, with about half of the students being Tutsi, including a number of genocide survivors on government scholarships. Because of a government emphasis on education, the student body had grown substantially, necessitating the construction of additional housing both on and off campus. Yet in many ways, the economy was weaker than in 1995–1996. The departure of most relief and development groups and the decline in foreign assistance deprived the community of resources, so that the restaurant at the Ibis was the only upscale restaurant left in town. Most of the nightclubs that had been flourishing just after the war had closed, and store shelves were much more bare. Butare seemed increasingly small and provincial compared with Kigali's growing prosperity and development.

---

[19] On prison conditions, see Human Rights Watch, "Rwanda: The Crisis Continues," 7, no. 1, April 1995.

A significant shift in ethnic relations had also taken place in Butare. First, the percentage of Tutsi in Butare had increased noticeably. The town of Butare had become a magnet for Tutsi genocide survivors from throughout Butare and Gikongoro prefectures who felt vulnerable and isolated in their home communities and were seeking to start a new life. Repatriated former refugees also moved primarily to urban areas like Butare. Although the government no longer gathered information on ethnicity, so there are no official statistics on the post-1994 ethnic breakdown, 48.0 percent of respondents to our 2002 survey identified themselves as Tutsi, compared to 37.3 percent who identified as Hutu. More subtly, an ethnic division of labor had emerged. Tutsi – particularly the repatriated – had come to dominate political, social, and economic life. Whereas immediately after 1994, many positions in the civil service, the university, and international organizations were occupied by Hutu, by 2001, Tutsi completely dominated professional positions. Many educated Hutu that I had worked with in 1995–1996 were unemployed; several had lost their jobs when they were imprisoned.

During the three years when my team was conducting research in Butare, the government underwent a restructuring in which communes were consolidated into larger districts. Butare was incorporated as a city and added several sectors formerly part of other communes. Elections for local government officials took place in March 2001, elections for gacaca court judges were held in October 2001, and a series of national elections were held in 2003. These elections were intended to mark a transition to democracy, yet in Butare we found manipulation of the political system from the smallest political unit to the highest level of power in the province. Our interview subjects told of considerable manipulation of the candidates for positions as councilors of sectors and coordinators of cells. Officials reported that they were instructed to run for office by Butare RPF officials, and several reported that they were later told to resign. In some cases, officials were threatened with imprisonment, Hutu on charges of participation in the genocide and Tutsi with charges of corruption. The councilor of Cyarwa-Cyimana Sector was fired in 2002 under accusations of corruption and "public misconduct," because she had two children out-of-wedlock. In 2003, Therence Kayigire, who had been a recent graduate of the NUR when he was elected mayor of Ngoma in 2001, was imprisoned on charges of corruption, along with the elected vice-mayors in charge of youth and social welfare and the executive secretary (a professional position, similar to a city manager in the United States). According to popular rumors, their arrests were because of their defiance of the Minister of Interior's directives on the allocation of land. In 2004, Governor Pierre Karemera, a Tutsi from the RPF, was removed from office after his friend, university rector Emile Rwamasirabo, a moderate member of the Central Committee of the RPF, was appointed ambassador to Japan, a move that was widely perceived as an effort by Kagame to consolidate his power within the RPF. Karemera spent nearly a year without work, before taking a clerical position in Kigali. People in Butare claimed that Karemera and Rwamasirabo were being punished in part for Butare's relatively low level of support for Kagame in the August 2003 presidential election.[20]

Mabanza Commune

Prior to 1994, Kibuye was the only prefecture in Rwanda without a paved highway, but at the time of the genocide, a World Bank-sponsored project was underway to pave the rough gravel road that linked Gitarama with the regional capital of Kibuye. After taking office, the post-genocide government completed the highway, and Kibuye, with its quaint guest houses along the stunningly beautiful shores of Lake Kivu, emerged as a preferred weekend destination for both expatriates and elite Rwandans from Kigali. Despite the relative difficulty of reaching Kibuye before the construction of the paved highway, the region had long been integrated into Rwandan national political life.

Mabanza was a rural commune in the high hills above Kibuye Town that underwent little RPF violence but experienced the genocide intensely and was the focus of several of the ICTR's earliest cases. The heart of Mabanza, the community of Rubengera, lay just beyond the highest point on the Gitarama-Kibuye road, past the continental divide that separated the Nile and Congo River basins. Rubengera had impressive views down toward Lake Kivu and, on clear days, across to the steep mountains on Idjwi Island in the DRC. With its commanding location, Rubengera served as the seat of a sub-chieftancy and a pre-colonial capital, one among a number of places dotted across the national landscape where the king maintained a residence and occasionally came to assert his authority. In the late 1800s, King Kigeli IV Rwabugiri directed his invasion of Idjwi Island from his residence in Rubengera. After the advent of colonial rule, when the monarchy worked collaboratively with European powers to centralize control over the territory, Rubengera was one of the first sites to establish a Protestant mission outpost, in 1909. After independence, Rubengera remained an important center for the Presbyterian Church of Rwanda, with a high school, health center, the national headquarters for Presbyterian youth

---

[20] Fieldnotes from observation in Butare.

activities, and a center for Protestant sisters whose activities included maintaining a large orphanage.

The commune of Mabanza spread out on either side of the Gitarama-Kibuye highway that bifurcated the commune before descending toward Lake Kivu and turning south into Kibuye Town's commune of Gitesi. An area of Mabanza along the shores of the lake was reached from the Kibuye-Gisenyi road that branched off from the highway at Rubengera. According to the 1991 census, the population of Mabanza was 53,555, spread out through fourteen sectors.[21] Rubengera was the largest community in Mabanza, with several streets lined with shops and homes that spread out to the north of the highway past the high school and on to the Presbyterian parish. The office of the commune, a large brick building, lay on a rise across the highway from Rubengera, along with several other communal buildings. The village of Kibirizi lay about a mile down the highway from Rubengera, just across a broad valley, and was the location of a large daily market and collection of small shops. Several other villages and centers dotted Mabanza's landscape further off the highway. The Catholic parish of Mushubati, founded in 1955, located five miles north of the communal office along the Gisenyi road, maintained a health center, with a small commercial area nearby. The Baptist Church, present in Mabanza only since 1976, had a large high school at Bumba. While most of Mabanza lay on the hills above Lake Kivu, on either side of the Gitarama-Kibuye highway, two sectors lay along the shores of the lake, accessible from the Kibuye-Gisenyi road. A large daily market took place along this road at Gitikinini.

Although most of Mabanza's elite – the teachers, nurses, pastors, and businessmen – lived in the small villages around the commune's religious, educational, and commercial centers, the vast majority of Mabanza's population were farmers who lived on the hillsides in the midst of their fields, sometimes several hours' walk from the nearest drivable road. Mabanza's farmers grew bananas, beans, sorghum, soybeans, peas, corn, and sweet potatoes. Farmers in the high hills near the Congo-Nile Crest also grew potatoes. Many people raised cattle, goats, and pigs, particularly in the high hills where there was more open land for grazing. Most of these food crops were for personal consumption, but farmers also sold their excess at the markets at Kibirizi and Gitikinini, where traders bought up goods to resell in the market in Kibuye Town. Most farmers made a small amount of cash from coffee production; in fact Mabanza was a fairly productive coffee growing region. Other than

---

[21] Government of Rwanda, "Recensement General de la Population et de l'Habitat au 15 Août 1991," Kigali, April, 1994.

farming, however, few opportunities existed for earning an income, and the commune – like most of Rwanda – was extremely poor. Electricity and running water were only available in or near a few of the village centers, but most residents lived in modest candle-lit mud-brick homes surrounded by banana groves and hand-tilled fields.

During the period of democratization in the early 1990s, Mabanza was an area of considerable political contestation. Kibuye Prefecture was part of the central-southern region that had dominated Rwanda under Kayibanda's First Republic. When Kayibanda's party was revived as the MDR in 1991, many people in Mabanza signed on. Yet Kibuye also bordered Gisenyi, home region of President Habyarimana, so support for the MRND remained strong. The political elite in Mabanza, as in communes throughout the country, owed their positions to Habyarimana and the MRND. Ignace Bagilishema, a native of Rubengera with only two years of high school education, had served as burgomaster since Habyarimana appointed him to the position in 1980, and he remained the local MRND leader. Prior to the genocide, Mabanza had a relatively high Tutsi population, due in part to Rubengera's history as a sub-chieftaincy seat and royal residence and the Presbyterian Church that employed Tutsi pastors, teachers, and others.

In the days immediately after President Habyarimana's death, Mabanza initially remained calm, but militia groups from neighboring Rutsiro Commune and Gisenyi began to attack Mabanza. Although Mabanza's residents at first repelled the militia from outside their commune, Tutsi began to leave their homes to seek refuge in central locations. Many Tutsi from the northern sectors of Mabanza, the areas first affected by violence, gathered on Gitwa, a high mountain, near the Congo-Nile Catholic parish on the border with Rutsiro Commune, where they fought off militia attacks for several days.[22] Tutsi from the areas around Rubengera initially gathered at the commune office, but apparently fearing that he could not protect them, Bagilishema arranged on April 12 to move the Tutsi to Kibuye Town, where most sought refuge in the regional Gatwaro Stadium, while others went to the Kibuye Catholic Church. National police and militia attacked both locations beginning April 17 and killed thousands. Some Mabanza residents sought refuge in the hills of Bisesero southeast of Kibuye Town in Gitesi and Gishyita. Tutsi there mounted the most effective defense in the country against militia attacks,

---

[22] Accounts of the genocide in Kibuye show some confusion between a hill called Gitwa in the Bisesero region in Gitesi Commune and another hill called Gitwa in Rutsiro. Tutsi fought off militia in both locations, but the one referred to here is the latter, which gained the nickname Nyamagumba, in reference to a hill in Ruhengeri where the RPF fought government soldiers.

protecting most of those who sought refuge until late June. Ultimately, however, most of the Tutsi there were killed, many after a contingent of French troops came to promise protection but swiftly withdrew to their camp in Kibuye. In all, an estimated 86 percent of Mabanza's Tutsi were killed, over one third at Gatwaro Stadium. Another third was killed within Mabanza.[23]

In the aftermath of the genocide, part of Mabanza was in the Zone Turquoise, the region under French military protection in late June 1994. Hence, in contrast to much of the country, Mabanza's Hutu population did not flee *en masse* at the end of the genocide, though a minority did go into Congo. The French troops left the region in late August, and the RPF occupied the commune. While some area residents fled at this time, the region experienced much less RPF-sponsored violence than those regions that the RPF occupied earlier, and a much smaller portion of the population ever experienced displacement than in Ngoma and other parts of the country.

Construction of the Gitarama-Kibuye highway resumed shortly after 1994, linking Mabanza more effectively with the rest of Rwanda. In 1997, Kibuye was among the prefectures touched by insurgent violence, leading to an increased RPF military presence. Mabanza was also among the first areas where the ICTR worked. The Prefect of Kibuye, Clement Kayishema was put on trial in 1997. Mabanza's burgomaster, Bagilishema, was also tried but acquitted in 2001.

Like Ngoma, Mabanza experienced considerable political intrigue surrounding the supposed transition to democratic government. In March 2000, as described in Chapter 5, Kibuye's former prefect, Assiel Kabera, an influential RPF member from Kibuye, was killed in Kigali in a heavily guarded area, apparently because he and his brothers, who were prominent in Rwandan civil society, had begun criticizing the government for failing to adequately address the needs of survivors.[24] In the 2001 administrative reforms, Mabanza was broken apart and incorporated into three separate districts. Rubengera sector was attached to the Municipality of Kibuye, while the rest of Mabanza was divided between Gisunzu and Rutsiro. The communal office of Mabanza served as the temporary home for the new Gisunzu District government while a more centrally located

[23] Philip Verwimp, "A Quantitative Analysis of Genocide in Kibuye Prefecture, Rwanda," Discussion Paper Series 1.10, Leuven: Center for Economic Studies, May 2001, analyzes in detail data on the genocide in Mabanza.

[24] Bjørn Willum, "Foreign Aid to Rwanda: Purely Beneficial or Contributing to War?" PhD Dissertation, University of Copenhagen, 2001, p. 78; International Crisis Group, "'Consensual Democracy' in Post-Genocide Rwanda: Evaluating the March 2001 District Elections," Africa Report 34, Nairobi and Brussels: International Crisis Group, October 9, 2001, p. 26.

office was being constructed. In the 2001 district elections, the man who had been burgomaster of Mabanza since 1994, "Joseph," was prevented by law from standing for mayor of Gisunzu because of his lack of a university degree and instead had to settle for a position as vice-mayor in charge of economic affairs. The man elected mayor of Gisunzu, "Alphonse," was a Hutu who had been a refugee in Congo until 1996. Joseph was himself a genocide survivor and head of the Kibuye chapter of Ibuka, and he reportedly resented both his demotion and becoming assistant to a Hutu. Joseph apparently colluded to organize genocide charges against Alphonse, who was arrested in August 2002. Investigations by a regional human rights group as well as our own research with the local population found that the charges against him were not well founded.[25] After Alphonse's arrest, Joseph became acting mayor.

In late 2004, the elected mayor of Rutsiro was also arrested on genocide charges. He was subsequently accused of having donated to the hate-radio station RTLM. In another case, a March 2005 article in the newspaper *Imvaho*, accused Deputy Julienne Kabanya, a PSD member of parliament from Mabanza, of participation in the genocide. She was forced to resign and was subsequently tried in a gacaca court. A number of lower-level officials in Mabanza were also forced to resign during the period from 2003 to 2005 under threat of genocide accusations. Several *Inyangamugayo* judges and sector counselors were denounced at gacaca sessions in Gisunzu and forced to resign. Those accused in the former Mabanza were all Hutu, and nearly all were replaced by Tutsi, so that the result of these arrests and forced resignations was an increasing domination of political positions in this region by Tutsi. Those Hutu left in office in the region were sufficiently cowed by the possibility of arrest or removal to become quiescent.

Buyoga Commune

The Commune of Buyoga lay north of Kigali and was the southernmost commune in Byumba Prefecture. Much of Byumba was historically part of the pre-colonial kingdom of Ndorwa, an area that was integrated late into the Kingdom of Rwanda. Some of Ndorwa became part of modern Uganda, and Byumba remained in many ways closely linked to Uganda, speaking a dialect of Kinyarwanda known as Kiga also spoken in

---

[25] LDGL, *Dynamique du paix et logiques de guerre: Rapport Annuel sur la situation des droits de l'homme au Rwanda*, May 2003. The LDGL reported that not only did the committee from Ntawuheziminsi's cell issue a letter to the prosecutor's office attesting to his innocence, but that survivors from his cell also "testified to his good conduct during the genocide."

southern Uganda. While the indigenous religion in most of Rwanda was the Cult of Lyangombe, the population of Byumba practiced the Cult of Nyabingi, which continued to be practiced by much of the population. The region had fewer Tutsi than were present in southern Rwanda, and in the early colonial era, resistance to the extension of central state power in this region manifested in part as anti-Tutsi sentiment.[26]

Buyoga Commune spread out around the small regional capital of Byumba. Part of Buyoga was easily accessible, lying along the main highway between Kigali and Kampala in a broad, marshy valley. A commercial center lay just off the highway at Zoko, with a daily market and a number of shops serving the truck drivers and other highway traffic. Most of Buyoga, however, was harder to reach, necessitating passing through Byumba Town, which lay on a high ridge some distance off the main highway. A winding dirt road descended south from Byumba town through a tree-filled valley to Kisaro, which lay at the intersection with the other important dirt road that cut across Buyoga from east to west. The Lasallian Brothers Catholic order ran a large agricultural development center at Kisaro that worked closely with ISAR and the Ministry of Agriculture on testing new crops and new agricultural methods. One major project of the Kisaro Center for Agricultural Development was the promotion of radical terracing, a means of fighting erosion by shaping land into steep steps. Farmers in the project worked cooperatively to create terracing on hills throughout the area, so that Buyoga looks physically different from much of Rwanda, reminiscent of fields in places such as Southeast Asia. The Kisaro Center sponsored several non-farm development projects for basket making and tailoring, and a sizable commercial area stood at the nearby crossroads. Continuing down the main dirt road eventually led to Buyoga center, near the banks of the Muyanza River that formed the southern border of Buyoga and fed nearby Lake Muhazi. The commune offices were located there, as well as a weekly public market. Following the river east a short distance was the Catholic parish of Muyanza, location of the commune's only health center. Beyond these few centers, Buyoga had little developed infrastructure, with no secondary schools or industrial enterprises.

Of the three case-study communes, Buyoga was the most dependent upon agricultural employment. A 2008 government report on economic development in Rulindo, the larger district into which Buyoga was incorporated in the 2006 administrative reforms, claimed that, "Almost the entire population of Rulindo lives from agriculture, even if practiced in

---

[26] Jim Freedman, *Nyabingi: The Social History of an African Divinity*, Butare: Institute National de Recherche Scientifique, 1984; Lemarchand, *Rwanda and Burundi*.

an archaic fashion."[27] Although the hills in Buyoga were less steep than places like Mabanza, the area had a high altitude that allowed the cultivation of crops not widely found elsewhere in Rwanda, such as wheat. Some cultivation of tea took place in parts of south-west Buyoga, serving a tea factory located outside the commune. In the valley along the Kigali-Kampala road, rice and sugar cane were cultivated. Beyond these, the main agricultural products were beans, sweet potatoes, sorghum, cassava, and vegetables such as tomatoes, carrots, and cabbage.

The Commune of Buyoga was deeply affected by the war between the RPF and the Habyarimana government. RPF attacks in 1992 drove thousands of refugees from northern Byumba into Buyoga, where they were housed at a camp for IDPs at Kisaro. In their June 1992 assault on northern Rwanda, the RPF bombed the Kisaro IDP camp. In their February 1993 assault, the RPF occupied most of Buyoga Commune, driving much of the population to flee. The RPF established a military post for the Fifty-Ninth Batallion at Kisaro and retained control over all but three of the commune's sectors for the remainder of the war, and much of Buyoga's population remained in IDP camps in Kigali-Rural for over a year, though a number of people initially displaced returned home after the Arusha Accords were signed in August 1993. After the Arusha Accords, the RPF-controlled sectors of Buyoga were officially part of the demilitarized zone, yet the RPF retained its military post at Kisaro.

The genocide affected only the three sectors of Buyoga outside RPF control, and the genocide stopped in these sectors once they were occupied by the RPF. With a comparatively small Tutsi population, the numbers killed in the genocide were relatively small. In the areas of Buyoga under RPF control, however, considerable violence took place. A number of people fleeing the outbreak of war passed through Buyoga, and in several cases, the displaced were apparently attacked by RPF troops even though they were unarmed civilians. Most displaced were directed to an IDP camp in Byumba Town, and some Buyoga residents also fled to this camp. Substantial evidence indicates that the RPF carried out summary executions and other killing at the camp and other sites in Byumba.[28] In Buyoga, the RPF called a public meeting on or around April 24 at Kisaro for people within the sector, promising a food distribution and discussion of security issues, and a number of men were apparently taken away from this meeting and shot. Similar meetings that ended in massacres apparently took place at Buyoga center, at

---

[27] République du Rwanda, Province du Nord, District de Rulindo, "Evaluation des Besoins en Renforcement des Capacités: District du Rulindo," Kigali, April 2008, p. xi.

[28] Des Forges, *Leave None to Tell the Story*; Rever, "Rwanda's Memory Hole."

Shagasha primary school near Muyanza parish, at Zoko, and perhaps a few other locations, where reportedly in some cases RPF soldiers simply fired into the crowd or threw grenades. Over the next several months, a number of Hutu from Buyoga, particularly intellectuals, disappeared and were apparently killed by the RPF.[29] Given Buyoga's experience of limited exposure to the genocide but considerable experience of RPF abuses, the region remained an area of concern for the RPF. Several incidents took place in Buyoga during the 1997–1998 insurgent uprising. Most seriously, in October 1997, Hutu militia killed a local official regarded as collaborating with the RPF and all the members of his household.[30]

After the 2001 administrative reform, Buyoga became the center of an expanded district called Kisaro. Elections were held in the district as elsewhere in the country, but the results were not made public. Instead, the Governor of Byumba simply named as mayor Alphonse, a Tutsi RPF member who was not from the district and did not live there. From the beginning, relations between Alphonse and the district council were tense. A few months after the council appointed an executive secretary, he faced charges of supporting former President Bizimungu's new political party, PDR-Ubuyanja. Despite a clear lack of evidence against him, he was convicted and sentenced to three years in prison. The population widely believed that Alphonse was behind the case, and the district council had difficulty recruiting a replacement to the executive secretary post. After two years of vacancy, a new executive Secretary took over, but he resigned after only three months. While he officially resigned "for personal reasons," he told us that it was because of the difficulty of working with Mayor Alphonse. The mayor was also involved in the removal of several of the elected counselors in the sectors, so that he could appoint people of his choosing to replace them. The growing public dissatisfaction with the mayor and increasingly vocal protests from the District Council led the central government ultimately to intervene. In late 2003, the government dismissed Mayor Alphonse and arrested him at his house in the Kicukiro neighborhood of Kigali on charges of corruption and dereliction of duty, charges based in part on his lack of residence in the district. The arrest was well received in Kisaro but widely seen as a government effort to appease the local population. Despite the vice-mayor for economic affairs assuming the position as interim mayor, political uncertainty in the district remained pronounced, as both counselors and

---

[29] Amnesty International, "Reports of Killings and Abductions"; Paul Rusesabagina, "Compendium of RPF Crimes – October 1990 to Present: The Case for Overdue Prosecution," Unpublished report, Brussels, November 2006, p. 5.

[30] Human Rights Watch, *World Report 1998*.

gacaca judges were dismissed in 2004 and 2005 under accusations of participation in the genocide or harassment of witnesses in the gacaca trials.

Early Reactions to Political Reforms

As this brief overview indicates, the experiences with both the genocide and RPF violence varied substantially between Ngoma, Mabanza, and Buyoga. These experiences shaped how people reacted to government policies. In the remainder of this chapter, I look at how people have reacted to the RPF regime's political initiatives. As should be clear from these three cases, for all the talk of national unity, at the local level ethnic and political tensions remained pronounced. The local political situation in Ngoma, Mabanza, and Buyoga was not one of the factors I considered in selecting these three sites as cases to study, yet during the period in which we were actively gathering data in these communes – the three years following the 2001 local elections – political intrigue was extensive in all three communes. Interviews and observations my research team and I carried out found considerable evidence of the type of manipulation of candidate lists that HRW and the International Crisis Group claimed preceded the elections, with individuals being forced either to withdraw their candidacies or forced to run for office against their will.[31] We found, however, that political manipulation did not end with the March 2001 elections. During the course of our research, the new district mayors were arrested in each of our case study sites (including the mayors of two of the three districts into which Mabanza was divided), while many other lower-level political officials were dismissed, forced out of office, or arrested. While the public played a role in selecting its own leaders in March 2001, higher-level party and government officials vetted the list of eligible candidates, apparently favoring people with the strongest loyalties to the RPF, and replaced officials once they were in office if they did not prove themselves sufficiently obedient to orders from above. The problems that local officials encountered in these communities contradicted the supposed move toward decentralization and democracy in Rwanda and indicated not a flourishing democracy, but a local political situation tightly monitored and controlled from above.

Given the obvious manipulation of the local political context, one might have expected to encounter a high level of cynicism in the

---

[31] International Crisis Group, "'Consensual Democracy' in Post-Genocide Rwanda"; Human Rights Watch, "No Contest in Rwandan Elections: Many Local Officials Run Unopposed," Press Release, New York: Human Rights Watch, March 9, 2001.

population. Yet in the years surrounding the transition, popular attitudes toward the expansion of elections, constitutional revision, decentralization, and other political reforms were often positive. Many people expressed support for the principles behind reforms such as democratization and decentralization, even as they said they were waiting to see the policies fully realized. Much of the population in these three communities remained relatively hopeful about the processes of decentralization and democratization during the period in the lead up to the 2003 national elections. People generally liked the idea of bringing government closer to them, and they appreciated having greater say in choosing their leaders, even as many expressed doubts over the implementation of the reforms. On decentralization, for example, most people said they liked the idea of giving districts substantial autonomy, so that they could make decisions over key issues for local communities rather than serving merely to implement decisions made by the central government in Kigali. Many people expressed hopeful sentiments similar to the woman in Butare who told us, "I think that [decentralization] will be an opportunity for each citizen to play a role. Before, it was difficult to develop a good relationship with the government, because it was based far from the population. And in most cases, it made decisions without consulting the people affected. I think that with decentralization, things will be able to change."[32] A nineteen-year-old woman in Buyoga likewise observed that decentralization was "aimed at bringing the administrative structures closer."[33]

At the same time, people also raised concerns about how decentralization would work in practice. Many doubted that local governments could become self-sustaining without substantial financial support from the central government. "It is too early for me to say, but it seems that if [decentralization] is ever achieved, we'll end up with something better than before. Only, I think it's just a dream to say that districts are actually going to be autonomous! Some of them can't even figure out how they're going to pay salaries."[34] Others objected that the reorganization of administrative units actually placed them farther from government offices than before. This was particularly the case in parts of Mabanza, some of which were incorporated into the City of Kibuye, a twenty-minute drive or several hours on foot. "These reforms are good for some people, but they are a bother for me, because of the fact that I now have to pay for a bus to go to Kibuye when before I could walk

---

³² Interview in Cyarwa-Cyimana, Butare, September 8, 2001.
³³ Interview in Mutete, Buyoga, Byumba, March 29, 2002.
³⁴ Interview in Kibirizi, Mabanza, Kibuye, September 15, 2001.

a few meters to go to the Commune of Mabanza. [Decentralization] actually separated us from our infrastructure making us depend on other governmental institutions further away."[35] A farmer in Mabanza similarly stated that, "We are waiting to see what [decentralization] brings us. Decentralization is not yet operational. And then, they put together three communes, for example, and I ask myself, is that decentralization?"[36] In principle, decentralization was designed to invest more authority in the sector, the level below the district, but historically sectors had enjoyed almost no independent authority, and in practice, little was done in the first years of decentralization to develop sectors, so districts remained the central government agency with which citizens needed to interact.

The idea of democratization, particularly at the local level, was also generally popular in these communities. People appreciated choosing their own local leaders in the 1999 and 2001 elections. A man in Cyarwa, Butare, for example, told us after the 2001 elections that, "I find that these elections are very useful, because they help us to put in place our own leaders, chosen freely through our own free choice. And even if [these leaders] disappoint us, we won't have anyone to blame but ourselves, because the choice was left to us."[37] Some of the strongest support for elections and for the process of political reform came from people who themselves were elected to office. One man who ran for office in Mabanza in the March 2001 local elections was very positive on the decentralization program:

[The elections] were well organized, above all because whoever wanted to was able to participate. They were based on competitiveness and each one had his chance. ... These reforms are good, because they are going to put an end to the monopoly that some political and administrative leaders have had, getting themselves confused with their posts, thinking that they paid for them and could occupy their posts permanently. But I'm afraid that poverty will be an obstacle to the process of decentralization.[38]

Another woman elected to local office in the same community was similarly positive on the process. "It is always better when the administrative structures are closer to the population."[39] If the regime was hoping to use elections and decentralization to implicate people in the political

[35] Interview in Kibirizi, Mabanza, Kibuye, December 8, 2001.
[36] Interview in Kibirizi, Mabanza, Kibuye, September 14, 2001.
[37] Interview in Cyarwa-Cyimana, Butare, September 7, 2001.
[38] Interview in Gacaca, Mabanza, Kibuye, December 6, 2001.
[39] Interview in Nyarugenge, Mabanza, Kibuye, December 6, 2001.

process, they clearly succeeded at least in part. Yet, as higher level officials continued to interfere with the functioning of local governments, many of these same local officials, many in office for the first time, grew increasingly sour about the political process and the failure to allow real political autonomy at the local level.

Some people went beyond raising concerns over whether political reforms would effectively accomplish their stated goals – bringing government closer to the people, expanding democracy, promoting rule of law – to challenging the true intentions of the government in implementing reforms. Some people we interviewed regarded the process of political reform with indifference or skepticism. "Every time there is a change of government, they have to have their innovations. Nothing should be surprising about these reforms, and maybe they'll help the government in power to put into practice their programs."[40] "Elections are elections. They ask you to vote and you vote, but you wait for results that never arrive. It is always the same everywhere."[41] A small number of people highlighted exactly the sort of manipulation of the electoral process that we found in all three communities and challenged the degree to which the government was actually allowing free choice in elections. A farmer near Rubengera told us, "[The elections] weren't at all democratic. They secretly prevented some people from posing as candidates at the same time that they forced others to run against their will."[42] A man in one of the communities raised similar concerns:

There were certain forms of tyranny and intimidation – lies, corruption, discrimination. I was a victim of it myself. I was mayor of X Commune for two years. When I posed my candidature for mayor of Y, they fomented lies against me, saying that I had advanced beyond the sector level [in the indirect voting system] because our sector privileged ethnic identity as the criterion for eligibility. So I was eliminated in the next round of voting.[43]

The rejection of candidates in the 2001 local elections under accusations of benefitting from ethnic voting foreshadowed the growth of the fight against "divisionism" that was used prior to the 2003 presidential and parliamentary elections to exclude the participation of both candidates

---

[40] Interview in Nyarugenge, Mabanza, Kibuye, December 6, 2001.
[41] Interview in Kibirizi, Mabanza, Kibuye, September 14, 2001.
[42] Interview in Gacaca, Mabanza, Kibuye, December 8, 2001. Local elections involved voting by lining behind candidates rather than through a secret ballot.
[43] Interview, December 17, 2001.

and entire political parties, such as Bizimungu's PDR-Ubuyanja and later the MDR.[44]

While the majority of the people that we interviewed in these three communities expressed guarded support for decentralization and democratization, this should not be understood as general support for the regime and its policies. Instead, it seems to have indicated the same sort of support for devolving power to the local level that I noted in Rwanda in the democratization period of the early 1990s. In research that I conducted in 1992–1993 in Butare, Kibuye, and Ruhengeri, people were skeptical of the emergence of multi-party politics and other changes at the national level but expressed support for political reforms that might bring power closer to them. "In short, the Rwandan masses supported changes that limited the activities and reach of the state, while they saw little promise in reforms that could have changed the personnel who occupied state office."[45] As during this period just prior to the genocide, the population ten years later continued to support reforms that might constrain the power of the central state while regarding reforms to the central state structures themselves with great skepticism.

Most people we interviewed regarded the process of constitutional reform that was underway during the first period in which we were conducting interviews as having little to do with them. Despite the fact that the Legal and Constitutional Reform Commission had undertaken an official program of public consultation, few people felt they had an opportunity to influence the contents of the constitution. Some people openly charged that the commission was a façade. A man in Buyoga, for example, told us, "I don't expect much [from the Constitutional Commission]. Personally, I'm afraid that this commission is playing around with us, asking our opinions when in reality it has already elaborated a plan."[46] Others argued that the constitution was less important than the actions of the government and challenged the exercise of adopting a new constitution as empty symbolism. "I hope that this time it is respected. A constitution as a text is not sufficient. It is necessary that it is respected and that it is lasting. You can't be content with a constitution that is always being amended and that changes with each regime."[47]

Many people in these communes reacted even more negatively to the change of flag, national anthem, and national seal, with most people

44 Human Rights Watch, "Preparing for Elections."
45 Timothy Longman, "Rwanda: Chaos from Above," in Leonardo A. Villalon and Phillip A. Huxtable, eds., *The African State at a Critical Juncture: Between Disintegration and Reform*, Boulder: Lynne Rienner, 1998, pp. 75–91.
46 Interview in Mutete, Buyoga, December 17, 2001.
47 Interview in Kibirizi, Mabanza, Kibuye, September 14, 2001.

dismissing the exercise as a diversion from the effort to change actual ideas and behavior. "Changing them or not doesn't matter to me. It wasn't the flag or the song that killed. There will always be some people ready to kill others."[48] "I don't know how to respond. For me, it is like changing pants that you have decided are too old and buying another, of another different color."[49] Some went further to suggest that the change of symbols was more about the new government exercising its power. A man in Buyoga said, "For me, I don't see how it is going to change the mentalities of Rwandans. It is not the words and colors themselves that killed. Those who were bad remain bad. I find it is a means of definitively erasing the traces of the defeated former regime."[50] An elder in Mabanza said:

Personally, I find that Rwanda risks continuing to have problems if each politician who gets into power has to change all the symbols of the country. I am afraid that what we praise today will be repudiated by another regime! I don't even see why they changed the symbols. I find that Rwandans are used to accepting whatever the authorities decide. As for myself, I would hope that Rwandans would adopt the only and the same symbols once and for all! We need something lasting.[51]

Ethnicity clearly influenced attitudes on at least some issues. Tutsi were much more likely to support most reforms. For example, a Tutsi who had been a refugee in Uganda reported that, "[The elections] were well organized, and it was particularly interesting for me, because it was the first time that I took part in voting. In Uganda, we didn't have the right to vote."[52] Another young woman repatriated from Uganda told us that, "The constitution should be for all of the people and not just for those in power or for a single ethnic group as it was in the past."[53] Opinions diverged most sharply along ethnic lines on the replacement of the national symbols, with Tutsi being much more likely to express support for the change to new symbols. A survivor in Mabanza told us, "the colors of the previous flag incited people to shed blood, but the colors of the new flag reconcile people."[54] A focus group for survivors in Matyazo, Butare, expressed strong support for the change of symbols:

SPEAKER 1: In the old national anthem that was suppressed, there was a part in which they spoke about ethnicities.
SPEAKER 2: In addition, in the old national symbols, there were bad ideas. The color red, for example, which symbolized the blood spilled by the Hutu to

[48] Interview in Kibirizi, Mabanza, Kibuye, December 8, 2001.
[49] Interview in Zoko, Buyoga, Byumba, December 20, 2001.
[50] Interview in Mutete, Buyoga, December 17, 2001.
[51] Focus group of elders, Mabanza, Kibuye, August 10, 2002.
[52] Interview in Mutete, Buyoga, Byumba, March 29, 2002.
[53] Interview in Zoko, Buyoga, Byumba, December 21, 2001.
[54] Interview in Rubengera, Mabanza, Kibuye, May 6, 2015.

liberate the monarchy. The CDR reinforced the same colors during the pre-genocide period to recall to Hutu that they would massacre the Tutsi.

SPEAKER 1:   Another bad thing that was in the flag was the hoe and the machete. These are objects that were used to massacre people.[55]

Since the change in symbols was justified by the regime as responding to the painful memories that the old symbols had for survivors, this support is perhaps not surprising. Yet, as on all issues, ethnicity alone did not determine individual opinions. In reference to the change of national symbols, one repatriated Tutsi man in Rubengera shared the opinion of many of his Hutu neighbors. "I don't think they're going to bring much change. It is more important to change hearts and attitudes than to change the colors of the flag or the couplets in a song."[56]

Rwanda's "Democratic Transition" Ten Years On

Follow up research in 2015 found much more cynicism in these communities about politics than in the early period of research when political reforms were underway. Few people considered Rwanda democratic in any substantial way, and many expressed resentment over the state's authoritarian practices. The regularization of local elections did little to bring legitimacy to local officials, as people widely rejected the legitimacy of the elections:

As for the current local authorities, we are afraid of them. We do what they ask us to do. If we don't do it, they will charge us with genocide ideology. The authorities already give us the names of those we're supposed to vote for. If you should not vote for those they've proposed, you will receive threats. During the vote, in the voting booth, there is often someone who guides you and forces you to vote for a particular candidate. And they do it because there are not any international observers to denounce the situation. If you resist this person who is placed in the voting booth, they take away your voting card and rip it up and send you to go get your fingerprint [to say you've already voted]."[57]

The only place where there is democracy is in the elections for leaders of the *imidugudu*. The reason that I say these are elected, is because only the population of the *umudugudu* vote for them. Only the population decides, saying this or that person can represent us. The population chooses themselves the person that they think capable of leading them. The candidates stand up front and those who want to vote for this or that candidate places themselves behind them ... This is done publicly. In other elections, I don't think that there is democracy. You know

<hr>

[55] Focus group interview with survivors in Matyazo, Ngoma, Butare, August 17, 2002.

[56] Interview in Kibirizi, Mabanza, Kibuye, December 7, 2001.

[57] Interview in Rubengera, Mabanza, Kibuye, May 12, 2015. Another interview in a neighboring community used similar words. "As for our authorities, we're afraid of them. They are named to office but claim to have been elected." Interview in Rubazi, Mabanza, Kibuye, May 8, 2015.

that the executive secretaries of the cells and sectors are not elected. They are named. And we don't know the process of how they are named.[58]

Do you think that you can convince me that in Rwanda there are elections in the true sense of the term? I don't think so. At first, it begins with something that we could qualify as lobbying. If there are three candidates competing for a post (whether they want to or not), the occupant of the post has already been decided in advance. It's just to go through the formalities. But because no one can dare denounce this – recall the military regime that I spoke to you about – if someone did try to denounce it, even if they weren't punished or imprisoned, some of their rights would disappear for having shown an ideology contrary to that of the political regime in place.[59]

Those we interviewed also complained about the shift of power in local governance to unelected executives. As one man in Butare said, "It's impossible to dismiss them. We have tried several times, but it hasn't worked. One time we asked that such an authority be dismissed, because she managed us badly and because we didn't want her. When she organized meetings, we did not participate. But we were surprised to see her continue in her post."[60]

At the time of our 2015 interviews, supporters of the president were mobilizing to amend the constitution to allow Kagame to run for a third term. The attitudes toward this proposal were quite revealing both about the political system and how people regarded it ten years after the purported democratic transition. Even many who supported Kagame opposed his attempt to seek a third term. A survivor in Butare who otherwise expressed quite positive views of the current situation nevertheless expressed strong support for term limits:

Personally, I think that the constitution should not be touched and that the President of the Republic ought to only seek two terms, and he should leave it others after. His right to seek a third term should be snatched away so that others can be left to direct the country. So, you work well during your time to work. If you let others use the seven years, they might also work well. So if you have worked well and your term is approaching its end, you need to let others carry on.[61]

One person expressed the belief that Kagame was seeking to hold onto power to protect himself and others in the RPF from the threat of prosecution:

It's true that after the genocide, President Kagame managed the country well. But this doesn't mean that it is only him who should remain eternally in power.

---

58 Interview in Rubengera, Mabanza, Kibuye, May 10, 2015.
59 Interview in Butare, July 12, 2015.
60 Interview in Butare, July 26, 2015.
61 Interview in Tumba, Ngoma, Butare, August 9, 2015.

But since the International Criminal Court is in the process of arresting other generals from the country who committed crimes during the war and after the genocide, Kagame can't give up power. That is why his subordinates and those close to him want him to stay in power to benefit from this protection.[62]

One survivor's explanation of the process of mobilizing for a third term demonstrated both the potential for popular support of the RPF based on its policies and the degree to which the RPF's use of heavy-handed tactics to achieve its goals undermined its potential support:

On our different hills, there is intensive mobilization of the local population in which there are people who pass through house to house obliging inhabitants to write their first and last names, the numbers of their identity cards, as well as their telephone numbers. On this paper, it says, "I want Article 101 of our constitution to be revised so that the mandate of the President of the Republic becomes unlimited and that it will be renewable each five years." ...

On the hills, in meetings organized by the RPF, they teach us how we are going to vote for another term for him ... There is rather a lot of mobilization on the hills. Here, the RPF speaks above all of its own accomplishments. They tell us that Kagame has done many things for his people, his own actions – notably the initiation of the national health insurance project, the electricity campaign – and people on the hills here understand quickly without asking questions, because on the hills, these projects function. ...

Because of this mobilization, those who want him to stay in power are numerous in the interior of the country. These folks work day and night to collect the signatures of the population. The proof is that almost every day, they drop off papers at the National Assembly that have been signed demanding another candidature of President Kagame. [63]

Note that, on the one hand the speaker recognized popular appreciation for RPF programs like health insurance and the plan to expand electricity, but on the other hand he described a process in which there was heavy mobilization and people were "obliged" to sign petitions. While people might be inclined to support the government because of its successful programs, its authoritarian practices alienated the population and fueled resentment. As another man in Mabanza said, "We live under the rule of the Kagame regime. If you don't want to submit to it, where can you go?"[64]

The 2015 interviews clearly revealed that people in both urban and rural Rwanda lived in fear of the government. Through personal and family connections in the communities where he conducted interviews, my research assistant was able to convince a number of individuals to speak frankly, but he also found considerable reticence and caution.

---

[62] Interview in Butare, July 12, 2015.
[63] Interview in Rubengera, Mabanza, Kibuye, May 7, 2015.
[64] Interview in Rubengera, Mabanza, Kibuye, May 5, 2015.

A number of people declined interviews, while some who agreed to speak were careful to say nothing controversial. As he reported to me, "The people with whom I tried to speak didn't say much useful, because they're afraid to express themselves on sensitive subjects."[65] Fear of speaking frankly was not limited to Hutu, since several of the genocide survivors we spoke with also avoided expressing any criticisms.[66] Some of the informants who were less inhibited complained about the restrictions on free expression:

People are not free as they should be. They don't have the right to express their opinions. The majority of people, rather than express their opinions, they prefer to keep silent so that they don't run into any problems or to avoid troubles that could result. People who try to express their opinions, they are arrested and imprisoned or they disappear in suspicious conditions, or they are charged with attacking the internal security of the state.[67]

Thomson discussed the practice of keeping silent, particularly in the presence of authorities, as an important Rwandan strategy for survival and resistance.[68]

The fear of speaking frankly has sharply increased since the earlier period of interviews in these communities. Particularly at the beginning of the research project in 2001, very few people refused to be interviewed. While most of our interview participants were cautious, particularly in focus groups, many expressed criticisms relatively explicitly. As our research continued, however, as the country began to mobilize for gacaca beginning in 2002 and for elections in 2003, as there was a crackdown on former President Bizimungu's political party and a new law on divisionism, we found growing reluctance among people to speak openly. After a decade of increasingly repressive laws and practices, people in 2015 were much more careful about what they said than they were even in 2003, though many still did offer criticisms.

Participants in our 2015 interviews complained about the government's regular mobilization of the population as a burdensome means of control. When local authorities called on people to support something, for example to attend a public meeting or to join a rally in support of a government policy, people felt obliged to participate, because they feared

---

[65] Personal email, July 18, 2015.

[66] One survivor in Butare, for example, claimed that there were absolutely no conflicts in his community. When pressed as to whether there were not occasionally ethnically based conflicts he reported, "Truly none at all." My research assistant noted, "The gentleman was characterized by fear and avoided making any criticisms." Interview in Butare, July 15, 2015.

[67] Interview in Butare, July 12, 2015.

[68] Thomson, *Whispering Truth to Power*, 145.

the consequences of failing to do so. An informant in Butare recounted seeing a rally in favor of changing the constitution to allow Kagame to stand for a third term:

Recently, in walking home, I encountered a big crowd of people and I asked an acquaintance of mine, "Why are there so many people? Where are you going?" He told me that they were going into the street to ask that the constitution be abolished. "Do you want it to be abolished?" I asked him, "because if it's like that, it's a coup d'état. Or is it that you want it amended?" This person, my acquaintance, finally responded that it was pretty much the same thing. This is just to say that there are people who follow the others, just to show that they participate and to avoid getting into trouble afterward for having failed to support the others. This shows that they take part in these programs knowing that they're not really interested.[69]

As a number of informants told us, there are usually no formal punishments for failing to participate in programs for which the government is mobilizing people, but those who fail to show up risk being marked as troublemakers and become vulnerable to official sanction:

Even today, if you don't want to march to the government's beat, you are badly viewed. For example, if they organize demonstrations to demand the liberation of this general who was arrested in London, if you don't want to take part in these demonstrations while your neighbors participated, you're going to be badly viewed, even though you haven't violated a law.[70]

Despite the growing resentment of the government's authoritarian practices, the research indicated that the regime's strategy of performance legitimation was at least partially successful. Many people we interviewed felt that Rwanda was well governed under the RPF and expressed a degree of respect for President Kagame in particular. Some linked their positive feelings directly to the benefits they received from government policies, like a Hutu man in Mabanza who said, "Politics in our community is going very well. For example, I didn't know how to read and write. Today, I know how to read and write."[71] A young survivor in Mabanza also mentioned the government's programs as evidence of good rule. "The President of the Republic does not tolerate any person who wants to ruin the country, whether it is on the Tutsi side or the Hutu side. He wants to develop Rwanda with incredible speed." Yet he went on to add:

Electoral democracy in Rwanda does not exist … In 2015, the situation appears good. I'm not afraid to say it: Rwanda after 1994 has had good governance.

[69] Interview in Butare, July 12, 2015.
[70] Interview in Butare, July 12, 2015.
[71] Interview in Nyarugenge, Mabanza, Kibuye, May 14, 2015.

I think that if there is calm today, it is thanks to the current authorities. Today, there is steady development. They build homes for the genocide survivors. They reinstall Rwandans who have been repatriated. This has allowed Rwandans to regain a taste for life. But if you look really closely, the situation shows that Rwandans only pretend to live together peacefully.[72]

Despite his generally positive assessment, the young man expressed concern that the current peace may be only a façade. The government was managing things well, but there was anger and resentment under the surface. Several other informants also made clear that the apparent compliance by the population and the peaceful appearance of Rwandan communities masked tensions underneath the surface:

In our community, I don't see any conflicts … That is to say, if there is a program or whatever activity that could bring people in the community together, like community work, then the objective is the success of this activity without taking account of people's ethnic membership or other small conflicts. Frankly, I don't see conflicts in my community. But if you look at it deeply there is an explanation for this. It is because our current power is a military regime. With a military regime in power, there is an obligation just to submit. The character of negotiation is absent.[73]

Conclusions

Although the communes that I discussed in this chapter differed in their experiences during the war and genocide, each of these communities has clearly felt the coercive power of the central state since 1994. The use of state violence was most pronounced just after the RPF's rise to power, though not equally experienced in all communities. When the research began in 2001 this active violence was rare, but thousands of residents from each community were in jail under genocide charges and the possibility of imprisonment remained a very real threat that hung over the heads of nearly all Hutu residents and helped to keep most from challenging the authority of the state in any visible fashion. Even after the conclusion of most genocide prosecutions, the possibility of being charged with divisionism or genocide ideology kept the threat of imprisonment tangible. Imprisonment was less a threat for Tutsi, as the accounts here indicate, but accusations of corruption could be used as a pretext for imprisoning Tutsi as well.

The near constant threat of imprisonment or official sanction created a highly constrained social climate in Rwanda. The fear of being charged

---

[72] Interview in Rubengera, Mabanza, Kibuye, May 10, 2015.
[73] Interview in Butare, July 12, 2015.

with divisionism or genocide ideology not only restricted people's ability to organize politically but also forced people to self-censor, avoiding openly discussing not just government policies but their own experiences and identities. The power of the government also forced people in these communities to accept the numerous government reforms largely without complaint.[74] The *imidugudu* program of forced villagization spared these three communes, but the exercise of state power was felt in many other ways. The population was increasingly mobilized to participate in government-sponsored initiatives that took more and more time away from productive activities. *Umuganda* community labor required every citizen to spend the last Saturday of the month working on community projects, and the local governments periodically required additional *umuganda*. Community residents were required to attend regular mandatory public meetings to instruct them about the 2001 local elections, the gacaca process, the gacaca elections, the new constitution, the 2003 elections, and other programs. In Buyoga and Mabanza, the population was already mobilized for the pilot phase of gacaca in June 2002, which not only took up a day every week but involved numerous public information sessions and other activities. From 2005 to 2012, gacaca mobilization was a weekly requirement for every citizen. In this highly restricted and politicized atmosphere, government policies like bans on public spitting and plastic bags, regulation of markets, and attempts to reform land tenure, were read as arbitrary exercise of state power.

That the residents of these communities generally hoped that decentralization, democratization, and other reforms would bring greater local autonomy and free them from interference from outside their communities is thus not surprising. In practice, however, people found that the heavy hand of the state was growing heavier as time passed. Our research began at a moment of optimism as the government promised that reforms would bring about a political transition. But the ostensible transition toward democracy was forcefully constrained by the mobilization against PDR-Ubuyanja and the MDR that affected people not only in Kigali but even in rural communities like Buyoga and Mabanza. The local elite had to be particularly careful about what they said and did. Teachers had to be cautious about what they taught in the classroom, as the campaign against "divisionism" spread in 2002.[75] Government administrators had to show near complete compliance with directives

---

[74] Thomson, *Whispering Truth to Power*, notes that "Individual facility in the art of disguising and concealing one's real feelings or opinions on a given matter is self-taught and culturally sanctioned; dissimulation and acquiescence are both common" (p. 144).

[75] Freedman et al, "Confronting the Past in Rwandan Schools"; Freedman et al., "Teaching History after Identity-Based Conflicts."

that came from above or risk not simply being thrown out of office but being thrown into prison. Andrea Purdeková described effectively how the exactions of the state steadily increased, as both demands on the time and financial resources of Rwandans and the surveillance apparatus to ensure compliance intensified. The complete compliance of local elected officials was guaranteed by the embedding of the executive secretaries named by the central government into each community and the *imihigo* performance contract system.[76] While most policymaking power was transferred to these unelected civil servants, a large portion of whom were repatriated Tutsi, the elected officials were largely relegated the responsibility of mobilizing the population in line with official policy.

We found people during the course of our research growing increasingly frustrated but also increasingly afraid to talk about their frustrations. As an informant in Mabanza said in 2015, "We are submissive. Here, politics is done by only a few people. And it can be seen that politics is played by only one political group, because others don't have political space."[77] People expressed fear of the local officials who were their main contact with the government. "If you don't respect [the local authorities], what can you do? They can take you. We are afraid of them. The authorities are named to office, and we line up behind them."[78]

The experience of my own research team effectively demonstrates the increasingly authoritarian nature of the state in Rwanda during this period. When I launched my research program in early 2001, I met with a wide range of ministers and others in government and sought formal permission for my projects from the Ministry of Higher Education and Research and the Ministry of Justice and from the mayor of each of the districts where we wanted to work. My research team and I received permission from the national body overseeing gacaca to attend gacaca sessions, and we received permission from the National Electoral Commission to observe the various stages of the 2003 election. A small group of researchers under my direction visited the three communes repeatedly beginning in May 2001, conducting individual and focus group interviews, attending gacaca sessions, and consulting local authorities. Nevertheless, when two of our researchers, including the research team leader who was a native of Mabanza, approached one of the polling places in Mabanza to observe the August 25, 2003, presidential elections, a small group of RPF supporters and intelligence officers stopped them. The researchers showed their letter from the National

---

[76] Purdeková, "Even if I Am Not Here"; Purdeková, *Making Ubumwe.*
[77] Interview in Kibirizi, Mabanza, Kibuye, May 5, 2015.
[78] Interview in Rubengera, Mabanza, Kibuye, May 5, 2015.

Electoral Commission granting permission to observe the voting, but the officers accused them of being agents for opposition candidate Faustin Twagirimungu and ordered them to leave. The two researchers then drove to another polling site within Mabanza, some distance from the first, but the officers had already broadcast a warning about their presence, and another group of officers stopped and turned back the researchers' car before arriving at the next site. Again at a third site, they were turned away:

At one site in Rubengera Sector, my colleague managed to record public reaction on his microphone before being stopped. The population complained about the way in which RPF supporters were following and intimidating them in their homes. Some claimed that RPF supporters were simply voting on their behalf for the RPF candidate. Following this incident where we were found speaking with the population, we ran into more serious problems. Our vehicle was stopped at a checkpoint, and our driver was charged RWF 20.000 (or about USD 50) for having forgotten his driver's license in his room, about a kilometer away.[79]

Being unable to observe the voting in Mabanza, the researchers decided to return to the Catholic guesthouse in Kibuye Town where they were staying. The driver was fined as they arrived at the entrance of town, and as the researchers then approached the guesthouse, a worker waved them down and warned them that police had searched their room and were waiting for them there. The researchers decided to turn around and head directly back home to Kigali.

This was not, however, the end of the affair. According to the team leader:

A few days after my return, I was surprised to hear my neighbors reporting a version of the incident in Kibuye that claimed that I was stopped by authorities as I was trying to influence electors to vote for a member of the Hutu ethnic group, like me, meaning Twagiramungu. According to my neighbors, the story was being spread by the counsellor of my cell. He told them that he had a mandate to put on the "red list" all people in his cell who had not been voting for the RPF. Apparently, authorities from Kibuye had contacted authorities in Kigali, and the counsellor had been told that he should put my name on the red list.

One month later, I was invited by an NGO to attend a weeklong meeting in Arusha, Tanzania. When I returned to Kigali, I was told by people that the same counsellor had publicly reported that I had fled the country, fearing the consequences of what I had tried to do during the elections, and that I had joined other political opponents in exile because our candidate, "our Hutu," had lost the elections. I approached the counsellor to discuss the rumors that he had been spreading, but he told me that it was other people he didn't mention who came to him and reported the news.[80]

---

[79] Fieldnotes, September 29, 2003.
[80] Ibid.

A few weeks after this incident, a group of police came to the researcher's home on a Sunday morning and conducted a search of the premises. "Without showing their authorisations, they started searching all the rooms in our house, without taking privacy into consideration. They said that they were searching for illegal arms held by some people within the area. One of the police asked me why I was keeping a lot of papers at my house like politicians and why I had a laptop at home."[81] The police confiscated the laptop and papers from our research project. Although the papers were eventually returned, the intimidating atmosphere continued, eventually forcing the researcher to flee the country with his family, fearing arrest and possible violence.

This story is indicative of the increasingly heavy hand of the state in Rwanda as the government, military and RPF sought to extend their control further and more effectively into public life. As I will discuss in the next two chapters, individual experiences with the state have affected how people have reacted to government policies, including programs to promote national unity and build rule of law. As the stories of Agnes, David, Eugene, and Patrick at the beginning of this chapter reveal, though ethnicity has remained a central element determining an individual's social status and influencing their encounters with the state, even in a single community among people of the same ethnic background, individual experiences of the genocide and of life in post-genocide Rwanda varied widely. The histories of these three communities and the stories of individual community members demonstrate that ethnicity is but one factor among many in determining experiences and attitudes. The division between those in Rwanda at the time of the genocide and those Rwandan refugees who subsequently returned to the country also greatly influenced individual experience. In some ways, the genocide was a shared experience for Hutu and Tutsi in Rwanda in 1994 that many repatriated refugees had difficulty fully grasping. In post-genocide Rwanda, repatriated refugees dominated not only the government but economic and social life as well, so that the repatriated experienced life in post-genocide Rwanda very differently from the rest of the population, enjoying a much greater degree of individual freedom and a greater sense of political openness. Yet as the arrest of the mayor of Kisaro District in Byumba suggested, the repatriated – even those who held public office – were themselves not immune from the strong arm of the Rwandan state.

This chapter sought to explain the local political context within which the government implemented policies to shape memory and promote justice. All three case-study communities experienced terrible violence in

---

[81] Fieldnotes, November 15, 2003.

1994, Mabanza primarily in the genocide, Buyoga primarily from RPF attacks, and Ngoma from both the genocide and the RPF. In the years after 1994, the level of active violence in all three communities declined, but government policies continued to be highly coercive. Thousands of people in each community were arrested on genocide charges and, as will be discussed in Chapter 8, gacaca served to heighten rather than alleviate fears of arrest. Crackdowns on "divisionism" and "genocide ideology" added to public apprehension. More and more restrictive public regulations and increasingly regular mobilization of the population for government programs promoted public obedience but created more fear and cynicism than agreement and loyalty. As I discuss in the next chapter, this authoritarian context sharply limited the ability of the government to convince the public to embrace its vision of the past in more than a superficial fashion. People learned to mouth the official government narrative, but their lived experience of an authoritarian regime undermined the government's efforts and kept counter-narratives alive.

> The politics of memory in Rwanda today are intimately connected to questions of identity. To remember is to assert a claim about one's own being.
>
> – Jennie Burnet, *Memory Lives in Us*

Alphonsine invited me to visit her home, which in Rwandan culture is an honor reserved for a friend. But she did not want to show me where she was living at the time nor the nearby house that she was currently building. Instead, she wanted to show me the place she considered her *real* home, where she had lived before – before the genocide, before the war, the place where she had lived much of her life, before her neighbors drove her away.

On a Saturday morning Alphonsine came over, and we headed to Cyarwa and Tumba, the ostensibly urban neighborhoods spread out on the hills south of Butare, where the homes are surrounded by banana groves and fields of beans and homesteads are distinguishable from rural farms only by their close proximity to one another and the small size of the plots of land. We turned off the highway onto a main dirt road that ran through Cyarwa, then followed a side road until the pick-up could go no further, even in four-wheel drive, so we parked the truck and began to walk. "Before the war this was a good road," Alphonsine muttered as we made our way on foot.

The further we got from the main road, the more spread out and rural the homes became. The houses seemed shabbier and poorer here as well; the distance from the road made it harder for these residents to go into the city to find work. Many of the homes were abandoned, and some were in ruins. As we walked, Alphonsine pointed out landmarks. Passing one home where only a few knee-high mud walls remained, she told me, "That family was killed in April," meaning that they were killed during the genocide. Just across the street another house was abandoned, its doors and windows missing. "This family was killed in July," she said, meaning that they were killed by the RPF after they took control of Butare.

A little further on she pointed to a field overgrown with weeds. "There is a mass grave there," she said.

"From April?" I asked.

"No," she said. "From July. Many people here lost their lives then." She pointed to a spot further up the road. "The grave from April is over there," she said.

When we arrived at her home, we walked around the grounds, and she told me her story from 1994. Everyone who was in Rwanda that year has a story to tell. Alphonsine was Hutu, but she claimed that she was not political, and as a woman, she was under no pressure to participate in the genocide. Nevertheless, as the situation in Butare began to deteriorate, she found herself increasingly vulnerable. She was a single mother with no family nearby, and before the genocide, she had worked as a cook and cleaner for European expatriate workers, so she had more means than many of her neighbors. "The war changed people," she said. Neighbors grew jealous of her and demanded bribes. Men passed by asking for sexual favors. The order of the community began to deteriorate, and what had been a targeted genocide at its outset in April began to descend into general lawlessness by June. Alphonsine had moved to Butare years before from the neighboring prefecture of Gikongoro, so her family was not known here. A rumor spread through the community that Alphonsine was actually a Tutsi trying to pass for a Hutu, which could be used as an excuse for killing her and pillaging her goods. Fearing for her life, Alphonsine fled her home to stay with a friend on the opposite side of Butare.

Alphonsine did not return to Cyarwa until after the RPF arrived in Butare. When she returned to her house, she found that it had been looted of everything worth carrying away – the furniture, her radio, her kitchen equipment. She moved back in, but she found that she could no longer live in her neighborhood. "There was too much suspicion, too many rumors and lies." She could not trust her neighbors anymore, and so she returned to the neighborhood north of Butare to which she had fled during the war and rented a room there. She was now building a house just up the road, trying to start a new life with new neighbors with whom she shared no history in a community where the landscape did not bear constant reminders – at least not for her – of the death and destruction and danger of 1994.[1]

[1] Based on fieldnotes, March 1996.

The Official Memory Project Confronting Lived Experience

I have taken many such walks in Rwanda since 1994. To those familiar with them, the hillsides of Rwanda are crowded with memorials.[2] Buildings and roads and fields that appear ordinary to the uninformed evoke troubling memories in those who lived through the terrible events of 1994. Homes destroyed during the genocide or left abandoned when people fled into exile as the RPF approached often remained untouched, walls gradually disintegrating into mud, standing as monuments to those who died. Even after years of disinterment and reburials in official genocide memorial sites removed the bodies from many of the original mass graves, locals still remembered the fields where the bodies lay and who killed them. Bloodstains that never fully disappeared from the walls and floors of some churches served as reminders of the massacres as the faithful gathered for worship each week. A crossroads that appeared ordinary to those new to the area reminded those who lived through the events of 1994 of the dangerous roadblock through which they had to pass each day.

Every person living in Rwanda in 1994 has a story to tell, though not everyone chooses to share his or her story. Whether they were targeted by the violence or participated in attacks or merely witnessed the horrors taking place around them, everyone had personal experience of traumatic events. In the three local communities where we conducted research, we asked people whether they talked about what happened in Rwanda with their family and friends. Most said that they talked at least with those to whom they were close and who shared similar experiences. Some told us that talking about the past was a moral responsibility, so that those who were lost would not be forgotten or so that the terrible things that happened would never be repeated. A Hutu man in Butare said, "We must commemorate, because this helps use realize where the error came from and how to prevent others, while looking for a means of correcting the errors of the past."[3] Others told us that talking about the past caused them too much pain. A survivor in Butare told us, "As a victim myself, I feel very ill at ease every time that I have to talk about these things."[4] A Hutu man in Buyoga said, "I personally don't see why

---

[2] The *Oxford English Dictionary* defines a memorial as "Something by which the memory of a person, thing, or event is preserved, as a monument, a custom, or an observance." Online version, Oxford University Press, 2013.

[3] Interview in Butare, September 2001.

[4] Interview in Cyarwa-Sumo, Butare, November 23, 2001.

we should talk about it. We can't easily talk about these horrors. I personally avoid it."[5] Still others seemed reluctant to speak about their own experience, because doing so was politically dangerous.

As described in Part I of this book, the post-genocide government of Rwanda undertook great effort to shape the collective memory of the population about the country's past. The government and its supporters developed and disseminated a specific historical narrative that they reinforced by creating numerous sites of memory – memorials, commemorations, and new national symbols. Yet the degree to which a government can manipulate collective memory, particularly for events that have occurred within people's lived experience, remains contested. Pierre Nora saw the sites of memory that have proliferated in France as a nostalgic attempt to recapture the connection with community and place that was challenged by modernity.[6] Margaret Farrar effectively explained Nora's perspective:

Pierre Nora argues that the reason for the proliferation of these *lieux de memoire* is because there are no longer real environments of memory: the places where collective memory is inculcated and thrives because of thick familial and cultural ties. Instead of the traditional, collective memory inherent in peasant culture, he argues, mass society produces history: "the reconstruction, always problematic and incomplete, of what is no longer." Rather than memory occurring spontaneously and naturally, in contemporary society we rely on the frenetic and deliberate approximation of memory; we anxiously assemble archives, invent or revive rituals, and organize celebrations, searching for traces of what we have lost. The less memory is experienced internally, Nora points out, the more it relies on "its exterior scaffolding and out ward signs."[7]

Rwanda has certainly experienced substantial disruption and detachment of populations from place. Hundreds of thousands were killed in the violence of 1994, millions were displaced, and thousands of them died, particularly in the wars in Congo. More than half a million Tutsi who had been living outside Rwanda as refugees, many since 1959, returned home after the RPF victory.[8] Some of the returnees settled in the newly created territory of Umutara, while a large portion moved to Kigali. Only a minority of returnees went back to their family homesteads in rural communities. Many of the genocide survivors, particularly from rural areas, left their original homes as well, moving either

---

[5] Interview in Muranzi, Buyoga, Byumba, March 27, 2002.

[6] Nora, *Les Lieux de Mémoire*.

[7] Margaret E. Farrar, "Amnesia, Nostalgia, and the Politics of Place Memory," *Political Research Quarterly*, 46, no. 4, December 2011, 723–735, citation p. 729.

[8] Kristin Scalzo, "The Rwandan Refugee Crisis: Before the Genocide," National Security Archive Electronic Briefing Book No. 464, George Washington University, March 31, 2014.

to the cities or into special *imidugudu*, collective villages, for survivors.[9] Many Hutu, particularly in the northwest of the country, were forced out of their homes into *imidugudu* as well, and many Hutu also moved to the cities.

Like the French government that used sites of memory to construct French republican identity, the post-genocide Rwandan government sought to manipulate memory to reshape Rwandan national identity. Yet Rwanda is not France. Eighty percent of the population still lives in rural areas, and the vast majority makes their living from farming the land. While many people have left their homes, the majority of Rwandans, particularly those in rural areas, have deep roots in their communities. Rwandans do not lack "thick familial and cultural ties," and most are more directly connected to their history than the situation Nora discusses in France. Many of those who live in cities continue to maintain strong relationships with their home communities and visit them regularly, something made easy by Rwanda's small size and good transportation system. Many Rwandans remain close to their families, and elders continue to pass down the stories of family, community, and nation to the next generation. Furthermore, much of the history that the government seeks to influence is recent, having happened within lived memory. Local residents continue to remember who resided in their communities before 1994, what happened to them, and where they are now. Any attempt to shape collective memory runs up against both individual lived experience and the familiar stories of family and community.

As I have argued in this book, the hand of the Rwandan state is extremely heavy. The government's attempts to promote a particular narrative and shape collective memory are backed by coercive force. The legal system imposed the official narrative through both genocide trials, where vast portions of the population have been implicated in the event that the narrative places at the center of Rwandan history, and arrests and prosecution for "divisionism" and "genocide ideology" for those who publicly articulate stories that challenge the official narrative. Attempts to develop and share alternative narratives that challenged the RPF's interpretation of the past, thus, were constrained by an oppressive political context in which mentioning realities like the suffering experienced at the hands of the RPF could have dire consequences.

---

[9] Human Rights Watch, *Uprooting the Rural Poor*; Integrated Regional Information Networks, "Rwanda: Government Implements Low Cost Housing for Returnees," OCHA, October 5, 2004, www.irinnews.org/report/51581/rwanda-government-implements-low-cost-housing-for-returnees.

In this chapter, I explore how people in Rwanda talk about the past in an attempt to understand how much the government memory project has been able to shape collective memory.[10] Drawing primarily on individual interviews, focus group interviews, and two surveys conducted during the period of transition from 2001 through 2005 and on additional interviews conducted in 2015, I consider how popular interpretations of Rwandan history and the events of 1994 compares with the approved narrative. On some points, popular historical narratives were consistent with the narrative promoted in government statements, sanctioned commemorations, and authorized memorials sites. At the very least, people were familiar with the official narrative and knew what they were *supposed* to say about the Rwandan past. Yet the stories that people told were not uniform and often diverged in important ways from the authorized narrative. People also objected to what they saw as blatant and cynical attempts to shape memory. In this chapter, I also discuss how the population interprets the memorials and commemorations that the government used to shape collective memory specifically of the genocide. The wide diversity of reactions to and understandings of these memorials and commemorations suggest real limitations to the government's ability to use them to force a particular idea of the immediate past.

Popular Narratives of the Rwandan Past

In our interviews for this book, my research team and I asked Rwandans about their perceptions of their country's history and the origins of conflict. Many Rwandans from all social groups talked about social harmony in pre-colonial Rwanda, reflecting the official narrative's key idea of the essential unity of Rwanda's people.[11] Many also discussed the divisive role of colonialism. A schoolteacher who returned to Rwanda from Uganda after the genocide effectively captured a perspective consistent with the official interpretation of history:

[10] While a number of people have looked at the rewriting of Rwandan history, official memorials, and other topics related to post-genocide memory, only a few other scholars have explored how the Rwandan population itself is remembering the past. See in particular Burnet, *Genocide Lives in Us*, which explores how genocide survivors confront the past. See also Chakravarty, "Navigating the Middle Ground," pp. 232–253; Hintjens, "Post-Genocide Identity Politics in Rwanda"; and Jens Meierhenrich and Martha Lagace, "Photo Essay: Tropes of Memory," *Humanity: An International Journal of Human Rights, Humanitarianism, and Development*, 4, no. 2, Summer 2013, 289–312.

[11] Chakravarty, "Navigating the Middle Ground," found in her interviews that "respondents accepted the RPF assertion that Rwandans had been united under pre-colonial Tutsi rule, but disagreed with the RPF's key premise for that claim. They argued that unity had been in large part the product of Hutu submission to elite Tutsi injustices" (p. 234).

In their practices, Rwandans lived in perfect harmony. They exchanged services without taking account of ethnicity … The principle cause [of the events of 1994] was that the authorities sowed hatred among Rwandans and exploited the ethnic card. The Rwandan authorities based their actions on the difference established by the colonial authorities, who grounded the differences on height, on physical traits, like the nose, among others. They preached that the Hutu had always been dominated by the Tutsi, preaching that at the time of Tutsi rule, the cows, the fields belonged to the Tutsi.[12]

Many people who were in Rwanda in 1994 gave similar accounts. The explanation of a small trader in Butare was typical. "The ethnic groups have always existed, but that didn't keep people from getting along. Then the whites came to make them understand that they were not equal."[13] A genocide survivor in Mabanza claimed that ethnic problems dated, "From the arrival of the whites. Before their arrival, Rwandans lived in perfect harmony and lived together peacefully."[14]

When asked about the origins of ethnic conflict in Rwanda, many referred to the history of colonial manipulations of identity. For example, a young woman in Mabanza reported:

The problems began with the colonial authorities and the Church, who subdi-vided Rwandans into ethnic categories and instituted identity cards that listed ethnic identities. They told the Hutu that they were numerous and that they ought to drive the Tutsi from power, and in 1959, there was the revolution that burned Tutsi homes. In 1973, the same thing, until 1994 where all those who hadn't previously fled were massacred without pity. My parents always told me that before the arrival of the whites, people lived in harmony without mistrust, that there were mixed marriages and such.[15]

A middle-aged Tutsi woman in Mabanza blamed *abazungu*, "whites" or "foreigners," for the country's divisions:

Our history tells us that the origins of the ethnic problems in Rwanda was the arrival of the *abazungu*. They classified the two groups of the Rwandan popula-tion according to their wealth and their poverty. Those who were rich were called Tutsi, the poor were called Hutu without consideration of their physical appear-ance. After successfully creating this division, the whites lined themselves up on the side of the Tutsi, giving them all the advantages. It's thus that they ordered the Tutsi to beat the Hutu. The Hutu thus bore a grudge until the revolution. With their revolution, the Hutu turned against the Tutsi. And then, the whites, realizing that the Tutsi were not following their wishes, they ordered the Hutu to oppress the Tutsi.[16]

---

[12] Interview in Matyazo, Ngoma, Butare, December 2, 2001.
[13] Interview in Matyazo, Ngoma, Butare, December 13, 2001.
[14] Interview in Rubengera, Mabanza, Kibuye, May 7, 2015.
[15] Interview in Kibirizi, City of Kibuye (formerly Mabanza), September 14, 2001.
[16] Interview in Rubengera, Mabanza, May 6, 2015.

We asked a youth focus group in Butare whether ethnicity had played a role in the genocide:

SPEAKER 1: Yes, because in times past, there was no ethnicity. Everyone was called Rwandan. The policies of the *abazungu* sowed the problem of ethnicity, the origin of the segregation of Rwandans. If there had been no ethnicity, there would have been no genocide.

SPEAKER 2: Wherever a Rwandan is, he should be considered as a Rwandan, not as a Tutsi or Hutu.

SPEAKER 3: In historic Rwanda, there was no ethnicity, but the herders were designated as Tutsi and the farmers as Hutu. And when a herder, that is to say a Tutsi, became poor, when his cattle disappeared, he was called a Hutu and vice versa for Hutu who became rich, they were called Tutsi.[17]

While blaming Rwanda's ethnic problems on colonial rule is consistent with the official narrative, it also resonates with people's own experience. Rwandans in 1994 still carried identity cards that stated their ethnicity, and they knew identity cards were first issued by the Belgian authorities. People old enough to remember the 1950s had direct memory of colonial policies on ethnicity and witnessed the shift in official support from the Tutsi to the Hutu. An elderly Hutu farmer in Byumba explained how colonial policy divided Rwandans, focusing on the elimination of the clientage system that happened in the last decade of colonial rule:[18]

Before, we had enough wealth to go around for everyone. Those who didn't have enough could go work for those who had more than them, and it was complementary. That changed at the moment where they banned the practice called *ubuhake*, or the cleavage of Tutsi against the Hutu. The colonial authorities were right in saying that it wasn't democratic. But people became poor and jealous toward the rich. They even required forced sharing and all that did nothing but stir up cases of conflict between the ethnic groups. The problems dated back way before 1994, very far back. In 1994, it was the realization of this frustration among the Hutu who were poor in spirit and material goods against other Hutu with more integrity and above all against the Tutsi, whom they considered like beings unworthy of the name human.[19]

Yet people were not unanimous in repeating the government's narrative. In Buyoga in particular, where RPF violence killed more people than the genocide, the majority of individuals we interviewed said that they knew nothing about the origins of ethnic conflict in Rwanda (in contrast

[17] Focus group with youths, Cyarwa, Butare, June 15, 2002.

[18] Newbury, *Cohesion of Oppression*, provides an excellent explanation of *ubuhake* and other systems of clientage that existed in Rwanda in the late colonial period. *Ubuhake* was a system of exchange of cattle between patrons (mostly Tutsi) and clients (mostly Tutsi) that was banned by King Rudahigwa, under international pressure, in the 1950s, because it was regarded as an unequal and exploitative system.

[19] Interview in Zoko, Buyoga, December 20, 2001.

to other regions, where most people offered responses), and many of those who did offer opinions blamed ethnic divisions on the RPF and its invasion of Rwanda. A young widow told us, "Everything began with the RPF war in 1992 ... There was first the war, then the genocide and massacres."[20] Another young woman farmer told us, "I think that the [ethnic] problems began with the war of 1990 and the political parties that were based on ethnic groups."[21]

In Butare and Mabanza, some people also identified the RPF invasion as a source of problems, but they usually did so in more qualified terms. For example, a man in Butare told us, "I hear on the radio that the Rwandan people were a people who lived together as one. This included farmers and herders. People shared cows, married together, and could share a beer during the harvest. But that was affected by the war, because those who entered the country came in killing, and those here killed as well, and that is how it broke down."[22]

The official narrative appeared to influence other elements of popular narratives. When I lived in Rwanda in 1992–1993, the Revolution of 1959 was a central element of the official discourse. The ruling party was called the National *Revolutionary* Movement for Development, and the elite justified their rule through claims they were realizing the promise of the 1959 revolution (even as they were in fact enriching themselves in the face of the country's general poverty). But in our 2001–2003 interviews, very few people referred to the events of 1959 as a revolution, and those who did generally qualified their remarks and portrayed the violence then not in heroic terms but as the beginning of the country's ethnic discord.[23] A former government official in Buyoga, for example, said that the ethnic problems in Rwanda, "Go back, in my opinion, to 1959 when the Hutu revolution attacked the Tutsi. That caused the first movement of refugees to the exterior of the country."[24] Many people tied the revolution to colonial manipulation. Not surprisingly, Tutsi were more likely than Hutu to see 1959 as the beginning of the country's ethnic discord. When asked about the origins of ethnic conflict in Rwanda, a young survivor in Rubengera told us, "I think that it was with the revolution of 1959, when they began to burn and destroy the property of others in order to drive them from

---

[20] Interview in Muranzi, Buyoga, December 17, 2001.
[21] Interview in Zoko, Buyoga, December 20, 2001.
[22] Interview in Cyarwa-Cyimana, Butare, August 22, 2001.
[23] Chakravarty's informants in "Navigating the Middle Ground" were more open to discussing 1959 in positive terms, but still with qualifications. Her informants "perceived the events of 1959 as a struggle for freedom from oppression, but did not believe that the means adopted had been just" (p. 243).
[24] Interview in Buyoga, December 17, 2001.

the country."[25] In a discussion of the sources of violence, a survivor in Mabanza said:

I want to add that the persecution of Tutsi began in 1959. Those who had the means took flight to neighboring countries where they multiplied. In this way, they were able to study and to seek the means to return to their native country. The Hutu authorities in the government of Habyarimana rejected the Arusha Accords. They promoted the idea that Rwanda was too small to welcome everyone. The Tutsi living outside the country did not accept the idea from the Rwandan authorities. Lacking other solutions, the high Rwandan authorities began to influence the population to kill the Tutsi population. In reality, everything began in 1959, until 1991. Many Tutsi were treated as traitors. I was myself written about in the newspapers like many other Tutsi, above all those whose families had means.[26]

In very few of our interviews did people dare to speak approvingly of the 1959 revolution. One middle-aged farmer in Kibuye said that in school:

They told us that the Tutsi accumulated all the power and their children were the only ones who could be admitted to school. And they told us that this was the reason for the revolution of 1959. In my opinion, this history was true, because the colonizers worked with the ruling class, which was the Tutsi. It was that which allowed them to have their children enrolled in school first, and it was to be expected, in my view. It was the revolution of 1959 that changed things.[27]

An elderly man in Buyoga took an even more risky position:

I talk about what I know, what I saw with my own eyes. The origin [of ethnic conflict] was 1958–1959. There were two groups, Hutu and Tutsi. In 1959, Hutu went and destroyed Tutsi houses, took their cattle, chased them from the country, some to Burundi, some to Uganda. The king had said that he had abolished *ubuhake*. He said that Tutsi should give Hutu cows. He wanted to make them equal. Then he went and died. That's when the fighting started. Those who were outside the country came to avenge what happened. The cause [of ethnic conflict] was those who came from outside to chase away the Hutu and take over power and rule the whole country.[28]

Sentiments of this sort were quite common in Rwanda before 1994, when the events of 1959 were always referred to as a revolution and even most people who were critical of the ethnic violence approved of the transfer of power to the majority.[29]

---

[25] Interview in Rubengera, Kibuye, December 7, 2001.

[26] Focus group with survivors, Rubengera, Kibuye, August 10, 2002. One interesting element of this answer is the resentment that it suggests against the Tutsi refugees, contrasting their success outside of the country with the suffering of the Tutsi within Rwanda.

[27] Interview in Rubengera, Kibuye, December 7, 2001.

[28] Interview in Burenga, Buyoga, Byumba, January 24, 2003.

[29] Based on my fieldwork, 1992–1993.

Most people we interviewed agreed with the official narrative that the teaching of Rwandan history before the genocide was biased and divisive. In fact, many people blamed the school system as a cause of the genocide.[30] Many people identified the content of the history taught in Rwandan schools, with its emphasis on Tutsi as foreign invaders who oppressed the Hutu, as a source of conflict. A young man in Butare explained:

The history of Rwanda – and I'm speaking here about the manner in which it was taught – contributed negatively to the destruction of the country and to the deterioration of relations among the three ethnic groups of Rwanda. Each time that one ethnic group rose to power, it was said that it pushed the others out, and that became the cycle of vengeance, up to today.[31]

A trader in Butare said that Rwanda's ethnic problems were caused by, "The bad teaching of the history of Rwanda that said the Tutsi ruled over the Hutu for centuries, depriving them of their possession and transforming them into their slaves."[32] A young man in Buyoga said:

Personally, I was shocked about what they said [in school] about the kings and the wickedness of the rulers. They went so far as to say that Queen Kanjogera killed a baby Hutu with her sword every morning! This was to encourage hatred between the ethnic groups and above all to demonize the deposed monarchical regime.[33]

In addition to the divisive history lessons, our interview subjects talked about practices of ethnic discrimination in schools. Shortly after Habyarimana's 1973 coup, his government put in place a quota system that limited Tutsi enrollment in each school to 10 percent of the student body. Habyarimana implemented the quota system in response to the popular uprising against Tutsi in academic establishments, seeking to placate Hutu ethnic resentments. While intended initially to stop ethnic instability, the quotas came to be viewed as an oppressive tool to identify Tutsi for discrimination. In order to adhere to the quotas, schools were required to keep track of the ethnicity of students, and Tutsi students were regularly singled out in class.[34]

Many of our informants mentioned the quota system and the practice of singling out Tutsi in schools. A woman in Buyoga told us, "From the young age of a school girl, I experienced this discrimination. In the

---

[30] King, *From Classrooms to Conflict in Rwanda*, provides an excellent overview of the history of education in Rwanda and its politicization both before and after the genocide.
[31] Interview in Matyazo, Butare, December 2, 2001.
[32] Interview in Matyazo, Butare, December 13, 2001.
[33] Interview in Zoko, Buyoga, December 20, 2001.
[34] King, *From Classrooms to Conflict in Rwanda*.

past, every time I had to raise my hand and accept my Tutsi ethnicity."[35] Another woman in Rubengera who attended school in the 1980s said, "Ethnic problems began when I was a young girl. At school they asked us our ethnic identity and I already sensed that there were dangerous reasons for this manner of doing things. Often I was afraid to raise my hand for fear of being the only Tutsi in class."[36] A Hutu mason in Buyoga told us, "There was discrimination in all sectors of national life during the time of Habyarimana. It was, for example, difficult to have a place or to sign up for school having a Tutsi ethnicity. The proof of this is that every year, they did a census of students according to their ethnicity in order to know, in my opinion, frankly how many it was necessary to expel or make fail."[37] The role of schools in promoting ethnic divisions is another case where the official narrative was widely accepted, because it resonated with people's lived experience. Both Hutu and Tutsi who attended schools in the 1970s and 1980s heard the history lessons that demonized Tutsi and painted them as outsiders, and everyone witnessed or personally experienced the singling out of Tutsi in class.

Another area where popular discourse generally coincided with the official narrative was in critiquing the previous regimes. According to a man in Butare, the cause of the genocide was, "Bad administration of the country. The government could have stopped soldiers from killing. If they had not encouraged people to kill, it would not have happened, especially here in Butare"[38] A young man in Buyoga said the violence in 1994 was caused by "bad administration that divided Rwandans rather than uniting them as a single nation."[39] Another in Mabanza said, "I don't think that it was the population that started this war. The war was above all a war for power. The authority was with the government. They had the power to stop this war."[40] In a focus group with women in Rubengera, one participant said that, "The causes [of the genocide] were due to bad governance of the country during that period that sowed segregationist ideas." Another added, "There was bad governance at the head that made bad ideas enter the heads of the population, without weighing the consequences that would follow one day." A third chimed in, "It was the thirst for power."[41]

[35] Interview in Muranzi, Buyoga, March 3, 2002.
[36] Interview in Rubengera, Kibuye, December 3, 2001.
[37] Interview in Muranzi, Buyoga, December 17, 2001.
[38] Interview in Butare, November 8, 2001.
[39] Interview in Buyoga, December 20, 2001.
[40] Interview in Rubengera, Mabanza, Kibuye, August 24, 2001.
[41] Focus group interview with women, Rubengera, Kibuye, August 10, 2002.

These attitudes may reflect the degree to which in retrospect the genocide seemed a terrible mistake, even for those involved in carrying it out, because the end result was to bring greater misery to their lives. According to a man in Byumba, "We say that the Hutu killed the Tutsi. But there were Hutu who lost their families in the refugee camps in Zaire. That is because of the genocide. If the genocide had not taken place, they would not have gone to die in Zaire."[42] A woman in Rubengera said, "We talk about it as a great tragedy. War only kills and destroys. It brings us no good. We lost our produce and our possessions. Whether Hutu or Tutsi, we all lost. The principle cause was bad governance that came from the old authorities. If not for them, the Rwandans were good."[43] Blaming government for the genocide also reflected a general perception that problems come from above, even today. A young man in Butare said, "What happened in Rwanda was terrible, and it was caused by bad governance and authorities." Another added, "The selfishness of authorities who pursued only their own interests."[44]

Many people tied social divisions to the advent of multiparty politics. In the focus group of elders in Buyoga, when asked about the events of 1994, they told us:

SPEAKER 1: It all began with the appearance of political parties. Before the parties came here, we lived in peace.

SPEAKER 2: It was the political parties that were at the source of our misfortunes. Wherever they passed, they sowed the spirit of hatred and divisions. Sometimes, they destroyed goods and their adversaries. They beat people.[45]

A young man in Butare said that conflicts, "Started with the arrival of the political parties. The different leaders stirred up their followers, and there were from time to time even fatal incidents. Next there was the campaign to treat all members of the opposition parties as accomplices of the Rwandan Patriotic Front and through that as enemies of the country."[46] In blaming multiparty politics, an elderly man traced the problem back, not to the 1990s but to the 1950s, when the first parties were formed. His critique, thus, is a more general critique of the elites who vie for power rather than a specific criticism of the regime that organized the genocide:

In the past, Rwandans lived in harmony, despite ethnicity. When someone needed help, everyone helped. When someone had an old home, everyone got

---

[42] Focus group interview with elders, Buyoga, Byumba, March 1, 2003.
[43] Interview in Rubengera, Mabanza, Kibuye, August 24, 2001.
[44] Focus group interview with youth, Cyarwa, Butare, June 15, 2002.
[45] Focus group with elders, Buyoga, March 1, 2003.
[46] Interview in Matyazo, Butare, December 2, 2001.

together to build a new home. When someone was sick, everyone worked in their field. When there was a marriage, everyone brought gifts. There was real sharing. I lived through that myself, and my grandparents. That ended with the beginning of party politics, which divided people, when one group said they wanted power for their group. And recent events were the final chapter. Neighbors no longer share. When you speak with people, they speak but they hide things.[47]

Overall, we found significant continuity between the official narrative about Rwanda's past and the ideas that people we interviewed expressed regarding their country's history. This seems to indicate a degree of success for the regime's attempt to promote its version of history. Yet it also seems important that on these points, the official narrative resonates with people's lived experience. For example, while research by scholars such as Catherine Newbury and Jan Vansina indicate that identity-based conflicts between Hutu and Tutsi were in fact expanding during the late colonial period,[48] Rwandans had a more direct connection to the last decade of colonialism, where they or their parents or grandparents witnessed colonial manipulations of identity that gave weight to the official narrative's claim that colonialism invented ethnic division. The pre-colonial period was sufficiently remote in time to fall outside most stories that relatives shared among themselves. Furthermore, blaming social divisions on outsiders deflected responsibility from Rwandans themselves, a tendency that we found throughout the individual narratives. On other points, the official narrative also resonated with the people we interviewed. Not only was speaking of 1959 as a revolution politically unacceptable in post-genocide Rwanda, but "revolution" also did not seem to accurately describe the events of 1959 and their aftermath. While the elite were driven from power, the masses were not empowered in their place. For three decades, leaders in Rwanda placed the rhetoric of revolution at the center of their political discourse, but at the same time, they were enriching themselves, even as the general population was becoming increasingly poor. Similarly, the chaos and loss of life and property that came from the policies of the previous regime gave resonance to claims about bad governance. The previous government clearly led the population down a path that brought them misery. In sum, the Rwandans we interviewed clearly knew the government's historical narrative, and they had adopted it to a substantial degree, particularly where it resonated with their own lived experience, yet they also adapted it in important ways to critique elites in general and not simply the Second Republic.

---

[47] Interview in Cyarwa-Sumo, Butare, November 22, 2001.
[48] Newbury, *Cohesion of Oppression*; Vansina, *Antecedents to Modern Rwanda*.

Talking About the Genocide

While the ways that the Rwandans we interviewed for this book talked about the more distant past overlapped with the official government narrative, popular discourses on the more recent past showed much less similarity. In our interviews, we asked people both general questions about what happened in Rwanda in 1994 and specific questions about what happened in their own community. The ways in which people talked about the events of 1994 often diverged from the official narrative on important points, particularly when describing local events. To avoid leading respondents, we asked open-ended questions that allowed them to select their own descriptive terms. For example, we asked, "What happened in your community in 1994?" and "Can you briefly explain in your own words what happened in Rwanda in 1994?"

Hutu we interviewed in 2001–2003 referred most often to *intambara*, the war, *ubwicanyi*, the killings, or more vaguely *ibyabaye*, the happenings, or *amahano*, horror or tragedy. A man in Mabanza, for example, said, "It was truly a horror [*amahano*]. It touched all Rwandans and was the first time in our history. People were basically exterminated, cleared away. Entire populations became refugees in countries far away and in disarray. Thousands dead in exile. And now, look at the thousands of people in prison, including some who are innocent."[49] In French, people commonly referred to "*les evenements*," the events. Many Hutu did mention *itsemba bwoko*, but usually in conjunction with *itsemba tsemba*, massacres, a term used to talk about massacres of Hutu. A middle-aged farmer in Butare said, "They have named it genocide [*itsemba bwoko*] and massacres [*itsemba tsemba*], so I call it that myself, like everyone else."[50] Not surprisingly, individuals we interviewed in Buyoga, where RPF killings took place in more areas than the genocide, referred to *intambara* and *itsemba tsemba* more regularly. The few Hutu in Buyoga who mentioned the genocide in individual interviews tied it to the war, like a young man who described what happened in Rwanda in 1994 as, "A genocide caused by the war."[51] Even some Tutsi in Buyoga characterized the conflict differently than those in other regions. For example, a Tutsi woman who herself was driven out of school in the anti-Tutsi attacks of 1973 but who was in the RPF zone in 1994 described the events of 1994 as "the war between the RPF and the FAR."[52] Most genocide survivors

49 Focus group interview with elders, Mabanza, August 10, 2002.
50 Interview in Cyarwa-Cyimana, September 7, 2001.
51 Interview in Zoko, Buyoga, December 20, 2001.
52 Interview in Muranzi, Buyoga, March 28, 2002.

labeled what happened in 1994 genocide. The majority of survivors interviewed in 2001–2003 invoked the Kinyarwanda term for genocide then in use, "*itsemba bwoko*," but toward the end of the research survivors began to use "*jenoside*," reflecting the official shift in language. Few Tutsi, whether survivors or repatriated refugees, mentioned *itsemba tsemba*. In 2015, the Tutsi survivors we spoke to uniformly used the term "*jenoside y'abatutsi*" to describe the events of 1994, following the new terminology, while Hutu also generally spoke of "*jenoside*" in 2015, though not the more specific "genocide of the Tutsi."

The most striking feature of the way in which people described what happened in their own communities was the degree to which they attributed local genocidal violence to outside forces. In all three communities, people said that militias from neighboring communes or soldiers who came from elsewhere initiated the killings.[53] In Butare, people reported that killings were launched by the intervention of the new president, Butare native President Sindikubwabo, or by his Presidential Guard, many based at his Tumba home. A young man in Cyarwa reported:

So here, everything began at the same time as elsewhere but it really got worse April 19, 1994, after the interim president, Sindikubwabo came on a visit to Butare where he gave a speech encouraging the Hutu to exterminate the Tutsi. Because he lived in this sector, his guards soon preached by example … The guards of President Sindikubwabo, who guarded his home here not far away, came and called on the people from here to do "like the others," in other words to kill. And they killed and pillaged until July 1994, when they fled to neighboring countries."[54]

Another woman in Cyarwa told us:

I've heard it said that it was the soldiers who started this. They came by plane. They parachuted. We heard gunfire in Tumba. It was Wednesday, I think. They began to speak to the population and to push them to carry out malicious acts, but the people here did not welcome these propositions while in other corners of the country there were already massacres. They said that Butare did not let itself get carried away in the rhythm of the rest of the country. That's why the Presidential Guard themselves had to begin the operations in Tumba and then in Cyarwa. The population was ignorant and then followed blindly.

A women's focus group in Matyazo on the other side of town reported a similar account:

---

[53] This tendency to blame outside forces was consistent with the research that I conducted on the genocide in 1995 and 1996, in which people in every community where I researched claimed that the violence was initiated in their community by outside forces. See Des Forges, *Leave None to Tell the Story*, chapters on local communities.

[54] Interview in Cyarwa-Sumo, Butare, September 9, 2001.

SPEAKER 1: I lived near the road, and at first I saw people fleeing the killings in the region of Bugesera. When you asked them what was happening, they said that they had seen dead bodies in the rivers. We didn't know what to do, whether to flee or to stay at home. Sometime after, we heard a plane land at the Ngoma airport, just across from here. A little later, there were the soldiers who arrived accompanied by some local individuals who served as guides in identifying the victims to attack. The Tutsi were singled out and driven in trucks toward an unknown destination.

SPEAKER 2: After the assassination of President Habyarimana, there were orders that we should stay in our houses. Those who went out of their homes were severely beaten. On the night of April 21, 1994, two days after the visit of the interim president Dr. Sindikubwabo Théodore and after the assassination of our Prefect at that time, who was opposed to the killings,[55] the GP [Presidential Guard] asked us to divide into two groups, the Tutsi on one side, the others on their other side.[56]

In Mabanza, people claimed that militia groups came from the north, from Gisenyi Prefecture and the Kibuye communes that bordered Gisenyi, like the man who explained:

People at first were afraid after the announcement of the death of the president. We knew that the country had been at war since 1990, but here it had been calm. Everyone waited, fearing what would happen after this death, because members of the parties close to the MRND [the ruling party] already swore to avenge the President. And then, attacks came from the north, from the communes of Gisenyi, Ramba Commune, and Gaseke, but also the neighboring commune Rutsiro [in Kibuye]. They incited the people from here to kill the Tutsi whose party, the RPF, had attacked President Habyarimana. The burgomaster did everything he could to stop it, but they said that people had gone crazy, and the authorities had no more power.[57]

Another young Hutu man gave a similar account but acknowledged local complicity a bit more:

In 1994, it was attacks supervised by the powerful. No one could oppose it. All the Tutsi were to be exterminated because they were thought to be behind the assassination of President Habyarimana. No one had the right to protect them, not even the authorities. Here the former Burgomaster tried, but in vain, because the Prefect was more involved. So, the attacks first came from Gisenyi and Rutsiro. They pillaged the furniture and destroyed buildings, killing each time. At first, the people from here wanted to organize themselves to counter the attacks that they thought up to then were strange and provocative. But that didn't accomplish anything, because on the radio, we heard that in other regions, including Kigali, RTLM called on the Hutu to eliminate the Tutsi enemy once and for all. So, the people from here submitted in their turn. Some among them,

---

[55] In fact, Prefect Habyalimana was dismissed from office on April 19, but he went into hiding and was not killed until later. Des Forges, *Leave None to Tell the Story*.

[56] Focus group of Women, Matyazo, Butare, August 17, 2002.

[57] Interview in Kibirizi, Kibuye, September 15, 2001.

above all the members of parties close to the former regime such as the MRND and the CDR began to commit shameful acts of genocide.[58]

The account of a survivor from Mabanza was consistent with these testimonies:

They killed President Habyarimana on April 6, and we were frightened. We saw attacks coming from the Congo-Nile ridge and homes burning. I learned that the authorities here called on the people to counterattack against these people coming from the north so that it [the violence] wouldn't come here. But in the end, the situation got worse. We took refuge at the Mabanza communal office. Arriving there, the burgomaster asked us to go to Kibuye to be protected by the prefectural authorities. In mid-path, some militia came to kill us. When we saw that some people were already cut by machetes, we turned around. I came back here and chose to hide in the area, rather than go to Kibuye with the others ... We lived in the bush. But there was a benefactor who took me in her home, a neighbor. I spent a month there. I stayed there until the end of the genocide.[59]

Those who spoke about the genocide in Buyoga also emphasized the importance of outside participation. One man told us, "I was in the army in 1994, but I have heard people say that in the former commune of Buyoga, the killings took place above all in the sectors of Mutete and Zoko [two of the sectors outside the RPF zone]. The principle authors of these killings were soldiers fleeing after the RPF seized the City of Byumba."[60] Another man said, "The soldiers who left Byumba called on the people from here to kill the accomplices of the RPF, the Tutsi and all others who opposed them."[61] Hutu were not alone in portraying the genocide as coming from outside. In the focus group of survivors in Buyoga the first speaker, from Zoko Sector, blamed attacks on people coming from Mutete Sector of Buyoga. The second speaker, from Mutete, said that attacks came from another commune:

SPEAKER 1: We were victims of an attack coming from Mutete Sector. It was the counselor of that sector who was at the head. He led the Interahamwe and gave them arms. At the beginning, the Hutu and Tutsi fought together. They didn't yet know that the genocide was being planned. We were on good terms with the soldiers who had their positions close to our home. We didn't know that they had been replaced, and it was their replacements who launched the killings in our community.

SPEAKER 2: A friend revealed to us that the Tutsi were going to be killed. We didn't want to believe it. A little after, we learned that almost all the Tutsi practically were killed. We were victims of attacks coming from Kinyami Commune.

[58] Interview in Kibirizi, Kibuye, September 14, 2001.
[59] Interview in Gacaca, Kibuye, August 23, 2001.
[60] Interview in Mutete, Byumba, December 17, 2001.
[61] Interview in Zoko, Byumba, December 20, 2001.

While both Hutu and Tutsi talked about violence coming from outside their communities, Hutu tended to emphasize the reluctance of the local people who eventually participated in the genocide. In their narratives about 1994, many Tutsi (particularly survivors) emphasized local complicity much more extensively, even as they acknowledge that attacks often came first from outside. Most revealing of the difference in perceptions was an exchange between a Hutu man and a Tutsi man in the focus group of elders in Mabanza:

SPEAKER 1 (HUTU): Here it was necessary to wait until April 14, 1994, for the massacres to really begin. At the time when the radio stations were calling for massacres, the inhabitants here didn't understand anything. They were instead desolated to learn what was happening in the neighboring commune of Rutsiro. The gendarmes had to raise public awareness about exterminating the Tutsi and had to bring Bakiga[62] from the north for Rubengera to know the sort [of violence] as other regions. The fact that the situation went on for two months made it so that some people from Rubengera [Mabanza], those weak in spirit, of course, were ultimately implicated in the massacres. But the population at the beginning refused to give into temptations.

SPEAKER 2 (TUTSI): I find all the same that we should not minimize too much the role played by the local population in the massacres. There was also a certain complicity evident on the part of some people, because the killers from, for example, Gisenyi or Rutsiro, couldn't have known the Tutsi in Gacaca Sector if people hadn't served to indicate who they were. That is a sign of the previous existence of a certain mistrust, of interethnic hatred in Rubengera.[63]

Both Hutu and Tutsi talked about the leading role of authorities in instigating and overseeing the violence. A survivor in Cyarwa, Butare, told us:

First there were the forces of the presidential guard who came from the City of Butare [the city center] looking for those they called accomplices [*ibyitso*] in the assassination of President Habyarimana. To come here, they had begun bringing along the youth from Tumba quarter, who were going to receive military training in the arboretum of the National University of Rwanda. It was the former counselor B. of Tumba who busied himself not only with the selection of the youths to train but also to sort out the people to kill. That's how the manhunt for Tutsi began, after they had erected roadblocks in our community.

---

[62] The term Bakiga literally refers to a population that lives in north-central Rwanda and southern Uganda, and speaks a distinct dialect related to Kinyarwanda. In modern Rwanda, however, the term Bakiga refers to anyone from northern Rwanda and is also used as a derogatory term to refer to unrefined people from more remote areas, equivalent to the terms "hayseed" or "hillbilly" in the United States. In this context, the speaker probably implies two meanings to describe those who attacked Mabanza; they were people from northern Rwanda, but in choosing the term Bakiga, he is also implying that they were backward.

[63] Focus group of elders, Mabanza, Kibuye, August 10, 2002.

I stayed hidden by my neighbors nearby. Of course, the situation was hard and confusing for me. It was alarming each time that I learned that someone in my family had just been killed. I lost three brothers and four sisters. My parents as well. I am left with only one brother, and I am nearly an invalid, because I was beaten and tortured during the events.[64]

A Hutu woman whose Tutsi husband and children were killed in the genocide talked about destruction, pillaging, and killing. When asked who was responsible, she said, "It was certain Hutu whom we knew well. They followed in the footsteps of the GP [Presidential Guard], but they [the Presidential Guard] didn't know who to kill like the Hutu who were our neighbors."[65] A survivor in Mabanza said that attacks had come from Gisenyi and Rutsiro, but also said that, "In April 1994, the actors walked around freely and operated without any worry. The former deputy M. and the former businessman R. themselves organized the attacks. They hoped in the end to take over the property of the fallen victims."[66]

In sharp contrast to the official narrative, participants in our research did not characterize the genocide as a mass movement with wide popular support and participation. Instead, people of all ethnicities emphasized the leading role of authorities, the ignorance of the population, and a general reluctance to engage in the killings. People we interviewed talked only rarely about ethnic hatred as a motivating force. Many people emphasized that the public had to be taught to view the Tutsi as enemies and to join in the killing. Those interviewed in French regularly used the term *"sensibiliser,"* which has no direct English equivalent but refers to raising public awareness or raising consciousness. Hutu in particular tended to emphasize the degree to which Hutu and Tutsi lived together peacefully prior to 1994. As a woman in Butare reported:

Before the war, the people lived together closely without any segregation, I mean at least on the hills where I personally lived. These massacres thus surprised us all. It is the authorities who must answer and give reasons about what pushed them to such a failure on their part. They deserve condemnation more severe than the population that blindly followed their bad example. Ordinarily, the peasant obeys political orders out of fear of being punished. So ... it was the bad leaders who drove the population to these massacres even though they lived in brotherhood before 1994.[67]

A young farmer in Mabanza made a similar point:

Before 1994, the inhabitants of our region were united and there were no ethnic problems. They even called the people from here *ibyimanyi* [hybrids] ... In

64 Interview in Cyarwa-Sumo, Butare, November 23, 2001.
65 Interview in Cyarwa-Cyimana, Butare, September 7, 2001.
66 Interview in Gacaca, Mabanza, Kibuye, December 6, 2001.
67 Focus group of women, Matyazo, August 17, 2002.

1994, when the plane of President Habyarimana was shot down, the inhabitants here kept calm, but the sounds of drums and the blowing of whistles rang out everywhere, calling everyone to vigilance. Three days later, the military barricades began to be erected. So-called security meetings took place in which they encouraged us to do patrols at night. Slogans like, "the enemy is the same" were hammered into the heads of the population. But up to then, no outbursts. Around April 10, 1994, people from the north, Kiga, came to threaten the inhabitants with reprisals if they didn't act like others in the region. And effectively, we were attacked by these people on April 14 and 15, 1994. Coming from Gisenyi, a band of assailants infiltrated our locality. Almost all the population evacuated their homes and fled to the mountains. Their goods were pillaged. That evening and the next day, the inhabitants returned one by one, but they were forced to collaborate with these assailants in the massacre of Tutsi. Thus, you collaborated in order to avoid having your goods pillaged.[68]

Even as they recognized that there had been waves of anti-Tutsi violence in the early 1960s and in 1973, many people denied that there were conflicts in their communities prior to 1994. Hutu in particular seem to have reflected a general reality that, despite occasional unrest, most Hutu had no intense hatred for Tutsi but instead lived beside them normally, interacting with them on a daily basis, sharing with them, attending church with them, even marrying into their families.[69] The periodic anti-Tutsi violence, thus, was exceptional and did not reflect the normal Hutu attitude toward Tutsi but rather something forced on the population first by colonial policies, then by modern political leaders. Among the Rwandans she interviewed, Susanne Buckley-Zistel similarly found that, "the past is remembered as harmonious and peaceful, with the genocide being a sudden rupture which took everybody by surprise."[70]

An elderly Hutu man who lost two of his children by a Tutsi mother in the 1994 genocide demonstrated well the contradictory perception of general ethnic harmony despite periodic waves of violence. When initially asked what happened in Rwanda in 1994, the man declared:

Only God can explain these horrors! I don't know how to make sense of those who conceived of this extermination! I've heard it said that Hitler did the same thing, but only God can be the judge to compare the two situations. The Hutu and Tutsi were like brothers. They were united. From the time of my birth during the time of Rudahigwa until very recently, they were united.[71]

---

[68] Focus group interview with youth, Rubengera, Kibuye, August 10, 2002.

[69] The idea that ideology and hatred were not the main forces pushing the population to participate in the genocide is a major theme in research on local participation. See Straus, *The Order of Genocide*; Fujii, *Killing Neighbors*; and my own, Longman, *Christianity and Genocide in Rwanda*.

[70] Susanne Buckley-Zistel, "Remembering to Forget: Chosen Amnesia as a Strategy for Local Coexistence in Post-Genocide Rwanda," *Africa* 76, no. 2, 2006, 131–150, citation p. 140.

[71] Interview in Cyarwa, Butare, September 7, 2001.

Yet when asked about the origin of Rwanda's ethnic conflicts, the man traced the divisions back to colonialism and acknowledged personal experience with anti-Tutsi attacks in previous waves of violence. In describing the source of ethnic conflicts, the man blamed colonialism:

Everything began in the colonial period, with the introduction by the Belgians of identity booklets then called *amabuku* [books]. Before that, they didn't officially distinguish between the ethnic groups ... The king could offer his gifts to everyone without any distinction and without taking account of ethnic membership or appearance. But the situation changed with the first political parties in 1959 to 1962, after the death of King Rudahigwa, dead in Bujumbura, betrayed by his Tutsi entourage and the Belgian colonials.... In 1959, when I was working for the Brothers of Charity, I helped two families escape, though they were unfortunately killed in 1994. [In 1959], they were threatened, and I appealed to the burgomaster at the time to let me take them to my home. In that period, you could stand up for a threatened Tutsi and save him.[72]

In other words, ethnic violence had sometimes occurred in Rwanda, but it was instigated from outside and the normal state of affairs was that Hutu would save threatened Tutsi. The events of 1994 thus seemed a break with the past to most Hutu.

Not surprisingly, Tutsi survivors spoke less about ethnic harmony prior to 1994, since many had direct personal or family experience with ethnic discrimination and sometimes arrest or violence. A survivor in Mabanza who was thirty at the time of the genocide said, "From when I was young, when we were in grade school, there were always signs of dissension for those who were able to notice it."[73] An exchange in the survivors' focus group in Buyoga about problems they faced before 1994 is telling:

SPEAKER 1: This is what we experienced. Ethnic discrimination was visible in the distribution of administrative posts. It was the same thing in the schools.
SPEAKER 2: In the army too. They recruited only Hutu.
SPEAKER 3: These conflicts dated back a long time. People attacked their neighbors, no one knows why.
SPEAKER 4: These conflicts were there. The events of 1994 only caused a volcano that was already active to erupt.
SPEAKER 5: The events of 1994 were not a surprise. When the political parties were born in Rwanda, no Tutsi could become member of a Hutu political party.
SPEAKER 3: Between 1990 and 1993, the Tutsi were killed because it was said that they were accomplices of the RPF.
SPEAKER 1: It was in this way that our Hutu friends began to pull away from us.[74]

[72] Interview in Cyarwa, Butare, September 7, 2001.
[73] Interview in Gacaca, Mabanza, Kibuye, December 6, 2001.
[74] Focus group interview with survivors, March 1, 2003.

Many survivors mentioned that a large number of Tutsi were arrested in 1990 when the government swept up supposed accomplices after the RPF attack. A survivor in Mabanza said:

From my perspective, the conflicts began on October 1, 1990. In this period, I saw people being imprisoned, and I said to myself that there was going to be a problem following the attack of the RPF. On October 4, 1990, there was gunfire in the City of Kigali as it was said that the RPF had just attacked. But it was a pretext for the Habyarimana government to arrest accomplices of the RPF. They began to imprison these accomplices. Our teachers, our neighbors were arrested. And these arrests operated on the basis of their Tutsi ethnic identity.[75]

Almost no Hutu mentioned the 1990 arrests.

Gender also proved relevant in responses to some questions, particularly on the topic of sexual assault. Despite the widespread use of rape as a weapon during the genocide,[76] the topic of sexual violence came up only rarely when people described the 1994 genocide. Those few who brought up the topic were all women and exclusively Tutsi. When asked to describe what happened in 1994, a survivor in Mabanza stated that, "I only saw people slaughtering their neighbors. I saw them in the midst of pillaging and raping. I don't know what to call such actions."[77] A Tutsi genocide widow in Butare told us that, "There were some people who went on attacks to kill people far from their communities and who could hide their intentions to commit other acts, like the rape of women and girls."[78] Overall, however, very few people spoke about sexual violence, probably reflecting the continuing shame associated with sexual assault.

The most significant point of departure between the narratives that we gathered and the official narrative was the inclusion of stories about violence perpetrated by the RPF and its supporters. Hutu respondents in particular mentioned that people from all ethnic groups died in 1994, even if they did not mention the involvement of the RPF in killings. A young man in Butare said something echoed by many others, "In 1994, many people were killed on both sides, though certainly the Tutsi were the most affected."[79] Some talked specifically about attacks by the RPF or its supporters, including in the period after the RPF took power:

I decided to leave here a bit late, in 1995, because I was very afraid. Not a small number of people were afraid at that time. We couldn't even go into the city center of Butare, because the youths were gathered together and tied up. I'm still

---

[75] Interview in Rubengera, Mabanza, Kibuye, May 7, 2015.
[76] Binaifer Nowrojee and Janet MacGaffey, *Shattered Lives: Sexual Violence During the Rwandan Genocide and Its Aftermath*, New York: Human Rights Watch, 1996.
[77] Interview in Mabanza, Kibuye, December 7, 2001.
[78] Interview in Matyazo, Butare, December 13, 2001.
[79] Interview in Matyazo, Butare, December 2, 2001.

traumatized by it all. My father was killed mysteriously after he left us in Kigali to come back here to check on the situation. Our neighbors who were survivors organized a plot against him. He thus disappeared, and we were left always thinking that he might be alive, maybe in prison somewhere. It was only later that we learned that he had been killed and what always troubled me was that we were never able to at least find his body where it fell. My mother is also in prison.[80]

Others talked about RPF attacks on the refugee camps in Congo, like a man from Mabanza:

We left for Zaire, me and all my family, after the French Operation Turquoise left. We were afraid of RPF vengeance. We stayed there until the war of Kabila of 1996 that drove us back home in January 1997. The conditions in the refugee camps were atrocious, despite the assistance of the international community … I still don't know the fate of my son whom I lost in Zaire when we were taking flight. I lost track of him in the gunfire … If at least I could know whether or not he's dead, so that I can mourn like the others.[81]

Some recounted their experiences of imprisonment or harassment at the hands of the RPF. A young man in Mabanza told us:

My parents left for Zaire, and they have not yet come back. People say that they died there, and perhaps it's true. They were too old to manage in the forests like I often hear about from those who have come back from Zaire. I myself stayed [here] until the end. The RPF arrived, and they put just about everyone in prison. As for me, a soldier saw me and said, "that one is too dirty and looks like an Interahamwe." He put me in the communal jail, and I spent two years there. I wasn't freed until after he was transferred. Everyone knew that I was innocent, but they were afraid of him … The OPJ [police detective] could let someone out of prison, but he was too afraid of the soldiers.[82]

In our survey, when asked to describe what happened in Rwanda in 1994, 10.8 percent of respondents chose the response, "The RPF waged war against Rwanda." When asked to choose the principal cause of the violence in 1994, 9.2 percent chose the RPF invasion. While a small percentage, it is surprising that even this many people in a survey blamed the RPF as a perpetrator of violence and cause of the problems in 1994, given the politically sensitive nature of these statements.

The most extensive RPF attacks in our case studies were in Buyoga, but people there were reluctant to speak openly about violence they witnessed at the hands of the RPF in an official interview setting. While Hutu in Buyoga generally characterized what happened in 1994 as war and massacres, rather than genocide, few were willing to expound on

---

[80] Ibid.
[81] Interview in Kibirizi, Mabanza, Kibuye, September 15, 2001.
[82] Interview in Kibirizi, Mabanza, Kibuye, September 17, 2001.

what specifically happened in their communities. Of the three case study sites, Buyoga was the most politically sensitive. The northern region of the country was the base of Habyarimana's support and was also the region most directly affected by RPF violence. A large portion of Byumba Prefecture was occupied by the RPF beginning in February 1993 and experienced violence at the hands of the RPF, particularly from April to July 1994. The RPF was highly sensitive to discussion of this violence, and people in Buyoga feared that speaking openly about what happened in their community could result in their being accused of divisionism or of other crimes, like supporting former president Bizimungu's banned political party.[83]

As a result, even as their interviews suggested that they or others they knew had experienced violence at the hands of the RPF, few people in Buyoga were willing to elaborate. Those who did give details made clear that RPF violence was widespread but much less severe and targeted than the violence associated with the genocide. One elderly man told me:

Where we were, there were no problems. There was no killing [of Tutsi] in this sector. Even in 1959, we didn't have killings in Burenga. The RPF came to Burenga but then left. It happened in one part of this sector. Around 8 p.m., there was a sort of rain, and people took shelter. There were 10 families killed. It was about one month after Habyarimana was killed. It was down the road, in the ditch. The soldiers stayed on the other side of the road. One RPF soldier came back to check to see that they were buried. It included many people that I knew – brothers, cousins, in-laws. This was the only killing in Burenga."[84]

A young woman from another part of Buyoga told me:

There were many dead. They died here. Many were killed by stray bullets running between places … Those who died are those who continued pushing in front of the front lines. Among those who came behind the lines, there were fewer killed. In our sector, only about 100 people died. There was no genocide in my area. Those who died were killed by government forces or killed by the RPF. Others were killed by the RPF, who may have thought they worked for the government.

Another woman told us, "There was combat between the RPF and the government. There were thus civilian victims of this war, including my husband, killed at my neighbors', where he was hiding. There were dead who were buried in their households, but they are never spoken of, unfortunately."[85] Many more of those interviewed in Buyoga were like

---

[83] The attacks on Canadian journalist Judi Rever for her article "Rwanda's Memory Hole," on the massacres in Byumba indicate the RPF's sensitivity on this topic. See Lara Santaro, "Terror as a Method: A Journalist's Search for Truth in Rwanda," *Foreign Policy Journal*, September 25, 2015.
[84] Interview in Burenga, Buyoga, Byumba, January 24, 2003.
[85] Interview in Muranzi, Buyoga, Byumba, March 27, 2001.

the woman who complained about justice and commemoration being one-sided when in fact people from all groups died yet was unwilling to give specifics about how Hutu died. "There was gunfire everywhere. Those who could, saved themselves. Others died in their fields ... It was a war."[86]

Most people in Buyoga were very careful about what they said in the context of our interviews, despite assurances of confidentiality. People in focus group interviews were particularly careful about what they said and were much less willing than those interviewed as individuals to explain the events in 1994 in terms of the RPF attack or even to discuss those killed by the RPF.[87] In the Buyoga focus groups, several participants mentioned that they were in the RPF-controlled zone, but only one young woman tailor in the youth focus group spoke up after others talked about the genocide to say, "It was war, and that's all. It was a war with guns. I did not see anyone take a machete and go cut up his neighbor. That didn't happen [where I lived]."[88] But others in the group, which included genocide survivors and repatriated Tutsi, were not willing to back her up. When asked what happened specifically in their community, one said:

SPEAKER 1:   Here in the District of Kisaro [of which Buyoga became a part in 2001], we didn't experience these problems. We maintained our unity until the end. In contrast, we welcomed our compatriots who were fleeing the neighboring zones threatened by the genocide. Here, there was no genocide.

SPEAKER 2:   I need to add to what he said. Perhaps he is not well informed. It was not because people of Kisaro were good people, but simply because they were in the neutral zone controlled by the RPF. Elsewhere, when you left this zone and you went to the zones controlled by Habyarimana's army, you were taken for an enemy, and vice-versa ...

SPEAKER 3:   [who came from the part of Buyoga where the genocide occurred] The genocidal spirit began here in 1990. When the war began that year, all of my family was imprisoned. In 1994, the genocide began. I myself was not here, because I had joined the RPF, and when I returned to see my family after the war, only a few of my family remained. In a few words, there was a part of Kisaro that suffered a lot and another in the neutral zone that experienced no problems.[89]

Beyond the one mention of war, none of the four focus groups explicitly discussed killings by the RPF. Instead, in these Buyoga focus groups, most participants spoke in glowing terms of the RPF regime. In fact, of

---

[86] Ibid.
[87] Burnet, *Genocide Lives in Us*, p. 201, made a similar observation of focus group participation.
[88] Focus interview with youth, Buyoga, Byumba, March 1, 2003.
[89] Ibid.

the focus groups in Buyoga, only the survivors' group spoke critically about the post-genocide government and continuing ethnic tensions in their community. The survivors complained vociferously about a range of government policies, including the release of prisoners, gacaca, and the failure to provide survivors with sufficient assistance.[90]

The fact that people were unwilling to talk about RPF violence in an interview setting does not indicate that people remained silent about their experiences. When asked if they talked about what happened in 1994, the overwhelming majority said that they did. An elderly man said, "Of course I talk about it. How could I forget the things I lost, like all my cattle."[91] Instead, people suggested that they speak only among those with similar experiences. One Hutu man said, "We talk about [what happened] with other neighbors who went to Zaire in 1994, sharing about the different conditions of life in the different refugee camps that we experienced."[92] Another, who lived in an *umudugudu*, a resettled village which housed mostly Hutu, said, "We talk about it in the *umudugudu*, above all because we see ourselves in these homes that are almost uninhabitable, when we used to have our own proper homes."[93] A survivor in Buyoga told us, "I don't talk about it because I don't see anyone in the same situation as me."[94]

Popular Opinions of Memorial Initiatives

Government efforts to shape collective memory about the events of 1994 are clearly seen in official commemorations and genocide memorials. Each April, beginning April 7, the government sponsors an official week of events commemorating the genocide, known by Rwandans as "the Week of Mourning." A large national commemorative event is held annually at a genocide site, with the president and cabinet ministers and foreign dignitaries. Each local community also organizes its own commemoration, where public officials talk about the genocide and how to keep such tragedies from happening again.

While the Week of Mourning happens once a year, memorial sites serve as an ever-present reminder of the genocide and its local manifestations. As described in Chapter five, major memorial sites are scattered throughout the country and serve as tourist destinations and pilgrimage

---

[90] Thomson, *Whispering Truth to Power*, found that survivors used gacaca as a forum to critique the government.
[91] Interview in Zoko, Buyoga, Byumba, December 20, 2001.
[92] Interview in Muranzi, Buyoga, Byumba, December 17, 2001.
[93] Interview in Mutete, Buyoga, Byumba, March 29, 2002.
[94] Interview in Muranzi, Buyoga, Byumba, March 28, 2002.

sites, visited periodically by school groups and visitors to Rwanda. But each community has its own sites as well. Butare hosts a major mass grave and memorial at the entrance to the university, near where hundreds of people were killed at a particularly brutal roadblock. The memorial is a raised platform and canopy built out of tan bricks with floral planters and a garden in a grove of large shade trees. This and a memorial at the Ngoma airport are the municipality's main genocide memorials, yet many other mass graves were scattered throughout the area. In the neighborhood of Ngoma, the government began a memorial along the main road, but for several years, nothing was completed but a brick marker with a few untended flowers planted around it. Meanwhile, in the neighborhood of Cyarwa, a mass grave was marked only by the remains of a deteriorating canopy of branches erected for the previous year's local genocide commemoration over an otherwise unremarkable open plot of land. On the day that I visited, goats were tethered to the canopy to graze on the plot's grass.

In Mabanza, the only memorial site was some distance from the sectors where we conducted interviews, at Nyamagumba, a high hill overlooking Lake Kivu on the border with Rutsiro Commune. Most people referred to the official site at the Gatwaro Stadium in Kibuye, the location to which many of Mabanza's Tutsi fled and where many were killed. This was the site to which people from the community went for the annual commemoration. A site was eventually built in the community, a small mausoleum where some local bodies were reburied. As one survivor told us, "It is an order of the government for each sector to construct a genocide memorial site."[95] At the time of our main research, there were no memorial sites in Buyoga, nor in the expanded district of Kisaro. As one person told us, "There are no sites properly said. Only individual and family graves that you see here and there."[96] Rulindo, the district into which Kisaro was incorporated in 2006, does have several genocide sites, including a memorial at Mvuzo, close to Kigali, and a small museum in Rusiga sector.

Although both Butare and Buyoga experienced killings at the hands of the RPF, neither had any sites acknowledging these incidents. In public discourse, all mass graves were assumed to be graves of people killed in the genocide. Public commemorations focused exclusively on those killed in the genocide. Hutu were mentioned only as killers or occasionally rescuers, but almost never as victims and certainly never as victims of RPF attacks.

[95] Interview in Rubengera, Mabanza, Kibuye, May 7, 2015.
[96] Interview in Muranzi, Mabanza, Byumba, December 17, 2001.

The opinions of people we interviewed about the annual commemorations and the memorial sites varied radically. Many people embraced these efforts to acknowledge the past, while others found them traumatizing or divisive. A focus group of women in Mabanza that included both Hutu and Tutsi demonstrated the variety and complexity of opinions:

SPEAKER 1.   Because we need reconciliation, we should keep inside these bad events, to avoid falling into the same trap. We should forget this passage of events and not talk about it publicly.

SPEAKER 2.   I find that it is not possible to forget, because it has already entered into the history of Rwandans. The child who is going to be born is going to know about it, even if we don't talk to him. Much better to speak about it in clarity to avoid everything that could cause us to return. It's not good to hide the truth.

SPEAKER 3.   It's good to commemorate the genocide.

SPEAKER 4.   I would add this: I don't find it good to return each time when we have need for reconciliation. When someone has asked for forgiveness and another has given it to him with a good heart, it is not good to show the fault that he committed. That could indicate that forgiveness has not been given, and the peace of heart will no longer be found ...

SPEAKER 5.   I find that it is not good to forget these events completely, but commemorating them is also not good, as we have done each year. For example, I have friends who are survivors. When the week of mourning arrives, I see that they are distressed. They remember everything that happened in the genocide. They become so traumatized that that don't want to speak to their neighbors.

SPEAKER 6.   I support having these memorials put before the eyes of Rwandans, but I want the days of mourning abolished. I am not ignoring that the genocide took place. But when the songs play on the radio, I feel upset. It touches me personally.

SPEAKER 5.   In my opinion, I find that this means of commemorating the genocide cannot bring us reconciliation, because when I remember an unhappy event, I find myself back in that situation. In this case, there can't be reconciliation, because I am grieving. It is said that there is reconciliation after you forget all that has happened and joy begins to burst forth.[97]

Opinions on commemorations did not fall easily along ethnic lines. Among Tutsi, most supported the official week of mourning held each April and the creation of genocide memorial sites. A survivor in Mabanza said, "for me, this memorial site is one of the proofs to show that the Tutsi genocide took place. They preserve the victims of the genocide in great dignity."[98] A repatriated Tutsi man in Butare said, "There are ceremonies that are prepared, like the maintenance of [memorial] sites, with prayers and testimonies. I myself go, because I believe it important that

---

[97] Focus group of women, Mabanza, Kibuye, August 10, 2002.
[98] Interview in Rubengera, Mabanza, Kibuye, May 7, 2015.

all the victims should be commemorated. Also, this site serves as one of the tools for the history of the genocide."[99] A genocide survivor told us that the annual commemoration:

Is an occasion to remember my personal suffering first and then to think of this tragedy that plunged an entire people into mourning. You would explode and go crazy if you didn't talk about it … We take ourselves to the sites where we hold prayers. The widows and orphans come together to continue the mourning in our own fashion. We also celebrate the victory of the RPA who saved us. Otherwise, we would have all been killed. Every time April 6 comes, I remember how my husband was killed by a crowd of people that came to take him from our home. I revisit the scenes of killings that took place in front of my house and you know that makes me feel bad. At first, I thought I was going to go crazy![100]

A survivor in Mabanza told us, "I find that a good part of the population is uninterested in the commemorations that are organized. Since the consequences of the genocide were felt by all Rwandans, this commemoration should be taken up by everyone."[101]

Nevertheless, some found the commemorations and memorials traumatizing, like a young woman in Mabanza who said, "Talking about it causes me problems and brings bad memories and sorrows."[102] An elderly woman in Mabanza doubted the sincerity of Hutu who participated in commemorations. "For those who attend, it is like turning a knife in the wound again. Who are those paying respects remembering? I see them, and I am traumatized."[103] A survivor in Butare said, "The problem is that each time the I think about it, I have the tendency to believe that it is going to happen another time … We have commemorations here. We take ourselves to the cemetery and have prayers. I go, of course. But it brings me bad memories of the people I lost and of having been displaced."[104]

Others felt that commemorations and memorials were not useful or were even potentially dangerous, like a woman from the focus group of survivors in Mabanza:

People speak about it differently, but I find that [memorials] impede unity and reconciliation, because when one looks at these displays of bones while those who killed them remain in their homes, the idea of coming together and reconciling seems difficult. It is necessary instead to proceed to the reparation of the hearts of those affected.[105]

[99] Interview in Matyazo, Butare, December 2, 2001.
[100] Interview in Matyazo, Butare, December 14, 2001
[101] Interview in Rubengera, Mabanza, Kibuye, December 7, 2001.
[102] Interview in Rubengera, Mabanza, Kibuye, December 7, 2001.
[103] Interview in Gacaca, Mabanza, Kibuye, April 29, 2015.
[104] Interview in Matyazo, Butare, December 14, 2001.
[105] Focus group of survivors, Mabanza, Kibuye, August 10, 2002.

Another young woman in Mabanza told us:

When we talked with our parents, they told about the old wars that happened in the past. They talked about 1959. They told us that at that time as well there was hunting for Tutsi. The same thing in 1973, when I was only 5 or 7. It was always a manhunt for Tutsi. Then in 1994 it was again the same thing ... To continue to talk about what happened risks infecting your children who didn't even witness it. It is better that they don't know that there were others who killed with machetes.[106]

Among Hutu, many acknowledged a need to commemorate the genocide. An elderly man in Mabanza said:

Personally, I think that the memorial sites are necessary and that everyone should look at them in the same fashion. I see that around the anniversary of the genocide, all the ethnic groups participate in the ceremonies and commemoration. I believe that it is a good thing, because it gives an occasion to pray and to meditate on the collective memory of those who, after all, were savagely killed even though they were innocents ... On the other hand, commemorative activities should not wake up hatred or the desire for vengeance.[107]

A woman in Mabanza made a similar observation. "For me, these sites offer a sense of respect and remembrance to all the innocent victims who perished in the 1994 genocide."[108] "We pay respects to the Tutsi who were killed. I go just to accompany others. We have neighbors who were killed during the genocide. Their disappearance shames us, even if I was accused and then won my case. If I participate in the mourning, it is because I had Tutsi friends, people who exchanged cattle with us, who were killed during the genocide."[109] Some Hutu, like their Tutsi neighbors, had ambivalent feelings about the commemorations. A young Hutu man whose father died after the RPF came to power told us, "Commemoration, or the practice of discussing what happened, helps many people, particularly the traumatized survivors. The problem is that the organization Ibuka [the umbrella group for survivors] focuses only on the Tutsi, when there were losses of human life on both sides."[110]

Yet some Hutu rejected the commemorations and memorials for being biased and failing to reflect the experiences of all who suffered, including Hutu. For example a Hutu widow in Buyoga whose husband was killed by the RPF said that she had no interest in the official commemorations. "I

---

[106] Interview in Gacaca, Mabanza, Kibuye, August 23, 2001.
[107] Focus group of elders, Mabanza, Kibuye, August 10, 2002.
[108] Interview in Nyarugenge, Mabanza, Kibuye, December 7, 2001. Note that by specifying the victims of the 1994 genocide, she is not generalizing to include Hutu who suffered at the hands of the RPF.
[109] Interview in Kabuga, Mabanza, Kibuye, April 27, 2015.
[110] Interview in Matyazo, Ngoma, Butare, December 2, 2001.

don't see myself concerned. The victims of the war here are marginalized and forgotten."[111] Another man in Buyoga said, "I deplore this fashion of commemorating a single ethnic group when there were other victims."[112] A man in Butare reported:

Some people in our community participate in these commemorations but reluctantly, because they also lost their own [family members]. In effect, they don't have the right to remember their own who were savagely killed just after the genocide. They bear a grudge in the depths of their hearts. Just after the genocide, young people, authorities, even if they didn't participate in the genocide, all of them were arrested and taken somewhere to be killed. In short, while during the week of mourning, everyone meets together, in reality they are not thinking about the same thing in the depths of their hearts.[113]

An elderly man in Butare combined several of the critiques:

It is not good to keep speaking about what happened. I know that you can write about it in books, but it should not be sung everywhere. That traumatizes people. Commemoration is not bad. To have a day to commemorate is okay. But not every day all year. One day to discuss, but talking about it every day is not good. We too have our dead, and they don't take time to commemorate them.[114]

Others rejected the commemorations and memorials because they were destructive and divisive. One man in Butare said that commemorations, "Are a complete humiliation … [During the commemorations], I think above all about my detractors who are always looking for a way to accuse me of having been involved in the genocide. They do this, because I have property that they could take if I were condemned in a court."[115] A man in Butare told us, "People should stop talking about and dramatizing what happened, because it hurts other people, above all the survivors and those whose families have their members in prison."[116]

People also expressed concern that the annual commemoration of the genocide had become a time for the regime to crack down on dissent. An ex-prisoner from Mabanza said, "It's better to forget. What good does it serve to think about the dead, when you don't know how to bring them back? Think instead about saving those still alive from destitution … The commemorations frighten some people. I see people during the week of mourning who hide until it's over. They say that they are afraid of the settling of scores by the survivors."[117] By 2015, the situation had become more serious:

[111] Interview in Muranzi, Buyoga, Byumba, March 27, 2002.
[112] Interview in Muranzi, Buyoga, Byumba, December 17, 2001.
[113] Interview in Butare, July 12, 2015.
[114] Interview in Cyarwa-Sumo, Butare, November 22, 2001.
[115] Interview in Matyazo, Butare, December 14, 2001.
[116] Interview in Matyazo, Butare, December 13, 2001.
[117] Interview in Kibirizi, Mabanza, Kibuye, September 17, 2001.

In the countryside, a lot of people are imprisoned during this week. For example, you hear that in one district, twenty people were imprisoned for genocide ideology …. During the national Week of Mourning that is commemorated every year from April 7 through 13, this period is the proof that shows that Rwandans are not yet reconciled. In other times of the year, you can't easily see that Rwandans are not yet reconciled. Here, people act as though they have forgotten. But during this national Week of Mourning, it is obvious directly to the eyes, that Rwandans are not yet reconciled. You find on the Hutu side, they say inflammatory things and still hold onto this ideology to kill the Tutsi, while on the Tutsi side, their lies against Hutu multiply. Here, for example, you can talk with the prosecutors, and they'll tell you that they have registered many cases related to the infraction of genocide ideology, but in the end, they find that they are lies.[118]

Most interesting were those who read their own interpretations into the commemorations and memorials. Some Hutu reinterpreted the commemorations and memorials to include their own personal experiences. Although the government clearly intended the memorials and the week of commemoration to focus specifically on the genocide of Tutsi, many Hutu chose to embrace them as expressions of what they personally went through in 1994 and the years that followed and the losses that they suffered. For example, a Hutu woman in Mabanza told me:

Personally, I commemorate what happened. I think I have suffered as others have suffered. I suffer because I can't raise my children well … I find that what I had happen has a place in the commemorations, because we commemorate the suffering that everyone suffered. If it hadn't been for the war, we wouldn't have suffered.[119]

Another man said, "We commemorate what took place and affected Rwanda. I think that all Rwandans ought to feel concerned and involved. I find myself entirely implicated in this commemoration, because I lost my own victims that I still mourn."[120] An older man in Rubengera told us, "We should not forget that a genocide was committed against members of the Tutsi ethnic group and that thousands of innocent Hutu are dead in exile in Zaire. It is thus necessary each time to remember this, so that such filth is never reproduced."[121] A woman in Butare told us, "We should remember all those who lost their families during this war … I have gone [to the commemoration at the memorial site] one time, because that gave me a chance to reflect on my mother who lost her life in Zaire."[122]

[118] Interview in Rubengera, Mabanza, Kibuye, May 10, 2015.
[119] Interview in Rubengera, Mabanza, Kibuye, August 23, 2001.
[120] Interview in Kibirizi, Mabanza, Kibuye, September 16, 2001.
[121] Focus group of elders, Mabanza, Kibuye, August 10, 2002.
[122] Interview in Butare, September, 2001.

Our interviews in 2015 found that over time, participation in genocide commemoration had become increasingly compulsory to the point that an elderly Hutu man in Mabanza told us, "I participate, because if I didn't that could land me in prison."[123] Another man said, "The authorities lead us to the place of commemoration and show us where to sit. They put together a list of those present. If not, personally I would not participate."[124] A young man in Mabanza explained in detail how officials enforced participation:

We commemorate the genocide that was committed against the Tutsi. If someone tells you that there is another sort of commemoration, they would be lying. The participation of the population is an obligation. Only, they don't say that it is an obligation. If you are absent, you could be considered as someone who rebels against the policies of the government. If you don't go, it's not that there are punishments laid out by the law. If you are sick and you decide not to go, you will not be well looked at by the authorities. If they find you busy playing music at home, or if you are in a bar having a glass to drink, that situation is not allowed. If you don't participate in the discussions organized during this national Week of Mourning, you are at risk of being punished, even if there's not a law. From my understanding, the authorities could investigate you for the infraction of genocide ideology, because they can ask you why you didn't participate like the others. This year of 2015, I remember well, I did not participate one day in these discussions, and they came to knock on my door to ask me why I didn't participate. They made me pay a 5,000 Rwandan Franc fine. But I didn't pay this sum, because I went to see them to explain nicely that on that day, I was feeling poorly. They believed me. So you understand what would have happened if they had found me playing music or doing anything else enjoyable. I was lucky.[125]

Talking About the Past

The diverse reactions people expressed to genocide commemorations and memorials and the varied interpretations people gave to them suggest limitations to the government's ability to shape collective memory. The people we interviewed had embraced the official narrative on the more remote past. Prior to 1994, even though scholarship had long debunked the idea that the ethnic groups in Rwanda had emerged out of migration, virtually every Rwandan regardless of ethnicity accepted the idea that Twa, Hutu, and Tutsi were completely distinct groups that

---

[123] Interview in Rubengera, Mabanza, Kibuye, May 5, 2015.
[124] Interview in Rubazi, Mabanza, Kibuye, May 8, 2015.
[125] Interview in Rubengera, Mabanza, Kibuye, May 10, 2015. Another man in Mabanza made a similar claim. "I participate because they come to search house by house to see if there is anyone who hasn't come. I commemorate, because the state requires it." Interview in Gisanze, Mabanza, Kibuye, May 6, 2015.

had come to Rwanda in successive migratory waves. In our research in the post-genocide period, most people seemed to have accepted the new version of history that emphasized the essential unity of Rwandans in the pre-colonial period, (though they did not necessarily agree that ethnicity had no meaning, as I discuss in greater detail in the concluding chapter). Even though the new historical narrative had its own disagreements with scholarship, as it downplayed ethnic divisions that research suggests actually existed, the government seemed to have succeeded in gaining buy in from most Rwandans. The idea of ethnic unity probably resonated with the experience of living generally at peace with neighbors, despite periodic waves of violence.

Blaming the *abazungu*, the white colonizers, also resonated with Rwandans. Prior to 1994, Rwandan national discourse lacked the anti-imperialist, anti-Western rhetoric that was common in many African states, including neighboring Burundi, Congo, Uganda, and Tanzania. The 1959 revolution was depicted as a revolution exclusively against the Tutsi rulers, not against the Belgian colonial state, which was criticized only insofar as it had previously privileged the Tutsi. The shift after 1994 to depicting the colonizers as the source of divisions and violence relieved Rwandans of their responsibility for what ultimately happened, allowing Hutu to feel less guilt and Tutsi to feel less threatened by their compatriots. Furthermore, for those old enough to remember, the new approach was consistent with their experience of the colonial state, which had after all exploited Rwandans. Life under the first and second republics also failed to live up to the rhetoric of revolution. The failure of the United Nations and others to stop the genocide showed how the *abazungu* continued to exploit and abuse Rwandans.

Thus, government efforts to shape popular historical understandings seem to have been moderately successful, at least where the new interpretation made sense to people and served their interests. Ideas that deflected blame for Rwanda's problems from average people and instead attributed problems to colonizers, foreigners, or the Rwandan elite seemed particularly popular. One man who participated in an *ingando* told us:

They talked about history beginning with the former governments up to the Second Republic of Habyarimana, not forgetting the government of national unity [that took power in 1992]. *Ingando* is a good thing in the sense that it allows an exchange of ideas about good governance. They told us, for example, about the administrative powers that drove the Rwandans to acts of genocide and that the responsibility of the population came in second place."[126]

[126] Interview in Matyazo, Butare, December 14, 2001.

At the very least, our research made clear that people were aware of the official narrative and could repeat many of its details.

Yet people were also keenly aware of the government's project to shape historical perceptions. A young Hutu man who began school under the old regime and finished under the new complained:

I personally think that there were omissions [from the history curriculum]. Because its version depended on the ethnicity of the teacher. You would say that there is no true history! That which was good yesterday is bad today. We need a true history and not a biased history. Whatever its version, it is our history. We must accept it as such and not try to transform it from one day to the next.[127]

A woman in a focus group in Buyoga told us, "Today, they recount history in the same manner [as before 1994]. Before the war, it was said that the Tutsi regime behaved badly. After the war, it was said that the Tutsi were not bad, but instead it was the regime that had to be condemned."[128] Of the respondents to our 2002 survey, 49.2 percent agreed or strongly agreed with the statement, "Whoever is in power rewrites Rwandan history to serve their own interests," while only 21.7 percent disagreed. A young man in Mabanza complained:

Rwanda is a nation without history. Whoever takes power invents his own version of history that he claims is the history of Rwanda. He praises himself and invents facts that are politically favorable to him. But we don't know exactly what to say about when and by whom Rwanda was formed and founded. Even what we teach in the schools, it's just bits that we've assembled from left and right or that comes from [the government newspaper] *Imvaho*.[129]

Nevertheless, people's attitudes toward the attempt to rewrite history seem to have depended at least in part on their attitudes toward the postgenocide government. A genocide survivor in a focus group in Buyoga insisted, "Previously, the governments transformed history to their advantage. Today, the authorities have given us the true version of the facts of our history."[130]

The variety of terms that people used to refer to the events of 1994, the diversity of narratives that they told, and the multiplicity of interpretations of genocide commemorations and memorials reveal important limitations in the ability of authorities to shape collective memory. While everyone in Rwanda knew that the approved label for what happened in 1994 was genocide, people we interviewed employed many other terms. Nearly all Hutu we spoke with acknowledged the genocide and the particular

---

127 Interview in Cyarwa, Butare, September 9, 2001.
128 Focus group of women, Buyoga, Byumba, March 1, 2003.
129 Focus group interview with youth, Rubengera, Kibuye, August 10, 2002.
130 Focus group of elders, Buyoga, Byumba, March 1, 2003.

suffering of the Tutsi. Many expressed deep regret and shame over what had happened. Yet popular narratives diverged from the official narrative on key points. Even if people accepted the broad outlines of the official historical narrative, the way that they talked about Rwanda's past did not indicate a belief that history had been building inevitably toward the genocide. Rather, Hutu in particular portrayed ethnic harmony as the norm, even after independence, and they saw ethnic violence as an occasional, exceptional event that was forced on the population by those in power.

Rwandans my research team interviewed, like those Thomson spoke with, "felt the RPF was manipulating the way the genocide is remembered to maintain its position of power and wealth rather than truly seeking to unify the country."[131] Our informants from both ethnic groups spoke very little about ethnic hatred and instead talked about the role of those from outside their communities in instigating the violence. They portrayed the killing as having been undertaken by relatively small groups of local people, directed by local elites. Many Hutu and some Tutsi also ignored the enforced silence in the official discourse about RPF violence. Even many who were unwilling to give details made clear that they had experienced tragic events outside the genocide. They were plainly aware, and often seemed resentful, of the fact that the official story excluded their experiences. Personal experience was a key element in shaping how people responded to the official narrative. Where the official line made sense based upon people's experience, they embraced it willingly. Where their own experiences challenged the official line, they either adapted the narrative to include their experiences or rejected those parts that they found false.

Finally, the continuing repression in Rwanda clearly shaped popular narratives. Most people could repeat the approved narrative about Rwanda's history, the genocide, and the RPF liberating Rwanda and stopping the killing, but often they clearly did not believe what they were saying. This was in part a result of the interview context, the peculiarity of speaking to a stranger about intimate facts in a formal setting, but also reflected the difficulty that Rwandans faced in sharing their narratives. In a context where people who said the wrong thing could face charges for complicity in the genocide or be arrested for promoting genocide ideology, they had to watch their words. "We can't speak freely, only in whispers. It is this fear that stays in people's hearts. They are afraid that if they speak about ethnicity, they may be accused of supporting hostilities."[132]

---

[131] Thomson, *Whispering Truth to Power*, p. 117. Purdeková, *Making Ubumwe*, finds the same.

[132] Interview in Rubengera, Mabanza, August 24, 2001.

Some said that because of the constraints, they did not speak at all about the past, like a market salesman in Mabanza, who said, "Who would I talk with about what happened? I don't have any family, so my family is the market, and the people of the market are crazy. They only talk about money, weights, and quality. I talked about it in prison. Here, people are afraid, probably because they don't want to do anything that could make the survivors get angry."[133]

In Rwanda's authoritarian context, people had to be careful what they said. A Hutu ex-prisoner told us, "The people in my community live together peacefully. Here there are no conflicts. We try to avoid causing any problems, to avoid getting charged with genocide ideology."[134] Talking about violence perpetrated by the RPF was particularly dangerous. At the beginning of our research project, people could still speak about ethnicity in certain contexts, provided they were very careful. But by the end of our research, talking openly about ethnicity had become nearly impossible. People had to practice self-censorship. As a researcher, I found myself having to be very careful what topics I broached. In my fieldnotes during the midst of my assessment of the Internews Newsreel project, I reflected on this problem:

I have realized how effective self-censorship can be. On the survey [developed for the project], there were a number of times where people said, No, you can't ask that. So topics and questions had to be taken out. The result is that public discourse gets tightly controlled, and we all end up contributing to this.[135]

Yet people do not, in fact, completely avoid discussing the past. Instead, they do so only in carefully selected circumstances. This generally means that people talk about the past openly mostly with people of their same background. A survivor told us, "We talk about [what happened] mostly in the meetings of widows."[136] The young man above who said that people don't talk because they are afraid of making the survivors angry added that they had talked more openly in prison, something that several other former prisoners confirmed.

The problem with constraining speech so completely is that it prevents people from unifying around a common understanding of the past. Everyone knows what they are supposed to say, and one side feels their experiences reflected, more or less, in the narrative. But others have experiences that are excluded from the narrative or contradict it. While they are careful what they say and to whom, they do not ultimately keep

---

[133] Interview in Kibirizi, Mabanza, Kibuye, September 17, 2001.
[134] Interview in Rubengera, Mabanza, Kibuye, May 5, 2015.
[135] Fieldnotes, October 23, 2004.
[136] Interview in Matyazo, Butare, December 13, 2001.

silent. Behind closed doors, in trusted company, they tell competing narratives. As a result, social divisions become reproduced. As one genocide survivor told us, "We don't speak the same language. When we talk about the genocide of April 1994 for the Tutsi, the Hutu talk about July 1994, saying that the RPF also committed acts of vengeance."[137]

The danger with the constraints on public discourse is that they mask real divisions and social challenges and prevent them from being confronted.[138] People pretend that all is well and publicly do as authorities tell them, but privately their anger continues to build:

Here, good relations and mutual understanding are considered like an order and not something worthwhile. It's sad that it is presented like that. When people are asked to show mutual respect, they do it, but there is something else hidden behind. We are not sincere. What I'm telling you is my personal experience. My parents always told me the opposite, that they always got along well with their neighbors, whether they were Tutsi or Hutu, but I don't believe it. This false calm, it is a wickedness where Rwandans have a habit of showing that all is going well, when in fact the contrary is true."[139]

Another person in Mabanza said, "If everyone were not trying to be understanding and tolerant, there would be problems. The people who have been in prison for a long time have families that hold it against those who denounced them. A part of the survivors would also loved to see all the Hutu pay in the place of the real authors of the genocide. It's a cycle of suspicion."[140]

Acknowledging only one type of suffering and denying the suffering of others seems unlikely ultimately to suppress individual or even collective memories. Most Rwandans still have thick cultural ties to their communities, and their families and communities will continue to share stories about the traumas that they have known, even if those stories fall outside what officials want them to discuss. If people find that their own experiences are being debased, they may not revise their private, personal narratives, but they are likely to feel resentful, and they may ultimately debase the suffering experienced by others. A constrained public discourse full of enforced silences and undermined by competing offstage narratives, does not seem a viable strategy for building long-term social harmony. The interviews conducted in 2015 indicate that even as

[137] Interview in Matyazo, Butare, December 14, 2001
[138] Hintjens, "Post-genocide Identity Politics in Rwanda," similarly argues, "whilst public expression of political identities has been largely 'de-racialized', this has been done in a very topdown and authoritarian manner. The result has prevented the emergence from below of potentially more complex forms of political identification, which could form the basis for more inclusive forms of Rwandan citizenship in future" (p. 6).
[139] Interview in Kibirizi, Mabanza, Kibuye, September 15, 2001.
[140] Interview in Nyarugenge, Mabanza, Kibuye, December 6, 2001.

commemoration of the genocide has become a required annual event and as genocide memorials have been set up throughout the country, the sense of social division – between ethnic groups, between people who were in Rwanda in 1994 or outside, between those who were refugees in different countries – has become more pronounced, not less. People all know the official history, but enforcing it has divided them rather than bringing them together.

     Politics by Other Means: Popular
       Opinion about "Transitional Justice"

> Contrary to the myth of legal neutrality, the law is always a form of poli-
> tics by other means, as it is normative as well as merely formal, rational
> and self-referential. Legal meaning is enmeshed in wider value systems,
> and is caught between other competing normative discourses which are
> political, cultural, and more often than not, nationalist.
>
> – Richard Wilson, *The Politics of Truth and Reconciliation in South Africa*

In the past, January was the most beautiful month in Rwanda. The clear
clean air of the short dry season created remarkable vistas. When conditions were perfect, the high volcanoes on Rwanda's northwest border
were visible from almost anywhere in the country, looming massive and
purple above the horizon. On the high mountain ridge that rises sharply
above Lake Kivu and slices through the province of Kibuye, where tem-
peratures this time of year can grow surprisingly chilly at night, you could
see the Island of Idjwi and even further across the lake to the high mountains of the eastern provinces of the Democratic Republic of Congo.

In recent years, however, the weather has changed, and the dry season – which is vital to the cultivation of certain staple crops such as
beans – is no longer dry. Rains now stretch unpredictably throughout the
year, stopping occasionally for a few weeks, but then returning in a heavy
deluge that waterlogs fields and makes the beans and sweet potatoes rot
before they grow to maturity. Many Rwandans say, "God is punishing us
for what we have done."

On a rare sunny January morning in 2003, a crowd of several hundred people gathered in a field behind a sector office in Mabanza.[1] The
roads leading to the location were still wet and muddy from the rains
of the night before, and the crowd was slow to gather. A table sat on a
low point just off the road, and three benches were arranged beside it,
where a mixed group of women and men, mostly older, but a few youths
as well, sat chatting. Part of the crowd arranged itself in rows in front of

---

[1] The following account is based on fieldnotes, January 2003.

the benches, but most people gathered along the raised sides, either in the shadow of the sector office or under the trees along a fence on the other side.

The meeting of this gacaca court, originally scheduled for 9 a.m., began around 10, with a local official standing in front of the crowd, thanking them for attending, and reading the rules for this phase of the gacaca process. The president of the gacaca court – a woman in her 30s who looked as though she might be a teacher – then stood and told the crowd, "As is our custom, let us stand for a moment of silence in memory of those who were killed." The crowd rose and stood quietly for a moment, until the president called for them to sit down. She said that they would begin Phase 6 today, listing the accused, but they first needed to complete Phase 5, listing those who suffered and what they lost. A few people took their turn standing and mentioning items that were pillaged from them in 1994, and others spoke up to confirm their claims, while an older man acting as court recorder jotted the claims in a notebook. Discussion ensued when a woman who ran a bar in her home claimed that the banana beer that the militia members drank after killing her neighbor was actually pillaged, because they did not pay. The president of the court questioned her, until a young woman rose excitedly and said, "They did not come as customers, but after killing Polidi. They had a machete to kill the old woman and forced her to give them the beer. They did not come as customers." The president then relented and let the woman list what had been taken, which included items that she sold out of her home in addition to the beer. The recorder came forward and asked if there were any other instances of pillage or destruction of property that needed to be listed and, seeing none, he sat down.

The president came forward again and explained that today was the last opportunity for people to confess, because once they began to draw up the list of the accused, it would be too late. "You need to have the courage to confess and ask forgiveness." She called on people to come forward and confess their crimes, but when no one immediately came forward, she called for those who had already been charged for pillaging and had repaid their debt to come forward. A group of five women and ten men came down and stood facing the judges. The president then clarified that only those who had themselves pillaged should confess, not those who merely repaid the debts of family members. All of the women and a few of the men then sat down. She then called for anyone else who wanted to confess, not just those who had already repaid debts.

The secretary of the court, a young educated man, came forward to speak for the first time. He addressed the crowd like an Evangelical preacher, exhorting people to come forward to confess. "This is a chance for us to work together to solve these problems ourselves, within our own community. If you have done something, come forward and ask forgiveness. You need to have the courage to say what you saw in the genocide. If you were involved, it is better to come forward yourself and confess rather than be denounced, because you will not benefit from the reduced penalties if you are denounced."

The president of the court stood back up. "We don't want just those who have pillaged to confess, but also those who killed. Anyone who has something to confess should come forward." A few more men rose and walked to the front. The secretary handed papers to people to take back to their seats and fill out with an explanation of their crimes and a list of those who joined with them. While the president and secretary were dealing with those who had confessed, a flurry of conversation and activity was taking place among the judges. An elderly judge who had gotten up several times and paced around the area now came forward and said that he wanted to confess. "I had children who pillaged, and I paid the fine." The secretary handed him a paper, but the president said that if he had not himself pillaged, then he should not confess, and the judge returned to his seat. Several people in the audience stood to ask questions about buying pillaged goods or taking goods that have since been returned to their owners.

"Why aren't there any women who have come forward?" the president asked. "Weren't there any women who were involved? Do you think that those who are writing will not accuse you because you are women?"

An older male judge stood up and spoke to the crowd. "You know there will be those who will accuse you of having killed. You know that there are those who will accuse you. There were people killed here. We all know it. The prisoners will be brought forward, and they will accuse you." Two more men stood and came forward to take papers. There was more action around the judges' table, and the elderly male judge who had come forward before got up and took a paper and left to join the crowd facing the judges' table.

The president announced, "His conscience won't let him stay. So he is no longer a man of integrity [*Inyagamugayo*]. He takes himself out."

A man in the crowd asked, "We have been taught that those who killed were those who used a machete to strike someone. But what about those who were in a group that killed even if they did not themselves strike? Should they confess?"

"I think that even those should confess," the president said. "Even if you just indicated where someone was hiding and you didn't kill them, you should come forward. If you were in a group, you may think that you weren't seen, but others may come forward and accuse you."

There was a pause while the judges waited for people to finish filling out their forms and to come forward. Talking spread through the crowd. A woman behind me said, "If people ask forgiveness, God will forgive them too." A man to my side complained, "This is going to last until night-time."

The secretary came forward to preach again. "I'm sorry to push you all from both sides, but this is the last opportunity to confess. There was a judge among us whose heart was heavy. He did not carry things away himself, but he feels responsible, because children in his home were involved. Kagina had children in his home who killed, so he does not feel that he can continue as a judge. He has set a good example for all of us."

Those who wanted to confess were then called forward one by one to give their testimony. A man came forward and handed his paper to the secretary, who read the statement. "I took the roof tiles off of the home of Hitimana. There was also a dead cow at the home of Dawidi. I took some of the meat from that cow. I ask pardon from God and from this assembly."

The president looks over his paper. "We asked you to name those who saw you and also those who participated with you." She returned to the judges' table, and as he mentioned names, she wrote them down on his paper. Those he named were all either dead or already in prison. "Weren't there any more who pillaged? Others who took meat from the cow?"

"I went to get meat for my little dogs," the man said. "Some people saw me with the meat and asked where the cow was, but when I took them, the meat was all gone. So those people did not take from the cow. That is all that I did." He sat down toward the front of the crowd.

Another man came forward and confessed to having pillaged and destroyed the home of a Tutsi family. He listed about five men as accomplices. "And who saw you?" the president asked. He named a man. "But he is already in prison."

Another judge spoke up, "You say that you destroyed a home and no one saw? It takes time to do that. Surely people saw you!"

"That is all that I know," the man responded. "Perhaps there were others, but I don't know them."

A man stood up and said that he did not want to confess, but that he wanted to list those he knew were involved in pillaging from him. He needed to get back to work, he said, and he wanted to give the names of those he knew were involved.

"We need to follow the rules," the president said. "There are rules for each phase of gacaca. We can't begin denouncing when we haven't finished letting people confess. Please be patient, and there will be time for you to speak." The man sat down, but he did not look happy.

One by one people wanting to confess came forward, admitted to crimes, listed those who participated with them, and asked for forgiveness. A few seemed genuinely repentant and sorry for their actions. The judge who had earlier recused himself confessed to the minor infraction of haven taken firewood from a home after it was pillaged, but he seemed deeply and sincerely distressed. A few seemed almost defiant in their confession, prompting the court president to burst out, "If you are asking forgiveness, you can't do it in anger. You need to be repentant."

Finally, the president rose and addressed the crowd. "Those who have confessed number fifteen people. They all participated in pillaging. But no one admits to having killed. So the role now falls on you the population. You need to say what you saw or heard. You need to have the courage to tell the truth about what happened."

A young man in a police uniform asked to be recognized:

Thank you, madam president. Since I have heard the list of those who have confessed, I would note that all those who came to testify confessed to crimes for which they had already been accused. One after another they said, I stole these tiles, and I have paid for them, I stole and I have paid. Everyone knows that Gasimba was killed, everyone knows that Polidi was killed, and yet they say only, I took this, I took that. They don't want to cite the name of anyone who participated in killing. My suggestion is that we need to ask those who said they stole to tell us where the proprietors of these homes were when they were pillaging.

The president explained that they would now go through the cases of those killed in the cell one by one and come up with a list of those accused of having participated in their killing. An older woman judge then stood to read the list of the dead. There were about twenty killed within the cell whose killers needed to be identified. There were also two dead whose identities were not known. Finally, there were twenty residents of the cell killed elsewhere.

The president announced that they would begin with the case of Polidi. The elderly woman who had earlier in the morning testified to being pillaged rose to her feet. She began speaking quickly, with intensity in her voice, and she did not stop for nearly twenty minutes:

"He was killed next to my house. That night, there was much commotion, and so I was hiding myself in my home. He was killed at dawn. I heard people shouting, and I heard him cry out. 'They're taking me! They're taking me!' I called out, 'Courage! Courage!' I left my bed. It was not yet dawn, so I couldn't see. I went out, and I couldn't see, but I could recognize voices. I found Polidi with a group of people. He told me, 'They found me, and they took me to my house and demanded a goat and a jerrican of banana beer. They said if I give them money, they will let me go. The only money I had was 4,000 francs. So I went to the home of Apollo, but he told me, "I don't have money for this one." Please, go ask the Counselor to give, and perhaps I will survive.' So I went to the Counselor and asked him to give money to save his life. He said, 'Do you think this will save him? If he is going to die, let him die.'

"I went back down to my house, and there were men around him. They took a large stick and Ntezimana took a machete and struck him. I said, 'Stop it! Leave him alone! Why kill someone like this?' But Kalisa hit him with the stick on his head, and Dusaidi hit him on the back. I said, 'Have you no charity?! Have you forgotten that his brother gave you to drink.' They said, 'Leave, old woman, or you will be killed too.' They chased me, and I fell. They were going to kill me, but the counselor stopped them. He said, 'You are going to kill an old lady?' They let me go.

"I went back to my home, and there were men there hitting him on the head, smashing in his skull, so that he would not be recognizable. They dragged him across to the banana grove. They were going to bury him. They tried to dig in the ground, but it was hard ground. So they left the body in the banana grove. That was when they came over to my place and ordered me to give them beer, because I had objected to their actions. I didn't want them in my home, so I tried to offer them money. But they said, 'We don't want your money.' They broke the lock on my door and forced their way in.

"That is what I saw. I saw also one of the judges there at this attack. There were many people. Niyitegeka, Nsabimana, Rutayisire."

"So we add three people?" the secretary asked.

"No," the woman said, "they didn't kill. They were just in the crowd."

Her young neighbor then stood to speak. "I will also say what I saw. What she said is a little different from what I saw."

"You should only say what you personally saw," the court president told her.

"I went out to see what was happening. There were some young men, I found them hitting Polidi on the head. Hitimana, Manirabo, Cyiza. I add these to the names already listed. There were others, but it was dark, so I could not identify them." The secretary then read back the names, to make sure that he had noted them correctly.

One of the men who had confessed and was still sitting toward the front of the crowd was then recognized to speak, because he had been named. "I heard cries, and I went to see what was happening. But when I arrived, he was already dead. I simply got my hoe to help bury him. We went to get clothes to bury him in."

A woman sitting in another part of the crowd was recognized and stood to speak. "Polidi knocked on my door around 11 p.m. I was afraid, because there had been many attacks in these days. He asked me for help, but I was afraid to open the door. He asked me for a goat to give to those who would kill him. He came with Dusaidi, who is dead, and Ntezimana. I gave a goat. A little later they came and asked me to give them a mattress, so I gave them a mattress, but they found that the children had urinated on the mattress, so they came and traded it for another."

The court president spoke. "I see that the story is long, so we will ask the prisoners for specifications when they come before us."

A middle-aged well-dressed man with a large belly that suggested prosperity then came forward to address the crowd. He was the former counselor, recently accused. "I arrived on the scene after he was killed. The old woman is not wrong, but she has left out some details. My wife and I came after we heard the cries to help him, but it was too late. They were going to kill the old lady. They had raised the machete, all ready to kill her, when I intervened."

The president interrupted. "We don't need a lot of explanations now, we just want the names of those who participated in the killing."

The old woman who had spoken before stood to speak once more. "Again, when I told the counselor and his wife what was happening, they said they could do nothing. They told me, 'What can you, an old woman, do? Go back to bed.'"

The crowd had become restive, with people wanting to speak and defend themselves. The younger neighbor jumped up and addressed the president with great passion. "Why won't you let us tell the truth?! Why won't they let us speak?! People were gathered outside. I thought it was a cow they were killing, but when I opened my window, I saw that it was a body. Kayumba [the counselor] says he was only there when they buried the body, but I saw him! I am ready to die, but I will tell the truth! He was there when they killed him. And when they buried him, he was there too!"

While the young woman was speaking, the president sat down and the secretary came forward. "Please! You can't say everything at once. You can't attack people when they talk. There are rules that have to be followed."

The young woman continued defiantly. "I want to list Batakanwa, Kabugu, Bizimana. It was the counselor himself who told me, they want to kill your mother, and I intervened. They were lowering him down. When Fidel said that they went to get clothes to cover him for burial, really they just took his jacket and wrapped him up."

The secretary spoke again, "We can't confuse things. This is not a trial. There will be a time for that. All we need to know now is who was there, and we will hold the trial later."

People in the crowd tried to interrupt, wanting to speak. "We have a list of 16 people who were sighted around the body. There were, I think, two groups. One group that killed, and another that stood around watching."

The young woman spoke, "Yes, there was a group that killed, while others watched."

A man rose to speak, "I have something to add. I think it is better to distinguish between those who killed and those who just watched."

A well-dressed, obviously educated man then rose to speak from the side of the crowd. "I am the coordinator of gacaca here. I want to say that this is not the time to confront one another. This is the time to list those who killed, those who are accused of killing. I would suggest that we also make a list of those who witnessed the killing. You should not get angry in your testimony. We can make a provisional list of witnesses to use in the actual trials."

The policeman then spoke. "This is a good idea, but this is difficult. We don't want to wrongly accuse people, but we need to have the names of the accused for trials. Unfortunately, in a big group, it is difficult to know who participated and who was just watching."

A discussion then arose over who might have just been watching and who actually participated. It was decided that two women who passed that way regularly to get water had certainly just been passing by, while in other cases, it was less clear. Finally, the secretary said, "This is not a perfect list. It is just a provisional list that will be sorted out later, in the trials."

The president came forward again. "The hours are moving forward. ... We can continue with this discussion next time. Maybe next time we can get testimony from the prisoners."

Another man added, "Perhaps we can place a request that prisoners who know something about this case be freed to come to the next meeting."

A man came forward. "My question is, I heard myself cited in one of the papers. Can I explain myself?"

"No, not now," the president responded. "This is not the time."

The young policeman then rose to speak:

"There are those here today who confessed, and in the coming days people will say, 'They are finished with this. They have asked forgiveness.' But notice that people came up to speak only of things they had already been accused of. There is still much more to uncover here. In leaving this meeting, some people will say to others, 'I know about what you did, but I didn't dare to speak. Unless you buy me a beer, I will accuse you.' For those of you who were involved, you need to speak up *before* you are accused.

"In leaving this meeting, don't go to the bar to start discussing all that has happened. Don't go around talking about what has happened here.

Don't sit around discussing who is guilty and who is lying. This can create anger and distrust among us. This kind of talk will bring about more genocide. These things should only be brought here to these meetings. This is my advice. This session has been very heated, but we need to leave it here."

The court president then announced, "Next Tuesday, we will continue to go through the list of those killed." The current counselor of the sector came forward to make a few announcements and hand out mail. Then the meeting ended, and the crowd quickly dispersed.

Grassroots Perspectives on Justice

This session of the gacaca court held in what was formerly the commune of Mabanza was but one of thousands of such meetings that were held across Rwanda between 2002 and 2012. There were initially over 9,000 gacaca jurisdictions in Rwanda, and almost the entire adult population of 11 million people was involved in the gacaca process. Yet despite their broad reach, gacaca courts represent only one of a number of judicial processes undertaken in response to the Rwandan genocide. As I described in Chapter 4, both the Rwandan government and the international community decided to pursue trials as a primary means of building rule of law and promoting peace and reconciliation in the aftermath of the catastrophe of 1994. The government spent more time, money, and energy on holding trials than on any other aspect of post-genocide social reconstruction, while for the international community, justice was also the most extensive and enduring means of contributing to the reconstruction of Rwandan society.

Yet the actual impact of this huge investment in judicial accountability has received far too little assessment. The moral requirement of seeking justice in the aftermath of an event as horrific as the 1994 genocide is incontrovertible. But the claims that trials of genocide perpetrators would deter future crimes, contribute to reconciliation, help ensure peace, provide a clear account of what happened in Rwanda in 1994, and bring closure to survivors have yet to be demonstrated. Typical for the literature on transitional justice, much of the writing on gacaca and other judicial initiatives in Rwanda is based on what Bert Ingelaere called "magical legalism," in which authors "depict a theoretical model that is primarily based on law or law talk" rather than on empirical evidence.[2]

---

[2] Bert Ingelaere, "From Model to Practice: Researching and Representing Rwanda's 'Modernized' *Gacaca* Courts," *Critique of Anthropology*, 32, no. 4, 2012. For examples, see various publications by the government and its official representatives, e.g., Frank Rusagara, "*Gacaca* as a reconciliation and nation-building strategy in post-genocide

While almost no scholarship has studied the impact within Rwanda of the national and international genocide trials,[3] a small body of empirical research has explored gacaca. The most extensive analysis of gacaca has been carried out by Phil Clark, who – while recognizing some problems – offers an overall positive assessment of the trials, contending that the trials should be judged by their own standards, according to which he feels they have largely succeeded.[4] Nearly all other empirically-based scholarly work, however, has been more critical of gacaca.[5] Most authors who studied gacaca in depth agree with Lars Waldorf's assessment that, "Far from being a model for future transitional justice efforts, gacaca offers some profound cautionary lessons about how local justice should be adapted after mass atrocity."[6]

In this chapter, I explore the impact of these judicial initiatives on ordinary Rwandans. The research in the case study communities began in 2001, when the ICTR and national trials had been underway for five years but gacaca was just beginning. The research continued through the implementation of gacaca's test phase in 2002 and national launch in 2005. A decade later in 2015, after the completion of gacaca and the end of most ICTR and national genocide cases, my research team was able to conduct follow up interviews in two of the communities. Based upon these data, I contend that the ICTR was mostly irrelevant for average Rwandans, who know very little about its operations and results and feel detached from its actions. People are better informed about national trials, but most regard them as corrupt and politicized.

Rwanda," *Conflict Trends*, no. 2, 2005, 20–25 and Roelof Haveman and Alphonse Muleefu, "The Fairness of Gacaca," in Dawn Rothe and Christopher Mullins, eds., *State Crime, Current Perspectives*, New Brunswick, NJ: Rutgers University Press, 219–244. See also works by legal scholars such as William Schabas, "Genocide Trials and Gacaca Courts," *Journal of International Criminal Justice* 3, no. 4, 2005, 896–919.

[3] Nicola Palmer, *Courts in Conflict: Interpreting the Layers of Justice in Post-Genocide Rwanda*, Oxford: Oxford University Press, 2015, is exceptional for including analysis of interviews with officials and judges at all levels – in the ICTR, national genocide courts, and gacaca courts. Gahima, *Transitional Justice in Rwanda*, draws on his years of personal involvement in the various judicial processes in Rwanda to discuss and assess each.

[4] Clark, *The Gacaca Courts, Post-Genocide Justice and Reconciliation in Rwanda*.

[5] See Waldorf, "Mass Justice for Mass Atrocity"; Chakravarty, *Investing in Authoritarian Rule*; Max Rettig, "*Gacaca*: Truth, Justice, and Reconciliation in Postconflict Rwanda?" *African Studies Review*, 51, no. 3, 2008, 25–50; Ingelaere, "Does the Truth Pass across the Fire without Burning?"; Christoph Bornkamm, *Rwanda's Gacaca Courts: Between Retribution and Reparation*, Oxford: Oxford University Press, 2012, while focused mostly on policy, includes data on observations of gacaca in two communities. Burnet, *Genocide Lives In Us*, pp. 200–212, and Thomson, *Whispering Truth to Power*, pp. 160–182, include sections on gacaca in their analysis of post-genocide life. Penal Reform International conducted extensive monitoring of gacaca throughout the process and has published a series of reports that are particularly useful sources of empirical information on gacaca.

[6] Lars Waldorf, "Mass Justice for Mass Atrocity: Rethinking Local Justice as Transitional Justice," *Temple Law Review*, 2006, 86.

The impact of gacaca appears more mixed. Rwandans had very high expectations about gacaca, because they saw it as a process that they would themselves control and that would allow them to remove the cloud of collective guilt from Hutu and expedite the release from prison of many wrongly accused individuals. In practice, though, gacaca realized very few of its goals, and disappointment in its results was widespread. The confession process encouraged perpetrators to seek reconciliation with survivors and provided important information about what happened in 1994. Learning the fate of specific relatives and, in some cases, being able to recover and rebury their bodies was particularly important to many survivors. Yet many people were frustrated at a general lack of truthfulness in gacaca. Many Hutu complained of false accusations, while Tutsi survivors complained that too many Hutu refused to admit their real role in the genocide or to implicate others. People of all ethnicities complained of corruption for and against the accused. Many Hutu were also frustrated that RPF crimes were excluded from consideration, something that explains in part low levels of attendance (until the law was revised to require attendance) and limited participation. Among those who attended Tutsi were disappointed that gacaca – as well as national trials – failed to provide them with significant reparations, one of their primary expectations from justice. On the whole, gacaca seems to have added to both ethnic and class tensions in the three case study communities more than it helped to advance reconciliation.

Attitudes Toward the International Criminal Tribunal for Rwanda

One variable differentiating the three case-study communities was their level of contact with the ICTR. During the bulk of our local-level research, 2001–2005, two cases directly tied to Mabanza had been completed, including the 2001 acquittal of Mabanza's burgomaster, Ignace Bagilishema.[7] A case against genocide leaders in Butare, including Minister of Women and Family, Pauline Nyiramasuhuko, and her son Shalom, and two men who served as mayor during the genocide, began in 2001 but proceeded very slowly. The judgment was not rendered until 2011 (two years after closing arguments), and the appeal was ongoing

---

[7] International Criminal Tribunal for Rwanda, "Bagilishema, Ignace (ICTR-95-1A), available at www.unictr.org/en/cases/ictr-95-1a. The other case related to Mabanza was of the Kibuye prefect, Clément Kayishema, a trial in which I testified in 1997. See, International Criminal Tribunal for Rwanda, "Kayishema et al. (ICTR-95-1) available at www.unictr .org/en/cases/ictr-95-1.

at the time of our 2015 interviews.[8] No cases with direct connections to Buyoga were undertaken by the ICTR.

The major observation about the ICTR drawn from our interviews was how poorly informed Rwandans felt about the court. Fully half of those we spoke with in one-on-one interviews claimed that they knew nothing or almost nothing about the court in Arusha. In our survey, only 0.7 percent of respondents claimed to be well informed about the ICTR, while 31.3 percent claimed to have no knowledge at all about the ICTR. Many people tied their lack of information about the ICTR to its location in Arusha and expressed regret that the court was not held in Rwanda. A woman in a Butare focus group told us, "I'm completely uninformed. It should come hold trials in Rwanda."[9] What people did tell us about the ICTR further indicated a lack of knowledge, like the man who mistakenly told us that the trials were held in Arusha, "Because it was in Arusha that the accords between Habyarimana and the *Inkotanyi* (RPF) were signed."[10] Significantly, research participants in Mabanza felt the best informed, while those in Buyoga felt the least informed, but even in Mabanza, a large number complained of a lack of information about the ICTR.

Among those who did express opinions, some reflected official criticisms of the ICTR for being slow, wasting money, judging too few cases, and mistreating witnesses. "We know that it is a tribunal … but we're uninformed about what it really does. We know that since its creation, only about 10 cases have been judged. I don't know if these judges do nothing but sit [in court], and for that [little amount of work] they still receive their salaries, and they're paid in dollars!"[11] Some people also complained that the ICTR did not have the death penalty, like a survivor in Mabanza. "The punishment of life in prison does nothing for *genocidaires*. If it comes out of the UN system, if that's their means of punishing criminals, I don't know. But in my opinion, it is not enough for this sort of criminal."[12] Many said they wished the ICTR were located in Rwanda. "The ICTR is located in Arusha. We wish that this court could be located in Rwanda, because it is judging people who committed their crimes in Rwanda."[13]

---

[8] International Criminal Tribunal for Rwanda, "Nyiramasuhuko et al. (Butare) (ICTR-98-42), available at www.unictr.org/en/cases/ictr-98-42.

[9] Focus group interview with women, Matyazo, Butare, August 17, 2002.

[10] Interview in Mabanza, Kibuye, May 7, 2015.

[11] Focus group interview with women, Buyoga, Byumba, March 1, 2003.

[12] Focus group interview with survivors, Rubengera, Kibuye, August 10, 2002. A few disagreed with this position, like a woman in Butare in who said "It's good, because it doesn't condemn people to the death penalty. I wish they could judge cases here as well." Focus group interview with women, Matyazo, Butare, August 17, 2002.

[13] Focus group interview with youth, Cyarwa, Butare, June 15, 2002.

Survivors were most likely to criticize the ICTR, as in a focus group in Buyoga:

SPEAKER 1: Personally, I'm completely uninformed about its functioning. I have only heard said that it has imprisoned the big *genocidaires*, and that the trials are taking a long time. I don't see what it has really done concretely. One would say that its agents aren't doing anything but crossing their arms and just eating up money. Apparently, they're doing nothing for Rwanda. This Arusha tribunal ought to change its methods to respond to the real interests of victims of the genocide. ...

SPEAKER 2: Unfortunately I'm not an authority able to change whatever I want, but I find that this tribunal minimizes the Rwandan genocide. It doesn't accept the true testimonies and it doesn't respect the rights of those who've been called to testify. You have the example of the women who were brought there and of whom the tribunal frankly asked, "show us what they did to you during the genocide." They returned with a sense of desolation and disappointment. [The ICTR] doesn't serve the interests of the survivors but above all of the accused. It doesn't do anything but seriously injure the survivors. I can only say about the tribunal what I have heard on the radio: the commentaries on this or that process, how one or another was arrested and transferred to Arusha. And when one tries to do an analysis, one remarks that the tribunal only supports the *genocidaires* because it completely ignored the people who suffered in the genocide.[14]

An exchange with a survivor in a 2015 interview in Butare indicates the degree to which people sometimes accepted government talking points on the ICTR even though they might recognize the court's success on specific cases:

The ICTR did not function well. How can it be said to function when only a single person is judged in a year? That's why Rwandan authorities chose to speed things up with the gacaca courts so that these trials could be finished up! Gacaca judged a million cases in a single year! The problem with the International Criminal Tribunal for Rwanda is that it acquitted *genocidaires* when there were proofs against these accused. The trials in Arusha were not judged as people hoped.

Q. – Do you now of the cases of the leaders from Butare judged at the ICTR?

I've heard speak of authorities but I don't know. ... Oh yes, I remember the example here, there was a woman named Nyiramasuhuko Pauline, who was judged by Arusha.

Q. – What do you think of this trial?

What I know is that there was a case in Arusha that grouped together the *genocidaires* from Butare. And, after her condemnation, she received punishment corresponding exactly to the infractions that she committed. If you consider

[14] Focus group interview with youth, Buyoga, Byumba, March 1, 2003.

the infractions that Pauline Nyiramasuhuko committed, her trial could not have been judged by gacaca. That is why her case was judged by the ICTR. ... Her trial lasted a whole year. Here in Rwanda, we were very pleased with her verdict. The inhabitants of Butare were very happy with the verdict.[15]

Later in the interview, he again mentioned that the ICTR acquitted individuals known to be guilty, but when pressed, he was unable to give any examples.

Overall, however, opinions about the ICTR were less negative than the government's uniformly critical public assertions suggest. People recognized several justifications for the ICTR. They acknowledged that most of the leaders of the genocide had fled the country and were not available to be tried in Rwandan courts.[16] A number of people felt it was important that the international community try cases, both because of its own complicity in the genocide and because the crimes committed in Rwanda were of international significance. Some people also mentioned the need for a competent court to try the difficult cases of powerful individuals. A small businessman in Mabanza said, "Even though the crimes of the genocide were committed against Rwandans, they also concern all of humanity to which returns the heavy responsibility of contributing to the total repression of a crime like genocide, by arresting notably the main authors who fled the country."[17] A market woman in Buyoga had a slightly different take. "The ICTR is there to take up the genocide cases of those who are outside the country. The main *genocidaires* are outside Rwanda, plus the international community has to take responsibility. Because it did not stop the genocide, it ought to contribute to managing the consequences of this tragedy."[18] Interestingly, repatriated Tutsi we spoke with were most likely to emphasize the international significance of the crimes, perhaps because of their own experience living outside Rwanda. A woman in Mabanza told us, "Such an international tribunal was necessary, because the genocide was a crime against all of humanity and not just a single nation."[19] A teacher and genocide survivor in Butare who was well informed about the Butare ICTR cases emphasized the greater competence of an international court. "I find that the Tribunal did very important work, because it judged those who planned the genocide. It focused notably on those who were authorities, big businessmen,

---

[15] Interview in Butare, July 26, 2015.

[16] "It judges the big fish, because all the government ministers responsible for the genocide have taken refuge outside the country." Interview in Mutete, Buyoga, Byumba, March 29, 2002.

[17] Interview in Muranzi, Buyoga, Byumba, December 17, 2001.

[18] Interview in Zoko, Buyoga, Byumba, December 20, 2001.

[19] Interview in Kibirizi, Mabanza, Kibuye, December 7, 2001.

high officers in the army as well as reknowned journalists who mobilized the population. Thus, these people needed to be judged by a tribunal with a more advanced judicial competence."[20]

Apart from positively assessing its purposes, some informants also praised its operations. Appreciation for the ICTR was strongest in Mabanza, where people we interviewed unanimously agreed with the decision to acquit Burgomaster Bagilishema. A young farmer said, "This tribunal is too slow, as has been said. But this slowness signifies for me wisdom and prudence. I think that it takes its time to better manage the investigations and to condemn those who are truly guilty."[21] An elderly man told us, "Concerning the tribunal in Arusha, apart from its slowness, I have appreciated its manner of carrying out investigations, above all with the former burgomaster of Mabanza, who was accused of participating in the genocide and who was in the end acquitted. This verdict was correct as anyone who knows this man would agree."[22]

On the whole, our research provides little evidence that the ICTR had a significant impact within Rwanda. A few informants felt that having the international community hold national leaders accountable provided a significant example. A university student observed, "Personally, I think that the tribunal contributed [to reconciliation], because Prime Minister Jean Kambanda recognized that there was a genocide in Rwanda. Thus, I believe that his confession provided a lesson to other Rwandans to accept that in Rwanda there was a genocide, even if at the beginning they didn't want to recognize it."[23] Yet the public overall had very limited knowledge of the ICTR. Rwandans we spoke to felt little connection to the ICTR and had little interest in its work. Whatever importance it may have had for international jurisprudence, the evidence from these case studies indicates that the ICTR had little direct relevance for people living inside Rwanda.

Attitudes Toward Rwandan Genocide Courts

Rwandans were much more directly affected by national genocide courts, as a larger number of people were tried in these courts. Most of the people we interviewed claimed direct knowledge of one or more cases in the genocide courts, though relatively few had actually attended a trial. Some of those who did were impressed by the seriousness and professionalism of the process, like the woman in Mabanza who said, "I was

[20] Interview in Ngoma, Butare, August 9. 2015.
[21] Focus group interview with youth, Rubengera, Kibuye, August 10, 2002.
[22] Focus group interview with elders, Rubengera, Kibuye, August 10, 2002.
[23] Interview in Mabanza, Kibuye, May 17, 2015.

able to attend a first-level court in Kibuye. I found that it did its work in clarity. They asked if you were an eyewitness of what you said and not to base statements on what you had heard. In general, it does its work well."[24]

A key point raised repeatedly in our interviews was that justice had two sides, that justice involved not only holding those who committed crimes accountable but also releasing those were found innocent. Many others echoed what a Mabanza youth said. "It's important that justice helps identify the guilty and the innocent, to punish the guilty and liberate the innocent."[25] This perspective was expressed equally by Hutu and Tutsi. A survivor in Butare said:

Justice for me signifies the fact that the guilty are punished for the bad they did. But also the innocent who have been unjustly pursued must be rehabilitated. The guilty must be punished according to the severity of the crimes committed. True justice ought to respect the testimonies and observation of all parties in the trial equally.[26]

The idea that justice should involve not only holding the guilty accountable but also releasing the innocent reflects a number of aspirations – hope for equitable justice free of corruption and taking no account of ethnicity or class, the problem of too many people in prison, a hope that trials would contribute to reconciliation. Many criticisms of the courts were direct reflections of disappointments with the performance on these aspirations. The most common criticism of the Rwandan courts was their slowness. Hutu complained the accused languished in prison with no opportunity to prove their innocence, while survivors complained that the failure to move cases forward was denying them justice. An elder in Butare said, "If these cases aren't decided, then people are going to waste their time in prisons rather than participating in activities of reconstructing the country."[27] A focus group in Buyoga echoed similar sentiments:

SPEAKER 1: I think that they have announced very few verdicts considering the large number of cases that are awaiting judgment. I am afraid that many of the victims will die without having been able to benefit from a trial. Some detained minors are growing old while remaining accused.
SPEAKER 2: Because of their slowness, some people will be acquitted after having spent years and years in prison, and without any kind of compensation.[28]

[24] Focus group interview with women, Rubengera, Kibuye, August 10, 2002.
[25] Focus group interview with youth, Rubengera, Kibuye, August 10, 2002.
[26] Focus group interview with survivors, Matyazo, Butare, August 17, 2002.
[27] Focus group interview with elders, Cyarwa, Butare, June 15, 2002.
[28] Focus group interview with women, Buyoga, Byumba, March 1, 2003.

This criticism was a direct response to the government's own justifications for gacaca,[29] but it also expressed real frustration at the problem of too many people in prison, and particularly a concern that a number of those in prison were innocent.

Corruption, both in the community and in the courts, was a major concern. Many people complained about the problem of false accusations, like a man in Mabanza who said, "Someone who is really guilty comes to take revenge on those who did not visit them in prison. They accuse others who were not involved, and then they are imprisoned. Often, when there is a conflict over property or when you had a fight, they accuse you, but it is not true."[30] Both Hutu and Tutsi complained of ethnic bias in the courts. Many Hutu complained that the courts treated them unfairly and failed to take their testimonies seriously. A youth in Buyoga told us:

We need to have a justice that punishes without distinction. It is true that some Hutu killed Tutsi. They ought to be punished according to the law. At the same time, Tutsi who bring false testimonies against Hutu should also be punished. Our justice system ought to operate transparently and above all fight corruption.[31]

While few people in our formal interviews dared to complain about the failure to bring cases against RPF soldiers for crimes that they committed during and after the genocide, many Hutu complained in private and off the record about the lack of accountability for RPF crimes, both past crimes and continuing RPF human rights violations. In formal interviews, people spoke to this indirectly and in coded language. "Justice needs to function better now to repair the wrongs caused by its failings. You know that there is still a culture of impunity in the country. People kill others and rather than being punished, they are promoted to a more elevated post."[32]

Many Tutsi survivors complained that they also felt the courts were ethnically biased against them. Survivors felt that Hutu had used their majority position in society to influence the courts and protect their ethnic fellows from facing the consequences of their actions. "There's a problem of corruption that plays a huge role in delaying the trials. A delay of three years is significant ... the survivors will die without coming to the end of the trials. You hear that case files have disappeared, and this has been done just to erase the traces."[33]

---

29 "At least these [gacaca] courts will be more efficient that the regular courts!" Focus group interview with women, Matyazo, Butare, August 17, 2002.
30 Interview in Rubengera, Mabanza, Kibuye, August 24, 2001.
31 Focus group interview with youth, Buyoga, Byumba, March 1, 2003.
32 Focus group interview with elders, Rubengera, Kibuye, August 10, 2002.
33 Focus group interview with survivors, Rubengera, Kibuye, August 10, 2002.

While ethnic bias was a concern, participants in our interviews were at least as concerned that economic and class issues distorted the judicial process. Women in a focus group in Buyoga implied that the implementation of justice was ethnically biased but spoke most critically about the judicial bias in favor of the rich and powerful:

SPEAKER 1: Justice will contribute to the unity of the country if it is neutral. We want an impartial justice that puts aside all ethnic sentiments. Those who committed a crime ought to be punished without consideration of whether you are a Prefect or someone rich. ...

SPEAKER 2: Our justice will contribute to the reconciliation of the country the day that it becomes impartial. We have witnessed that when they imprison a leader, he enjoys certain advantages. His trial advances very quickly and he is often freed very quickly at the same time that a peasant spends years and years in prison without even having a case file. We are really astonished when we learn that there are social classes in prison. There are some detainees who employ others as grooms, as washers. It's really astonishing![34]

Many people complained that judges were corrupt and that justice therefore favored the small percentage of the population that was wealthy and powerful, while the majority of the population languished in prison or was found guilty because they could not pay bribes:

Justice in Rwanda is handicapped by poverty, so that judges easily agree to be corrupted and to let themselves be influenced. At the same time, I think that without a justice where truth is king, it will not be possible to have reconciliation in Rwanda."[35]

The regular courts lack a lot and have a lot of weaknesses. They have a problem of incompetence at the level of their agents. Our jurists haven't yet realized the value of the human person. To render justice, you have to absorb the value of every human person. Instead, in favoring the powerful because of corruption, the judges degrade the human person and you can't talk anymore about justice.[36]

Some complained about the police, like a man in Butare who told me:

If we tell what people did, in the genocide or other crimes, today you take a crook to the police. The next day, he is on the hill, and he goes after you. I don't know if these people [the police] are not well trained or if they don't make enough money, but they are easily corrupted.[37]

For survivors, the failure of courts to provide reparations was a major disappointment:

---

[34] Focus group interview with women, Buyoga, Byumba, March 1, 2003.
[35] Focus group interview with elders, Rubengera, Kibuye, August 10, 2002.
[36] Focus group interview with youth, Rubengera, Kibuye, August 10, 2002.
[37] Interview in Butare, November 8, 2001.

What I can say about trials in Rwanda is that they have not developed into something positive, satisfying. Because once a judgment is finished and pronounced, the person found guilty is classified in his category with his punishment to submit to and then the file is put away and it's finished. The payment of damages and interest ought to be done as quickly as possible in favor of the beneficiaries. Up to now, I don't know if anyone has obtained damages and interest.[38]

Although the law made no provisions for reparations related directly to trials in ordinary courts, many survivors believed that without reparations, there was no justice. As one Rwandan legal expert said simply, "Rwandan ideas about justice involve reparations."[39] Many survivors we spoke with believed that corruption was preventing the payment of reparations:

The question of genocide trials is treated like a game. People who carried out the genocide, even those who have confessed from their own mouths are in complete security. They are more at ease than we are. The survivors who are waiting impatiently for judgments, most are dead waiting while the criminals are not being pursued. The damages that survivors deserve ought to come to the beneficiaries. The state ought to work to speed up the functioning of the fund intended to reimburse the survivors of the genocide in order to help them with their daily problems and to support the orphans that are in their care.[40]

Attitudes Toward Gacaca

Having begun research in these communities before gacaca elections in 2001, conducted interviews and observation throughout the pilot phase, then held follow up interviews in 2015 after gacaca's completion, the data provide before, during, and after perspectives on the gacaca process. In the research that we conducted as gacaca was being launched, most people were optimistic about gacaca's potential. In our 2002 survey, conducted after judges had been elected throughout the country but before trials had begun anywhere, we found that more than 80 percent of respondents had a positive attitude toward gacaca;[41] 82.9 percent agreed or strongly agreed with the statement, "I have confidence in the gacaca process." In our interviews, we found people of all ethnicities recognized

---

[38] Focus group interview with survivors, Rubengera, Kibuye, August 10, 2002.

[39] Interview with Alice Karekezi, Center for Conflict Management, National University of Rwanda, Butare, August 11, 2001.

[40] Focus group interview with survivors, Rubengera, Kibuye, August 10, 2002.

[41] See Timothy Longman, Phuong Pham, and Harvey Weinstein, "Connecting Justice to Human Experience: Attitudes Toward Accountability and Reconciliation in Rwanda," in Eric Stover and Harvey Weinstein, eds., *My Neighbor, My Enemy: Justice and Community in the Aftermath of Mass Atrocity*, Cambridge: Cambridge University Press, 2004, pp. 206–225, where the gacaca attitude scale is explained in greater detail.

that keeping large numbers in prison indefinitely without judging them was an obstacle to national reconstruction. A survivor in Mabanza said, "All the *genocidaires* must be judged. Otherwise, it is a burden for their families who must take them provisions all the time and for the country that doesn't know what to do with them."[42] Some survivors were optimistic that gacaca would reveal what actually happened to their family members:

We're waiting impatiently for the testimonies in order to know exactly what happened. Many people were killed in our absence, after we fled our homes. We weren't in a place to follow exactly what happened. The means used to kill our people and their goods will be announced by those who were present in the place. We're bothered by not knowing the graves where our family members have been buried who were refugees at the communal office and were massacred. We want to know who is in these graves and the identity of those killed.[43]

Others hoped gacaca would lead to reparations. "There has been no compensation or interest above all for our homes destroyed. Everything needs to be repaired in a conciliatory fashion."[44]

Confidence in gacaca seems to have been based on people's perception that gacaca was something that they themselves would control. A participant in the elders focus group in Butare said, "What we're waiting for from gacaca is that the innocent should be freed and the guilty punished. It will be justice rendered by the population itself."[45] A survivor in Mabanza made a similar assertion. "Gacaca courts will be composed by known agents, chosen by us, coming from this region."[46] A woman in Butare said that she supported gacaca, "Because they say the prisoners will be released and there will be changes. It will be before our eyes, so that we can judge the process for ourselves. We will ourselves give testimony."[47]

People did express some concerns about gacaca. Fifty-six percent of respondents to our survey agreed with the statement, "I am concerned that the gacaca judges are not well qualified." Whereas 35.6 percent

---

[42] Interview in Kibirizi, Mabanza, Kibuye, December 8, 2001. While Clark, *The Gacaca Courts, Post-Genocide Justice and Reconciliation in Rwanda*, found in his interviews that "Both survivors and suspects discuss minimally gacaca's contribution to processing the backlog of genocide cases" (p. 173) and that "the population generally views little connection between gacaca and economic development, particularly at the individual or communal levels" (p. 179), both of these elements featured more prominently in my own interviews.

[43] Focus group interview with survivors, Rubengera, Kibuye, August 10, 2002.

[44] Interview in Kibirizi, Mabanza, Kibuye, December 8, 2001.

[45] Focus group interview with elders, Cyarwa, Butare, June 15, 2002.

[46] Focus group interview with women, Rubengera, Kibuye, August 10, 2002.

[47] Interview in Rubengera, Mabanza, Kibuye, August 24, 2001.

agreed that, "I am concerned that the gacaca judges are corrupt."[48] Some worried that gacaca would increase tensions in their community

The principle worry involves the consequences of testimonies at the level of families and the good relations on the hills. I don't see how someone can testify against his father who raised him! If that were the case, what would the results be? I find that it is necessary to retake and intensify the campaigns of public education so that people are prepared psychologically.[49]

I think that gacaca is going to increase cases of trauma. For example, a mother will be required to denounce her own child. The child in his turn will say to his survivor friend that despite their friendship, he killed his mother. These are not easy things! In addition, the liberation of some detainees could create insecurity. On the one hand, the survivors will try to seek vengeance. On the other hand, the families of the detained who have been provisionally released will do the same thing under the pretext that their family members have been unjustly imprisoned. Don't you see how gacaca could be another source of hatred? And if gacaca points the finger at a person who society has up to now considered innocent, the consequence will be hatred![50]

One testimony in Butare put the concerns of survivors in particularly stark terms:

Personally, I am the only survivor on my hill. There is nothing and no one that encourages me to go participate in the gacaca meetings. I find the idea ridiculous to have to go accuse all on my own someone who is accompanied by his wife, his uncle, his aunt, and his five children. It's ridiculous to me. This is why I won't participate in gacaca courts. What good will come of accusing someone who will not be caught?[51]

Some people also expressed hope that gacaca would judge RPF crimes. A Hutu woman in Buyoga expressed a common sentiment among her neighbors, who were deeply affected by the 1990–1993 civil war, in arguing about gacaca's potential contribution to reconciliation that, "For me, it would be possible, if it also judged our victims killed before 1994 during the war."[52] Despite these concerns, the majority of participants in our research were hopeful overall that gacaca would prove more useful than destructive.

We continued interviews as gacaca sessions got underway, and also observed gacaca in Buyoga and Mabanza and found evidence both of

---

[48] This concern came up in our interviews as well. "I am worried that the judges will be tempted by corruption, because there is no salary planned for them. I say this, because I am one of these judges myself." Focus group interview with elders, Rubengera, Kibuye, August 10, 2002.

[49] Focus group interview with youth, Rubengera, Kibuye, August 10, 2002.

[50] Focus group interview with women, Buyoga, Byumba, March 1, 2003.

[51] Focus group interview with survivors, Matyazo, Butare, August 17, 2002.

[52] Interview in Muranzi, Buyoga, Byumba, March 28, 2002.

some successes and of rising concerns within the population. The gacaca court session in Mabanza described at the beginning of this chapter highlights both the extraordinary potential that gacaca possessed to transform Rwandan society and the disappointing limitations that the process often experienced in practice. On the one hand, the session revealed a willingness on the part of many in the community to come to terms with the 1994 genocide. The session involved sharp confrontations, as some individuals sought to share what they had witnessed during the genocide, while others endeavored to defend their honor and deflect responsibility. There was deep soul searching on the part of some participants who sought to wrestle with their own actions in the terrible events of 1994.

Yet on the other hand, the bureaucratic nature of the process militated against a full and open discussion among community members. According to the regulations, this session was supposed to focus on listing crimes committed and naming those accused of the crimes, either through confession or accusation. As a result, efforts to discuss the specifics of what happened, to explain accusations and to mount a defense, were silenced. "This is not the time to confront one another," the gacaca official declared, and the moment of honest confrontation between community members, a moment in which the weak mustered the courage to challenge the powerful for their complicity, was quashed, with no guarantee that this potentially fruitful reckoning would ever occur again, since the accused would have time to pressure the accusers into silence or to prepare a more spirited – and less honest – defense.

Another problem highlighted in this session was the lack of full and honest participation by community members. The session was well attended both by the judges and the community, and a number of people spoke with a degree of frankness, but the community's engagement was limited in important ways. Several authors have noted silences that characterized the gacaca process.[53] In this case, despite considerable exhortation, the number of those who confessed was quite low, and all of them confessed to property crimes, rather than more serious offenses. As the gacaca secretary proclaimed, "There were people killed here. We all know it." Yet at this phase, not a single person outside prison confessed to having killed. Because only confessions that implicated others were accepted, those who confessed gave names, but all were careful to

---

[53] Rettig, "Gacaca," notes three types of *ceceka* ("keeping silent" in Kinyarwanda), in which: "Hutus agree not to give testimony against other Hutu" (p. 40); "Nonsurvivors fear that if they defend the accused they will be accused themselves" (p. 41); and "the inability of nonsurvivors who serve as judges to make their voices heard during deliberations" (p. 41). See also Burnet, *Genocide Lives in Us*, p. 199, and Thomson, *Whispering Truth to Power*.

list only those already named by others or in prison or those who were dead or in exile. While people responded to the incentives for confession built into the gacaca process, the majority in this initial phase sought to confess to the least serious crimes and make no new accusations, demonstrating the least engagement possible while still receiving the benefits of confession.

In our observation of gacaca in Buyoga, we noted that attendance became a major problem. While a huge crowd came to the first sessions, once officials made clear that people would be prevented from discussing RPF crimes, most stopped attending.[54] The judges themselves showed little commitment. One session in September 2002, scheduled to begin at 9 a.m., reached a quorum of residents at 11 a.m. but did not have a quorum of judges until 12:25, so the session began over three hours late. Another began at 11:57, while a third began at 12:30.[55] The problem of participation experienced during the pilot phase of gacaca led the government to make several revisions to the gacaca law, including making participation in gacaca mandatory, consolidating levels of gacaca courts, and reducing the number of judges in each court from nineteen to nine.[56]

A concern that survivors expressed during the pilot phase was the possibility that some gacaca judges were not in fact "people of integrity" but had themselves been involved in the genocide. This was a concern that the survivors' group, Ibuka, the National Gacaca Authority, and other official voices raised during the pilot phase of gacaca that received considerable coverage in the press.[57] While the people we spoke with may have been reflecting this official discourse, they also gave some specific examples, as in a focus group in Mabanza:

---

[54] Most gacaca observers noted problems with attendance and participation. Rettig, "Gacaca," notes that a much larger portion of respondents to his survey in Sovu claimed to have attended gacaca each week than actually did, and that those who attended limited their participation. "Most attendees were little more than passive bystanders" (p. 36).

[55] Fieldnotes Buyoga August 8, 2002; August 14, 2002; September 11, 2002, and September 23, 2002.

[56] Government of Rwanda, *Organic Law No 16/2004 of 19/6/2004 Establishing the Organisation, Competence and Functioning of Gacaca Courts*, Kigali, June 19, 2004, Articles 8, 13, and 29. The number was further reduced in 2007 to seven, with two alternates, Government of Rwanda, *Organic Law No 10/2007 of 1/03/2007 Modifying and Complementing Organic Law No 16/2004 of 19/6/2004 Establishing the Organisation, Competence and Functioning of Gacaca Courts* Kigali, March 1, 2007, Article I.

[57] C.f., "Le Role des Juridictions Gacaca dans la Reconciliation des Rwandais," special presentation on Radio Rwanda, October 13, 2002; Morning news in Kinyarwanda, Voice of America, April 4, 2003. Bornkamm, *Rwanda's Gacaca Courts* reports that according to government statistics, 5 percent of judges in the pilot phase were forced to resign because of genocide charges (p. 43).

SPEAKER 1: When you analyze it, you find that among the gacaca court judges, there are some criminals. The Ministry of Justice promised that it would conduct an inquiry on this subject before all the courts began. Only non-guilty people should be selected as judges. Some prisoners have written to their fellows to ask why and how they could be a judge when during the war they were together in the massacre of Tutsi.

SPEAKER 2: They were elected by their families, and when someone else wants to have himself elected, they hold themselves back and can't have any voice behind them.

SPEAKER 3: In our cell, they voted for someone who searched homes, someone who was imprisoned for three years and they say that he was innocent. We don't understand how gacaca can function having judges like that.[58]

With the process having been completed in the communities a few years before, the interviews that we conducted in 2015 focused extensively on people's opinions of gacaca, inquiring about how gacaca transpired in their community and whether it contributed to reconciliation or social division. We found that popular perceptions of gacaca were mixed, with appreciation that some issues between perpetrators and survivors had been improved yet concern as well that gacaca was used to falsely accuse many people, had increased tensions in the community, and was used to intimidate and constrain the population. Some of those we interviewed felt that gacaca had contributed – at least in part – to reconciliation. They identified the process of confession and requesting forgiveness as important for bringing together the survivors and those who killed. One Hutu man in Butare expressed his belief that gacaca had pushed some in his community to come to terms with their crimes:

Many people are troubled by the crimes they committed, such that those who committed crimes, on their return to the hills, they sought to reconcile with the victims of the genocide. Truly, some among them, after their liberation, once they returned to their hills, they were sorry about the persons they killed. They asked forgiveness from the families to whom they had caused harm, and most of the victims of the genocide have truly offered them forgiveness.[59]

The president of a gacaca court in Butare, himself a survivor, was the strongest advocate we encountered for the power of gacaca to promote reconciliation:

---

[58] Focus group interview with survivors, Rubengera, Kibuye, August 10, 2002. A survivor in a focus group in Buyoga raised a similar complaint. "It will be difficult to speak the truth. There were, for example, those elected as *inyangamugayo* in gacaca and then you learned afterward that they had participated in attacks against the innocent at the time of the genocide. And even someone who was elected who did not kill, he may have participated in acts of pillage at the time of the genocide. It's a problem. We can't hope that these people are going to effectively carry out their mission." Focus group interview with elders, Mabanza, Kibuye, August 10, 2002.

[59] Interview in Butare, July 12, 2015.

The objective of the gacaca trials was to bring those who had committed crimes to reconcile with their victims. Those who didn't want to reconcile, they had to at least be punished in order to put an end to this problem. If there had never been gacaca trials in Rwanda, there would be many conflicts in Rwandan society … Gacaca trials contributed much to the reconciliation of Rwandans. If gacaca had never existed, reconciliation would never be achieved. If they hadn't thought about putting together people to speak face-to-face, reconciliation could not have been achieved. Thus reconciliation was the fruit of this action of putting together the suspects and the victims to speak the truth. And this pushed many suspects to officially express their forgiveness.[60]

Yet further conversation revealed that much of the reconciliation he discussed in fact occurred outside the formal gacaca process. The gacaca law did have provisions for asking forgiveness from victims. Those seeking a reduced sentence in exchange for confession were required not only to give "a detailed description of the confessed offence" and to "reveal the co-authors, accomplices and any other information," but also had to "apologise for the offences that he or she has committed."[61] As described in the revised law, the apology could be given publicly during a gacaca session or written out.[62] Yet this gacaca judge took it upon himself to intervene outside the formal gacaca process to promote a more private form of reconciliation between perpetrators and victims:

The president of the gacaca jurisdiction had to be active in the reconciliation process. The first step, I had to educate so that these two people, one or the other, would accept to meet, to speak with the other. When the killer decided to approach the victim of the genocide, he came to see me and I gave him a clean sheet of paper for him to take to the victim. Once arriving at his victim's home, he exposed the motive of his visit. He told the other everything that happened during the genocide, how he killed her family. In the end, he asked for forgiveness. The victim could forgive or not. If she pardoned, the two drew up an agreement on the paper, either the killer or the victim would bring it to me, and I put the gacaca stamp on it. Later the killer of his own accord came to me to ask that I accompany him to his victim's home bringing along a jerrican full of banana beer for a celebration, because she had agreed to forgive him and so that the president of the gacaca court in our cell could hear what was said between the two people who had agreed to reconcile. The victim spoke up first, saying, "This person came to see me and asked for forgiveness, and I have forgiven him. Also, he has brought this and that and I want you to know it." In my turn, I encouraged them by asking that they rise and embrace and that everyone should do like

<hr>

[60] Interview in Butare, July 26, 2015.
[61] Government of Rwanda, *Organic Law No. 16/2004*, Article 54.
[62] "Apologies shall be made publicly to the victims in case they are still alive and to the Rwandan Society … [P]etitioners of confessions, guilt plea, repentance and apologies shall do it orally during the floor given to them, or by means of written declaration bearing his or her signature or fingerprint." Ibid., Articles 54 and 62.

them. I took the paper on which I had attached my signature, and that was the end of the problem.[63]

Genocide survivors identified learning the fate of their loved ones who were killed as the most important positive outcome of the gacaca process. Finding out through gacaca testimonies where the dead were buried and being able to recover their bodies and provide them with an appropriate burial was particularly meaningful for many survivors.[64] What one elderly survivor in Mabanza mentioned was typical of many others we spoke with in 2015:

Gacaca resolved a lot of problems. I appreciated its work, because it contributed to the discovery of the remains of our family members and afterward, we were able to rebury them with dignity. Those who confessed helped to show where we could find our family's remains.[65]

A Hutu man in Mabanza offered a similar assessment:

Gacaca in our community told the truth. In our community, those who killed were known. Yes, gacaca contributed to reconciliation, because our neighbors did not know where their family members were thrown. Gacaca allowed them to be buried in dignity.[66]

Release from prison was also seen as a positive contribution of gacaca. Despite the long delay in implementing gacaca nationwide and the massive number of people tried and found guilty in the trials, the process did ultimately result in a decline in the prison population.[67] Many Hutu who were themselves released from prison or had family members released because of gacaca expressed appreciation that gacaca allowed them to return home. A man in Mabanza found guilty in gacaca but then released from prison felt gacaca had a positive social impact:

Gacaca contributed a lot to reconciliation. Because, in my case, I was accused in gacaca. I was arrested and then imprisoned. After gacaca began its work,

---

[63] Interview in Butare, July 26, 2015.

[64] The gacaca law required those who confessed to "give a detailed description of … persons victimized and where he or she threw their dead bodies." Government of Rwanda, *Organic Law No. 16/2004*, Article 54.

[65] Interview in Mabanza, Kibuye, May 6, 2015. Ingelaere, "Does the Truth Pass Across the Fire Without Burning?" identifies this type of information as "forensic truth," contrasted with deeper sorts of truths. He reports that in his gacaca observations he "often heard testimonies indicating who, where, when, against whom and how something happened, almost never why" (p. 516).

[66] Interview in Mabanza, Kibuye, May 14, 2015. Burnet, *Genocide Lives in Us*, also emphasizes the importance to survivors of finding out what happened to their loved ones.

[67] According to the International Center for Prison Studies at the University of London, Rwanda's prison population declined from 145,000 in 1998 to 112,000 in 2002 after the first provisional release related to gacaca to 58,461 in 2011. www.prisonstudies.org/country/rwanda.

I was brought to my local community to be judged, and then I was condemned. Gacaca condemned me to a penalty equal to the time that I had already spent in prison, and then I was released.[68]

Some Hutu who were acquitted also praised gacaca, feeling that their acquittal demonstrated the success of the process:

In gacaca, there were people who did not speak the truth, and that is the reason that I was imprisoned, because they protected those who killed. If not, I would never have been imprisoned. But gacaca really contributed to reconciliation, because those who had been charged with crimes were liberated. Gacaca showed the truth. In my case, for example, gacaca found me innocent, because I was unjustly accused.[69]

Yet even most supporters of gacaca recognized serious limitations to the contributions gacaca made to reconciliation. The gacaca court president who asserted so strongly that gacaca promoted reconciliation also recognized that the process was traumatizing for many survivors. "During the gacaca trials, when the *genocidaires* recounted how they had savagely killed people, the survivors learned how their families were savagely killed, they were traumatized. That was the problem that we encountered most often. We couldn't do anything else for them but to console them."[70] He recognized that some Hutu perpetrators also refused to seek forgiveness:

There was a handful of people who refused to ask forgiveness. For example, there are certain killers who did not want to ask forgiveness from their victims, and I asked them why they did not want to approach them. In a very hard tone, they responded to me that they could not go express this [request for] forgiveness. It was because the victims were people who were very poor, while their killers generally were very rich and did not want to go bend down to poor people to ask for forgiveness. The government has to intervene. It punishes those who don't want to ask for forgiveness.[71]

He also recognized that some survivors remained unwilling to accept reconciliation. "The cohabitation of these two people [Hutu and Tutsi] is perfect, but it is not everyone who lives together perfectly. I can say that ten percent don't want to live together with their executioners. They have refused to offer forgiveness."[72]

In our interviews, many survivors clearly seemed to resent the gacaca process. We encountered a number of survivors who rejected the

---

[68] Interview in Mabanza, Kibuye, May 12, 2015.
[69] Interview in Mabanza, April 20, 2015.
[70] Interview in Butare, July 26, 2015.
[71] Interview in Butare, July 26, 2015.
[72] Interview in Butare, July 26, 2015.

pressures on them to offer forgiveness to those who killed their family members. Many felt that Hutu lied during the process rather than speaking fully and honestly about their role in the genocide.[73] The gacaca trials strengthened the sense of isolation for many Tutsi, particularly many women survivors, who felt vulnerable if they spoke up in gacaca about the loved ones they lost, since Hutu were the vast majority in their communities and those they might accuse had large families to defend them. An elderly survivor in Mabanza expressed a complete rejection of the trials. "Gacaca worked like the killers hoped it would. Who was going to testify for us, when it is these executioners who have killed them? Why would I want to find reconciliation with them? I have no interest in reconciling with them."[74] One survivor who served as an *inyangamugayo* reflected the continuing tensions in her community. "During gacaca, Hutu sought to hide what they had done, but we discovered it. They lied. I too was in the seat [as a judge]. Gacaca let us have our past, to find out what was untold. But not reconciliation. Reconciliation doesn't exist, because they continue to threaten us. Gacaca allowed us at least to know where our people are buried."[75]

The issue of reparations was quite contentious for survivors.[76] In contrast to the regular genocide courts, the gacaca law contained provisions for reparations, requiring those found guilty of property crimes either to return what was stolen or the, "Repayment of the ransacked property or carrying out the work worth the property to be repaired."[77] In practice, however, these provisions produced few results. In the initial presentation of gacaca in the early 2000s, most Rwandans assumed that the provisions for "community services" (usually known by the French acronym, TIG, *travail d'intérêt général* – work in the public interest) in exchange for reduced sentences would involve work to benefit the survivors. In practice, TIG consisted mostly of community projects, like repairing roads and bridges, and

---

[73] Clark, *The Gacaca Courts*, notes that, "As gacaca has developed … some [government] officials have expressed growing concerns over widespread false testimony during gacaca hearings" (p. 190). Within the population, he noted considerable hope about the potential of gacaca to reveal truth but also found widespread concerns over the lack of truth telling that occurred in practice in gacaca (pp. 192–201, 206–219).

[74] Interview in Mabanza, Kibuye, April 29, 2015.

[75] Interview in Mabanza, Kibuye, May 13, 2015. My own research is consistent with the observation in Thomson, *Whispering Truth to Power*, that "A common thread I noted in the narrative of survivors when speaking about *gacaca* was the constant sense of insecurity they felt" (p. 173).

[76] Waldorf, "Mass Justice for Mass Atrocity: Illiberal Peace-Building," noted the lack of a compensation fund to supply reparations as one of the main structural weaknesses of gacaca (pp. 193–195).

[77] Government of Rwanda, *Organic Law No. 16/2004*, Article 73.

much of it was done in labor camps outside peoples' home communities. Only those who committed property crimes were required to make reparations, but as analysis by Brehm, Uggen, and Gasanabo indicates, the median fine for those found guilty of property crimes was 7,100 RWF, or approximately $11, and half the fines were 25,000 RWF or less (under $40).[78] Yet survivors complained that even these limited fines had not been paid. A survivor in Mabanza complained that those found guilty refused to pay:

Those who participated in the genocide must ask for forgiveness, but also they need to pay those from whom they stole and whose property they destroyed during the genocide of 1994. Up to now, there are those who have not wanted to repay what they stole or destroyed during the genocide, not because they are poor, but because they lack the will.[79]

The gacaca court president in Butare identified failure to pay fines as a continuing problem:

As for the third category, there was not a lot of forgiveness, because those in this category were required to pay what they had been charged with. In this category, there are always problems, because the people never pay, being given perhaps a fine of one million Rwandan francs, where are you going to find that money? ... The government will take things in hand and find a solution to this problem. These people who don't carry out their sentence will be forced to do public works, that's all.[80]

Considering the fact that two-thirds of gacaca cases involved property crimes and that guilty verdicts were issued in over one million cases,[81] this issue clearly has the potential to serve as a continuing source of social tensions. A survivor in Butare discussed the larger problem that frustrated many survivors: the loss of family members had a huge economic impact on them, but there was no compensation for the loss of human life. "If you take a survivor, the members of her family have been killed, but there is not monetary value that exists to pay them. But according to the law, they ought to be compensated for the fact that they lost their families."[82]

[78] Hollie Nyseth Brehm, Christopher Uggen, and Jean-Damascène Gasanabo, "Genocide, Justice, and Rwanda's Gacaca Courts," *Journal of Contemporary Criminal Justice*, 30, 3, 2014, pp. 333–352.

[79] Interview in Mabanza, Kibuye, May 6, 2015.

[80] Interview in Butare, July 26, 2015. Brehm, Uggen, and Gasanabo, "Genocide, Justice, and Rwanda's Gacaca Courts," find that only "1% of fines exceeded 680,953 RWF, or US$1,049," (p. 340).

[81] National Service of *Gacaca* Jurisdictions, "Summary of the report presented at the closing of Gacaca court activities," Kigali, Rwanda, 2012.

[82] Interview in Ngoma, Butare, August 9. 2015.

Many people we interviewed were reluctant to criticize gacaca openly, responding when first asked their opinions of gacaca that the process went well in their community. Yet when pressed, they raised a number of complaints that revealed serious concerns with how gacaca transpired. Most Hutu did not appear to believe that the massive number of cases treated by gacaca courts reflected the actual breadth of participation but rather that it showed the degree to which the process was abused. Many Hutu who were forced to defend themselves or their family members of charges of participation in the genocide claimed that accusations raised in gacaca were false, motivated by revenge, personal vendettas, and greed. Complaints of unjust accusations were widespread:

Gacaca tried to do its work, but there were those who accused and condemned others unjustly. Many people were imprisoned even though they hadn't done anything. Gacaca helped bring reconciliation for only one part of the population, but there are many who were accused unjustly. For example, my father was accused unjustly. He was accused of having killed Tutsi.[83]

One elderly man complained that he had been charged and found guilty of genocide crimes, because he had criticized a local family that refused to protect the children of a Tutsi in-law during the genocide. "During the gacaca trials, they came and charged you with whatever they wanted. I spent ten years in prison even though I did nothing."[84]

A common complaint about gacaca was that the process was corrupted by money. As one man in Kibuye complained, "There was injustice. Those who were rich were acquitted. They charged me with crimes at Bisesero, and I was imprisoned."[85] Another man also complained about false accusations and the role of money:

Gacaca was very difficult. They charged us with whatever they wanted. They even had put together associations that charged us falsely. For example, my wife was several times pursued and they wanted to imprison her, saying that she participated in the killings. I had to spend a lot of my means so that she was not imprisoned. The Tutsi are responsible for what happened in 1994, because they were the first to start shooting on the plane that was carrying President Habyarimana. They provoked their own chaos knowing that they were not strong.[86]

---

[83] Interview in Mabanza, Kibuye, May 5, 2015.

[84] Interview in Mabanza, Kibuye, May 5, 2015. Chakravarty, "Navigating the Middle Ground," found similar anger over false accusations. One of her informants said, "Once you are accused, it is hard to prove you are innocent … unless you have the backing of powerful people," (p. 250).

[85] Interview in Gisanze, Mabanza, Kibuye, May 6, 2015.

[86] Interview in Rubazi, Mabanza, Kibuye, May 8, 2015. Thomson, *Whispering Truth to Power,* includes testimony from a Tutsi woman who admits to having denounced someone under pressure from powerful individuals in her family and community. "I never saw him before, but I denounced him" (p. 171).

Since those accused in gacaca were not allowed to hire lawyers, when this interview participant discussed spending money to defend his wife, he was implying the need to buy off either accusers or *inyangamugayo* or both. His anger over his gacaca experience leads him directly to question the government's official narrative about the genocide. His blaming the Tutsi for the events of 1994 is particularly significant since it is an assertion that is highly controversial in Rwanda today and could easily lead to arrest.

Some people pointed out a different form of corruption that occurred in gacaca, the attempt to extort the wealthy and powerful or to get revenge on them by charging them falsely with crimes. A survivor in Butare recounted a case involving a man who had become a local government authority after the genocide, but then had a conflict with a few survivors who brought charges against him. Ultimately he was condemned to thirty years in prison:

To a large extent, those in society who were victims of the gacaca courts were the intellectuals, the business people and others with a lot of money. It was sufficient that they have a problem with a survivor, and he would ask himself whether he couldn't pursue something in this system that was underway, because it was the only means to snatch his money away. And if he was a Hutu who was there during the genocide, it was very easy to find an infraction against him, and that would go very well. … It was sufficient to find a witness who had been corrupted with a little sum of money to charge him.[87]

Some also complained of the politicization of gacaca and the constraints on the process created by the repressive political climate:

The *Inyangamugayo* carried out their mission under something that I would qualify as pressure or fear. If you analyze it carefully, you're going to see that in the country today, Rwandans live at peace and appear to be reconciled, when they're not. To really see that people are not reconciled, you have to go to educational establishments, and that is going to prove to you that Rwandans are not yet reconciled. Also in matters of seeking work, you can see that people are not yet reconciled. In a few words, even if there aren't conflicts linked to what happened in 1994, truly it is clear that reconciliation has not yet been attained, even though you're not allowed to say certain things. Those who say them will run into problems. It's fear that has invaded people."[88]

What happened in one Butare sector is particularly troubling, as it indicates a willingness simply to ignore the official structures in response to political concerns:

In my community, the population participated massively in the gacaca trials, and they went well, because everyone tried to talk about what happened during

---

[87] Interview in Tumba, Butare, August 9, 2015.
[88] Interview in Rubengera, Mabanza, Kibuye, May 10, 2015.

the genocide. Even those who wanted to speak lies, others in the community contradicted them. But there were two phases of gacaca ... At the time when the first phase was about to finish, the general direction of gacaca courts determined that the information gathered wasn't well done, and they decided to restart a second phase of information gathering. Frankly, this second phase of information gathering happened badly, because this second phase of gacaca trials was characterized by terror or panic. Personally, I think that it was as if, after having done an evaluation of the first phase, they found that they had imprisoned an insufficient number of *genocidaires*. And because of this, they sought to imprison a big number. During this phase, every time there were new names that came to their attention, they were imprisoned. And then, another aspect is that during the second phase, people arrested couldn't explain themselves, couldn't bring witnesses, whether for or against. So you could see that this phase was just looking to maximize the number of people who could be imprisoned or be punished. These people really had no rights.[89]

Conclusions: Justice and Social Control

My research indicates that the legacy of judicial responses to the Rwandan genocide is mixed, but viewed from the perspective of the lived experience of average Rwandans, the various judicial initiatives appear to have done more to strengthen the current regime's hold on political power than to promote justice and reconciliation. For all of its expense and international prominence and whatever its contributions to international law, the ICTR has contributed almost nothing to the processes of social reconstruction within Rwanda, other than serving as a lustration tool to prevent those involved in the genocide from regrouping outside Rwanda and presenting themselves as a viable alternative to the RPF.[90] Rwandans are very poorly informed about the ICTR, undermining the potential for justice to "be seen to be done" by the ICTR.[91] People understand the ICTR to be a tool for holding prominent individuals involved in the genocide accountable. The failure to bring even a single case against anyone associated with the RPF has allowed the current regime to strengthen its international moral authority and tighten its

[89] Interview in Butare, July 12, 2015. Few of my research participants were as explicit as the young Hutu who told Thomson, "For me, *gacaca* is just a way for the government to put us Hutu in prison and to make sure we don't make more genocide for them. It [genocide] could happen because Hutu are no longer welcome here" (*Whispering Truth to Power*, 172), yet the sense that gacaca was mostly about putting Hutu in prison seems to have been shared by many of my Hutu informants.

[90] A major point in Akhavan, "Beyond Impunity," is that the ICTY and ICTR "have helped to marginalize nationalist political leaders and other forces allied to ethnic war and genocide" (p. 9).

[91] Lord Chief Justice Hewart in *R v. Sussex Justices, Ex Parte McCarthy*, 1924 famously wrote that, "Not only must Justice be done, it must also be seen to be done."

control over Rwandan society. While the RPF has officially maintained a negative view of the court, the ICTR has ironically helped to consolidate the RPF's power within Rwanda.

The Rwandan population perceived the national courts to be tools used by the regime to enforce its power. Whatever improvements may have taken place in due process standards within Rwanda's national courts,[92] most Rwandans did not appear to believe that the primary purpose of the courts was to mete out justice – to convict the guilty and free the innocent – but rather saw the courts as tools of state power. Rwandans did not make a distinction between the special genocide courts and other courts used to punish people for genocide ideology and other blatantly political crimes, giving the impression – to Hutu in particular – that the courts are biased, corrupt, and highly political. The slowness of these courts, a point that the government itself admitted in its explanations of gacaca, was seen not as a problem just of limited capacity but as a reflection of policy. For Tutsi survivors, the lack of reparations in national courts greatly reduced their relevance. For most Hutu, the national courts were not about justice but about coercion.

The impact of gacaca is more complicated. Despite some organized opposition,[93] the population as a whole was very hopeful about gacaca before its launch, and in fact the gacaca initiative did succeed to a limited degree in achieving its goals of providing accountability for the genocide and promoting reconciliation. Many people who participated in the genocide were tried and found guilty, while a number of accused were acquitted. The process of confession encouraged many who participated in the genocide to come to terms with the crimes that they committed in 1994. Gacaca encouraged many of the confessed Hutu perpetrators to seek a rapprochement with the Tutsi whose families they had killed, and in some cases, relations between victims and perpetrators were improved.[94] The information that gacaca provided – particularly the specific information about where and how individual Tutsi were killed and where their bodies were interred – was important to many survivors. For Hutu, the fact that by the end of gacaca the prison population was reduced by half was particularly important.

---

[92] Centre de Documentation et d'Information sur les Procés de Génocide, *Quatre Ans de Procés de Génocide: Quelle Base Pour les Juridictions Gacaca?* Kigali: LIPRODHOR, 2001, found that due process had improved.

[93] Jennie Burnet, "The Injustice of Local Justice: Truth, Reconciliation, and Revenge in Rwanda," *Genocide Studies and Prevention,* August 2008, 173-193.

[94] My own interviews do indicate that, as Clark claims in *Gacaca Courts, Post-Genocide Justice and Reconciliation in Rwanda* (pp. 165–168, 220–256), in some cases gacaca did encourage positive engagement that helped to contribute to reconciliation, but my research indicates that this engagement was less widespread than Clark found.

Yet certain elements inherent to gacaca undermined its ability to promote reconciliation. At a time when official government policy banned the use of ethnic labels in an attempt to promote national unity, ethnic identification was at the heart of how the gacaca courts functioned. Ethnicity determined whether or not a crime could be included in gacaca, since gacaca focused only on genocide crimes, and genocide was defined in ethnic terms. If a crime were against a Tutsi, then it could be included in gacaca, but if it were against a Hutu, it generally could not. The multiplication of cases to nearly two million, involving charges against over one million individuals, meant that a massive portion of the Hutu population became labeled as *genocidaires*. While the cases of those charged with murder seem to have been treated fairly seriously in most communities, demonstrated in part by a fairly high acquittal rate, the property crimes that represented two thirds of cases had an acquittal rate of only 4 percent. While property crimes were regarded as much less serious, they nevertheless marked those convicted officially as *genocidaires*, and with convictions in 1,266,632 cases (with no opportunity for appeal), a substantial portion of the Hutu population was effectively removed from the possibility of engagement in public life.[95] When reforms to the gacaca law consolidated the number of jurisdictions and reduced the number of *inyagamugayo* in each from nineteen to nine, the portion of judges who were Tutsi increased sharply.[96] The effect of gacaca, thus, was to solidify ethnic categories, defining Hutu as perpetrators and Tutsi as victims, witnesses, and judges.

The retributive powers of the gacaca courts and the confrontational nature of the trials had the effect of reinforcing ethnic tensions rather than helping reduce them.[97] Despite some who emphasized the potential for gacaca to promote reconciliation, like the gacaca president from Butare quoted above, gacaca was at its heart a process of retributive, rather than restorative, justice. Gacaca trials were court proceedings whose main

---

[95] Rwandan Patriotic Front, "Gacaca Courts Genesis, Implementation, and Achievements," www.rpfinkotanyi.org/en/?gacaca-courts-genesis. Bornkamm, *Rwanda's Gacaca Courts*, notes that according to Article 76, "Those convicted under the Gacaca Law are deprived of their rights to be elected to public office and to serve in certain official functions" (p. 83). In reality, the sanction goes further, since those marked officially as *genocidaires* are marked as social problems who must be careful to avoid appearing oppositional or face future prosecution on charges such as genocide ideology.

[96] Since the government does not recognize ethnicity and keeps no ethnic statistics, this conclusion is based on the observations of a number of informants and the fact that nearly all of the people we interviewed who identified themselves as *Inyangamugayo* were Tutsi.

[97] My own research in the three case-study communities supports Rettig's observations in Sovu that, "Gacaca is fueling – or at least exposing – conflict, resentment, and ethnic disunity" ("Gacaca," p. 29).

function was to judge and punish perpetrators, and they operated under what Ingelaere has termed a "prosecutorial logic."[98] While confession encouraged a minority of perpetrators to accept guilt, the majority of the accused were found guilty in cases that pitted mostly Tutsi accusers against Hutu defendants. As Minow has pointed out, the process of accusation and defense is highly confrontational and compromises the ability of trials to promote reconciliation.[99] Many Rwandans felt that the gacaca process was unjust. Survivors complained that the perpetrators lied and evaded justice, while many Hutu complained about the multiplication of unfounded accusations. Many informants offered some version of the complaint that, "They charged us with whatever they wanted."[100] Evidence from these three communities supports Gerald Gahima's assertion that, "In many communities, the retributive aspect of Gacaca had the impact of transforming Gacaca into a bitter, partisan contest between survivors and relatives and sympathizers of people accused of genocide."[101]

A major focus of this book has been to understand the effectiveness of the attempt by the post-1994 Rwandan government to use the tools of transitional justice to shape collective memory in the effort to promote national unity and solidify political power. I argued in Chapter 4 that the regime used trials to focus national and international attention on the genocide, to imply collective guilt on the part of all Hutu, and to erase memory of the RPF's own war crimes and other human rights abuses. I visited each of the three case study communities when I lived in Rwanda in 1995 and 1996, and at that time, people spoke relatively freely about abuses by the RPF. In the early part of this research project, many people still expressed a belief that RPF members involved in crimes should be held accountable in trials. In our 2002 survey, 55.2 percent of survey respondents who expressed an opinion agreed or strongly agreed with the statement that, "The Arusha Tribunal should try members of the RPF who committed war crimes," compared to 28.1 percent who disagreed or strongly disagreed.[102] Of the

---

[98] Ingelaere "Does the Truth Pass Across the Fire?" notes that the legalistic approach contrasted with traditional gacaca. "The prosecutorial logic of the modern Gacaca process limits the restorative aspects connected with the system as it functioned previously: the quasi-ritualistic purification of the social order by bringing parties in conflict together and re-creating harmony between families in dispute" (p. 12).

[99] Minow, *Between Vengeance and Forgiveness*.

[100] Interview in Rubazi, Mabanza, Kibuye, May 8, 2015.

[101] Gahima, *Transitional Justice in Rwanda*, p. 169.

[102] Ethnicity was significant on this question, as 74.2 percent of respondents who identified themselves as Hutu agreed that the RPF should be tried in Arusha, compared to only 30.7 percent of Tutsi.

respondents, 42.4 percent with an opinion also agreed with the statement, "Crimes committed by the Rwandan Patriotic Army should be included in gacaca." Among Hutu, support was 52.0 percent. A Hutu woman in Buyoga expressed a common sentiment in her community, deeply affected by the 1990–1993 civil war, that gacaca could contribute to reconciliation "if it also judged our victims killed before 1994 during the war."[103]

The overwhelming time and attention paid to prosecuting genocide crimes did not erase the memory of RPF abuses or convince Hutu that they were in fact collectively responsible for the genocide, but it has crowded out any thought of bringing members of the RPF to trial for their crimes. Like the memorials and commemorations, trials have helped to maintain a hegemonic focus on the genocide as Rwanda's singularly important historical event. My research indicates that the extraordinary emphasis on accountability for genocide crimes has effectively excluded completely from popular consideration the idea of accountability for RPF crimes. In their assessments of gacaca, people in our 2015 interviews did not mention the failure to hold the RPF accountable at all, because the idea had become simply unimaginable.[104]

My research also indicates that the genocide trials effectively intimidated the population, making them increasingly cautious and compliant.[105] By forcing every adult in Rwanda to participate in the gacaca process, particularly as the charges leveled in gacaca became increasingly specious, Rwandans were in effect being required to participate in their own subjugation. Hundreds of thousands of Hutu were convicted as *genocidaires*, even if most were only found guilty of property crimes, and as a result, they were effectively excluded from national, regional, and community leadership. As convicted *genocidaires*, they must be careful to avoid any appearance of dissent or they could easily be accused of a recidivist embrace of genocide ideology. The Tutsi survivors were forced, whether they wanted to or not, to return again and again to the story of the genocide, and they were under heavy pressure to encounter and ultimately forgive those who killed their families. In short, in Rwanda's authoritarian context trials

---

[103] Interview in Muranzi, Buyoga, Byumba, March 28, 2002.

[104] Thomson, *Whispering Truth to Power*, similarly contends, "That Tutsi might be guilty of serious crimes against Hutu is publicly unimaginable and something that is rarely discussed among Rwandans in private, let alone in a public space like *gacaca*" (p. 172).

[105] I recognize Thomson's point in *Whispering Truth to Power*, that people do find ways to protest and resist, so they are not completely powerless and passive. Nevertheless, the state is sufficiently strong and authoritarian that the majority of people must seek to limit their contact with the state and generally to comply in order to survive.

became tools for exercising state control rather than just meting out justice.[106]

My research in the three case-study communities revealed one important issue that has been largely neglected in the literature on transitional justice – the economic context within which post-conflict judicial initiatives take place. As described in Chapter 5, Rwanda has experienced an economic renaissance that has brought economic growth but has also fueled the frustrations of average Rwandans. While the majority of the population has gained limited benefits, such as improved access to education and healthcare, they perceive a small elite – mostly people linked to the government – to have prospered disproportionately. Urban areas are booming, with skyscrapers, fancy new homes, and high-end restaurants, but this new cosmopolitan life is available to only a small portion of Rwanda's people, while the majority finds themselves continuing to struggle to get by. The condescension with which the members of the country's new elite treat the majority exacerbates popular tensions.[107]

The population of Rwanda experienced judicial initiatives in this context of inequality, with gacaca in particular being understood as just one of a number of top-down government initiatives for popular mobilization alongside *umuganda* community labor, *ingando* re-education camps, and administrative decentralization. In our observation of gacaca, we found that government officials – mostly repatriated former Tutsi refugees – intervened regularly in gacaca proceedings, ensuring that they stayed on track and served the interests of the regime.[108] The "second phase of gacaca" that was described in Butare indicated the willingness of authorities to step in more aggressively if they found that proceedings were not to their liking. As a result, even though gacaca was based

---

[106] According to Susan Thomson and Rosemary Nagy, "Law, Power, and Justice: What Legalism Fails to Address in the Functioning of Rwanda's *Gacaca* Courts," *International Journal of Transitional Justice*, 5, 2011, 11–30, their "research shows that, even if gacaca is legally acceptable in a harmonized way, it is nevertheless a state-run legal system that reinforces a particular version of reconciliation and, as such, not only renders most Rwandans largely powerless in individual processes of reconciliation but also serves to maintain a climate of fear and insecurity in their everyday lives," p. 13.

[107] Thomson, *Whispering Truth to Power*, does a particularly nice job of explaining the condescending attitudes of the elite, primarily the returned refugees, and how average Rwandans of all ethnicities bristle at their treatment.

[108] Clark, *Gacaca Courts, Post-Genocide Justice and Reconciliation in Rwanda*, observed similar government intervention: "The government rarely discusses the extensive involvement of state actors in gacaca, including providing judges with dossiers detailing suspects' crimes and confessions, and sometimes intervening when hearings are perceived to diverge from the statutes and norms of the Gacaca Law and Gacaca Manual" (p. 146). A good example of this sort of intervention can be witnessed in the gacaca sessions presented in Anne Aghion's documentaries *The Notebooks of Memory* (2008) and *My Neighbor My Killer* (2009).

in the local community and depended on extensive community engagement, Rwandans experienced gacaca as an instrument of state power. Regardless of their sense of vulnerability, susceptibility to trauma, or personal interest in moving on from a focus on the genocide, Tutsi survivors were forced to participate in the gacaca proceedings as judges and the most important witnesses. Many Hutu experienced gacaca as a mechanism designed primarily to intimidate and control them, backed up by the possibility of conviction under charges of genocide ideology should they object.[109]

In our interviews people felt both that the rich were treated differently by the justice system, including in gacaca, and that bribery and fraud were widespread in all the judicial processes. As I recounted in Chapter 4, when I visited a prison, looking for those who had organized the killing of my friends, I was told that, "There are only peasants here now. All the important people, all those with influence, they have been released." This experience was common for Rwandans, who complained widely in our interviews that money and power corrupted the judicial process. The poor who were the mere foot soldiers of the genocide have been much more likely to face imprisonment and other punishment than community leaders, who could bribe their way out of charges or use their influence to reduce their sentence. Many poor Hutu felt that they were unfairly charged yet lacked the means to secure acquittal or a reduced sentence, and the debts with which they were laden by property crime prosecutions places them in a permanently vulnerable position. The judicial processes also limited the prospects of the prominent Hutu, as their implication in the genocide and the threat of facing genocide ideology charges makes them vulnerable and forces them to remain quiescent and accommodating.

Economic issues also affected how Tutsi genocide survivors interpreted gacaca and other judicial initiatives. In post-genocide Rwanda, many survivors live in abject poverty and struggle to make ends meet. A large portion lost their homes in the genocide, and the homes that have replaced them – often built in government programs – are generally inadequate. Having lost most of their families, they lack the networks that most Rwandans rely on for financial security and support. Thus, reparations were the most important priority for survivors, and they have been deeply disappointed by the failure of Rwanda's judicial initiatives to provide significant reparations. Like poor Hutu, many survivors felt that

---

[109] My interviews reaffirm Thomson's assertion "that the *gacaca* process is for many ordinary Rwandans an oppressive form of state power that forces them to participate in ways that are not necessarily in line with their own lived realities," (*Whispering Truth to Power*, p. 169).

the wealthy who had organized the genocide were able to use corruption to avoid stiff punishment, but many were also frustrated at Rwanda's new wealthy, the repatriated, who forced them to participate in gacaca, pressured them to seek reconciliation with the Hutu who killed their families, and who benefited from exploiting the genocide while sharing very few of the benefits with the survivors. Many survivors are angry not only because of the genocide but also because of their continuing low social status twenty years later. From this perspective, the various judicial initiatives have offered very little justice.

Sadly, if the judicial initiatives in Rwanda have largely failed to promote reconciliation, they have also done little to promote the rule of law. The perception that national trials and gacaca were biased and corrupt compromised their ability to promote the idea of equality under the law and respect for justice. The one-sided nature of the various judicial initiatives in particular undermined their ability to promote rule of law. As Lars Waldorf noted, "Despite the RPF's insistence on the need to end impunity in Rwanda it has consistently prevented its (then mostly Tutsi) soldiers from being held accountable for war crimes and crimes against humanity committed against Hutu civilians during the 1990–1994 period."[110] To many Rwandans, trials appear to be tools for disciplining Hutu rather than institutions promoting justice.

---

[110] Waldorf, "Mass Justice for Mass Atrocity: Rethinking Local Justice," p. 61.

Part III

Conclusion

 "We Pretend to Live Together": Assessing the Impact of Transitional Justice Mechanisms in Rwanda

---

Ahabaye inkovu hada subirana

A wound never heals completely.

– Kinyarwanda proverb

"Espérance" was a friend from my first sojourn in Rwanda in the early 1990s. When I returned to the country in 1995, we renewed our friendship. Over the months, I gradually learned the story of her experiences in 1994. She had been living and working in a community an hour's drive (or several hours on foot) from where she had grown up. During the genocide, her life was threatened and she was raped, but she ultimately survived because of a few kind neighbors who took her in and hid her from the militia groups. After the RPF arrived in July 1994 and most of the people where she was staying fled – both those who had tormented her and those who had protected her – she returned to her home community, where she found that her parents and grandparents, all of her brothers and sisters, all of her aunts and uncles – in fact, everyone in her entire extended family except two second cousins – had been killed. She took her two surviving cousins with her and made her way to Kigali, where she worked to start a new life.

In early 1996, Espérance came to me seeking help. The government was requiring all Rwandans to return to their home communities to register and receive a new official identity card. She was afraid to go back to her home. "All the Tutsi have been killed. There's no one left," she told me. So I agreed to accompany her as she returned to her community to register.

On a morning in March, Espérance and I loaded up in my Toyota Hilux pickup truck and drove to the commune where she was born and grew up. We drove an hour off the main paved road on a small dirt road and stopped at the ruins of a home. We walked around the mud walls, melting into the growing brush, and she said, "This was my aunt's home." We got back into the truck and drove on. When the road became too rough, we parked the truck and began to walk a lightly worn path up a mountainside. Near the summit, we came to the ruins of another home. "This was my house," she told me. Nearby were the ruins of her grandparents' home and the ruins of an uncle's home. We walked around a bit, silently looking at what was left of her childhood.

While we were looking around, an elderly woman came running up from a house a short distance down the path. Her home had a thatched roof, something that only the poorest people in this region would have. She ran up to Espérance, clapping her hands in pleasure and bowing her head in respect.

"Oh, Espérance! Espérance! I have been waiting for you!" She said. "I have some things from your home. I have some roof tiles and some cooking pots! I have been saving them for you. Let me get them."

Espérance smiled wryly and shook her head. "You keep them. I don't need them. I've started a new life in Kigali."

She looked around at the barren land surrounding the ruined homes, the fields lying fallow and overgrown.

"And these fields," she said to the woman. "Go ahead and cultivate them. I will never come back here to farm them."

The woman bowed her head in thanks and walked back to her home. As the woman walked away, Espérance said to me, "Her family killed my family."

She looked around one last time, shook her head and said, "This is no longer my home. I won't come back here."

We walked back down the hill and headed to the communal office for her to register.

In the aftermath of a cataclysm as horrific as the 1994 Rwandan genocide, the widespread desire for a story of transformation and redemption is understandable. The media, usually focused on Africa's wars, famine, poverty, and corruption, have embraced post-genocide Rwanda as a different sort of tale, newsworthy because it is unusual in its apparent hopefulness. The narrative that has gained wide circulation is that, despite all odds, Rwanda is being successfully rebuilt. The victim group in the genocide has chosen to reject revenge and embrace forgiveness and reconciliation and, as a result, Rwanda has become peaceful and prosperous. A tale of forgiveness like Espérance's willingness to offer her land to the family that murdered her own kin fills us with hope and faith in humanity and becomes a symbol of a society transformed. This hopeful narrative has inspired many charitable groups, development organizations, and corporations to invest heavily in Rwanda.[1]

---

[1] C.f., Marc Gunther, "Why CEOs Love Rwanda: As a Small African Nation Recovers from Genocide, Google, Starbucks, and Costco Lend a Hand," CNNMoney.com, April 3, 2007.

But the situation in Rwanda is complex and cannot be reduced to a simple story of a country rising like a phoenix fully healed from the ashes of the 1994 genocide and war. Even in a country with a flawless regime whose policies were beyond reproach, reconstructing a society as deeply broken as Rwanda in 1994 would have been a challenge. Yet as I have attempted to demonstrate in this book, the post-genocide regime in fact has a mixed record at best – strong on maintaining order, promoting a clear economic and political vision, and running government efficiently and effectively, yet widely criticized for extensive use of repression, a very poor record on civil and political rights, and lack of meaningful citizen representation.

The central argument of this book has been that the various mechanisms and institutions to advance rule of law, justice, reconciliation, healing, peace, and national unity, often considered together under the heading of "transitional justice," function within a political context that influences how the population receives and reacts to them. The Rwandan people do not experience the regime's programs to promote memory and accountability for the 1994 genocide as a distinct "transitional justice" policy category but instead as part of a broader program of far-reaching social, economic, and political transformation. As discussed in Chapter 5, the RPF used extensive violence in its first years of rule to establish its authority and subdue or eliminate those it viewed as threats. Since 2000, though the RPF regime has used less open violence, it has continued to rule in a highly authoritarian fashion. Rwanda's leadership has not simply tolerated very little dissent but gone further to insist that all Rwandans demonstrate open support for the regime, its initiatives, and its narrative. Those who fail to show active support or who articulate alternate ideas about the past or the future have been regularly punished.

In this chapter I assess the overall impact of the extensive transitional justice initiatives that have been implemented in Rwanda, given the country's highly controlled, highly authoritarian context. I separately consider three possible areas where transitional justice may have made contributions in Rwanda – to democratic consolidation, peace and reconciliation, and justice – and find that despite some positive contributions to social reconstruction, overall transitional justice has contributed to neither transition nor justice in Rwanda.

"Transitional Justice" in an Authoritarian Context

Transitional justice, both as an area of public policy and a field of academic study, is deeply rooted in the experience of societies that have used truth commissions, trials, memorialization, and other tools to help

in the transition from brutal authoritarian rule to popular democracy.[2]
In reviewing the origins of the term "transitional justice," Paige Arthur
argues that, "'Transition' – and more specifically, 'transition to democracy' – was the dominant normative lens through which political change
was viewed."[3] The influential collection of writings and documents edited
by Neil Kritz of the US Institute for Peace in 1995 was titled, *Transitional
Justice: How Emerging Democracies Reckon with Former Regimes*. Although
the cases explored in Kritz's edited volumes include a few post-conflict
contexts, such as Denmark, France, and Italy after the Second World
War, the overwhelming focus is on post-authoritarian transitions.[4] The
idea that transitional justice is something implemented as democracies
are "emerging" has remained influential, even as the principles of transitional justice have been applied increasingly in post-conflict settings
like Rwanda, Sierra Leone, Timor Leste, Cambodia, and Kosovo, where
transition to democracy has not necessarily been expected.

The experiences of Argentina, Chile, and South Africa (and to a lesser
extent Brazil and Uruguay) have been particularly influential in shaping
ideas about transitional justice, with many of the most important figures
in the field, both activists and academics, emerging from these countries.[5]
The general success of transitional justice in these countries in helping
to consolidate democracy by exposing the truth about abuses committed
by previous regimes, encouraging public conversation about the past,
re-integrating victim populations into the political community, and promoting rule of law through accountability has profoundly shaped perceptions of transitional justice and its potential to have a similar impact
in other settings. As a result, much of the literature on transitional justice

---

[2] Lawrence Weschler, *A Miracle, A Universe: Settling Accounts with Torturers*,
Chicago: University of Chicago Press, 1998, saw the "attempt to move from dictatorial
to democratic systems of governance" (p. 242), as *the* central concern for transitional
justice mechanisms.

[3] Paige Arthur, "How 'Transitions' Reshaped Human Rights: A Conceptual History of
Transitional Justice," *Human Rights Quarterly*, 31, 2009, 321–367.

[4] Neil J. Kritz, *Transitional Justice: How Emerging Democracies Reckon with Former Regimes*,
Four Volumes, Washington: USIP, 1995.

[5] Activists from these countries who have played leading roles in transitional justice efforts
include Luis Moreno Ocampo, an Argentine lawyer who became the first chief prosecutor of the International Criminal Court; Juan Mendez, an Argentine lawyer and
human rights activist who served as president of the International Center for Transitional
Justice (ICTJ) and UN Special Adviser on the Prevention of Genocide; José Zalaquett,
a Chilean lawyer and influential academic; Alex Borain, the vice-president of South
Africa's Truth and Reconciliation Commission who became founding president of the
ICTJ. Many of the leading scholarly advocates of transitional justice also worked in these
countries, including Marc Osiel, Naomi Roht-Arriaza, Elizabeth Jelin, Katherine Sikkink,
Leigh Payne, David A. Crocker, Tricia Olsen, and Priscilla Hayner. See Arthur, "How
'Transitions' Re-Shaped Human Rights."

suffers from a teleological tendency to sees trials, truth commissions, and the like, as contributing to an inexorable improvement of societies as they transition from authoritarianism to democracy, from division to unity, and from war to peace. This perspective has influenced the wide embrace for transitional justice among policymakers in both the international community and countries overcoming authoritarianism and war.

In the Rwandan case, transitional justice mechanisms were implemented at the very time the country was undertaking a purported transition to democracy, though the two processes were not necessarily linked in government assertions. In his extensive list of the Rwandan government's goals for gacaca, Clark significantly does not include democratic consolidation.[6] Nevertheless, since democratization *is* one of the central goals for transitional justice in many societies and in much of the literature, some advocates of transitional justice in Rwanda listed democratization among the hoped for outcomes. Aneta Wierzynska, for example, argued that by encouraging participation and contestation, gacaca would help build Rwandan civic culture and thereby promote democratic consolidation.[7]

The Rwandan case urges considerable caution, however, in assuming the direction in which transitional justice will move a country. Whether or not the ICTR, national genocide trials, gacaca, historical revision, memorialization, commemoration, and other policies contributed to reconciliation, peace, and justice in Rwanda, something I consider below, they plainly failed to support a transition to democracy but instead helped the RPF consolidate authoritarian rule. As my research unambiguously demonstrates, although the RPF regime mouthed the language of democracy and free public discourse, in practice it implemented the tools of transitional justice in an authoritarian fashion and used them to promote its interests. To argue, like Wierzynska, that, "The fulfillment of Gacaca's potential for engendering civic culture will depend *solely* on whether the Rwandese people take advantage of the floor given to them to express their concerns and find solutions to them,"[8] represents the sort of naïve neglect of the political context that undermines much of the literature on transitional justice in Rwanda and beyond. Rwanda is an authoritarian state where public free exchange of ideas is not allowed.

[6] According to Clark, *Gacaca Courts, Post-Genocide Justice and Reconciliation in Rwanda*, p. 32, the government of Rwanda's goals for gacaca, including the "profound objectives" of truth, peace, justice, healing, forgiveness, and reconciliation and the "practical objectives" of "processing the massive backlog of genocide cases; ... improving living conditions in the jails; and ... facilitating economic development."

[7] Aneta Wierzynska, "Consolidating Democracy through Transitional Justice: Rwanda's Gacaca Courts," *NYU Law Review*, November 2004, 1934–1969.

[8] Ibid., pp. 1968–1969. My emphasis.

This authoritarian context constrains the potential of transitional justice mechanisms to contribute to positive social change.

My research is replete with examples of the ways in which transitional justice actually supported a consolidation of authoritarian governance. In the 2004–2006 project to revise the Rwandan high school history curriculum, the officials from the Ministry of Education and professors from Rwandan universities with whom we worked told me and my colleagues repeatedly that they embraced principles of democratic education that encouraged students to think independently and debate historical issues rather than merely teaching facts. In practice, however, the teaching materials developed by our partners promoted a single narrative – the official version of the Rwandan past endorsed by the regime – and teachers trained in our program feared allowing real democratic discourse in their classes.[9] One Rwandan affiliated with this project found in interviews that he conducted in Byumba that many people talked about their experience of violence perpetrated by the RPF in 1994, but when he discussed this with a senior colleague, he was told, "That's not what we're looking for." As a result, he felt that he could not include these data in his analysis.[10]

Memorials have similarly constrained rather than encouraging democratic discourse. In contrast to countries where memorials became sites of key contestation over public memory of past atrocities, the authoritarian context in Rwanda constrained the process of memorialization, preventing meaningful public participation in their conceptualization and creation. The degree to which genocide survivors have been allowed to interpret their own experience has been highly restricted, even as their suffering has been exploited to justify the regime's policies. Memorials and official commemorations promote the official single narrative, focusing exclusively on the genocide and pointedly excluding mention of other atrocities. All Rwandans are required to participate in annual community mourning events, forcing them not only to acknowledge the importance of the genocide with their physical presence but also to enact the organized amnesia of atrocities perpetrated against many of them. The amplified silence around RPF crimes is pointed. While, as I discussed in Chapter 7, some people gave their own meanings to these commemorations, many viewed them as one more example of the heavy hand of the state forcing their participation in an attempt to shape them and exercise control. If individuals were publicly to mourn their family members killed by the RPF, they would face harsh punishment.

---

[9] Freedman et al., "Teaching History after Identity-Based Conflicts"; and Freedman et al., "Confronting the Past in Rwandan Schools."

[10] Fieldnotes, September 7, 2002.

Trials have been especially important tools for the RPF to consolidate its rule. Not only did they reinforce the RPF's narrative that highlights the centrality of the genocide and encourages organized amnesia about RPF crimes, but they also serve as valuable instruments of social control. As I described in Chapter 5, immediately after taking power, the RPF used extensive violence to enforce its rule and widely employed detention to command and intimidate the population with little regard for rule of law. With the change to open RPF control in 2000, the regime shifted to more subtle means of controlling the population, depending much more significantly on legal mechanisms to assert state authority and dominate subjects.

While Rwanda has never formally adopted a lustration law, in practice, any politician facing substantial charges of involvement in the genocide has been forced from office. No one tainted by genocide charges could make a realistic run for office today, even if the charges were never proven in court. Accusations of genocide crimes have been grounds for dismissal from employment, particularly in state institutions. Those who have faced serious accusations of genocide crimes remain permanently suspect and encounter heightened public scrutiny that discourages them from getting involved in political parties, taking an active role in civic organizations, speaking critically about the government and its policies, or engaging in other activities that the regime and its supporters might regard as potentially disruptive.[11] With over one million individuals charged in the gacaca process, gacaca has effectively excluded from full participation in public life a massive portion of the population.

Genocide trials constrained democratic participation even for those who did not face genocide charges. Because of public ostracism, potential loss of employment, imprisonment, and other dire consequences associated with accusations of participating in the genocide, the *threat* of facing accusations has had a serious chilling effect on the broader Hutu population. Laws against divisionism and genocide ideology have reinforced this chilling effect, seriously constraining public engagement by Hutu. The dark side of the otherwise laudable extensive engagement of women in Rwandan politics[12] is the reality that men are much more vulnerable to genocide charges, forcing many out of active political participation.

Wierznyska's assertion that the gacaca trials themselves created a space for democratic engagement because of the extensive public participation they entailed failed to consider the authoritarian political context. While

---

[11] This is a central point in Chakravarty, *Investing in Authoritarian Rule*, that gacaca in particular served to control the population by both coercing and coopting the Hutu majority.

[12] Longman, "Rwanda: Achieving Equality or Serving an Authoritarian State?"

in my observations of gacaca, I did encounter instances of dramatic public confrontations (as in the hearing I discussed in the previous chapter), in general participation in gacaca was highly constrained and became increasingly so as gacaca advanced. Survivors and others were reluctant to testify against powerful individuals for fear of facing retribution from their friends and family, while people were also hesitant about speaking in defense of the accused for fear of being seen as genocide sympathizers or, worse, facing charges themselves. Far from allowing a free and open discussion of Rwanda's past, gacaca was highly regulated. Government officials intervened regularly to keep gacaca within prescribed parameters, excluding discussion of RPF crimes, following the calendar for listing crimes, naming the accused, and holding trials, and ensuring that gacaca jurisdictions did not have too high a rate of acquittal. Rwandans acted out their required roles in the gacaca process, but few regarded gacaca as an opportunity for communities to speak openly and develop a common understanding of what went wrong in 1994.

In short, the Rwandan case demonstrates that the tools of transitional justice do not inherently promote democratization. Because the ideas of transitional justice are rooted so deeply in the Latin American and South African experiences, many advocates fail to realize that in undemocratic contexts like Rwanda, the tools of transitional justice can be used to consolidate the power of authoritarian regimes. A few authors have noted that even in more democratic contexts, transitional justice has been politicized. For example, Richard Wilson argues that in South Africa, the Truth and Reconciliation Commission served above all to help build the nation and the state and to legitimize the ruling African National Congress (ANC) rather than serving the lofty goals of fighting impunity, promoting human rights, and bringing reconciliation that its advocates claimed.[13] In my own research in South Africa, I have noted that museums and other memorials consistently promote a narrative highlighting the heroism of the ANC while obscuring the role of other organizations and encouraging amnesia about the ANC's own failings.[14] If transitional justice in comparatively democratic South Africa was politicized, then my claim that the authoritarian state in Rwanda has effectively employed the tools of transitional justice to reinforce its power should not be shocking.

---

[13] Based on the South African case, Wilson, *The Politics of Truth and Reconciliation in South Africa,* contends that, "Truth commissions are one of the main ways in which a bureaucratic elite seeks to manufacture legitimacy for state institutions, and especially the legal system" (p. 19).

[14] I have conducted research in South Africa in 2007, 2008, and 2010 in addition to numerous professional visits.

Peace, Reconciliation, and the Enduring Challenge of Identity

In contrast to democracy promotion, the government of Rwanda has made extensive assertions about the contributions they hoped various transitional justice institutions would make to peace and reconciliation. In changing the historical narrative, setting up memorials, holding commemorations, and organizing both national and gacaca trials, the Rwandan regime hoped to uncover the truth about what happened in 1994, establish a common account of the past, acknowledge the suffering of Tutsi victims, encourage forgiveness, promote the re-establishment of relations between perpetrators and victims, fight impunity, deter future ethnic violence, and promote peace and stability, among other goals. An overarching goal was to create a new collective memory about the Rwandan past that would ultimately push Rwanda's people to revise their understanding of their own identities, seeing themselves as a unified people rather than members of distinct and incompatible ethnic groups. With a shared collective memory and unified national identity, RPF leaders hoped that their own status as members of a cultural minority would no longer matter and their hold on power would become more secure.

As my discussion in the previous three chapters indicates, the various transitional justice mechanisms enjoyed some success on these goals. They contributed to a better understanding of what happened in many communities in 1994. In gacaca hearings, communities identified the losses in human life and property that they experienced in the genocide. Gacaca provided information about the fate of victims that was particularly important to survivors. The regime also successfully promoted a specific narrative of the more distant Rwandan past. Although the regime was not able to impose a singular narrative of the genocide, as average Rwandans still saw the genocide as largely elite driven, rather than popular, and imposed on their communities from the outside, the relentless emphasis on the genocide crowded out consideration of other atrocities, particularly violence committed by the RPF, and successfully established the genocide as the central focus of Rwandan history. Even critics of the regime have come to use the official terminology that defines Rwanda in the past twenty years as "post-genocide" rather than "post-war" or "post-conflict." The idea of accountability for RPF crimes, still seen as a possibility when the research for this book began in 2001, has disappeared from popular consideration.

On the specific question of creating a unified national identity, however, my research indicates that transitional justice has largely failed – or even been counterproductive. The regime closely tied the idea of reconciliation in Rwanda to the goal of national unity, and diminishing the importance of ethnicity is a central aspiration of the regime's national unity program. When the research for this book began, talking about ethnicity was already taboo, but ethnic identification soon became formally illegal through laws divisionism and ethnic ideology. Yet in reality, ethnic identities remain quite strong in Rwanda. As the biographies I recounted at the beginning of Chapter 6 indicate, ethnicity alone does not explain people's political opinions, as people of the same ethnicity may live through very different experiences. Nevertheless, ethnicity does influence how people experience social, economic, and political life in Rwanda, and transitional justice highlighted rather than diminishing the importance of ethnic identities.

My interviews indicated that Rwandans were aware of the government's goal of suppressing ethnic identity, and a minority of people supported the goal. For example, a Hutu widow from Butare who lost her Tutsi children in the genocide said, "I myself am Rwandan, like the state has asked us to say and as my identity card says! I am nothing other than Rwandan!"[15] Yet many more regarded the suppression of ethnic identity as unnecessary or counterproductive:

I don't see why one should not talk about what exists. You exist. I exist. We say in Kinyarwanda, "Someone who does not want people to talk about him should have stayed in his mother's womb." So why not talk? That's reconciliation. It is between you and me. It is between Tutsi and Hutu, between Hutu and Hutu, between Tutsi and Tutsi, between all the different ethnic groups. So how can you arrive [at reconciliation] without talking about what is good or bad, what is favorable or not for this reconciliation?[16]

Another man said that reconciliation would come, "Only when they [Rwandans] have learned to know and mutually respect each other in their differences. The differences have to exist. Even children coming from the same father and the same mother don't necessarily resemble each other. So why are Rwandans afraid and ashamed of their differences?"[17]

Regardless of their opinions about the desirability of suppressing ethnic identification, people in my research overwhelmingly felt that ethnic divisions remained important. From the earliest interviews conducted for this research, people claimed that open talk about ethnicity was no longer possible even though most felt that ethnicity remained significant. A man recently released from prison was surprised to find that people rarely talked about ethnicity. "In prison, we talked about it more than

---

[15] Interview in Cyarwa-Cyimana, Butare, September 8, 2001.
[16] Interview in Kibirizi, Kibuye, September 14, 2001.
[17] Interview in Cyarwa-Sumo, Butare, September 9, 2001.

outside."[18] Another told us, "We don't speak about ethnicity any more. No one dares to say you are Hutu or Tutsi … At least not in public." A woman in Mabanza reported, "We don't speak freely about ethnicity, because they have told us to think of ourselves only as Rwandan. The church teaches us the same thing, that we are all Rwandans."[19]

Even as speaking about ethnicity has become off-limits, in practice ethnic divisions have become more pronounced with less, rather than more, interaction across ethnic lines. A Hutu man told us, "People don't share a glass at the cabaret any more."[20] A young orphaned survivor in Mabanza reported that he used to have Hutu friends, "But today this friendship has disappeared. We were children at the time, but now that we have grown up and become adults, we play hiding games like all the others."[21] A Tutsi survivor complained that, "The father of my son is a Hutu soldier … The family of this soldier refused to allow him to take charge of me or even to recognize his child. I have to get by on my own."[22] A Hutu man told a parallel story about his sister that showed continuing ethnic consciousness on the other side. "A case that I can mention here is that of my older sister. She had a child with a Tutsi soldier after the war. The child lives here, because his father did not want to recognize him because of his ethnicity."[23] A survivor told us that she did not support programs to promote reconciliation. "It's better to stay like we are now. Because people can lie and say that they are reconciled, when in fact they are planning to kill others. In 1994, we thought that everything was going well."[24]

Over the course of the main field research for this project from 2001 to 2005, even as gacaca and other transitional justice programs were being implemented, no evidence emerged of a diminution of ethnic identification. In the 2015 follow up research conducted after completion of gacaca and other genocide trials, the persistence of ethnic divisions became starkly clear. Despite the dangers of talking about ethnicity, many people in the 2015 interviews spoke frankly about ethnic animosities or complained about ethnic discrimination. One elderly survivor told us, "People from the same ethnic group live together well. But conflicts do exist, and they are based on ethnicity."[25] Another survivor reported that, "There are not really relations [between Hutu and

---

[18] Interview in Nyarugenge, Mabanza, Kibuye, December 6, 2001.
[19] Interview in Rubengera, August 23, 2001.
[20] Interview in Butare, November 8, 2001.
[21] Interview in Gacaca, Mabanza, Kibuye, December 7, 2001.
[22] Interview in Mabanza, Kibuye,
[23] Interview in Matyazo, Butare, December 2, 2001.
[24] Interview in Kibirizi, Mabanza, Kibuye, September 17, 2001.
[25] Interview in Gacaca, Mabanza, Kibuye, April 29, 2015.

Tutsi] in the community. We pretend to live together. We live together, because the authorities teach us to live together. But there are hidden suspicions … This one person had a problem with another, and he said to the other, 'Even if you're a survivor, you can't frighten me.' "[26] Another man reported, "Some people say that if they criticize openly what's not going well, they risk imprisonment. And the Hutu don't feel free. To live, they must play along with what's required … But on the hills, you find that Hutu and Tutsi hate each other openly."[27]

Rather than diminishing ethnic divisions, Rwanda's transitional justice mechanisms exacerbated them in troubling ways. Even as the government implemented policies seeking to suppress ethnic identity, genocide trials reinforced the centrality of ethnicity. The ethnicity of the perpetrators and the victims determined whether cases were admissible in trials in both national courts and gacaca courts. Human rights activist Aloys Habimana explained the problem of denying the reality of ethnicity while organizing trials inherently defined by ethnicity:

You cannot say that one million people died and go before the Tribunal and say that they were Tutsi, and then say that ethnicity does not exist. Ethnicity is a social creation. People changed their ethnic identities to get advantages. So yes ethnicity is a social creation, but that doesn't mean that it does not exist. When being Hutu or Tutsi does not give any advantages, then they will lose their meaning.[28]

Because it required weekly participation in a public hearing where ethnicity was a defining element, gacaca in particular raised the importance of ethnicity in individual's lives. Many Hutu felt that memorials, commemorations, gacaca and other genocide trials were all used to define Hutu as perpetrators and Tutsi as victims. A man in Butare told us, "I can talk about my ethnicity only when I'm at ease with the people around me. In most cases, being Hutu means being responsible for the genocide, being an assassin."[29]

While Gacaca provided valuable information about what happened to victims during the genocide, for many survivors, this information did not bring closure and make healing possible, as some advocates of transitional justice suggest truth telling can. Instead, the details of what happened often increased the distance between survivors and their Hutu neighbors, as my 2015 interviews strongly indicated. A survivor in Mabanza told us, "Why should I reconcile with them, when they killed

[26] Interview in Mabanza, Kibuye, May 6, 2015.
[27] Interview in Mabanza, Kibuye, May 10, 2015.
[28] Interview with Aloys Habimana, Kigali, June 3, 2002.
[29] Interview in Matyazo, Butare, December 13, 2001.

members of my family? What's more, I have no interest in hearing talk about reconciliation. How can I reconcile with the Hutu when they killed my people?"[30] Another widowed survivor told us, "We pretend to be able to live together. I don't have a choice. Except that it sometimes happens when they provoke us. That is to say, the Hutu remind us of the hard moments that we knew in bringing the ideology of the genocide ... We pretend to be reconciled. But is it possible for you to reconcile with someone who has filled your life with mourning?"[31] A third survivor made similar comments, "Relations [between the ethnic groups] have completely disappeared, because during the genocide, they tried to kill us. I can't talk with people who don't share my ethnicity, because I just can't trust them."[32]

Many people, including some who supported the goal of suppressing ethnic identity, felt that the officials implementing programs promoting national unity were hypocritical, because they did not personally believe in the ideas they were promoting. A student told me that he knew of several cases of the children of government ministers who attended his school who got in trouble for dating someone from another ethnic group. "The very ministers who are publicly denouncing ethnic difference would not accept someone from the other group in their home and punish their children for ignoring ethnic identity."[33] Another respondent told us:

In different public meetings, in seminars, on the radio ... the political will is manifest, but there is also a problem. What is said is often the opposite of what is in the heart. You know of the ex-Prime Minister Rwigema and his lectures on unity and reconciliation. Now when he is in exile in Chicago, he has changed his language. You could say that they are all opportunists without any conviction, the politicians I mean. Others will say [they support reconciliation], and the next day you hear that they have imprisoned someone unjustly or that they are occupying the homes of others.[34]

A survivor in Kibuye told us, "These district mayors are designated according to their ethnicity. For example, in the district of Bisesero, where survivors are dominant, you could not have a campaign by a Hutu for this post, because the survivors need to feel calmed by a Tutsi."[35] A man in Butare

---

[30] Interview in Gacaca, Mabanza, Kibuye, April 29, 2015.

[31] Interview in Gacaca, Mabanza, Kibuye, May 13, 2015.

[32] Interview in Rubengera, Mabanza, Kibuye, May 6, 2015. Karen Broneus, "Truth-Telling as Talking Cure: Insecurity and Retraumatization in Rwanda's Gacaca Courts," *Security Dialogue*, 39, no. 1, 2008, 55–76, found that speaking in gacaca hearings did more to retraumatize victims than to help them heal.

[33] Personal communication, Kigali, January 2005.

[34] Interview in Butare, September 9, 2001. After Rwigema fled Rwanda in 2000, he became a regime critic.

[35] Interview in Mabanza, Kibuye, May 7, 2015.

said, "What could reconcile Rwanda is if the authorities could get along. Then the problems would be gone."[36] Whether or not government officials are in fact being hypocritical in suppressing ethnic identity for others while continuing to act in favor of their own ethnic group, the popular perception of official hypocrisy is widespread and undermines the goal of pushing Rwandans to embrace a stronger unified national identity.

Identity and Economic Opportunity

I was sitting in a bar in Kigali with a friend, talking about identity politics in Rwanda.

"People say that identity no longer matters, that we are all just Rwandan," he said. "But at the university, people still put themselves in groups. You still see the different tendencies" – a delicate phrasing that avoided talking explicitly about ethnicity. "At lunch, as I walk around, I see there is a group of those from Burundi, and there is another group of those from Congo, and another group of those from Uganda. And there are the *Abarokore* [the Born Again Christians] who all sit together. And then there is the group of those who were in Rwanda before."

"Just one group?" I asked.

"Oh no, the survivors are in their group, and the Hutu are in theirs."

The bar we were in was a nice place. Formerly only a bakery and butchers, the owner had added a terrace a couple of years previously, where people could order drinks and eat the snacks purchased inside. A few steps from the main roundabout in downtown Kigali, the bar was well situated and had become quite popular.

"What about this place?" I asked. "Is this crowd mixed?"

"Oh, no! There is only one tendency here. There is only one group that can afford to come to places like this. The other group cannot afford this."

"So where does the other group go? Where do the Hutu go?"

"Maybe to the small cabarets [modest local bars] where they serve banana beer. But, Kigali is more and more a Tutsi city."

"Not entirely," I said. "Isn't it still mostly Hutu who do the gardening and the cooking? It's mostly Hutu who build the roads and do the other hard jobs."

"Perhaps," he said, "But the city is mostly Tutsi now."[37]

A conclusion that I had not anticipated when I began this project, in part because the literature on memory and transitional justice largely ignores the topic, was the importance of economics in shaping how

---

[36] Interview in Matyazo, Butare, November 8, 2001.
[37] Fieldnotes in Kigali, June 2006.

people regarded trials and other transitional justice mechanisms. As the contrasting individual portraits in Chapter 6 suggest, even people from the same ethnic group sometimes had very different perceptions of post-genocide Rwanda based on their lived experience. While ethnic and other identities were an important element in shaping individual life experiences and therefore were significant to the research, these identities alone did not determine people's perceptions. The minority of people who were doing well in the current context, people who had managed to secure salaried appointments, for example, were often less pessimistic, while people who struggled with poverty were much more likely to be critical.

Again and again in my research, however, people expressed concern that Rwanda's social, political, and economic life was being increasingly dominated by a single social group: former Tutsi refugees who had returned to Rwanda after 1994. Many people – Hutu and Tutsi alike – expressed the opinion that even as the country's leaders were forbidding ethnic identification, they were actively discriminating in favor of their own group. The truth of this perception is difficult to establish, in no small part because of the policies preventing ethnic identification. The perception, however, is widespread, and my own qualitative observation certainly backs up the idea that Tutsi returnees have come increasingly to monopolize salaried employment in both the public and private sectors. When I returned to Rwanda in 1995, many Hutu held important positions in government, the civil service, business, NGOs, schools, and elsewhere. Many of these were moderates who had opposed the genocide and in some cases were targeted by the perpetrators of the genocide. Yet over the past twenty years, the vast majority of these individuals were forced out of their positions. Some were found guilty of genocide crimes and imprisoned. Others were accused of genocide ideology and fled the country to escape arrest. Although some of them may have been genuinely guilty, I know of enough specific cases where charges appear specious to raise serious concerns.

The example of one couple I knew and kept in touch with over the years is emblematic. The husband was the local director of an international NGO immediately after the genocide. In the late 1990s, he was accused, not of genocide crimes but of failing to protect people during the genocide. He was acquitted of the charges, but government officials nevertheless pressured the NGO to fire him, and he was subsequently unable to find salaried employment. The couple moved to a neighboring province, where his wife, who was a Tutsi survivor, had found work as a secretary in a regional government office. A few years later, though, she was told that her position was being eliminated, and she was let go.

She subsequently discovered that shortly after her termination, her position was reinstated and filled with a Tutsi returnee with connections to the regional leadership. Since beginning the research for this book in 2001, I have heard countless similar stories of both Hutu and Tutsi genocide survivors being pushed out of their positions in favor of returnees. Outsiders traveling to Rwanda often ask my advice on how to understand what is going on in the country. I tell them to keep an eye out for evidence of this economic differentiation that has taken place. Since they cannot reasonably ask people in Rwanda today about their ethnic identity, I suggest instead that they ask where people they meet were in 1994. Nearly all of these travellers confirm that in office after office, almost all the people they encounter were outside Rwanda in 1994.

Many Hutu we interviewed expressed the belief that they were actively discriminated against. For example, one young Hutu in Mabanza complained in 2015 that:

When there is a job available, you find that it is only those of the Tutsi ethnicity who have the information on the opening, while the Hutu are not informed. For example, in our community, there could be work to do, and I wouldn't be afraid to tell you that 80% of the work would go to Tutsi, because they are the first to receive the information about the opening."[38]

As I described in the previous chapter, many people felt that gacaca and other genocide trials were corrupt and served the interests of the elite. For many Hutu, the elite is defined in ethnic terms, so they see the various trials as having served the interests of the Tutsi.

Yet Tutsi survivors also expressed considerable economic frustration that affected their perceptions of post-genocide Rwanda and shaped the impact of transitional justice. The testimony of survivors indicated a sharp divide between them and the Tutsi returnees. Some complained of discrimination, like a woman who was dismissed from an administrative post and said of politicians that, "Their speeches often differ from their behavior and their actions. They speak only so that they can maintain their posts. They seek above all to walk around ethnic identity rather than promoting mutual respect for the different ethnic groups."[39] Among survivors, the loss of their economic standing was among the most significant lasting effects of the genocide, which targeted not just Tutsi lives, but their property as well, destroying their homes, killing their cattle, and stealing their possessions. While the government and international community built homes for some survivors, they were generally greatly inferior to the homes that had been destroyed. Poverty has been a major

---

[38] Interview in Mabanza, Kibuye, May 10, 2015.
[39] Interview in Mabanza, Kibuye, December 6, 2001.

challenge for survivors. Having lost much of their family, survivors lack the important social networks that Rwandans rely on not just for opportunity, but for survival. Before the genocide, the majority of Tutsi – like the majority of all Rwandans – were farmers, and the death of family members meant that after the genocide, there were fewer hands to work on the farms. Furthermore, many survivors were displaced; fearing staying in the communities where they had been targeted, they abandoned their lands and moved to the city or one of the *imidugudu* set up for survivors, where their access to farmland was much more limited. As I described in Chapter 8, the failure to provide substantial reparations was a major disappointment with transitional justice among survivors and has compromised the ability of transitional justice to contribute to reconciliation. A survivor in Mabanza claimed in 2001 that, "There will never be reconciliation in the midst of this poverty. The victims have to be returned to their rights and then Rwandans can be called to become again the Rwandans from before 1994."[40] The testimony from survivors in 2015 shows that their continuing poverty remained a strong source of resentment that colored their perceptions of Rwandan society.

In writing about the enduring challenge of identity in post-genocide Rwanda, I will almost certainly be condemned by some for perpetuating ethnic division. Given the role that scholars have in fact played in the past in helping to define and reinforce differences in Rwanda, raising this concern is fair and understandable. Yet my analysis is based firmly on the data that I have collected. In the research conducted for this project, identities mattered. The lived experiences of Hutu and Tutsi in Rwanda have differed, and these differences affected respondents' perceptions of the past and present and their opinions about the government and its transitional justice programs. In this book, I talk about ethnicity in Rwanda, because many Rwandans still believe that ethnicity is important for determining their life chances.

Yet ethnicity is clearly not the only politically relevant identity in Rwanda today. While the regional divide between northern and southern Rwanda that was highly salient when I was conducting research in Rwanda in 1992 and 1993 has largely disappeared, on many issues, the most important divide since 1994 has been between those who were in Rwanda at the time of the genocide and those who returned after. The community of returnees generally experiences Rwanda in very different ways from those who were in the country in 1994. While those who were in Rwanda before lived in communities that were ethnically mixed and often had members of the other ethnic group in their family, many returnees (particularly from

---

[40] Interview in Rubengera, Mabanza, Kibuye, December 7, 2001.

Uganda) grew up with only Tutsi and had no Hutu neighbors, friends, or relatives. Since the returnees were not in Rwanda during the genocide, their understandings of what actually happened are based on second-hand knowledge, not personal experience. Hence, they have much more fully embraced the official narrative that portrays the genocide as a massive popular uprising, a perspective that makes them much more suspect of the general Hutu population than even many survivors. The perspective of survivors is shaped by their personal experiences in 1994. One survivor told us, "We talk about [what happened in 1994], but each time that we try to talk about it, those who weren't in Rwanda in 1994 think that we're exaggerating."[41] Survivors often told us that they felt that the returnees regarded them with suspicion, assuming that they must have betrayed their Tutsi identity in some way to stay alive.

Even among the returnees, important social divisions affected how they experience post-genocide Rwanda. The RPF emerged out of Museveni's NRM, and the bulk of the early RPF soldiers were Rwandan refugees in Uganda. After the RPF took power, this Anglophone group was best placed to assume top positions, particularly in government and business. Subsequent government policies like the integration of Rwanda into the East African Community and membership in the Commonwealth have favored English speakers. Rwandan refugees in Burundi and Zaire were more integrated into their host countries and had greater opportunities for education, so Francophone returnees initially dominated the education sector. But the regime shifted education in Rwanda to English, forcing out many of the Francophone teachers and professors and creating openings for the Anglophone.[42] A joke going around Kigali in the early 2000s said that if you ask a Hutu about the Rwandan government, they say it is a Tutsi regime. If you ask a Tutsi, they say that it is a regime of returnee Tutsi. If you ask a returnee, they say it is a regime of returnees from Uganda. If you ask a returnee from Uganda, they say it is a regime of people from Kagame's refugee camp. The point is that identity still strongly influences the distribution of power in Rwanda but that perceptions of who actually controls Rwanda today vary depending on an individual's group identity.

A major challenge for reconciliation is the perception that the benefits of Rwanda's economic growth are not being evenly distributed. Even if the regime has, as it claims, reduced poverty and addressed issues like access to healthcare and reducing adult illiteracy,[43] a view exists that the

---

[41] Interview in Muranzi, Buyoga, Byumba, March 27, 2002.

[42] Chris McGreal, "Rwanda to Switch from French to English Schools," *The Guardian*, October 13, 2008.

[43] Filip Reyntjens, "Reduction of Poverty and Inequality, the Rwandan Way. And the Aid Community Loves It," Analysis and Policy Brief, No. 16, Institute of Development and

majority of the population remains poor, while the Anglophone returnees have gotten rich. Rwandans from other groups believe the Anglophone returnees not only dominate the government and other salaried positions in all sectors but that they have gotten rich by monopolizing business opportunities. Whether or not this is true, the perception is widespread.

As I suggested in Chapter 5, President Kagame regards Singapore as a model, believing that if he can bring prosperity to the population, they will not care about civil and political rights. But the perception that the benefits of Rwanda's economic growth are being unevenly distributed is problematic for this model. Ted Gurr's influential work on sources of social conflict argues that it is not simply poverty or even a gap between the rich and the poor that leads to social unrest but rather relative deprivation, frustration over the gap between expectations and actual opportunities.[44] Gahima argued that, "Rwanda has a history of social conflict going back centuries. The principal driver of the conflict is grievances over perceptions of social, economic and political marginalization and exclusion"[45] In Rwanda currently, much of the population is frustrated over their perceived marginalization and the sense that a limited social group is reaping all of the benefits of the country's prosperity. While I do not believe that conflict is imminent – the regime has far too strong a grip on power for any uprising to be possible – I would contend that the perception that the RPF regime's primary constituency (repatriated former Tutsi refugees) has consolidated control over social, political, and economic life and become rich while everyone else remains poor undermines popular support for the regime and its policies. The potential of transitional justice initiatives to contribute to reconciliation is undermined by the perception that trials, commemorations, and other programs are being implemented cynically to subdue the general population and justify the dominance of the country's new elite.

How Just Was Rwanda's Transitional Justice?

If transitional justice cannot generally be said to have made an overall positive contribution to either democratic transition in Rwanda or transition to peace, at least as defined in terms of reconciliation and positive peace,

Policy Analysis, University of Antwerp, December 2015, contends that the Rwandan government's recent claims to have reduced poverty are based on a manipulation of the statistics. "The genuine comparison from 2010/11 to 2013/14 therefore is not from 45% to 39% but from 33% to 39%. In other words, rather than a decrease of 6 points in poverty, what the EICV4 actually shows is an increase of 6 points" (p. 2).

[44] Gurr, *Why Men Rebel*.

[45] Gahima, *Transitional Justice in Rwanda*, p. 51.

the question remains whether it has at least brought justice. Following an event as appalling as the 1994 genocide, judicial accountability was an absolute moral imperative. The systematic slaughter of Rwanda's minority Tutsi population was so clearly an act of genocide and the nature of the violence inflicted against the Tutsi so brutal and cruel that almost no one inside or outside Rwanda has denied the need for at least the organizers to be tried and punished for their crimes. In fact, between the international community and the domestic Rwandan judicial system, an impressive number of the key perpetrators of the Rwandan genocide have been brought to justice. Although a few key individuals evaded justice, such as President Sindikubwabo, who died in exile in the DRC, the ICTR successfully tried a number of important government ministers, military commanders, and leaders in the media, religious organizations, and business, including Prime Minister Kambanda, who pled guilty to genocide and other charges in 1998. The Rwandan court system tried a number of government officials and military officers, though generally of lower rank than those tried in Arusha, including Léon Mugesera, a key anti-Tutsi ideologue who was extradited from Canada.

Despite the degree to which trials have established extensive accountability for crimes related to the 1994 genocide, two problems undermine the claim that transitional justice has provided justice in Rwanda. First, while trials convicted many of those responsible for the genocide, they also failed to distinguish effectively between the guilty and the innocent. As my research indicated, at least at the local level, wealthier and more powerful individuals were often able to avoid conviction or at least to receive more lenient sentences, even though they generally bore greater responsibility for what happened than the common farmers and youths who were simply following orders but have faced harsher sentences. Furthermore, subtle shifts in legal standards as the judicial processes developed had outsized impacts that undermined the quality of justice. In the test phase of gacaca that began in 2002, defendants who could demonstrate that they were coerced into participating in the genocide could be acquitted, and only those who actively participated in acts of violence were held accountable, while those who simply participated in patrols or in manning roadblocks (as was required by the government of the time) were not punished if they were not directly involved in killing. These legal standards had been applied in genocide trials in regular courts since 1996, yet as gacaca was launched nationally in 2005, without any formal shift in the law, gacaca courts stop making allowances for coerced participation. In addition, testimony that an individual was present when someone was killed also became sufficient grounds for conviction. As a result, as I described in Chapter 4, gacaca actually served to promote the idea of collective Hutu guilt – and collective Tutsi victimhood – rather than to differentiate between the innocent and the guilty. My research indicated that, while a large majority of Rwandans supported the idea of accountability for genocide crimes, the public perception was that both national trials and gacaca were politicized (a view held largely by Hutu) and corrupt (a view held largely by Tutsi survivors).

The second major problem confronting the claim that justice has been done in Rwanda is the complete lack of accountability for crimes committed by the RPF. A primary point of trials in the aftermath of mass atrocity is to fight impunity and hence build rule of law, yet to pair an overuse of trials for genocide crimes with an almost complete lack of accountability for crimes committed by those currently in power actually undermined rule of law and promoted impunity. Strong evidence indicates that the RPF tortured and killed civilians during the 1990–1993 civil war, then attacked civilians again as they advanced across Rwanda in 1994. After taking power in July, the RPF carried out a large number of summary executions and continued to use extensive violence to establish control in the first years of its rule.[46] Evidence also indicates that the RPF was involved in atrocities in the 1996 and 1998 invasions of neighboring Congo.[47] Yet only a handful of cases have been prosecuted against those accused of participation in these atrocities, and the punishments of the few found guilty have been exceedingly mild.

The failure of the ICTR to pursue even a single case against an RPF official seriously compromised the entire project of international justice in Rwanda, undermining both the domestic and international impact of the significant cases successfully prosecuted against genocide perpetrators. Despite a few attempts to pursue cases against RPF officials by France – perhaps the worst-placed country to seek accountability for the RPF, given France's failure to confront its own complicity in the genocide – Rwandans have been left with the impression that the international community is less interested in promoting justice in Rwandan than in advancing its political interests, which seem to align with the Kagame regime. The most compelling lessons that trials in the Rwandan case seem to have offered are to ensure that your side wins the war and therefore can dictate the terms of transitional justice and to make sure that you have a great propaganda machine that justifies your cause to the international community.[48]

---

[46] Des Forges, *Leave None to Tell the Story*.
[47] Longman and Des Forges, "Attacked by All Sides"; Longman, "Eastern Congo Ravaged."
[48] Pottier, *Re-imagining Rwanda*, compellingly analyzes the RPF's successful propaganda machine.

Lessons from the Rwandan Case

As the data presented in this book indicate, despite extensive transitional justice interventions, post-1994 Rwanda has experienced little transition and only limited justice. The case of Rwanda thus challenges the orthodoxy that transitional justice serves to bring positive transformation to post-conflict societies. After reviewing the degree to which the concept of transitional justice grows out of the Latin American post-*authoritarian* experience, Arthur suggests that for post-*conflict* societies, "Perhaps new norms and methods of realizing them need to be identified and refined. Should those working in transitional justice develop a new set of measures to address the specific justice concerns of transitions to peace?"[49] Based on the Rwandan case, one would have to answer with a resounding yes. But without a context more tolerant of civil and political rights, any mechanisms that might successfully promote truth, reconciliation, justice, and other goals of transitional justice are hard to imagine. In part by exploiting the international community's fixation on the transition paradigm, the post-genocide Rwandan government has used the tools of transitional justice to consolidate autocratic rule. While transitional justice advocates assume that trials, truth commissions, and other mechanisms help countries consolidate democracy and promote reconciliation, in fact, the experience of Rwanda indicates that a basic protection of human rights must already exist for transitional justice mechanisms to accomplish most of the diverse goals that their advocates profess.

For the post-1994 Rwandan government, memory and justice were tools for transforming society in ways that they believed would both promote justice, unity, and peace and also increase their hold on power. Believing that the genocide occurred because of a distorted conflation of ethnic identity with national identity and the popular embrace of an anti-Tutsi ideology based on a warped reading of history, the RPF regime sought to reconstruct popular understandings of Rwanda's past in order to reshape social identities. Yet, several contradictions undermined the regime's social engineering program. While the regime sought to replace ethnic identities with a unified national identity, the country's new elite remained highly suspicious of those Rwandans who were in the country in 1994 and believed that it needed to retain power for the foreseeable future in order to protect the Tutsi minority. The regime has, thus, sought to suppress ethnic identities for the general population while remaining highly conscious of ethnicity in practice. While professing support for democracy and human rights and going through a formal process of

---

[49] Arthur, "How 'Transitions' Reshaped Human Rights," p. 360.

democratization, the regime in fact consolidated its hold on power and strengthened authoritarian control of the population. Authoritarian rule was driven both by continuing suspicion of the population and factors that motivate dictatorship more widely – arrogance of power (i.e., the belief among leaders that no one else can rule the country as well as they) and a desire to hold onto the benefits that control provides. Although the RPF leadership has limited high-level corruption, their tight hold on power has brought significant economic benefit to their core constituency of returned Tutsi refugees from Uganda, which has come to dominate both salaried employment and the business sector. The resultant growing inequality in the country and resentment over the regime's authoritarian practices have actually heightened social divisions and undermined attempts to create a collective memory and unified national identity. Although the post-genocide government has been highly successful at establishing order and driving economic development, whether restricting personal liberties and ruling with a heavy hand were necessary to accomplish these goals remains in doubt. The role that transitional justice has played in helping the regime exercise its authority, however, is clear.

The judicial mechanisms used in response to the genocide highlight the contradictions inherent in the government's program. In the aftermath of the 1994 genocide, accountability was unequivocally necessary. Given the scope of the violence and its extreme cruelty, those responsible for the genocide indisputably needed to face justice. Some analysts suggested that an approach that focused on trials and punishment for those who bore the greatest responsibility – the political, military, business, and social leaders who were the chief ideologues and architects of the genocide – combined with restorative justice measures such as a truth commission for the majority of genocide perpetrators might have provided not only more peace and reconciliation but also more justice.[50] Yet critiques of hybrid approaches in other contexts and the limitations of truth commissions – I think in particular of the incisive works of Kimberly Theidon on Peru[51] and Rosalind Shaw on Sierra Leone[52] – caution

---

[50] Sarkin "The Necessity and Challenges of Establishing a Truth and Reconciliation Commission," made this claim back in 1999.

[51] Kimberly Theidon, *Intimate Enemies: Violence and Reconciliation in Peru*, Philadelphia: University of Pennsylvania Press, 2012; Kimberly Theidon, "Justice in Transition: The Micropolitics of Reconciliation in Post-War Peru," *The Journal of Conflict Resolution*, 50, no. 3, 2006, 433–457.

[52] Rosalind Shaw, "Memory Frictions: Localizing the Truth and Reconciliation Commission in Sierra Leone," *International Journal of Transitional Justice*, 1, no. 2, 2007, 183–207; Rosalind Shaw, "The TRC, the NGO, and the Child: Young People and Post-Conflict Futures in Sierra Leone," *Social Anthropology*, 22, no. 3, 2014, 306–325.

against an assertion that this alternative would have avoided the pitfalls of gacaca and other trials in Rwanda. The authoritarian context would certainly have limited the functioning and impact of a potential Rwandan TRC, and the troubling impact of truth telling in gacaca, particularly on survivors, suggest problems with the assumption that truth inevitably promotes reconciliation. Yet the approach ultimately taken in Rwanda clearly undermined rather than promoting not only democratic consolidation but also peace and reconciliation.

Perhaps if transitional justice mechanisms had included accountability for the RPF, they would have been more effective. The lack of any accountability for crimes committed by the RPF seriously undermined attempts to build rule of law and fight impunity. Though genocide is an extremely serious crime that demands accountability, there is no particular magic to the term "genocide" that erases all other crimes and makes them irrelevant. To ignore or dismiss the tens of thousands of people killed by the RPF between the invasion of Rwanda in October 1990 and the peace deal in Congo in July 2003 makes it very difficult for many Rwandans who lost family members in this violence to come to terms with the losses experienced in the genocide. The erasure of RPF crimes has empowered the RPF and its leaders to continue to act with impunity.

Yet to assert that if only the RPF had been held accountable, transitional justice would have worked may be another example of "magical legalism." The problem may be a larger problem with the conceptualization of transitional justice. While the atrocities perpetrated in Rwanda certainly demanded justice, framing trials in Rwanda as *transitional* justice ultimately undermined both justice and transition. Thomas Carothers has argued that the international focus on transition has actually undermined attempts to promote positive reform in many societies. "Many countries that policymakers and aid practitioners persist in calling 'transitional' are not in transition to democracy ... Sticking with the paradigm beyond its useful life is retarding evolution in the field of democratic assistance and is leading policymakers astray in other ways."[53] Framing various policies in Rwanda such as memorials, commemorations, and historical revision as transitional justice has similarly undermined the important "labors of memory"[54] demanded in the aftermath of the terrible events that unfolded in Rwanda. To view the constructed display of bodies at a site like Murambi as an unproblematic expression of Rwanda's collective memory is to ignore

---

[53] Thomas Caruthers, "The End of the Transition Paradigm," *Journal of Democracy*, 13, no. 1, 2002, 5–21, citation p. 6.

[54] This term from Jelin, *State Repression and the Labors of Memory*.

the political context that has highlighted certain stories of suffering while suppressing others. In practice, despite some noble motives, the regime's memory and justice programs have done more to consolidate authoritarian control than to promote national unity, reconciliation, and justice.

For some observers of Rwanda, the unique circumstances of the post-genocide situation justify the regime's authoritarian practices. Many believe that the social divisions that drove the genocide make democracy impossible, and they express confidence that Kagame is a benign leader who is truly committed to promoting the best interests of the Rwandan people. Gourevitch, for example, acknowledges President Kagame's authoritarian practices but praises the accomplishments of the regime, noting, "Rwanda is one of the safest and the most orderly countries in Africa. Since 1994, per-capita gross domestic product has nearly tripled, even as the population has increased by nearly twenty-five per cent, to more than ten million. There is national health insurance, and a steadily improving education system."[55]

While acknowledging that the social divisions and devastation left by the genocide represented a difficult legacy and that Kagame and other RPF leaders may have many noble motivations, I would nevertheless contend that consigning the Rwandan population indefinitely to authoritarian rule does not serve the long-term interests of the country and its people. The failures of transitional justice in Rwanda reveal that an authoritarian context undermines even well intentioned programs. Without the constraints of popular oversight and control, public programs are easily redirected to serve the interests of those in power rather than the public interest. The increasing consolidation of power and wealth in the hands of a limited social group has intensified social divisions in Rwanda and fed popular resentment that may one day manifest itself in destructive actions. The Rwandan population is not likely to embrace a narrative of national unity as long as ethnicity and other social identities remain relevant to people's lived experience. To most Rwandans, transitional justice has not been about bringing Rwanda peace, reconciliation, unity, or justice but rather about allowing those in power to consolidate their rule. My research reveals that many Rwandans regard the current regime with growing cynicism, believing that they are constantly being controlled and mobilized and sacrificing their civil and politic rights merely to increase the wealth of those in power. While the regime's oppressive policies are successfully maintaining order at present, the strategy of domination and indoctrination is not likely to maintain stability in the long term.

[55] Gourevitch, "The Life After."

A Final Word of Hope ... and Caution

When I was in Rwanda on a research trip in 2006, Espérance and I met for tea, and she updated me on her life. Since we had visited her home ten years before, she had managed to get a scholarship to a business college outside Rwanda and earned a degree in business administration. After returning to Rwanda, she found a job running a multi-ethnic development program. She had put her two cousins through school, and they were now in university themselves. She was doing well. She lived in a comfortable room in a house with several other survivors.

On this visit, Espérance wanted to tell me about something that had happened in gacaca. She had not gone to her home community to attend any of the sessions, but someone contacted her to say that her sister's case had come up during one of the general assembly meetings. A young man had confessed to being involved in her murder, and he had information about it. Espérance traveled to her home community in what was now Southern Province so that she could meet with the confessed killer. She met with the young man, and he shared with her the story of how he had been among those who attacked and killed her sister. He told her where the body had been buried, and as a result Espérance had been able to exhume the body and was planning to give her sister a proper burial. For Espérance, being able to give at least one of her close family members a decent burial was highly significant and allowed her to achieve at least some degree of closure. After speaking with Espérance, I was reassured that despite all of its shortcomings, gacaca was at least producing some positive results. Uncovering elements of the truth of what happened in Rwanda in 1994 was important to many survivors.

But in a series of emails a couple of years later Espérance undermined this reassurance. She wrote to tell me that because of facts that were revealed in gacaca, she was experiencing increasing distress:

Recently, I have had a hard time because of people who confessed in gacaca court about the sexual violence they have done to me. I have never been open on this matter. I kept it to myself, due to the number of people whom I could not identify, because all happened at night. Now I know some of the others. This is a hard time for me. I am deeply troubled ... Since this happened, all things have changed, so that all of my memories have turned to the genocide.

She expressed a need to leave Rwanda for a time, to take a break so that she could find ways to understand what had happened to her. The truth had most certainly not set her free.

In the aftermath of events as terrible as what took place in Rwanda in 1994, there are no easy solutions. The Rwandan government and international community have drawn on a variety of tools from the transitional justice arsenal to attempt to bring healing, reconciliation, truth, and justice to a traumatized population and a divided country. Sadly, as my research has shown, these tools have proven inadequate. Healing and justice and reconciliation are never easy, and stories like that of Espérance demonstrate the confounding complexity of overcoming the legacies of the past. Rwandan history did not stop in 1994. Life has moved on, as survivors, bystanders, and perpetrators have all sought to rebuild their daily existences. Their ongoing experiences – their ability to make a decent living, success in caring for their children, and interactions with their neighbors – have affected how they react to the past and to the government's efforts to confront the past. Just as the ongoing experiences of life affect how individuals regard the past, ongoing political interests shape official attempts to confront the past. As my research has shown, programs to promote social healing, reconciliation, and national unity and to provide justice for the terrible crimes committed in Rwanda have been undermined by a continuing mistrust of the population and overriding concern for retaining power. Sadly, despite extensive time and energy and resources put into transitional justice programs intended to reshape popular understandings of the past, unify the population, and allow Rwanda to move forward into a brighter future, the population of Rwanda continues to wait impatiently for both justice and transition.

Bibliography

Adam, Heribert. "Trading Justice for Truth." *The World Today*, January 1998: 11–13.

Aegis Trust – Rwanda. "10 Years After: Shaping the Memory of the Rwandan Genocide." Kigali, April 7, 2004.

Africa Watch, Fédération Internationale des Droits de l'Homme (FIDH), Union Inter-africaine des Droits de l'Homme et des Peuples (UIDH), et al. "Rapport de la Commission Internationale d'Enquête sur les Violations des Droits de l'Homme au Rwanda depuis le 1er Octobre 1990 (7–21 Janvier 1993)." Paris: FIDH, March 1993.

Agbénonci, Aurélien A. "Introductory Remarks." *Delivering as One: Annual Report 2009*. Kigali: United Nations Rwanda, 2010.

Akhavan, Payam. "Beyond Impunity: Can International Criminal Justice Prevent Future Atrocities?" *American Journal of International Law*, 95, 7, 2001: 7–31.

"The International Criminal Tribunal for Rwanda: The Politics and Pragmatics of Punishment." *American Journal of International Law*, 90, 3, 1996: 501–510.

Amnesty International. "Amnesty International Report 1996." London: Amnesty International, January 1, 1996.

"Pre-Election Attacks on Rwandan Politicians and Journalists Condemned." London: Amnesty International, August 4, 2010.

"Rwanda: 23 Public Executions Will Harm Hope of Reconciliation." London, Amnesty International, April 23, 1998.

"Rwanda Abolishes the Death Penalty." London: Amnesty International, August 2, 2007.

"Rwanda: Civilians Trapped in Armed Conflict, 'The Dead Can No Longer Be Counted.'" AFR 47/043/1997, London: Amnesty International, December 19, 1997.

"Rwanda: Deeper into the Abyss – Waging War on Civil Society." AFR 47/013/ 2004, London: Amnesty International, July 6, 2004.

"Rwanda: Ending the Silence." AFR 47/32/97, London: Amnesty International, September 25, 1997.

"Rwanda: Escalating Repression against Political Opposition." AFR 47/004/ 2003, London: Amnesty International, April 22, 2003.

"Rwanda: The Hidden Violence: 'Disappearances' and Killings Continue." London: Amnesty International, June 22, 1998.

"Rwanda: Human Rights May Be the Main Casualty of Tensions in the Rwandese Government." AFR 47/18/95, London: Amnesty International, August 30, 1995.

"Rwanda: Human Rights Overlooked in Mass Repatriation." AFR 47/02/97, London: Amnesty International, January 1997.

"Rwanda: Independent Forensic Inquiry and Urgent Protection Needed for Internally Displaced Persons Following the Massacre of Several Thousands." AFR 47/09/95, London: Amnesty International, April 24, 1995.

"Rwanda: Jean RUBADUKA, Magistrate and Human Rights Activist Abbé André SIBOMANA, Acting Bishop and Human Rights Activist and Other Human Rights Activists." AFR 47/23/95, London: Amnesty International, November 30, 1995.

"Rwanda: Official Interference in Affairs of Human Rights NGO Places Independent Human Rights Work in Peril." London: Amnesty International, August 16, 2013.

"Rwanda: Reports of Killings and Abductions by Rwandese Patriotic Army, April–August 1994." AFR 47/16/94, London: Amnesty International, October 19, 1994.

"Rwanda, Two Years After the Genocide: An Open Letter to President Pasteur Bizimungu." AFR 47/42/96, London: Amnesty International, April 4, 1996.

"Safer to Stay Silent: The Chilling Effects of Rwanda's Laws on 'Genocide Ideology' and 'Sectarianism.'" AFR 47/005/2010, London: Amnesty International, August 2010.

Anderson, Benedict. *Imagined Communities: Reflections on the Origin and Spread of Nationalism*. New York: Verso, 1983.

André, Catherine, and Platteau, Jean-Philippe. "Land Relations Under Unbearable Stress: Rwanda Caught in the Malthusian Trap." *Journal of Economic Behavior and Organization*, 34, 1, 1998: 1–47.

Ansoms, An. "Striving for Growth, Bypassing the Poor: A Critical Review of Rwanda's Rural Sector Policies." *Journal of Modern African Studies*, 46, 1, 2008: 1–32.

"Re-engineering Rural Society: The Visions and Ambitions of the Rwandan Elite." *African Affairs*, 108, 431, 2009: 289–309.

"Views from Below on the Pro-Poor Growth Challenge: The Case of Rural Rwanda." *African Studies Review*, September, 2010: 102.

Ansoms, An, Cioffo, Giuseppe, Huggins, Chris, and Murison, Jude. "The Reorganization of Rural Space in Rwanda: Habitat Concentration, Land Consolidation and Collective Marshland Cultivation." In An Ansoms and Thea Hilhorst, eds. *Losing Your Land: Dispossession in the Great Lakes*. Suffolk: James Currey, 2014: 163–185.

Ansoms, An, and Marysse, Stefaan, eds. *Natural Resources and Local Livelihoods in the Great Lakes Region in Africa: A Political Economy Perspective*. New York: Palgrave Macmillan, 2011.

Ansoms, An, and Murison, Jude. "De 'Saoudi' au 'Darfur': L'Histoire d'un Marais au Rwanda." In Filip Reyntjens, Stef Vandeginste, and M. Verpoorten, eds. *L'Afrique des Grands Lacs: Annuaire 2011–2012*. Paris: L'Harmattan, 2012: 375–396.

Ansoms, An, and Rostagno, Donatella. "Rwanda's Vision 2020 Halfway Through: What the Eye Does Not See." *Review of African Political Economy*, 39, 133, September 2012: 427–450, 441–442.

Arendt, Hannah. *Eichman in Jerusalem: A Report on the Banality of Evil*. New York: Penguin, 1991, 1992: 253.

Arthur, Paige. "How 'Transitions' Reshaped Human Rights: A Conceptual History of Transitional Justice." *Human Rights Quarterly*, 31, 2009: 321–367.

Association Rwandaise Pour la Defense des Droits de la Personne et des Libertés Publiques (ADL). "Rapport sur les Droits de l'Homme au Rwanda." Kigali: ADL, December 1992.

Autesserre, Séverine. *The Trouble with the Congo: Local Violence and the Failure of International Peacebuilding*. Cambridge: Cambridge University Press, 2010.

Bal, Mieke, Crewe, Jonathan, and Spitzer, Leo, eds. *Acts of Memory: Cultural Recall in the Present*. Hanover, NH: Dartmouth University Press, 1999.

Barahona De Brito, Alexandra, Aquilar, Paloma, and Gonzalez Enriquez, Carmen, eds. *Politics of Memory: Transitional Justice in Democratizing Societies*. Oxford: Oxford University Press, 2001.

Begley, Larissa. "'Resolved to Fight the Ideology of Genocide and all of its Manifestations': The Rwandan Patriotic Front, Violence and Ethnic Marginalisation in Post-Genocide Rwanda and Eastern Congo." PhD diss., University of Sussex, March 2011.

Bloxham, Donald. *Genocide on Trial: The War Crimes Trials and the Formation of Holocaust History and Memory*. Oxford: Oxford University Press, 2001.

Booth, David, and Golooba-Mutebi, Frederick. "Developmental Patrimonialism? The Case of Rwanda." *African Affairs*, 111, 444, May 2012: 379–403.

Bornkamm, Christoph. *Rwanda's Gacaca Courts: Between Retribution and Reparation*. Oxford: Oxford University Press, 2012.

Brazemore, Gordon. "Restorative Justice and Earned Redemption: Communities, Victims, and Offender Reintegration." *American Behavioral Scientist*, 41, 6, 1998: 768–814.

Brehm, Hollie Nyseth, Uggen, Christopher, and Gasanabo, Jean-Damascène. "Genocide, Justice, and Rwanda's Gacaca Courts," *Journal of Contemporary Criminal Justice*, 30, 3, 2014: 333–352

Brown, Eric. "Rwandan Genocide: Is Rwanda Gearing up for Another Genocide." New York: Human Rights First, February 23, 2010.

Brownlee, Jason. *Authoritarianism in an Age of Democratization*. New York: Cambridge University Press, 2007.

Brody, Reed. "Justice: The First Casualty of Truth? The Global Movement to End Impunity for Human Rights Abuses Faces a Daunting Question." *The Nation*, April 30, 2001.

Broneus, Karen. "Truth-Telling as Talking Cure: Insecurity and Retraumatization in Rwanda's Gacaca Courts." *Security Dialogue*, 39, 1, 2008: 55–76.

Buckley-Zistel, Susanne. "Remembering to Forget: Chosen Amnesia as a Strategy for Local Coexistence in Post-Genocide Rwanda." *Africa*, 76, 2, 2006: 131–150.

"Between Past and Future: An Assessment of the Transition from Conflict to Peace in Post-genocide Rwanda." Osnabrück: *Deutsche Stiftung Friedensforschung*, 2008.

Burnet, Jennie E. "Gender Balance and the Meanings of Women in Governance in Post-Genocide Rwanda." *African Affairs*, 107, 428, May 2008: 361–386.

"The Injustice of Local Justice: Truth, Reconciliation, and Revenge in Rwanda." *Genocide Studies and Prevention*, August 2008: 173–193.

"Women Have Found Respect: Gender Quotas, Symbolic Representation, and Female Empowerment in Rwanda." *Politics and Gender*, 7, 3, September 2011: 303–334.

Genocide Lives in Us: Women, Memory, and Silence in Rwanda, Madison: University of Wisconsin Press, 2012, 216.

Burris, Beverly H. *Technocracy at Work*. Albany: SUNY Press, 1993.

Byanafashe, Dèogratias. "La famille comme principe de coherence de la société rwandaise traditionnelle." *Cahiers Lumière et Société*, 6, August 1997: 3–26.

Call, Charles T. "Is Transitional Justice Really Just?" *Brown Journal of International Affairs*, Summer/Fall 2004: 101–111.

ed., *Building States to Build Peace*. Boulder: Lynne Rienner, 2008.

Cardozo, B. Lopes, Vergara, A., Agani, F., and Gotway, CA. "Mental Health, Social Functioning, and Attitudes of Kosovar Albanians following the War in Kosovo." *Journal of the American Medical Association*, 286, 2001: 555–562

Carothers, Thomas. "The End of the Transition Paradigm," *Journal of Democracy*, 13, 1, 2002: 5–21.

Caryl, Christina. "Africa's Singapore Dream: Why Rwanda's Leader Styles Himself as the Heir to Lee Kuan Yew." *Foreign Policy*, April 2, 2015.

Cassese, Antonio. "Reflections on International Criminal Justice." *Modern Law Review*, January 1998: 1–10.

Cazenave, Odile, and Célérier, Patricia. *Contemporary Francophone African Writers and the Burden of Commitment*. Charlottesville: University of Virginia Press, 2011.

Centre de Documentation et d'Information sur les Procès de Génocide (CDIPG). *Quatre Ans de Proccés de Genocide: Quelle Base pour les "Juridictions Gacaca?"* Kigali: LIPRODHOR, July 2001: 36–38.

Cepl, Vojitech, and Gillis, Mark, "Making Amends After Communism." *Journal of Democracy*, October 1996: 118–124.

Chakravarty, Anuradha. *Investing in Authoritarian Rule: Punishment and Patronage in Rwanda's Gacaca Courts for Genocide Crimes*, New York: Cambrdge University Press, 2016.

"Navigating the Middle Ground: The Political Values of Ordinary Hutu in Post-Genocide Rwanda." *African Affairs*, 113, 451, 2014: 232–253.

Chalk, Frank, and Jonassohn, Kurt. *The History and Sociology of Genocide: Analyses and Case Studies*. New Haven: Yale University Press, 1990.

Chrétien, Jean-Pierre, ed. *Rwanda: Les Medias du Genocide*. Paris: Karthala, 1995.

Le Défie de l'Ethnisme: Rwanda et Burundi: 1990–1996. Paris: Karthala, 1997.

Clark, John F., ed. *The African Stakes of the Congo War*. New York: Palgrave MacMillan, 2002.

Clark, John F. and Gardinier, David E., eds. *Political Reform in Francophone Africa*, Boulder: Westview Press, 1996.

Clark, Phil. *The Gacaca Courts, Post-Genocide Justice and Reconciliation in Rwanda: Justice without Lawyers*. New York: Cambridge University Press, 2011.

Cole, Elizabeth. "Transitional Justice and the Reform of History Education." *The International Journal of Transitional Justice*, 1, 2007: 115–137.

Cole, Elizabeth, and Barsalou, Judy. *Unite or Divide? The Challenges of Teaching History in Societies Emerging from Violent Conflict*. Washington, DC: United States Institute of Peace, Special Report, 2006.

"Conclusion Generale." *Cahiers Lumière et Société*, December 1999: 73–76.

Corey, Allison, and Joireman, Sandra F. "Retributive Justice: The *Gacaca* Courts in Rwanda." *African Affairs* 103, 2004:73–89.

Costy, Alexander. "The Peace Dividend in Mozambique, 1987–1997," in Taisier M. Ali and Robert O. Matthews, eds., *Durable Peace: Challenges for Peacebuilding in Africa*. Toronto: University of Toronto Press, 2004: 42–182.

Cruvellier, Thierry. *Court of Remorse: Inside the International Criminal Tribunal for Rwanda*. Madison, University of Wisconsin Press, 2006.

François, D., and Maurice, M. "The Ones that Got Left Behind in Kigali's Demolished Shantytown." *Les Observateurs*, March 12, 2010.

Davenport, Christian, and Stam, Allan. "What Really Happened in Rwanda." *Truthout*, 6, October 2009.

David, Roman, and Yuk-ping, Susanne Choi, "Victims on Transitional Justice: Lessons from the Reparation of Human Rights Abuses in the Czech Republic." *Human Rights Quarterly*, May 2005: 392–435.

"Debats des Deputés sur le Rapport de la Commission Parlementaire de Controle sur les Divisions au Sein du Parti MDR." April 14, 2003.

de Lacger, Louis. *Le Ruanda: Aperçu Historique*, Kabgayi, 1939 and 1959.

de Lame, Danielle. *A Hill Among a Thousand: Transformations and Ruptures in Rural Rwanda*. Madison: University of Wisconsin Press, 2005.

de Soto, Hernando. *The Mystery of Capital: Why Capitalism Triumphs in the West and Fails Everywhere Else*. New York: Basic Books, 2000.

Des Forges, Alison. "The Ideology of Genocide." *Issue: A Journal of Opinion*, 23, 2, 1995: 44–47.

Leave None to Tell the Story: Genocide in Rwanda, New York: Human Rights Watch, 1999.

Des Forges, Alison, and Gillet, Eric. "Rwanda: The Crisis Continues." New York: Human Rights Watch, 7, 1, April 1995.

Des Forges, Alison, and Longman, Timothy. "Legal Responses to Genocide in Rwanda." In Harvey Weinstein and Eric Stover, eds. *My Neighbor, My Enemy: Justice and Social Reconstruction in Rwanda and the Former Yugoslavia*. Cambridge: Cambridge University Press, 2004.

Deutsch, Karl W. *Nationalism and Social Communication: An Inquiry into the Foundations of Nationality*. New York: John Wiley and Sons, 1953: 163.

Diop, Boubacar Boris. *Murambi: The Book of Bones*. Bloomington: Indiana University Press, 2006.

"'Disturbing Events' Marred Rwandan Leader's Re-Election, US Says." *New York Times*, August 15, 2010.

Dobson, William J. *The Dictator's Learning Curve: Inside the Global Battle for Democracy*. New York: Random House, 2012.

Domeniconi, Marco. "Gacaca Takes off Slowly." Foundation Hirondelle, 14, October 2002.

Dyregrov, A., Gupta, LRG, et al. "Trauma Exposure and Psychological Reactions to Genocide Among Rwandan Children." *Journal of Traumatic Stress*, 13, 2000: 3–21.

Easterly, William. *Tyranny of Experts: Economists, Dictators, and the Forgotten Rights of the Poor*. New York: Basic Books, 2015.

Eaton, Kent. "Decentralization's Undemocratic Roots: Authoritarianism and Subnational Reform in Latin America." *Latin American Politics and Society*, 48, 1, 2006: 1–26.

"Risky Business: Decentralization from Above in Chile and Uruguay." *Comparative Politics*, 37, 1, October 2004: 1–22.

Eaton, Kent, Kaiser, Kai, and Smoke, Paul. *The Political Economy of Decentralization Reforms: Implications for Aid Effectiveness*. Washington: World Bank, 2010.

Edelman, Murray. *The Symbolic Uses of Politics*. Urbana: University of Illinois Press, 1964.

Elster, Jon, ed. *Retribution and Reparation in the Transition to Democracy*. Cambridge: Cambridge University Press, 2006.

Eltringham, Nigel. *Accounting for Horror: Post-Genocide Debates in Rwanda*. London: Pluto Press, 2004.

Emerson, Ralph Waldo. "History." *The Essays of Emerson*, vol. 1, London: Arthur L. Humphries, 1899: 8.

Ensign, Margee. "Rwanda at 50: Reflections, Reconstruction, and Recovery." Huffington Post, July 3, 2012.

Epp, Marlene. "The Memory of Violence: Soviet and East European Mennonite Refugees and Rape in the Second World War." *Journal of Women's History*, 9, 1, Spring, 1997: 58–88.

Esbenshade, Richard S. "Remembering to Forget: Memory, History, National Identity in Postwar East-Central Europe." *Representations*, 49, Winter 1995: 72–79.

European Union Election Observation Mission. *Rwanda: Élection Presidentielle 25 Aôut 2003; Élections Legislatives 29 et 30 Septembre, 2 Octobre 2003* (final report). Brussels: European Union, 2003.

"Final Report: Legislative Elections to the Chamber of Deputies, 15–18 September 2008." Brussels: European Union, September 2008. www .euromrwanda.org/EN/Final_Report.html.

Fairbanks, Michael. "Nothing Good Comes Out of Africa." Huffington Post, May 3, 2010.

Farmer, Paul et al. "Reduced Premature Mortality in Rwanda: Lessons from Success." *BMJ*. January 2013.

Farrar, Margaret E. "Amnesia, Nostalgia, and the Politics of Place Memory." *Political Research Quarterly*, 46, 4, December 2011: 723–735.

Fein, Helen. *Genocide: A Sociological Perspective*. London and Newbury Park: SAGE, 1993.

Fierens, Jacques. "*Gacaca* Courts: Between Fantasy and Reality," *Journal of International Criminal Justice*, 3, 2005: 896–919.

"First Trial in Rwanda of Suspects of '94 Killing," *New York Times*, December 28, 1996.

Fletcher, Laurel E, and Weinstein, Harvey M. "Violence and Social Repair: Rethinking the Contribution of Justice to Reconciliation." *Human Rights Quarterly*, 2002: 573–639.

Ford, Jenny. "Rethinking Relocation in Rwanda." *The Chronicles*, May 30, 2012.

Forest, Benjamin, and Johnson, Juliet. "Unraveling the Threads of History: Soviet-Era Monuments and Post-Soviet National Identity in Moscow." *Annals of the Association of American Geographers*, 92, 3, 2002: 534–547.

"France Issues Rwanda Warrants," BBC News, November 23, 2006.

Freedman, Jim. *Nyabingi: The Social History of an African Divinity*. Butare: Institute National de Recherche Scientifique, 1984.

Freedman, Sarah Warshauer, Kambanda, Déo, Samuelson, Beth Lewis, et al. "Confronting the Past in Rwandan Schools." In Eric Stover and Harvey Weinstein, eds. *My Neighbor, My Enemy: Justice and Community in the Aftermath of Mass Atrocity*. Cambridge: Cambridge University Press, 2004: 248–264.

Freedman, Sarah Warshauer, Weinstein, Harvey M., Murphy, Karen, et al. "Teaching History after Identity-Based Conflicts: The Rwanda Experience," *Comparative Education Review*, 52, 4, 2008: 663–69.

French, Howard. "U.N. Report on Congo Offers New View of Genocide Era." *New York Times*, August 28, 2010.

Fritz, Nicole, and Smith, Alison. "Current Apathy for Coming Anarchy: Building the Special Court for Sierra Leone." *Fordham International Law Journal*, 25, December 2001: 391.

Fujii, Lee Ann. *Killing Neighbors: Webs of Violence in Rwanda*. Ithaca: Cornell University Press, 2011.

Gahiji, Innocent. "Rwanda: Districts Need Decentralization of Budgets for Sectors, Cell Levels." *Africa News*, July 5, 2012.

Gahima, Gerald. *Transitional Justice in Rwanda: Accountability for Atrocity*. New York: Routledge, 2013.

Gakuba, Alexis. "Le Kinyarwanda: Instrument de l'Unité Nationale." *Les Cahiers Evangile et Société*, 3, June 1996, 59–67.

Gellner, Ernest. *Nations and Nationalism*. Ithaca: Cornell University Press, 1983.

Goldhagen, Daniel Jonah. *Hitler's Willing Executioners: Ordinary Germans and the Holocaust*. New York: Vintage Books, 1997.

Gourevitch, Philip. *We Wish to Inform You That Tomorrow We Will be Killed Along with our Families: Stories from Rwanda*. Picador, 1999.

"The Life After: 15 Years after the Genocide in Rwanda, the Reconciliation Defies Expectations." *The New Yorker*, May 4, 2009.

Government of Rwanda. *Organic Law No 16/2004 of 19/6/2004 Establishing the Organisation, Competence and Functioning of Gacaca Courts*, Kigali, 19, June 2004.

"Constitution of the Republic of Rwanda." June 4, 2003.

Organic Law No 10/2007 of 1/03/2007 Modifying and Complementing Organic Law No 16/2004 of 19/6/2004 Establishing the Organisation, Competence and Functioning of Gacaca Courts, Kigali, 1, March 2007.

"Organic Law 13/2008 of 19/05/2008 modifying and complementing Organic Law 16/2004 of 19/06/2004, Establishing the Organization, Competence and Functioning of Gacaca Courts Charged with Prosecuting and Trying the Perpetrators of the Crime of Genocide and other Crimes Against

Humanity Committed between October 1, 1990 and December 31, 1994 as Modified and Complemented to Date." *Official Gazette of the Republic of Rwanda*, 47, 1, June 2008.

"National Itorero Commission (Strategy)," Kigali, November 2011.

Graybill, Lyn S. *Truth and Reconciliation in South Africa: Miracle or Model?*. Boulder and London: Lynne Rienner Publishers, 2002.

Guichaoua, André. *Les Crises Politiques au Burundi et au Rwanda (1993–1994)*. Lille: Université des Sciences et Technologies de Lille, 1995.

From War to Genocide: Criminal Politics in Rwanda 1990–1994, Madison: University of Wisconsin Press, 2015.

Rwanda 1994: Les Politiques du Genocide à Butare. Paris: Karthala, 2005.

Gunther, Marc. "Why CEOs Love Rwanda: As a Small African Nation Recovers from Genocide, Google, Starbucks, and Costco Lend a Hand." CNNMoney. com, April 3, 2007.

Gurr, Ted Robert. *Why Men Rebel*. Princeton: Princeton University Press, 1971.

Hakizimana, Emmanuel, and Gasana, Gallican. "Le Président Kagame Veint de Révéler sa Plus Grand Peur," *L'Aut' Journal*, April 17, 2014.

Halbwachs, Maurice. *On Collective Memory*. Edited and translated by Lewis A. Coser. Chicago and London: University of Chicago Press, 1992.

Hasselskog, Malin, and Schierenbeck, Isabell. "National Policy in Local Practice: the Case of Rwanda." *Third World Quarterly*, 36, 5, 2015, 950–966.

Haveman, Roelof, and Muleefu, Alphonse. "The Fairness of Gacaca." In Dawn Rothe and Christopher Mullins, eds. *State Crime, Current Perspectives*, New Brunswick, NJ: Rutgers University Press: 219–244.

Hayner, Priscilla B. *Unspeakable Truths: Confronting State Terror and Atrocity: How Truth Commissions Around the World are Challenging the Past and Shaping the Future*. New York and London: Routledge, 2001.

Hayward, Fred M., ed. *Elections in Independent Africa*. Boulder: Westview Press, 1987.

Hehir, Aidan, and Robinson, Neil, eds. *State Building: Theory and Practice*. New York: Routledge, 2007.

Hewart, Lord Chief Justice Gordon. *Rex v. Sussex Justices ex parte McCarthy*. 1924.

Hintjens, Helen. "Post-Genocide Identity Politics in Rwanda." *Ethnicities*, 8, 1, 2008.

Hite, Katherine. "'The Eye that Cries': The Politics of Representing Victims in Contemporary Peru." *A Contra Coriente*, Fall 2007: 108–124.

Hobsbawm, Eric. J. *Nations and Nationalism Since 1780: Programme, Myth, Reality*. Cambridge: Cambridge University Press, 1990.

Hodgkin, Katharine, and Rodstone, Susannah. "Introduction: Contested Pasts." In Katharine Hodgkin and Susannah Radstone, eds. *Contested Pasts: The Politics of Memory*. London and New York: Routledge: 1–21.

Hoepken, Wolfgang. "War, Memory, and Education in a Fragmented Society: The Case of Yugoslavia." *East European Politics and Societies*, 13, 1, 1999:190–227

Holland, Emily. "Dispatches from a Humanitarian Journalist: Dispatch I: Kibuye, Rwanda." *McSweeney's*, September 4, 2007.

Holmquist, Frank. "Kenya's Antipolitics," *Current History*. May 2005: 209–215.

Horowitz, Donald L. *Ethnic Groups in Conflict*. Berkeley: University of California Press, 2000.

Huggins, Christopher. "Seeing Like a Neoliberal State? Authoritarian High Modernism, Commercialization and Governmentality in Rwanda's Agricultural Reform." PhD Dissertation, Carleton University, 2013.

"'Control Grabbing' and Small Scale Agricultural Intensification: Emerging Patterns of State-facilitated 'Agricultural Investment' in Rwanda." *The Journal of Peasant Studies*, May 14, 2014.

"Land Grabbing and Land Tenure Security in Post-Genocide Rwanda." In An Ansoms and Thea Hilhorst, eds. *Losing Your Land: Dispossession in the Great Lakes*. Suffolk: James Currey, 2014: 141–162.

Human Rights Watch. "Human Rights Watch and FIDH Commend Peaceful End to Kibeho Crisis but Warn Rwandan Judicial System Needs Immediate Action." New York: Human Rights Watch, May 11, 1995.

"No Contest in Rwandan Elections: Many Local Officials Run Unopposed." Press Release, New York: Human Rights Watch, 9, March 2001.

"Preparing for Elections: Tightening Control in the Name of Unity." New York: Human Rights Watch, May 8, 2003.

"Rwanda." *World Report 1996*, New York: Human Rights Watch, December 1995.

"Rwanda." *World Report 1997*, New York: Human Rights Watch, December 1996.

"Rwanda." *World Report 1998*, New York: Human Rights Watch, December 1997.

"Rwanda." *World Report 1999*, New York: Human Rights Watch, December 1998.

"Rwanda: The Crisis Continues." New York: Human Rights Watch, 7, 1, April 1995.

"Rwanda: Deliver Justice for Victims of Both Sides." New York: Human Rights Watch, August 2002.

"Rwanda: The Search for Security and Human Rights Abuses." New York: Human Rights Watch, April 1, 2000.

"Rwanda: Uprooting the Rural Poor." New York: Human Rights Watch, May 1, 2001.

"Zaire: Transition, War and Human Rights." New York: Human Rights Watch/Africa, April 1997.

Hyden, Goran. *Beyond Ujamaa in Tanzania: Underdevelopment and an Uncaptured Peasantry*. Berkeley: University of California Press, 1980.

Ingelaere, Bert. "Do We Understand Life After Genocide? Center and Periphery in the Construction of Knowledge on Rwanda." *African Studies Review*, 53, 1, April 2010: 41–59.

"Does the Truth Pass across the Fire without Burning? Locating the Short Circuit in Rwanda's *Gacaca* Courts." *Journal of Modern African Studies*, 2009.

"From Model to Practice: Researching and Representing Rwanda's 'Modernized' *Gacaca* Courts." *Critique of Anthropology*, 32, 4, 2012.

"Living the Transition: A Bottom Up Perspective on Rwanda's Political Transition." Discussion Paper 2007.06, Institute of Development Policy and Management, University of Antwerp, November 2007: 37.

"Peasants, Power and Ethnicity: A Bottom-up Perspective on Rwanda's Political Transition." *African Affairs* 109, 435, 2010: 228–289, 273-292.

Integrated Regional Information Networks. "Jury Still Out on Effectiveness of 'Gacaca' Courts." United Nations Office for the Coordination of Humanitarian Affairs (OCHA), 23, June 2009.

"Rwanda: Focus on UN Tribunal," OCHA, Dar es Salaam, February 3, 2004.

"Rwanda: Government Implements Low Cost Housing for Returnees." OCHA 5, October 2004.

International Criminal Tribunal for Rwanda. *The Prosecutor vs. Aloys Simba*, Case No. ICTR-01-76-T. Judgement and Sentence. Arusha, December 13, 2005.

"Bagilishema, Ignace (ICTR-95-1A)", available at www.unictr.org/en/cases/ictr-95-1a.

"Kayishema et al. (ICTR-95-1) available at www.unictr.org/en/cases/ictr-95-1.

"Nyiramasuhuko et al. (Butare) (ICTR-98-42), available at www.unictr.org/en/cases/ictr-98-42

International Crisis Group. "International Criminal Tribunal for Rwanda: Justice Delayed." Brussels: International Crisis Group, 7, June 2001.

"'Consensual Democracy' in Post-Genocide Rwanda: Evaluating the March 2001 District Elections." Africa Report 34, Nairobi and Brussels: International Crisis Group, 9, October 2001.

"Rwanda at the End of Transition: A Necessary Political Liberalization." Brussels: International Crisis Group, November 13, 2002.

"Tribunal Penal International pour le Rwanda: Pragmatisme de Rigueur." Brussels: International Crisis Group, 26, September 2003.

International Justice Tribune. "Questions Pile up for Swamped Gacaca." *Radio Netherlands Worldwide*, 23, October 2005.

Jefermovas, Villia. *Brickyards to Graveyards in Rwanda: From Production to Genocide in Rwanda*. Albany: SUNY Press, 2002.

Jelin, Elizabeth. *State Repression and the Labors of Memory*. Minneapolis: University of Minnesota Press, 2003: 18.

Jenkins, Kate, and Plowden, William. *Governance and Nationbuilding: The Failure of International Intervention*. Northampton, MA: Edward Elgar, 2006.

Kagame, Alexis. *La Poésie Dynastique au Rwanda*. Brussels: Institute Royal du Congo Belge (IRCB), 1951.

Le Code des Institutions Politiques du Rwanda Precolonial. Brussels: IRCB, 1952.

L'histoire des Armées Bovines dans l'Ancien Rwanda. Brussels: ARSOM, 1963.

Kagame, Paul. Speech on the Occasion of the Day of Patriotism. Radio Rwanda, October 1, 2002.

"Discourse of the President of the Republic on the 8th Anniversary in the Memory of the Genocide and the Massacres of 1994." Nyakibanda, 7, April 2002.

"Speech on the Day of Heroes." Nyange, Kibuye. Radio Rwanda, February 1, 2003.

"Beyond Absolute Terror: Post-Genocide Reconstruction in Rwanda." Speech to the Commonwealth Club of California, San Francisco, March 7, 2003.

"Speech Given at the National Commemoration of the Ninth Anniversary of the 1994 Genocide," Mwurire, Rwangana, Kibungo, Broadcast on Radio Rwanda, April 7, 2003.

"Speech to the Woodrow Wilson International Center for Scholars." Washington, DC, 21, April 2004.

"Preface." In Phil Clark and Zachary D. Kaufman, eds. *After Genocide: Transitional Justice, Post-Conflict Reconstruction and Reconciliation in Rwanda and Beyond.* London: Hurst, 2008.

Kagire, Edmund. "Kagame Drops Last Two RPF 'historicals.'" *The East African,* June 1, 2013.

Kalimba, Célestin. "Rwanda: Les Frontiers." In *Rapport de Synthese du Seminaire sur l'Histoire du Rwanda.* Butare, December 14–18, 1998.

Kalisa, Armstrong Gatete. "Kiyovu Residents Decry Demolitions." *The Rwanda Focus,* July 29, 2008.

Kamanzi, Pierre. "Révolution ou Régression?" *Cahiers Lumière et Société,* 16, December 1999: 61–72.

Kanimba, Misago. "Le Peuplement du Territoire Rwandais: a la Lumière Archéologiques." *Les Cahiers Lumière et Société,* 5, May 1997: 68–79.

"Peuplement Ancien du Rwanda: à la Lumière de Récentes Recherches." *Cahiers du Centre de Gestion des Conflits,* 5, 2003: 8–44.

Karekezi, Alice. "Juridictions Gacaca: Lutte contre l'Impunité et Promotion de la Réconciliation Nationale." *Cahiers du Centre de Gestion des Conflits,* 3, May 2001: 9–96.

Karimi, Faith. "Rwandan Genocide Survivor Finds Solace in Gacacas." CNN. com, July 2009.

Kayihura, Michaël. "Composantes et Relations Socials au Rwanda Pre-colonial, Colonial, et Post-colonial: Hutu, Tutsi, Twa, Lignages et Clans." In *Rapport de Synthèse du Seminaire sur l'Histoire du Rwanda,* Butare, December 14–18, 1998.

Kayoboke, Ferdinand. "Le M.D.R. Parmehutu et la 1ère République." In *Rapport de Synthèse du Seminaire sur l'Histoire du Rwanda,* Butare, December 14–18, 1998.

"Keep Looking Ahead Rwanda." *The Economist,* January 13, 2007.

Kimanuka, Oscar. "Rwanda: Giving Power to the People." *The East African,* January 10, 2006

Kimonyo, Jean-Paul. *Rwanda's Popular Genocide: A Perfect Storm.* Boulder: Lynne Reinner, 2016.

Kimonyo, Jean-Paul; Twagiramungu, Noël; and Kayumba, Christophe. "Supporting the Post-Genocide Transition in Rwanda: The Role of the International Community." Democratic Transitions in Post-Conflict Societies Project, Working Paper 32, The Hague: The Netherlands Institute of International Relations Clingendael, December 2004.

King, Elisabeth. *From Classrooms to Conflict in Rwanda.* New York: Cambridge University Press, 2013.

Kinzer, Stephen. *A Thousand Hills: Rwanda's Rebirth and the Man Who Dreamed It.* Hoboken, NJ: John Wiley and Sons, 2008: 1–2, 336.

Koonz, Claudia. "Between Memory and Oblivion: Concentration Camps in German Memory." In John R. Gillis ed. *Commemorations: The Politics of National Identity,* Princeton: Princeton UP, 1994.

Kritz, Neil J. ed. *Transitional Justice: How emerging Democracies Reckon with Former Regimes. Volume II: Country Studies,* Washington, USIP, 1995.

Kron, Josh. "Rwanda Joins British Commonwealth." *New York Times,* November 29, 2009.

Kundera, Milan. *The Book of Laughter and Forgetting*. New York: Perennial Classics, 1996.

Kuperman, Alan J. "Provoking Genocide: A Revised History of the Rwandan Patriotic Front," *Journal of Genocide Research*, 6, 1, 2004.

Lawyers Committee for Human Rights. "*Prosecuting Genocide in Rwanda: A Lawyers Committee report on the ICTR and National Trials*." New York, 1997.

LDGL. *Dynamique du Paix et Logiques de Guerre: Rapport Annuel sur la Situation des Droits de l'Homme au Rwanda*. May 2003.

Leebaw, Bronwyn Anne. "The Irreconcilable Goals of Transitional Justice." *Human Rights Quarterly*, January 2008: 95–118.

Lemarchand, René. "Bearing Witness to Mass Murder." *African Studies Review*, 48, 3, December 2005: 93–101.

The Dynamics of Violence in Central Africa. Philadelphia: University of Pennsylvania Press, 2009.

"Genocide in the Great Lakes: Which Genocide? Whose Genocide?" African Studies Review, 41, 1, April 1998: 3–16.

Rwanda and Burundi. New York: Praeger Publishers, 1970.

Lenin, V.I. "Report on the Unity Congress of the R.S.D.L.P." 1906. www.marxists.org/archive/lenin/works/1906/rucong/viii.htm.

Levitsky, Steven, and Way, Lucan A. *Competitive Authoritarianism*. New York: Cambridge University Press, 2010.

Lijphard, Arend. *Thinking About Democracy: Power Sharing and Majority Rule in Theory and Practice*. New York: Routledge, 2008.

Linden, Ian, and Linden, Jane. *Church and Revolution in Rwanda*. New York: Africana Publishing Company, 1977.

Longman, Timothy. *Christianity and Genocide in Rwanda*. Cambridge: Cambridge University Press, 2010.

"The Complex Reasons for Rwanda's Engagement in Congo." In John F. Clark, ed. *The Continental Stakes in the Congo War*. New York: Palgrave, 2002: 129–144.

"Eastern Congo Ravaged." New York: Human Rights Watch, May 2000.

"Forced to Flee: Violence Against the Tutsi in Zaire." New York: Human Rights Watch/Africa, July 1, 1996.

"Justice at the Grassroots? Gacaca Trials in Rwanda." In Naomi Roht-Arriaza and Javier Mariezcurrena, eds. *Beyond Truth Versus Justice: Transitional Justice in the New Millenium*, Cambridge University Press, 2006.

"Nation, Race, or Class? Defining the Hutu and Tutsi of East Africa." In Joseph Feagin and Pinar Batur-Vanderlippe, eds. *The Global Color Line: Racial and Ethnic Inequality and Struggle from a Global Perspective*. JAI Press, Bingley, UK, 1999: 103–130.

"Rwanda: Achieving Equality or Serving an Authoritarian State?" In Gretchen Bauer and Hannah Britton, eds. *Women in African Parliaments*. Boulder: Lynne Rienner, 2005.

"Rwanda: Chaos from Above." In Leonardo A. Villalon and Phillip A. Huxtable, eds. *The African State at a Critical Juncture: Between Disintegration and Reform*, Boulder: Lynne Rienner, 1998: 75–91.

"The Uses and Abuses of the Media: Rwanda Before and After the Genocide." In Clara Ramirez-Barat, ed. *Transitional Justice, Culture, and Society: Beyond Outreach*. New York: Social Science Research Council, 2014.

Longman, Timothy, and Des Forges, Alison. "Attacked by All Sides: Civilians and the War in Eastern Zaire." 9, 1(A), New York: Human Rights Watch, March 1997.

Longman, Timothy, Pham, Phuong, and Harvey Weinstein, "Connecting Justice to Human Experience: Attitudes Toward Accountability and Reconciliation in Rwanda." In Eric Stover and Harvey Weinstein, eds. *My Neighbor, My Enemy: Justice and Community in the Aftermath of Mass Atrocity.* Cambridge: Cambridge University Press, 2004, 206–225.

Lyons, Beth. "Between Nuremberg and Amnesia: The Truth and Reconciliation Commission in South Africa." *Monthly Review,* 49, September 1997: 5–23.

Maja-Pearce, Adeale. "Binding the Wounds: Resentment, Anger and the Desire for Revenge Threaten to Undermine the Truth Commission's Attempt to Reconcile Victims and Oppressors." *Index on Censorship,* 5, 1996: 48–53.

Maindron, Gabriel. *Des Apparitions à Kibeho: Annonce de Marie au Coeur de l'Afrique.* Paris: O.E.I.L., 1984.

Malkki, Liisa. *Purity and Exile: Violence, Memory and Cosmology among Hutu Refugees in Tanzania.* Chicago: University of Chicago Press, 1995.

Mamdani, Mahmoud. *When Victims Become Killers: Colonialism, Nativism, and the Genocide in Rwanda.* Princeton: Princeton University Press, 2001.

Manirakazi, Vincent, and Ansoms, An. "'Modernizing Kigali:' The Struggle for Space, in the Rwandan Urban Context." In An Ansoms and Thea Hilhorst, eds. *Losing Your Land: Dispossession in the Great Lakes.* Suffolk: James Currey, 2014.

Manor, James. *The Political Economy of Democratic Decentralization.* Washington: World Bank, 1999.

Maquet, Jacques J. *The Premise of Inequality in Ruanda: A Study of Political Relations in a Central African Kingdom.* London: Oxford University Press, 1961.

Marschall, Sabine. "Gestures of Compensation: Post-Apartheid Monuments and Memorials." *Transformation* 2004: 78–95.

Master Plan Team, The (OZ Architecture, EDAW, Tetra Tech, ERA, and Engineers without Borders). "Kigali Conceptual Master Plan," prepared for the Rwanda Ministry of Infrastructure. November 2007.

Mayr, Otto. "The Enola Gay Fiasco: History, Politics, and the Museum." *Technology and Culture* 39, 3, July 1998: 462–473.

Mbonimana, Gamaliel. "Ethnies et Eglise Catholique: Le Remodelage de la Société par l'École Missionaire (1900–1931)." *Cahiers Centre Saint-Dominique,* 1, August 8, 1995: 52–67.

"Le Rwanda État-Nation au XIXe siècle." In *Rapport de Synthese du Seminaire sur l'Histoire du Rwanda.* Butare, December 14–18, 1998.

McAdams, A. James, ed. *Transitional Justice and the Rule of Law in New Democracies.* South Bend, IN: University of Notre Dame Press, 1997.

McGreal, Chris. "Rwanda to Switch from French to English Schools," *The Guardian,* October 13, 2008.

"Survivors Condemn Tribute to Top Hutus: Rwanda's Government 'Wants to Forget the Genocide.'" *The Guardian,* April 5, 1995.

McKinley, James C. "76,000 Still in Jail in Rwanda Awaiting Trial in '94 Slayings." *New York Times,* 24, June 1996.

McVeigh, Tracy. "Rwanda Votes to Give President Kagame Right to Rule until 2034." *The Guardian*, December 19, 2015

Medecins Sans Frontiers. "Report on Events in Kibeho Camp, April 1995." Paris: MSF, May 25, 1995.

Meierhenrich, Jens. *Lawfare: Gacaca Jurisdictions in Rwanda*. Unpublished Manuscript.

Meierhenrich, Jens, and Lagace, Martha. "Photo Essay: Tropes of Memory." *Humanity: An International Journal of Human Rights, Humanitarianism, and Development*, 4, 2, Summer 2013: 289–312.

Meldrum, Andrew. "One Million Rwandans to Face Killing Charges in Village Courts." *The Manchester Guardian*, 15, January 2005.

Mendez, Juan. "Accountability for Past Abuses." *Human Rights Quarterly*, 19, 2, 1997: 255–282.

Meredith, Martin. *Coming to Terms: South Africa's Search for Truth*. Washington: Public Affairs: 19.

Mgbako, Chi. "*Ingando* Solidarity Camps: Reconciliation and Political Indoctrination in Post-Genocide Rwanda." *Harvard Human Rights Journal*, 201, 2005: 201–224.

Michnik, Adam. "Reflections on the Collapse of Communism." *Journal of Democracy*, January 2000: 119–126.

Ministry of Finance and Economic Planning. "Rwanda Vision 2020." Kigali: Government of Rwanda, July 2000: 11–19.

Minow, Martha. *Between Vengeance and Forgiveness: Facing History after Geonocide and Mass Violence*. Boston: Beacon Press, 1998.

Misago, Augustin. *Les Apparitions de Kibeho au Rwanda*. Kinshasa: Faculté Catholique de Kinshasa, 1991.

Morrill, Constance. "Show Business and 'Lawfare' in Rwanda: Twelve Years after the Genocide." *Dissent*, Summer 2006: 14–20.

Morris, Madeleine H. "The Trials of Concurrent Jurisdiction: The Case of Rwanda." Special Symposium Justice in Cataclysm: Criminal Trials in the Wake of Mass Violence. *Duke Journal of Comparative and International Law*, Spring 1997: 349–374.

Mudoola, Dan M. "Institution Building: The Case of the NRM and the Military in Uganda, 1986–9." In Holger Bernt Hansen and Michael Twaddle, eds. *Changing Uganda*. Athens. OH: Ohio University Press, 1991: 230–246.

Mugisha, Alex and Rwema, Frances. "In Rwanda, Rapid Urbanization Chases the Poor Out of Town." *Inyenyeri News*, March 6, 2012.

Mulimbiri, Jean. "Remise en Cause et Reprise en Mains de Notre Histoire." *Cahiers Centre Saint-Dominique*, 1, May 8, 1995: 7–18.

Müller, Jan-Werner. "Introduction: The Power of Memory, the Memory of Power, and the Power over Memory." In Jan-Werner Müller, ed. *Memory and Power in Post-War Europe: Studies in the Presence of the Past*. Cambridge: Cambridge University Press, 2002, 1–35: 18.

Mungarulire, Pierre. "Le Revolution de 1959 au Rwanda." In *Rapport de Synthèse du Seminaire sur l'Histoire du Rwanda*. Butare, December 14–18, 1998.

Munyaneza, James. "City authorities need to review strategy on 'illegal' houses." *The New Times*, January 10, 2011.

Munyura, Pierre. "Rwanda Decentralization Assessment." Kigali: Strategies 2000 SARL, for USAID, July 2002.

Musahara, Herman, and Huggins, Chris. "Land Reform, Land Scarcity, and Post-Conflict Reconstruction: A Case Study of Rwanda." In Chris Huggins and Jenny Clover, eds. *From the Ground Up: Land Rights, Conflict, and Peace in Sub-Saharan Africa*. Pretoria: Institute for Security Studies, June 2005.

Mutakaganzwa, Domatilla. "Byuma Francois Xavier's Case." Kigali: National Service of Gacaca Jurisdictions, 12, June 2007.

Muzungu, Bernardin. "Ethnies et Clans." *Cahiers Centre Saint-Dominique*, 1, August 8, 1995.

"Le Prejugé de Race." *Les Cahiers Evangile et Société*, 4, December 1996: 20–29.

"Les Mythes." *Cahiers Lumière et Société*, 5, Mayu 1997, 23–36: Citation 34.

"Un Mensonge Politique." *Cahiers Lumière et Société*, 10, May 1998: 26–46.

"Les Signes d'Espoir." *Cahiers Lumière et Société*, 11, August 1998: 7–20.

"A qui Profitent nos Malheurs?" *Cahiers Lumière et Société*, March 1999: 35–54.

Nantulya, Paul, Alexander, Karin, Kanyugu, Didace, et al. "Evaluation and Impact Assessment of the National Unity and Reconciliation Commission (NURC)." Kigali: Institute for Justice and Reconciliation, November 2005.

National Census Service. "The General Census of Population and Housing, Rwanda: 16–30 August 2002: Report on the Preliminary Results." Kigali: Ministry of Finance and Economic Planning, February 2003.

National Service of Gacaca Jurisdictions. "Summary of the Report Presented at the Closing of Gacaca Court Activities." Kigali, Rwanda, 2012.

"Gacaca Jurisdictions: Achievements, Problems, and Future Prospects," www .inkiko-gacaca.gov.rw/En/EnObjectives.htm, 2012.

National Unity and Reconciliation Commission. "Itorero Ry-Igihugu." Kigali: NURC, January 12, 2010.

Ndayambaje, Jean-Damascène. "Le Genocide des Tutsi: Genese et Execution." In *Rapport de Synthèse du Seminaire sur l'Histoire du Rwanda*, Butare, December 14–18, 1998.

Neier, Aryeh. *War Crimes: Brutality, Genocide, Terror, and the Struggle for Justice*. New York: Random House, 1998.

"New Rwandan Prosecutor Named," London: BBC News, August 29, 2003.

Newbury, Catharine. *The Cohesion of Oppression: Clientship and Ethnicity in Rwanda, 1860–1960*. New York: Columbia University Press, 1988.

"Ethnicity and the Politics of History in Rwanda." *Africa Today*, 45, 1, January-March 1998: 7–24.

"High Modernism at the Ground Level: The *Imidugudu* Policy at the Ground Level." In Scott Straus and Lars Waldorf, eds. *Remaking Rwanda: State Building and Human Rights After Mass Violence*. Madison: University of Wisconsin Press, 2011: 223–239.

"Rwanda: Recent Debates over Governance and Rural Development." In Goran Hyden and Michael Bratton, *Governance and Politics in Africa*. Boulder: Lynne Reinner, 1992, 193–219.

Newbury, David S. "Canonical Conventions in Rwanda: Four Myths of Recent Historiography of Central Africa," *History in Africa*, 39, 2012, 41–76.

"The Clans of Rwanda: An Historical Hypothesis." *Africa: Journal of the International Africa Institute*, 50, 4, 1980: 389–403.

Nora, Pierre, ed. *Les Lieux de Mémoire*. Paris: Gallimard, Vols 1–3, 1984–1992.

Norman, Wayne. *Negotiating Nationalism: Nation-building, Federalism, and Secession in the Multinational State*. Oxford: Oxford University Press, 2006.

"Nouvelle Strategie du 'Double Genocide, La.'" *Cahier Lumière et Société*, 9, March 1998.

Nowrojee, Binaifer, and MacGaffey, Janet. *Shattered Lives: Sexual Violence During the Rwandan Genocide and Its Aftermath*, New York: Human Rights Watch, 1996.

Ntagungira, Godfrey. "Rwanda: KCC Evicts Kiyovu Kiosk Owners." *The New Times*, June 21, 2008.

"Demolished Kiosk Owners Drag KCC to Court." *The New Times*, July 14, 2008.

Nyamwasa, Kayumba, Rudasingwa, Theogene, Karegeya, Patrick, et al. "Rwanda Briefing." www.greatlakesdemocracy.blogspot.com/2010/09/rwanda-briefing-by-gen-kayumba-nyamwasa.html, August 2010.

Ntahombaye, Philemone, Ntabona, A, Gahama, Joseph, et al. *L'Institution des Bashingantahe au Burundi: Etudes Pluridisciplinaire*. Bujumbura, 1999.

Nyirimanzi, Gérard. "Les Solidaritiés Traditionneles." *Les Cahiers Lumière et Société*, 14, June 1999.

Nyirubugara, Olivier. *Complexities and Dangers of Remembering and Forgetting in Rwanda*. Sidestone Press, 2013.

Nzongola-Ntalaja, Georges. *Congo: From Leopold to Kabila*. London: Zed Books, 2002.

Oloku-Onyanga, J. "The National Resistance Movement, 'Grassroots Democracy,' and Dictatorship in Uganda." In Robin Cohen and Harry Goulbourne, eds. *Democracy and Socialism in Africa*. Boulder: Westview Press, 1991.

Olsen, Tricia D., Payne, Leigh A., and Reiter, Andrew G. *Transitional Justice in Balance: Comparing Processes, Weighing Efficacy*, Washington: United States Institute for Peace, 2010.

Olson, Jennifer M. "Land Degradation in Gikongoro Rwanda: Problems and Possibilities in the Integration of Household Survey Data and Environmental Data." Rwanda Society Environment Project, working paper 5, East Lansing: Michigan State University, 1994.

Orwell, George. "As I Please." February 4, 1944.

Osiel, Mark. *Mass Atrocity, Collective Memory and the Law*. New Brunswick and London: Transaction Publishers, 1997.

Pagès, A. *Un Royaume Hamite au Centre de l'Afrique: Au Rwanda sur les bos du Lac Kivu*. Brussels: Van Campenhout, 1933.

Palmer, Nicola. *Courts in Conflict: Interpreting the Layers of Justice in Post-Genocide Rwanda*. Oxford: Oxford University Press, 2015.

Parliament of Rwanda. "La où l'Idéologie Génocidaire se Fair Observer au Rwanda." Kigali, June 2004.

Penal Reform International. "From Camp to Hill: The Reintegration of Released Prisoners." *Research Report on the* Gacaca *VI*, Paris: May 2004.

"Monitoring and Research Report on the Gacaca Community Service, Areas of Reflection." London: PRI, March 2007.

Peskin, Victor. "International Justice and Domestic Rebuilding: An Analysis of the Role of the International Tribunal for Rwanda." *The Journal of Humanitarian Assistance*, October 1999.

"Pierre Celestin Rwigema, the Rwandan Exiled Prime Minister Returns as Revealed Before." *Umuvugizi*, October 24, 2011.

Pitcher, M. Anne. "Forgetting from Above and Memory from Below: Strategies of Legitimation and Struggle in Postsocialist Mozambique." *Africa*, Winter 2006: 88–112.

Plowden, William and Jenkins, Kate. *Governance and Nationbuilding: The Failure of International Intervention.* Northampton, MA: Edward Elgar, 2006.

Post, Robert C. "A Narrative of Our Time: The Enola Gay 'and after that, period.'" *Technology and Culture*, 45, 2, April 2004: 373–395.

Pottier, Johan. *Re-Imagining Rwanda: Conflict, Survival and Disinformation in the Late Twentieth Century.* Cambridge: Cambridge University Press, 2002.

Pouligny, Béatrice, Chesterman, Simon, and Schnabel, Albrecht, eds. *After Mass Crime: Rebuilding States and Communities.* New York: United Nations University Press, 2007.

Power, Samantha. "The Stages of Justice." *The New Republic*, March 2, 1998: 32–38.

   A Problem from Hell: The United States in the Age of Genocide. New York: Basic Books, 2002.

Press, Robert M. "In Rwanda's 'Slave Ship' Prisons, Life Is Grim for Suspected Killers." *The Christian Science Monitor*, 18, November 1994.

"Prosecutor Loses Rwanda Role," London: BBC News, August 28, 2003.

Pross, Christian. *Paying for the Past: The Struggle over Reparations for Surviving Victims of the Nazi Terror.* Baltimore: Johns Hopkins University Press, 1998.

"Protests as Rwandan Government Frees Detainees." *Business Day*, 12, February 1997.

Prunier, Gerard. *Darfur: The Ambiguous Genocide*, Ithaca: Cornell University Press, 2005.

   The Rwanda Crisis: History of a Genocide. New York: Columbia, 1995.

Purdeková, Andrea. "Even if I am not here, There are so Many Eyes." *Journal of Modern African Studies*, 49, 3, September 2011: 475–497.

   Making Ubumwe: *Power, State, and Camps in Rwanda's Unity-Building Project.* NewYork: Berghan Books, 2015.

   "Repatriation and Reconciliation in Divided Societies: The Case of Rwanda's 'Ingando.'" RSC Working Paper No. 43, Working Paper Series, Queen Elizabeth House, Department of International Development, University of Oxford, January 2008.

Raghavan, Sudarsan. "Rwanda's Success Story Fails to Silence Concerns about Rights: Slayings and Censorship Mar Campaign Season, Top Opponents Barred." *Washington Post*, August 9, 2010.

Ratner, Steven R. and Abrahams, Jason S. *Accountability for Human Rights Atrocities in International Law: Beyond the Nuremberg Legacy*, Oxford: Oxford University Press, 2001.

Recker, Sterling. "Vision 2020: An Analysis of Policy Implementation and Agrarian Change in Rural Rwanda." PhD Dissertation, University of Missouri-St. Louis, July 2014.

Reporters without Borders. "Rwanda, the Arrest of Father Guy Theunis: An Investigation of the Charges, the Legal Action, and Possible Reasons." Brussels: Reporters without Borders, November 2005.

Republic of Rwanda, National Assembly. "Rapport de la Commission Parlementaire de Contrôle Mise en place le 27 décembre 2002 pour Enquêter sur les Problèmes du MDR." Accepted by the National Transitional Assembly, April 14, 2003.

Republic of Rwanda. "Report on the Reflection Meetings Held in the Office of the President of the Republic from May 1998 to March 1999." Kigali: Office of the President of the Republic, August 1999.

Republic of Rwanda, Office of the President of the Republic. *The Unity of Rwandans: Before the Colonial Period and Under Colonial Rule; Under the First Republic*. Kigali, August 1999.

République du Rwanda, Province du Nord, District de Rulindo. "Evaluation des Besoins en Renforcement des Capacités: District du Rulindo." Kigali, April 2008.

Rettig, Max. "*Gacaca*: Truth, Justice, and Reconciliation in Postconflict Rwanda?" *African Studies Review*, 51, 3, 2008: 25–50.

Rever, Judi. "Rwanda's Memory Hole," *Foreign Policy Journal*, April 14, 2015.

Reyntjens, Filip. "Constructing the Truth, Dealing with Dissent, Domesticating the World: Governance in Post-Genocide Rwanda." *African Affairs* (2010): 1–34, Citation p. 2.

  "Le *gacaca* ou la Justice du Gazon au Rwanda." *Politique Africaine*, 40, December 1990: 31–41.

  The Great African War: Congo and Regional Geopolitics, 1996–2006. Cambridge: Cambridge University Press, 2009.

  Political Governance in Post-Genocide Rwanda. New York: Cambridge University Press, 2014.

  "Reduction of Poverty and Inequality, the Rwandan Way. And the Aid Community Loves It," Analysis and Policy Brief, No. 16, Institute of Development and Policy Analysis, University of Antwerp, December 2015.

  "Rwanda Ten Years On: From Genocide to Dictatorship," *African Affairs* 103, 2004: 177–210.

Reyntjens, Filip and Vandeginste, Steff. "Rwanda: An Atypical Transition." In Elin Skaar, Siri Gloppen, and Astri Suhrke, eds. *Roads to Reconciliation*. Lanham MD: Lexington Books, 2005.

Ricouer, Paul. *Memory, History, Forgetting*. Chicago and London: University of Chicago Press, 2004.

Robinson, Neil, and Hehir, Aidan. *State Building: Theory and Practice*. New York: Routledge, 2007.

Roht-Arriaza, Naomi. "Reparations in the Aftermath of Mass Violence." In Eric Stover and Harvey Weinstein, eds. *My Neighbor, My Enemy: Justice and Community in the Aftermath of Mass Atrocity*. Cambridge: Cambridge University Press, 2004: 121–139

  "State Responsibility to Investigate and Prosecute Grave Human Rights Violations in International Law." *California Law Review*, March 1990: 449–513.

Roht Arriaza, Naomi, and Mariencurrena, Javier, eds. *Transitional Justice in the Twenty-First Century: Beyond Truth versus Justice*, Cambridge: Cambridge University Press, 2006.

Rosen, Jonathan W. "Dissident 'Choirboy': Rwandan Gospel Star on Trial." Al Jazeera English, December 11, 2014.

Rosenberg, Tina. "Recovering from Apartheid." *The New Yorker*, 18, November 1996: 86–95.

Roth, Brad R. "Peaceful Transition and Retrospective Justice: Some Reservations: A Response to Juan Méndez." *Ethics and International Affairs*, 15, 1, 2001: 45–50.

Roth, Philip. "The Most Original Book of the Season." Interview with Milan Kundera. *The New York Times*, November 30, 1980.

Rousso, Henry. *The Vichy Syndrome*. Cambridge: Harvard University Press, 1991.

Rugagi, Jean Nizurugero. "Decolonisation et Democratization du Rwanda." *Cahiers Lumière et Société*, 7, October 1997, 43–54.

"Les Factuers Favorables à l'Identité Citoyenne dans l'Histoire du Rwanda des Origins à 1900." In *Rapport de Synthèse du Seminaire sur l'Histoire du Rwanda*, Butare, December 14–18, 1998.

Rusagara, Frank. "*Gacaca* as a Reconciliation and Nation-building Strategy in Post-genocide Rwanda." *Conflict Trends*, 2, 2005: 20–25.

Rusesabagina, Paul. "Compendium of RPF Crimes – October 1990 to Present: The Case for Overdue Prosecution." Unpublished report, Brussels, November 2006.

Rutaremara, Tito and Muzungu, Bernardin. "Qui Liberera le Rwanda de l'Idéologie Divisionniste?" *Les Cahiers Evangile et Société*, 3, June 1996: 46–56, citation p. 49.

Rutayisire, Paul. "Le Catholicisme Rwandais en Process." In *Rapport de Synthèse du Seminaire sur l'Histoire du Rwanda*, Butare, December 14–18, 1998.

Rutayisire, Paul and Muzumgu, Bernardin. "L'ethnisme au Coeur de la Guerre." *Cahiers Centre Saint-Dominique*, 1, August 8, 1995: 68–82.

Rutembesa, Faustin. "A propos de l'usage du concept 'féodalité' dans l'etude de la société rwandaise." In *Rapport de Synthese du Seminaire sur l'Histoire du Rwanda*, Butare, December 14–18, 1998.

Rutijanwa, Médard. "Le MRND et la IIème République Rwandaise: Essai d'Analyse Critique du Système Politique et Idéologique du MRND." In *Rapport de Synthèse du Seminaire sur l'Histoire du Rwanda*, Butare, December 14–18, 1998.

Rwanda Development Board. "Kigali Conceptual Master Plan," brochure. www .kcps.gov.rw/index.php/?id=21#Master%20plan.

"Rwanda: Government Said Planning to Redraw Provincial Boundaries." *The East African*, September 6, 2005.

"Rwanda Cuts Relations with France." BBC News, November 24, 2006.

"Rwanda: Trying to Move On." Public Radio International's *The World*, Jeb Sharp, producer, 2007.

Rwandan Patriotic Front, "Gacaca Courts Genesis, Implementation, and Achievements," www.rpfinkotanyi.org/en/?gacaca-courts-genesis.

"Rwandan Senate Votes to Allow Third Term for Kagame," Aljazeera, November 17, 2015.

Samset, Ingrid and Dalby, Orrvar. "Rwanda: Presidential and Parliamentary Elections 2003." Oslo: Norwegian Center for Human Rights, 2003.

Sanders, Edith R. "The Hamitic Hypothesis: Its Origin and Functions in Time Perspective." *Journal of African History*, 10, 4, 1969.

Santaro, Lara. "Terror as a Method: A Journalist's Search for Truth in Rwanda," *Foreign Policy Journal*, September 25, 2015.

Sarkin, Jeremy. "The Necessity and Challenges of Establishing a Truth and Reconciliation Commission in Rwanda." *Human Rights Quarterly*, 21, 3. 1999: 767–823.

Scalzo, Kristin. "The Rwandan Refugee Crisis: Before the Genocide." National Security Archive Electronic Briefing Book No. 464, George Washington University, 31, March 2014.

Schabas, William. "Genocide Trials and Gacaca Courts." *Journal of International Criminal Justice*, 3, 4, 2005: 896–919.

Scharf, Michael P. "The Prosecutor v. Dusko Tadic: An Appraisal of the First International War Crimes Trial Since Nuremberg." Paper presented on the panel, "Conceptualizing Violence: Present and Future Developments in International Law." Adjudicating Violence: Problems Confronting International Law and Policy on War Crimes and Crimes Against Humanity, *Albany Law Review*, 60, 861, 1997.

Schoenbrun, David Lee. *A Green Place, A Good Place: Agrarian Change, Gender, and Social Change in the Great Lakes Region to the Fifteenth Century.* Portsmouth, NH: Heinneman, 1998.

Schwedler, Jillian and Chomiak, Laryssa. "And the Winner Is ... Authoritarian Elections in the Arab World." *Middle East Report*, Spring 2006.

Scott, James C. *Seeing Like a State: How Certain Schemes to Improve the Human Condition Have Failed.* New Haven: Yale University Press, 1998.

Sebarenzi, Joseph and Mullane, Laura Ann. *God Sleeps in Rwanda: A Journey of Transformation.* New York: Atria Books, 2009.

Semujonga, Josias. "Le Discours Scientific comme Porteur du Stereotypes: Le Cas de l'Historiographie Rwandaise." In *Rapport de Synthese du Seminaire sur l'Histoire du Rwanda*, Butare. December 14–18, 1998.

"Senior Aid in Rwanda Coalition is Killed." *New York Times*, March 5, 1995.

Sezibera, Richard. "The Only Way to Bring Justice to Rwanda." *Washington Post*, 7, April 2002.

Shanmugaratnam, N., ed. *Between War and Peace in Sudan and Sri Lanka: Deprivation and Livelihood Revival.* Oxford: James Currey, 2008.

Shaw, Rosalind. "Memory Frictions: Localizing the Truth and Reconciliation Commission in Sierra Leone." *International Journal of Transitional Justice*, 1, 2, 2007: 183–207.

"The TRC, the NGO, and the Child: Young People and Post-Conflict Futures in Sierra Leone," *Social Anthropology*, 22, 3, 2014: 306–325.

Sherman, Daniel J. "Art, Commerce, and the Production of Memory in France after WWI." In John R. Gillis ed. *Commemorations: The Politics of National Identity*. Princeton: Princeton UP, 1994.

Shoup, Brian. *Conflict and cooperation in Multi-ethnic States: Institutional Incentives, Myths, and Counter-Balancing.* New York: Routledge, 2008.

Sibomana, André. *Hope for Rwanda: Conversations with Laure Guilbert and Hervé Deguine.* London: Pluto Press, 1999.

Siegloff, Roland. "Rwanda's Legal System Facing Paralysis over Backlog of Genocide Trials." Deutsche Presse-Agentur, March 8, 1997.

Sikkink, Kathryin. *The Justice Cascade: How Human Rights Prosecutions are Changing World Politics*. New York: WW Norton, 2011.

Sirven, Pierre. *La Sous-urbanization et les Villes du Rwanda et du Burundi*. Published by the author, 1984.

Slater, Dan. *Ordering Power: Contentious Politics and Authoritarian Leviathans in Southeast Asia*. New York: Cambridge University Press, 2010.

Smith, David. "Rwanda's Former Spy Chief 'Murdered' in South Africa." *The Guardian*, January 2, 2014.

Sommers, Marc. *Stuck: Rwandan Youth and the Struggle for Adulthood*. Athens, GA: The University of Georgia Press, 2012.

Sprecher, Drexel A. *Inside the Nuremberg Trial: A Prosecutor's Comprehensive Account*. Lanham, MD: University Press of America, 1999.

Stearns, Jason K. *Dancing in the Glory of Monsters: The Collapse of the Congo and the Great War of Africa*. New York: Public Affairs, 2011.

Straus, Scott. *The Order of Genocide: Race, Power, and War in Rwanda*. Ithaca: Cornell University Press, 2006.

"How Many Perpetrators Were There in the Rwandan Genocide: An Estimate," *Journal of Genocide Research*, 6, 1, March 2004.

Straus, Scott, and Waldorf, Lars, eds. *Remaking Rwanda: State Building and Human Rights after Mass Violence*. Madison: University of Wisconsin Press, 2011.

Straus, Scott, and Waldorf, Lars. "Introduction: Seeing Like a Post-Conflict State." In Scott Straus and Lars Waldorf, eds. *Remaking Rwanda: State Building and Human Rights After Mass Violence*. Madison: University of Wisconsin Press, 2011: 3–21.

Stren, Richard. "Decentralization: False Start or New Dawn?" United Nations Human Settlement Program, *Habitat Debate*, 8, 1, March 2002: 1–2.

Sundaram, Anjan. *Bad News: Last Journalists in a Dictatorship*, New York: Doubleday, 2016.

Tawil, Sobhi, and Harley, Alexandra, eds. *Education, Conflict and Social Cohesion: Studies in Comparative Education*. International Bureau of Education/UNESCO, 2004.

Teitel, Ruti. *Transitional Justice*. Oxford: Oxford University Press, 2002.

Theidon, Kimberly. *Intimate Enemies: Violence and Reconciliation in Peru*, Philadelphia: University of Pennsylvania Press, 2012.

"Justice in Transition: The Micropolitics of Reconciliation in Post-War Peru." *The Journal of Conflict Resolution*, 50, 3, 2006, 433–457.

Thompson, Allan. *The Media and the Rwandan Genocide*. London: Pluto Press, 2007.

Thomson, Susan. "Reeducation for Reconciliation: Participant Observation on Ingando." In Scott Straus and Lars Waldorf, eds. *Remaking Rwanda: State Building and Human Rights after Mass Violence*. Madison: University of Wisconsin Press, 2011, 331–339.

Whispering Truth to Power: Everyday Resistance to Reconciliation in Post-Genocide Rwanda. Madison: University of Wisconsin Press, 2013.

Thomson, Susan, and Nagy, Rosemary. "Law, Power, and Justice: What Legalism Fails to Address in the Functioning of Rwanda's *Gacaca* Courts." *International Journal of Transitional Justice*, 5, 2011, 11–30

Topping, Alexandra. "Kigali's Future, or Costly Fantasy? Plan to Reshape Rwandan City Divides Opinion." *The Guardian*, April 4, 2014.

Tunbridge, J. E. and Ashworth, G. J. *Dissonant Heritage: The Management of the Past as a Resource in Conflict*. Chichester, New York: J. Wiley, 1996.

Turner, Thomas. *The Congo Wars: Conflict, Myth, and Reality*. London: Zed Books, 2007.

Tutu, Desmond. "Healing a Nation." Interview. *Index on Censorship*, 5, 1996: 39–51.

Ugirashebuja, Octave. "L'ideologie du Tutsi Oppresseur." *Les Cahiers Evangile et Société*, 4, December 1996: 57–67.

Umbreit, M. *Victim Meets Offender: The Impact of Restorative Justice and Mediation*. Monsey, NY: Criminal Justice Press, 1994.

Umutesi, Marie Béatrice. *Surviving the Slaughter: The Ordeal of a Rwandan Refugee in Zaire*. Madison: University of Wisconsin Press, 2000.

UNESCO Institute for Statistics. "UIS Statistics in Brief: Education in Rwanda." www.stats.uis.unesco.org/unesco/TableViewer/document.aspx?ReportId= 121&IF_Language=eng&BR_Country=6460.

UNICEF. "Rwanda: Education." www.unicef.org/rwanda/education.html.

United Nations High Commission for Human Rights. "Democratic Republic of the Congo, 1993–2003: Report of the Mapping Exercise Documenting the Most Serious Violations of Human Rights and International Humanitarian Law Committed within the Territory of the Democratic Republic of the Congo between March 1993 and June 2003." Geneva: UNHCHR, August 2010.

Uvin, Peter. *Aiding Violence: The Development Enterprise in Rwanda*. West Hartford: Kumarian, 1998.

Uvin, Peter, and Mironko, Charles. "Western and Local Approaches to Justice in Rwanda." *Global Governance*, 9, 3, April–Jun 2003: 219–231.

Van Hoyweghen, Saskia. "The Urgency of Land and Agrarian Reform in Rwanda." *African Affairs*, 98, 392, July 1999: 353–372.

"The Rwandan Villagisation Programme: Resettlement for Reconstruction?" In Didier Goyvaerts, ed. *Conflict and Ethnicity in Central Africa*. Tokyo: Institute for the Study of Languages and Cultures of Asia and Africa, 2000: 209–224.

Van't Spijker, Gerard. *Les Usages Funéraires et la Mission de l'Église: Une Etude Anthropologique et Théologique des Rites Funéraires au Rwanda*. Kampen: Uitgeversmaatschappij J.H. Kok, 1990: 51–128.

Vansina, Jan. *Le Rwanda Ancien: Le Royaume Nyinginya*. Paris: Karthala, 2001.

Antecedents to Modern Rwanda: The Nyiginya Kingdom, Madison, WI: University of Wisconsin Press, 2004.

Vasagar, Jeevan. "France Blamed as Rwanda Marks Genocide Date." *The Guardian*, April 8, 2004.

Verwimp, Philip. "A Quantitative Analysis of Genocide in Kibuye Prefecture, Rwanda." Discussion Paper Series 1.10, Leuven: Center for Economic Studies, May 2001.

"Testing the Double-Genocide Thesis for Central and Southern Rwanda." *The Journal of Conflict Resolution*, 47, 4, August 2003: 423–442.

Vidal, Cluadine. "Les Commémorations du Génocide au Rwanda." *Les Temps Modernes* 613, 2001: 1–46.

Wagner-Pacifici, Robin, and Schwartz, Barry. "The Vietnam Veterans Memorial: Commemorating a Difficult Past." *American Journal of Sociology*, 97, 2, September 1991: 376–420.

Waldorf, Lars. "Censorship and Propaganda in Post-Genocide Rwanda." International Development Research Center, 2006.

"A Justice 'Trickle Down': Rwanda's First Post-Genocide President on Trial." In Ellen Lutz and Caitlin Reiger, eds. *Prosecuting Heads of State*. Cambridge: Cambridge University Press, 2009: 151–75.

"Mass Justice for Mass Atrocity: Rethinking Local Justice as Transitional Justice." *Temple Law Review*, 79, 1, 2006.

"Mass Justice for Mass Atrocity: Transitional Justice and Illiberal Peace-Building in Rwanda," PhD Dissertation, National University of Ireland, Galway, November 2013.

"Instrumentalizing Genocide: The RPF's Campaign against 'Genocide Ideology.'" In Scott Straus and Lars Waldorf, eds. *Remaking Rwanda: State Building and Human Rights after Mass Violence*. Madison: University of Wisconsin Press, 2011: 48–66, 54.

Waller, Michael. *Democratic Centralism: An Historical Commentary*. New York: St. Martin's Press, 1981.

Watson, Catharine. "Exile from Rwanda: Background to an Invasion." Washington: US Committee for Refugees, February 1991.

Waugh, Colin M. *Paul Kagame and Rwanda: Power, Genocide and the Rwandan Patriotic Front*. London: McFarland and Co., 2004.

Weschler, Lawrence. *A Miracle, A Universe: Settling Accounts with Torturers*. Chicago: University of Chicago Press, 1998.

"What Happens after Re-Demarcation?" *The New Times*, September 12, 2005.

Wierzynska, Aneta. "Consolidating Democracy through Transitional Justice: Rwanda's Gacaca Courts." *NYU Law Review*, November 2004, 1934–1969.

Williams, Melissa, Nagy, Rosemary, and Elster, Jon, eds. *Transitional Justice*. New York: New York University Press, 2012.

Willum, Bjørn. "Foreign Aid to Rwanda: Purely Beneficial or Contributing to War?" Ph.D. Dissertation, University of Copenhagen, 2001.

Wilson, Richard A. *The Politics of Truth and Reconciliation in South Africa: Legitimizing the Post-Apartheid State*. Cambridge: Cambridge University Press, 2001.

World Bank. "Net Official Development Assistance Received (Current US$)." www.data.worldbank.org/indicator/DT.ODA.ODAT.CD.

"Country Data: Rwanda." www.data.worldbank.org/country/rwanda.

"Rwanda at a Glance." Washington: World Bank, September 24, 2008. www.devdata.worldbank.org/AAG/rwa_aag.pdf.

"Rwanda Urban Infrastructure and City Management Project," www.web.worldbank.org/WBSITE/EXTERNAL/COUNTRIES/AFRICAEXT/0,,contentMDK:23277000~pagePK:146736~piPK:226340~theSitePK:258644,00.html.

World Economic Forum. "The Global Competitiveness Report 2010–2011." www.gcr.weforum.org/gcr2010/.

Yacoubian, George S. "Releasing Accused Genocidal Perpetrators in Rwanda: The Displacement of Preventive Justice." *Loyola University Chicago International Law Review*, 3, 21, Fall–Winter 2005: 21–39.

Young, James Edward. *The Texture of Memory: Holocaust Memorials and Meaning.* New Haven: Yale University Press, 1988, 1993.

Young, Crawford, ed. *Ethnic Diversity and Public Policy: A Comparative Inquiry.* New York: Palgrave, 1998.

Young, Crawford, Young, H. Edwin, and Emmerson, Ruppert, eds. *The Accommodation of Cultural Diversity: Case Studies.* New York: St. Martin's Press, 1999.

Zalaquett, Jose. "Confronting Human Rights Violations Committed by Former Governments: Principles Applicable and Political Constraints." In Neil J. Kritz, ed. *Transitional Justice.* Washington, D.C.: United States Institute of Peace Press, 1995: 3–31.

Zehr, Howard. "Restorative Justice: The Concept: Movement Sweeping Criminal Justice Field Focuses on Harm and Responsibility." *Corrections Today*, December 1997: 68–70.

Index

Abega clan, 61
administrative reorganization, 160–63
  popular opinions of, 214–16
  purpose of, 161
Aegis Trust, 12
  Kigali Memorial Centre, 5, 80–81
  Murambi genocide memorial, 6, 7, 8
African National Congress, 320
agricultural policy, 175–77
Amnesty International, 29, 98
amplified silence, 87
Angola
  involvement in Congo war, 146
Ansoms, An, 174, 177, 180, 184
anthem, national
  popular reactions to, 218
  replacement of, 160
Arbour, Louise, 107
Arendt, Hannah, 98
Argentina, 14, 316
Armenian genocide, 99
Army of the King, 149
arrest
  under false accusations, 21, 119, 123,
    131, 193, 205, 210
  of *genocidaires*, 93, 149, 204, 262,
    284, 296
  as intimidation, 29, 31, 120, 142,
    149, 156, 169, 192, 203, 229, 252,
    253, 267
  of journalists, 31, 171
  of political opponents, 149, 164, 165
  politically motivated, 13, 123, 141, 169,
    172, 196, 213, 214, 223, 229, 235,
    301, 327
Arthur, Paige, 316, 334
Arusha Peace Accords, 75, 141, 150, 158,
    203, 212
Ashworth, G.A., 72
Association Modeste et Innocent, 169
Association of Genocide Widows Agahozo.
    See AVEGA

Astrida. *See* Butare, city of
AVEGA, 170

Bagilishema, Ignace, 208, 209, 281, 285
Banyamulenge, 145
Bashingantahe, 111
Belgium
  colonial rule, 49–50, 82
  genocide trials, 95
  post-colonial influence, 84
Benebekire, 200
Bisesero
  community, 325
  genocide massacre, 76, 77, 208, 300
  genocide memorial, 5, 77, 88, 94
Bizimungu, Pasteur, 141, 147, 154
  foundation of opposition party,
    164, 168
Bizumuremyi, Bonaventure, 133
Bosnia-Herzegovina, 14
Brasilia, 157
Brazil, 14, 316
Brothers of Charity, 197
Buckley-Zistel, Susanne, 251
Bugesera, 67, 202
Bujumbura, 198
Bumba, 207
Burnet, Jennie, 87, 231
Burundi, 197, 198, 202, 265
  Bashingantahe system in, 111
  involvement in Congo war, 144
  as place of refuge, 117, 119,
    190, 201
  Tutsi refugees in, 44, 46, 136, 138, 149,
    203, 240, 330
Butare
  city of, 18, 19, 118, 190–94, 196–206
  province of, 117, 197, 202
Butare prison, 204
Buye, 198
Buyoga commune, 18, 210–14
Byanafashe, Déogratias, 46

Byuma, François-Xavier, 132
Byumba
    city, 211
    province, 18, 21, 255

Cahiers Lumière et Société, 53
Call, Charles T., 102
Cambodia, 97, 316
Canada
    genocide trials, 95
Cassese, Antonio, 99
Catholic Church, 62–63
    in Butare, 199
    in Buyoga, 211
    and ethnicity, 45, 49
    implication in 1994 genocide, 55
    in Kibuye, 208
    reconciliation programs, 169
ceceka, 292n. 53
Central African Republic, 97
Chakravarty, Anuradha, 156
Chile, 14, 316
Chrétien, Jean-Pierre, 42
Churchill, Winston, 35
civil society
    before 1994, 10, 62
    dangers of participation in, 141
    domination by returnees, 130
    involvement in research project, 35
    suppression of, 31, 88, 132, 143,
        147, 168–72
Civil Society Platform, 170
clans, 38, 47
Clark, Phil, 280, 317
Coalition for the Defense of the
    Republic, 41
colonialism
    as source of social division, 49–50,
        265
community service, 179
    as alternative to prison, 116, 124,
        298
competitive authoritarianism, 166
Congo, Democratic Republic of, 14, 47
    attacks by RPF in, 109, 121, 143, 204
    attacks on refugees, 32
    corruption in, 131
    first war, 108, 125, 144
    Hutu refugees in, 11, 12, 140,
        150, 201
    and International Criminal Court, 97
    invasion by RPF, 58
    second war, 108, 146, 153
    Tutsi refugees in, 44
Congo-Nile Crest, 207

constitution of 2003, 16
    popular opinions of, 218, 219
    reform process, 163
    term limits in, 167
Convention on the Prevention and
    Punishment of the Crime of
    Genocide. *See* Genocide Convention
Côte d'Ivoire, 97
Cruvellier, Thierry, 109
Cyanika genocide massacre, 2, 3
Cyarwa, 199

Darfur, 97
Day of Heroes, 80
decentralization, 160–63
    popular opinions of, 214–16
Del Ponte, Carla, 107
democracy movement, 9
Democratic Green Party of Rwanda, 165
Democratic Republican Movement, 54,
        141, 154, 218
    in Butare, 200
    parliamentary committee on, 59, 164
    suppression of, 164
democratization, 163–65
    in Mabanza commune, 208
    popular opinions of, 216–18, 220–21, 224
    purpose of, 163
Denmark, 316
Des Forges, Alison, 39
Deutsch, Karl, 36
Dialogue, 132
Diop, Boubacar Boris, 5
divisionism, 56, 57, 58, 217
    accusations against MDR, 164
    impact of law, 225
    law against, 168, 170, 223, 226, 230,
        235, 255, 319, 322
Dobson, William, 166
double genocide theory, 58, 127

East Timor, 14
economy of Rwanda
    prior to 1994, 9
    since 1994, 12, 184–85, 204
education
    bias in, 6, 49, 240, 241–42
    reform of, 17, 146
    as tool of transitional justice, 15
Egypt, 166
Eichman, Adolf, 98
El Salvador, 14
elections
    critiques of, 163–66
    for gacaca judges, 205

1999 local, 163
2001 local, 163, 205, 214
2003 constitutional referendum, 163
2003 parliamentary, 163, 164
2003 presidential, 163, 164, 227–29
2008 parliamentary, 165
2010 presidential, 165
2017 presidential, 167
Enola Gay controversy, 72
Episcopal Church, 147
  in Butare, 199
ethnicity
  centrality to gacaca courts, 127, 304,
    324
  colonial policy, 38–40, 49–50
  de-ethnicization, 159
  origins of conflict, 237, 238
  origins of Hutu, Tutsi, and Twa, 37, 47
  popular perceptions of, 236–38
  quota system, 40
  restrictions on discussing, 146
  role in 1994 genocide, 41–44
  in trials, 128–31

FARG. *See* National Fund for Genocide
    Survivors
Farmer, Paul, 28
Finland
  genocide trials, 95
First Republic, 50–52, 85, 208
flag
  popular reactions to, 218–19
  replacement of, 160
Forces Armées Rwandaise. See Rwandan
    Armed Forces
Forces démocratiques unifiées Inkingi. See
    United Democratic Forces-Inkingi
forgetting, sites of, 84–87
Forum of Political Parties, 152, 154, 170
France. *See also* Zone Turquoise
  charges against RPF officials, 333
  collective memory in, 71, 234
  Loiret-Butare development project, 198
  relations with Rwanda, 198
  role in 1994 genocide, 54
  transitional justice in, 316
Frazier, Jendayi, 71
Free Methodist Church, 147
Fujii, Lee Ann, 42

gacaca courts, 95, 123–26, 271–79
  corruption in, 300–01
  creation of, 111–13
  exclusion of RPF crimes, 124, 125
  goals of, 113–17

historic precedent, 111
  impact of, 305
  operation of, 113
  politicization of, 301
  popular opinions of, 289–302
  problem of participation in, 292
  structure of, 112
Gahima, Gerald, 106, 115, 129, 305, 331
Gatwaro Stadium, 208
Gatzinsi, Marcel, 200
Geneva Conventions, 96
genocidaires, 306
  actions in the genocide, 108
  arbitrary execution of, 262
  arrest of, 93, 121, 149, 204
  community service by, 179
  confessions by, 133, 281
  denunciation of, 122, 304
  equation of Hutu with, 130
  in gacaca, 296, 297
  in ICTR, 283
  impact of ICTR on, 108
  imprisonment of, 121, 282, 302
  involvement in reconciliation by, 115,
    124, 294, 297, 303
  need for accountability for, 120
  outside Rwanda, 106, 143
  reasons for participation in genocide, 42
  trials of, 16, 123, 290, 305
genocide
  causes of, 50–55, 242
  centrality to Rwandan history, 52–56
  failure of United Nations to stop, 105
  history of 1994 Rwandan
    genocide, 10–11
  need for trials, 103
  popular interpretations of, 245–53
  responsibility of international
    community, 5, 54, 56, 77, 105, 284
  role of ethnicity, 41–44
  words for in Kinyarwanda, 245
Genocide Convention, 97
genocide ideology
  accusations against MDR, 164
  belief in persistence of, 157
  charges against Victoire
    Ingabire, 165
  impact of law, 220, 225, 230, 263, 264,
    267, 306, 308
  law against, 169, 235, 319
  parliamentary committee on, 170
Gikongoro province, 6, 11, 67, 205
  genocide in, 1–3, 200
Gisenyi province, 150, 208
Gisovu prison, 91–95

Gisunzu commune, 209
Gitarama province, 122
Gitesi commune, 207
Gitikinini, 207
Gitwa, 208
Goldstone, Richard, 107
Golias, 63
Gourevitch, Phillip, 28
Groupe Scolaire, 197, 199, 201
Guatemala, 101
guilt, collective, 130, 304, 324
Gurr, Ted, 185, 331

Habyalimana, Jean-Baptiste, 199
Habyarabatuma, Cyriaque, 200
Habyarimana, Juvénal, 40, 43, 54,
    84, 208
  assassination of, 10, 190, 192, 247,
    248, 251
  government of, 10, 21, 41, 51, 53, 56,
    92, 126, 138, 265
  opposition to, 62
  policies of, 82, 173, 199, 241
Halbwachs, Maurice, 35
Hamitic hypothesis, 39
handicapped
  representation in parliament, 168
high modernism, 156
history
  curriculum revision project, 19, 34,
    60–64, 318
  moratorium on teaching, 46
  official narrative, 44–60, 266
  popular narratives, 236–57
  role in 1994 genocide, 37
Hobsbawm, Eric, 36
Hodgkin, Katharine, 36
Huggins, Christopher, 175–76
human rights organizations, 62, 70,
    98, 112, 122, 147, see Amnesty
    International, Human Rights Watch,
    LIPRODHOR
Human Rights Watch, 3, 98, 149, 151,
    201, 214
  office in Rwanda, 3, 13, 20, 63, 117,
    121, 122, 204
Hutu. See also ethnicity
  attacks by RPF on, 85, 142, 145
  attitudes of RPF toward, 157
  definition of, 38
  discussion of RPF attacks by, 253–57
  experiences during the
    genocide, 231–32
  imidugudu policy and, 235
  imprisonment of, 202

interpretations of the genocide by, 249
intimidation of, 132, 142, 149
language for 1994 violence, 245
opinions of gacaca, 296, 308
opinions on commemorations, 261
opinions on ethnic relations, 250–51
opinions of pre-genocide
    governments, 126
participation in the genocide, 53,
    55, 129
perspectives on revolution of
    1959, 239–40
post-genocide experienes of, 193–94
in post-genocide government, 141
in pre-genocide governments, 51, 54
refugees. See refugees: Hutu
RPF attacks on, 30, 8, 11,
    145, 148
sites of forgetting and, 86
social divisions among, 94, 131
as target of false accusations, 119, 123
Hutu militia
  in the DRC, 145, 146
  in the insurgency in the
    northwest, 145
  involvement in 1994 genocide, 1–3,
    5, 10, 76, 92, 129, 200, 201, 208,
    246, 272
  after 1994, 143, 213
  participation in ingando camps, 158
  training by France, 54
Hutu Power, 43, 54, 140, 142n. 20, 192

Ibis Hotel and Restaurant, 198, 204
Ibuka, 55, 171, 261, 293
identity cards, 40, 57, 146, 149, 222,
    237, 238
ideology. See also genocide ideology law
  anti-Tutsi, 34, 41, 43
Idjwi Island, 206
imidugudu policy, 145, 149–51, 175,
    226, 235
imihigo contracts, 162
Imvaho, 210
Indonesia, 97
Ingabire, Victoire, 165
ingando, 133, 155, 158–60, 307
  popular opinions of, 265
Ingelaere, Bert, 162, 183, 279
Inkiko gacaca. See gacaca courts
insurgency in the northwest from
    1997–1998, 145
Interahamwe. See Hutu militia
Internally Displaced People, 85, 142–45,
    157, 212

International Covenant on Civil and Political Rights, 97

International Covenant on Economic, Social, and Cultural Rights, 97

International Criminal Tribunal for Rwanda, 18, 95, 97, 103–09
  Butare cases, 281, 283
  exclusion of RPF crimes, 303, 333
  impact of, 302
  Kibuye cases, 206, 281, 285
  popular opinions of, 281–85
  relations with Rwandan Patriotic Front, 109

International Criminal Tribunal for the Former Yugoslavia, 97, 99, 108

International Crisis Group, 214

International Federation of Human Rights
  office in Rwanda, 3, 13, 20, 63, 117, 121, 122

Internews Newsreel Project, 93–95, 268

Inyangamugayo, 111, 112, 125, 210
  corruption among, 301
  political pressures on, 301

Inyumba, Aloysia, 158

Iraq, 97

IRST. *See* Rwandan Institute for Scientific Research

ISAR. *See* National Agricultural Research Institute

Italy, 316

itorero, 159

Jallow, Hassan, 107

Jelin, Elizabeth, 86

journalists
  intimidation of, 143, 171
  limits on, 148, 170

justice. *See* trials, *see* transitional justice

Kabanya, Julienne, 210

Kabera, Assiel, 171, 209

Kabgayi, 62, 89

Kabila, Laurent, 144
  tensions with Rwanda, 145

Kaduha genocide massacre, 2, 3

Kagame, Paul
  assessment of, 337
  challenges to authority of, 149, 164, 172
  on civil society, 172
  on commemoration, 78
  elections of, 164, 166
  family of, 61
  on France, 53
  on gacaca, 114–15, 116
  and genocide commemorations, 78–79
  on genocide survivors, 59
  on history, 47, 52
  on ICTR, 106
  on justice, 114
  on 1994 genocide, 52, 54, 79
  popular opinions of, 193, 221–22, 224
  praise of, 28
  rise to presidency, 151–55, 163
  on RPF crimes, 58
  on Rwandan Patriotic Front, 59, 137
  term limits, 167, 221, 224
  as vice-president, 147
  vision for country, 30, 56, 174, 178, 331

Kalimba, Célestin, 46

Kambanda, Jean, 200, 285, 332

Kanyamashuli, Janvier, 171

Kanyarengwe, Alexis, 153, 154

Kanyarwanda, 70

Karegeya, Patrick, 172

Karemera, Pierre, 205

Kayibanda, Grégoire, 82, 84
  death of, 84
  government of, 40, 51, 138, 208
  house of, 84
  and Parmehutu, 59, 199

Kayigire, Therence, 205

Kayihura, Michaël, 50, 57

Kayishema, Clement, 209

Kenya, 97
  corruption in, 131

Kibeho
  genocide massacre, 2
  genocide memorial, 76
  RPF massacre, 85, 124, 143

Kibirizi, 207

Kibungo province, 21, 150

Kibuye
  city of, 76, 206, 207, 215
  province of, 18, 19, 76, 171, 209

Kiga, 210, 251

Kigali, 198

Kigali Conceptual Master Plan, 177–82

Kigali Genocide Memorial Centre, 5, 65–66, 80–84, 87

Kigali-Rural province, 150, 202

Kinyamateka, 62

Kinyarwanda, 38, 47, 210
  news broadcasts in, 139, 171
  terms for violence and genocide in, 83, 245

Kinzer, Stephen, 28
Kirinda, 19, 20, 92, 94
Kisaro, 211
Kivu, Lake, 76, 206, 258, 271
Koonz, Claudia, 73
Kosovo, 316
Kritz, Neil, 316

land reform, 175–77
Lasallian Brothers, 211
Leebaw, Bronwyn Anne, 102
Legal and Constitutional Reform
    Commission, 163, 218
Levitsky, Steven, 166
Liberal Party, 153, 199
Liberation Day, 79
Libya, 97
LIPRODHOR, 132, 169, 170
Lizinde, Théoneste, 148, 154
local government, 220–21
    manipulations of, 205, 209–10,
        213, 214
Loiret-Butare project, 198
Lumière et Société, 46
lustration, 101, 302, 319
Lyangombe, 211

Mabanza commune, 18, 206–10
    during the 1994 genocide, 208
    under the RPF, 209–10
magical legalism, 279, 336
Makuza, Bernard, 154
Malaysia, 166
Malkki, Liisa, 44
Mamdani, Mahmood, 42
Manirakiza, Vincent, 180
massacres. *See also* Bisesero: genocide
    massacre, Kaduha genocide massacre,
    Kibeho, Murambi genocide massacre
    1990-1993, 10
Matyazo, 198
Mbonimana, Gamaliel, 46
Media High Council, 170
memorials. *See* Bisesero genocide
    memorial, Kigali Genocide Centre,
    Murambi genocide memorial,
    Ntarama genocide memorial,
    Nyamata genocide memorial,
    Nyarabuye genocide memorial
    impact of, 264, 318
    popular opinions of, 257–64
    theories of memorialization, 71–74
memory
    collective, 35, 37, 60, 235, 257, 264, 305
    labors of, 336
    sites of, 36, 71, 234

theories of memorialization, 71–74
Mendez, Juan, 100
Mgbako, Chi, 159
Mihigo, Kizito, 171
Ministry of Agriculture, 211
Ministry of Education, 34, 318
Ministry of Youth, Sports, and
    Culture, 9, 76
Minow, Martha, 99, 114
Mobutu Sese Seko, 144
monarchy, Rwandan, 1, 61
    and colonial administration, 39, 206
    in exile, 154
    and *imihigo*, 162
    role in national unity, 48, 60
Mouvement Démocratique Républicain. See
    Democratic Republican Movement
Mugesera, Antoine, 171
Mugesera, Léon, 41, 332
Muhazi Lake, 211
Müller, Jan-Werner, 71
Murambi, 12
    debate over numbers killed, 8–9
    genocide massacre, 1–3, 10
    genocide memorial, 1, 3–9, 67,
        71, 88
Murigande, Charles, 135–40
Murison, Jude, 177
Murumba, Anastase, 171
Museveni, Yoweri, 138
Mushubati, 207
Muvara, Father Félicièn, 62
Muvunyi, Tharcisse, 200
Muyanza parish, 211
Muyanza River, 211
Muzungu, Bernardin, 46, 56

Nairobi, 148
National Agricultural Research Institute,
    197, 211
National Assembly, 112, 152, 153
National Fund for Genocide
    Survivors, 171
National Human Rights Commission, 158
National Museum of Rwanda, 198
National Revolutionary Movement
    for Development, 41, 200, 208,
        239, 248
National Service of Gacaca Jurisdictions,
    117, 132
national symbols, 160
    popular reaction to, 218–20
National Unity and Reconciliation
    Commission, 78, 158–60, 167,
        171, 173
National University of Burundi, 136

National University of Rwanda, xi, 6, 34,
    46, 137, 192, 197, 199, 203, 205, 249
nationalism
    theories of, 36
Ndangiza, Fatuma, 158
Ndayambaje, Jean-Damascène, 52
Ndoba, Gasana, 54
Ndorwa, 210
Neier, Aryeh, 98
Never Again International, 9
Newbury, Catharine, 40
Newbury, David, 61
Ngoma commune. *See* Butare, city of
Nikuze, Bernard, 203
Nkubito, Alphonse-Marie, 141, 147, 148
Nora, Pierre, 36, 234
Nsanzabaganwa, Richard, 148
Ntahobali, Shalom, 200, 281
Ntarama genocide memorial, 5,
    68–70, 88
Ntezimana, Laurien, 169
Nuremberg trials, 96
Nyabarongo, 41
Nyabingi, 211
Nyakizu commune, 200
Nyamagumba, 258
Nyamata genocide memorial, 4, 5,
    67–68, 88
Nyamwasa, Kayumba, 172
Nyanza, 89, 122
Nyarabuye genocide memorial, 88
Nyiginya clan, 48, 61
Nyiramasuhuko, Pauline, 200, 281
Nyirimanzi, Gérard, 49, 51
Nyungwe Forest, 6

Office of Memorials, 9, 75, 78, 89
Open Society Institute, 98
Osiel, Mark, 100

Parmehutu, 52, 199
Parti Social Démocrat. See Social
    Democratic Party
Party for Democratic Renewal-Ubuyanja,
    58, 164, 168, 213, 218, 226
Pentecostal Church, 147
perpetrators
    see *genocidaires*
Peru, 72, 101, 335
Peskin, Victor, 106
popular mobilization, 155
    popular reactions to, 223
    required, 173
post-traumatic stress disorder, 15–16
Pottier, Johann, 13
Power, Samantha, 105

Presbyterian Church of Rwanda, 92, 206,
    208
Prosper, Pierre, 71
Prunier, Gerard, 45
Purdeková, Andrea, 159

quality of life laws, 182–83, 226

Radio Rwanda, 41
Radio-Television of the Thousand Hills,
    41, 210
rapatriés. See returnees
reconciliation
    Catholic Church and, 169
    collective memory and, 194
    contribution of
        commemmorations to, 55
    contribution of gacaca to, 281,
        291, 294–97
    contribution of ICTR to, 285
    contribution of *ingando* to, 159
    contribution of memorials to, 72
    contribution of trials to, 99–100, 113–17,
        120, 134, 279, 286
    contribution of truth commissions to, 101
    as goal of ICTR, 104
    government policies, 12, 13, 57, 78,
        302, 309
    historical narratives and, 34
    popular opinions of, 157, 195, 259, 260,
        288, 289–302
    role of truth telling in, 15
    in transitional justice theory, 16
    undermining of, 141, 186, 304, 305
refugees
    attacks on camps, 12, 121, 144
    Hutu, 12, 150, 254
    Tutsi, 12, 21, 44, 45, 203
regroupment, *see imidugudu* policy
reparations, 101, 308
    desire for, 289
rescapés. See survivors of 1994 genocide
restorative justice, 16, 101, 102, 123,
    304, 335
    gacaca as, 115
retributive justice, 14, 98, 114, 115
    alternatives to, 129
    gacaca as, 120, 123, 304
returnees, 12, 13, 44, 150, 203
    as audience for memorials, 8, 89
    dissent among, 165
    perceptions of the genocide, 330
    political and economic domination by,
        131, 185, 205, 327
    relations with survivors, 328
    settlement by, 234

returnees (*cont.*)
  social divisions among, 330
  support for RPF, 335
revolution of 1959
  interpreted as genocide, 50, 51, 138
  political uses of, 52, 84, 239, 265
  popular interpretations of, 237,
    239–40, 244
Reyntjens, Filip, 111
Riceour, Paul, 73
Rodstone, Susannah, 36
Roht-Arriaza, Naomi, 100
Rostagno, Donatella, 184
Rubengera, 206
Rubona, 89
Rudahigwa, King Kigeli IV, 252
Rugagi, Jean Nizurugero, 46
Ruhango, 89
Ruhengeri province, 150
Rulindo, 211
Russia, 166
Rutagengwa, Bosco, 171
Rutaremara, Tito, 163, 167
Rutayisire, Paul, 46, 55
Rutembesa, Faustin, 46
Rutsiro commune, 208, 209
Rwabugiri, King Kigeli IV, 206
Rwamasirabo, Emile, 206
Rwanda Vision 2020, 30, 173–83
Rwandan Armed Forces, 11, 53,
  75, 79
Rwandan Institute for Scientific Research,
  197, 199
Rwandan Patriotic Front, 3
  assessment of, 32, 56–60
  attacks on refugees, 12, 121, 144,
    204, 254
  in Butare city, 201–06
  consolidation of Paul Kagame's power
    within, 151–55, 206
  human rights abuses by, 11, 21, 102,
    125, 142, 143–44, 145, 202, 254,
    256, 333
  invasion of the Democratic Republic
    of Congo. *See* Congo, Democratic
    Republic of, wars
  invasion of Rwanda 1990–1993. *See*
    War of October
  origins of, 45
  popular fear of, 222–25
  popular opinions of, 239
  public policies, 57, 135–40
  response to insurgency in the
    northwest, 145
  role in stopping genocide, 56
  social engineering programs, 156–57

strategies of social control by, 29,
    168–73
Rwangabo, Pierre-Claver, 203
Rwigema, Pierre-Célestin, 154
Rwigyema, Fred, 138

School for Junior Officers, 197, 199, 200
Scott, James, 156
seal, national
  popular reactions to, 218
  replacement of, 160
Sebarenzi, Joseph, 153, 155
Second Republic, 50–52
self-censorship, 22, 223, 226, 268
  by journalists, 171
Sendashonga, Seth, 141, 147, 154, 203
  assassination of, 148
sexual violence, 74, 253, 338
Shagasha, 213
Shaw, Rosalind, 335
Sibomana, Father André, 62–63, 143, 148
Sierra Leone, 101, 316, 335
Simba, Aloys, 200
Sindikubwabo, Théodore, 200, 332
Singapore, 174, 331
Social Democratic Party, 141
social engineering, 12, 156–57, 174
Social Party-Imberakuri, 165
Songa, 89
South Africa, 316
  Truth and Reconciliation Commission,
    100, 116, 320
state structures
  revisions to, 160
Straus, Scott, 42
Sudan, 97
Sundaram, Anjan, 171
Supreme Court, 122
survivors of 1994 genocide. *See also* Ibuka
  experiences in the genocide, 10, 76, 77,
    93, 129, 330
  genocide memorials and, 7, 67–70, 80,
    259, 261, 262
  government policies for, 150, 225
  harassment by RPF, 153, 201
  impact of transitional justice on, 306,
    308, 321, 324, 336
  in *imidugudu*, 235
  interpretations of the genocide by, 246,
    248, 249, 252, 318
  involvement in false accusations, 123
  justice for, 104
  in Kagame's speeches, 59
  at NUR, 203
  opinions of gacaca, 290, 291, 293, 296,
    297, 299, 303, 305

opinions of ICTR, 283
opinions of national symbols, 160, 220
opinions of the RPF, 127, 149, 209, 257
opinions of transitional justice, 308, 329
opinions of trials, 286, 287
policies for, 17
post-genocide experiencecs of, 22, 117,
    119, 151, 190–93, 203, 313–14, 326,
    328, 330, 338
reconciliation and, 281, 294, 297
relations with Hutu, 324
reparations and, 288, 290, 298, 303, 308
RPF harassment of, 171
self-censorship of, 223
settlement in cities by, 178, 205, 234
suspicion of, 53
Sweden
    genocide trials, 95
Switzerland
    genocide trials, 95

Taba, 198
Tanzania, 265
    Burundian refugees in, 44
    Hutu refugees in, 11, 12, 150
    ujamaa program, 157
term limits, 167
    revision of, 167, 221–22
Theidon, Kimberly, 335
Theunis, Guy, 132
Thompson, Allan, 148
Thomson, Susan, 159, 223
TIG. *See* community service
Timor Leste, 101, 316
Tokyo trials, 97
transitional justice. *See also* trials,
    gacaca courts
    contributions to
        democratization, 315–20
    critique of, 102, 315–33
    development of in Rwanda, 152
    following Second World War, 96
    impact of economics on,
        307–09, 326–31
    meaning of, 14
    political uses of, 119–33
    use of trials in, 14
    use of truth commissions in, 14
trials. *See also* Eichman, Adolf
    corruption in, 131, 287–88, 333
    ethnic bias in, 129
    exclusion of RPF crimes, 124, 333
    goals in Rwanda, 102
    one-sided nature of, 128
    opinions about Rwandan national
        genocide, 285–89

political uses of, 119–33, 306, 319
politicization of, 333
promotion of collective guilt
    through, 127–29
purposes of, 102
Rwandan national genocide, 95, 110,
    120, 303
as tool of transitional justice, 14,
    95, 96–103
truth commissions
    as tool of transitional justice, 14, 101
Tumba, 199, 202
Turnbridge, J.E., 72
Tutsi. *See also* ethnicity
    attacks on in 1959, 51, 240
    attacks on in 1990s, 51
    definition of, 38
    opinions on commemoration, 260
    perspectives on revolution of
        1959, 239–40
    refugees. *See* refugees:Tutsi
    repression by RPF, 149
Twa, 60, 81, *see also* ethnicity
    definition of, 38
Twagiramungu, Faustin, 141, 147, 154
    presidential candidacy, 59, 164, 228
Twagiramungu, Noel, 172

ubuhake, 238, 240
Uganda
    and International Criminal
        Court, 97
    involvement in Congo war, 144
    and Rwandan territorial claims, 47
    Tutsi refugees in, 13, 21, 44, 45, 61,
        219, 330
ujamaa, 157
Umuco, 133
umuganda, 155, 173, 226, 307
umusozi, 150
Umutara province, 150, 234
Union of Baptist Churches in Rwanda,
    197, 207
United Democratic Forces-Inkingi, 165
United States Institute for Peace, 316
Universal Declaration of Human
    Rights, 97
University of Namur, 136
Uruguay, 316
Uwilingiyimana, Agathe, 54, 78, 80

van Hoyweghen, Saskia, 151
Vansina, Jan, 44
Venezuela, 166
Vietnam Veterans Memorial, 66, 72

374 Index

Village Urugwiro meetings, 111, 112, 123,
    151, 152n. 52, 158
Vision 2020, *see Rwanda Vision 2020*

Waldorf, Lars, 169, 280, 309
War of October, 9, 126, 239, 256
    impact on Buyoga, 212
    RPF interpretation of, 56
    RPF reinterpretations of, 56
Way, Lucan A., 166
Week of Mourning, 78, 79, 89, 257
    popular reactions to, 259–64
Wierzynska, Aneta, 317, 319
Wilson, Richard, 320

women
    political participation of, 167
    representation in parliament, 168

youth
    representation in parliament, 168
Yugoslavia, former, 99, 103

Zaire. *See* Congo, Democratic Republic of
Zimbabwe
    involvement in Congo war, 146
Zoko, 211, 213
Zone Turquoise, 11, 18, 53, 76, 105, 117,
    201, 209